Embodying Geopolitics

Embodying Geopolitics

GENERATIONS OF WOMEN'S ACTIVISM
IN EGYPT, JORDAN, AND LEBANON

Nicola Pratt

UNIVERSITY OF CALIFORNIA PRESS

University of California Press
Oakland, California

Library of Congress Cataloging-in-Publication Data

Names: Pratt, Nicola Christine, author.
Title: Embodying geopolitics : generations of women's activism in Egypt,
    Jordan, and Lebanon / Nicola Pratt.
Description: Oakland, California : University of California Press, [2020] |
    Includes bibliographical references and index.
Identifiers: LCCN 2020010790 (print) | LCCN 2020010791 (ebook) |
    ISBN 9780520281752 (hardcover) | ISBN 9780520281769 (paperback) |
    ISBN 9780520957657 (ebook)
Subjects: LCSH: Women political activists—Middle East—History. |
    Women's rights—Political aspects—Middle East—History. | Women
    political activists—Egypt—History. | Women political activists—Jordan—
    History. | Women political activists—Lebanon—History.
Classification: LCC HQ1236.5.M628 P84 2020 (print) | LCC HQ1236.5.M628
    ebook) | DDC 305.420956—dc23
LC record available at https://lccn.loc.gov/2020010790
LC ebook record available at https://lccn.loc.gov/2020010791

Manufactured in the United States of America

27 26 25 24 23 22 21 20
10 9 8 7 6 5 4 3 2 1

CONTENTS

CONTENTS

ACKNOWLEDGMENTS

First and foremost, I thank the British Academy for awarding me a Mid-Career Fellowship in 2013–2014, which enabled me to conduct the research for this book. I also thank the University of Warwick and the Department of Politics and International Studies for providing extra funding for field-work and awarding me study leave in the academic year 2014–2015, which allowed me to write the first draft of this book.

Several of the women that I interviewed are people whom I met during earlier research trips, including short visits to Lebanon, Jordan, and Egypt in 2007–2008, funded by a British Academy small grant, as well as personal relationships that I developed from living and working in Egypt after 1994. I am very grateful for further suggestions of potential interviewees that I received from my initial interviewees as well as other friends and acquaintances. In particular, I would like to acknowledge the following individuals who were very generous with their time in suggesting potential interviewees and providing contact information: in Lebanon, Samia El Tabari, Myriam Sfeir, Sonya Knox, Dima Dabbous, and Chantal Sarkis; in Egypt, Mandi Fahmy, Aida Seif El Dawla, Mozn Hassan, Arab Loutfi; in Jordan, Samar Dudin, Hala Ghosheh, Oroub Al Abed, Sara Ababneh, and Marta Petrobelli. Their assistance was invaluable. I also thank Sherene Seikaly for lending me her apartment in Cairo, Amal Sabbagh, Haifa Jammal, and the late Rula Quawass in Jordan for sharing their time, memories, and invaluable insights, and Kholoud in Lebanon for enabling me to conduct some interviews in Borj al-Barajneh camp among refugee women living there. While I did not end up using these interviews in this book, the perspectives of these women provided a contrast that enabled me to better understand the significance of class and citizenship status in shaping the subjectivities, identities, and activism of those women who are the focus of this study.

I spent my study leave in Jordan, writing my book, where the British Institute in Amman (Council for British Research in the Levant) provided a wonderful place for working and the opportunity to discuss ideas with the many fellows and scholars passing through. Thank you to the director, Carol Palmer, for creating such a welcoming, intellectual space. I also greatly benefitted from feedback that I received from the audience to a lecture that I delivered at the British Institute in May 2015.

I am very grateful to Nadje Al-Ali, Shirin Rai, Rebecca Roberts, and Charles Tripp for reading and commenting on earlier drafts of various chapters. Feedback from the reviewers of the first draft manuscript were constructive but also disheartening. Thank you to Sara Salem for reading the entire first draft and to Nicki Smith for reading the entire final manuscript. Their enthusiasm and praise kept my spirits afloat in the midst of self-doubt. Thank you to the reviewers of the revised version of the manuscript for their feedback, which I have attempted to address in the final version of this manuscript. Overall, this was a very challenging book to write, and it took me a lot longer to finish and many more cups of tea than I had anticipated. I apologize to my husband for all the weekends and holidays that I spent working to finish this book, and thank him for all the cups of tea. I thank my editor, Niels Hooper, for his patience. Thank you to my colleagues Richard Aldrich, Shirin Rai, and Mat Watson for their excellent advice and support on dealing with reviewer reports. I am also very grateful to a number of friends on Facebook for an engaging discussion over possible book titles and, particularly, to Aya Nassar for suggesting the final book title and some of the chapter headings.

I also want to take this opportunity to recognize my friend and former coauthor Nadje Al-Ali, whose work on the Egyptian women's movement and Iraqi women inspired me to become interested in the politics of gender in the Middle East.

Finally, and most vitally, I am grateful to all the women who gave their time to be interviewed and without whose cooperation this book would not have been possible. I dedicate this book to them and the many other women and men across the Middle East and North Africa who give their time, often at great personal sacrifice, in the struggle for a better world. All royalties from this book will be donated to the Palestinian Women's Humanitarian Organization in Borj al-Barajneh refugee camp, Lebanon.

ABBREVIATIONS

AAW	Alliance for Arab Women, Egypt
ABAAD	Resource Center for Gender Equality, Lebanon
ACT	Appropriate Communication Techniques for Development, Egypt
ADEW	Association for the Development and Enhancement of Women, Egypt
ANM	Arab Nationalist Movement
ARDD	Arab Renaissance for Democracy and Development, Jordan
AUB	American University of Beirut
AUC	American University in Cairo
AWO	Arab Women Organization of Jordan
AWSA	Arab Women's Solidarity Association, Egypt
AWU	Arab Women's Union, Jordan
CBO	Community Based Organization
CEDAW	Convention on the Elimination of all Forms of Discrimination against Women
CEWLA	Center for Egyptian Women's Legal Assistance
CRTD-A	Collective for Research and Training on Development–Action (Lebanon)

DFLP	Democratic Front for the Liberation of Palestine
DLM	Democratic Left Movement, Lebanon
ECWR	Egyptian Center for Women's Rights
EFU	Egyptian Feminist Union
EIPR	Egyptian Initiative for Personal Rights
EISA	Electoral Institute for Sustainable Democracy in Africa
EOHR	Egyptian Organization for Human Rights
EPCSP	Egyptian Popular Committee for Solidarity with the Palestinians
ESDP	Egyptian Social Democratic Party
EU	European Union
FGM/FGC	Female Genital Mutilation/Female Genital Cutting
FJP	Freedom and Justice Party, Egypt
GFJW	General Federation of Jordanian Women
GUPS	General Union of Palestinian Students
GUPW	General Union of Palestinian Women
HASHD	Jordanian Democratic People's Party
HRW	Human Rights Watch
IAF	Islamic Action Front, Jordan
ICG	International Crisis Group
ICPD	International Conference on Population and Development
IFES	International Foundation for Electoral Systems
IMF	International Monetary Fund
IR	international relations
IWSAW	Institute for Women's Studies in the Arab World (now the Arab Institute for Women), Lebanon
JCP	Jordanian Communist Party
JNCW	Jordanian National Commission for Women

JNM	Jordanian National Movement
JWU	Jordanian Women's Union
LADE	Lebanese Association for Democratic Elections
LAU	Lebanese American University
LCW	Lebanese Council for Women
LECORVAW	Lebanese Council to Resist Violence against Women
LGBTQ	Lesbian, Gay, Bisexual, Transgender, Queer/Questioning
LLWR	League for Lebanese Women's Rights
LNM	Lebanese National Movement
LNRF	Lebanese National Resistance Front
LWDG	Lebanese Women Democratic Gathering
MB	Muslim Brotherhood
MENA	Middle East and North Africa
MEPI	Middle East Partnership Initiative
NCLW	National Commission for Lebanese Women
NCW	National Council for Women, Egypt
NGO	nongovernmental organization
NPA	Norwegian People's Aid
NWF	New Woman Foundation, Egypt (previously NWRC)
NWM	National Women's Machinery
NWRC	New Woman Research Center, Egypt (now called NWF)
OAC	Organization of Communist Action
OpAntiSH	Operation Antisexual Harassment, Egypt
PFLP	Popular Front for the Liberation of Palestine
PLO	Palestine Liberation Organisation
PSP	Progressive Socialist Party, Lebanon
PWU	Progressive Women's Union, Egypt
RAND	League of Democratic Women, Jordan

SADAQA	Jordanian NGO seeking to create a women-friendly work environment
SCAF	Supreme Council of the Armed Forces, Egypt
SIGI	Sisterhood Is Global Institute, Jordan
UNDP	United Nations Development Programme
UNHCR	United Nations High Commissioner for Refugees
UNRWA	United Nations Relief and Works Agency
USAID	United States Agency for International Development
USJ	L'Université Saint-Joseph
WB	World Bank
WIDF	Women's International Democratic Federation
WMF	Women and Memory Forum, Egypt
WWL	Working Women's League, Lebanon
WUJ	Women's Union in Jordan

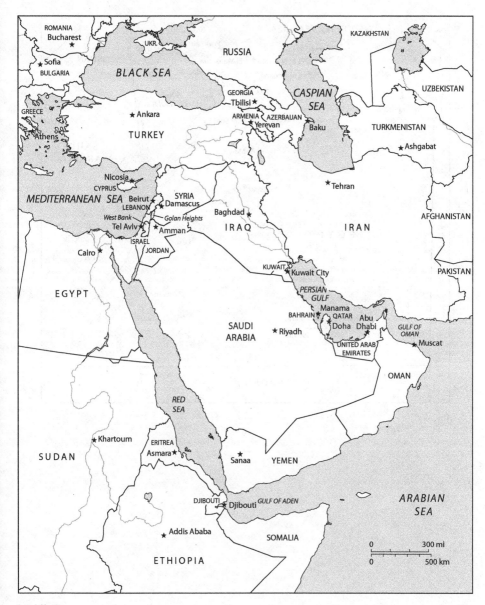

Middle East

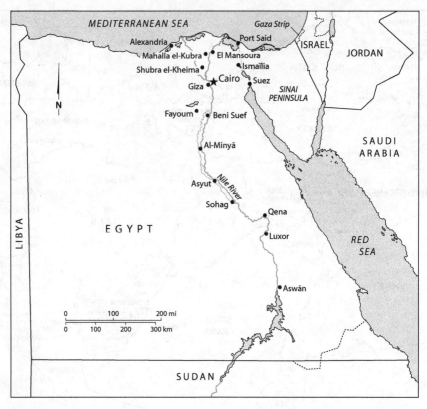

Egypt

Jordan

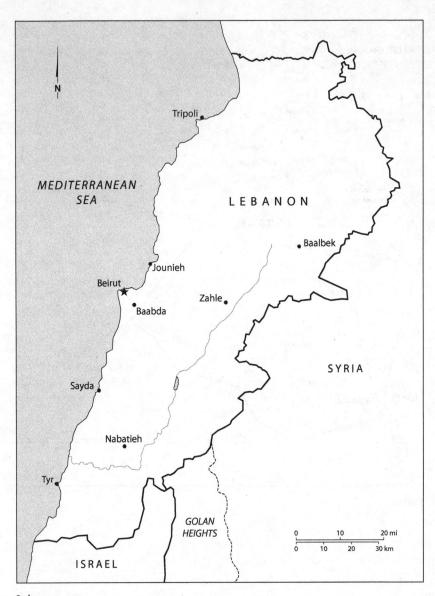

Lebanon

Introduction

EMBODYING GEOPOLITICS IN THE MIDDLE EAST AND NORTH AFRICA

Somehow when you get involved, [. . .] [there's] this sense of obligation that grows with you, and it always makes you feel like "I can't go, I can't leave." [. . .] And it's weird that you have that sense, because a lot of people who were also involved didn't have; they left and they emigrated, so I have always been thinking, why do some of us have that sense? And it's a false sense because life does go on without you, so why one has that sense that it's important to be in the middle of these things, I have no idea, I am trying to make sense, but I have no idea why.

HALA SHUKRALLAH
former student activist in the 1970s, development consultant, women's rights activist, former president of the Dastour Party, 2014–2015, Cairo, Egypt

Since we were [. . .] children, my father used to tell us [. . .], "It's a duty in Islam to give away some of what you have, as much as you can."

NUHA NUWAYRI SALTI
physician and founder of an outreach clinic in Shatila refugee camp, Beirut, Lebanon

Mainly because I was attached to politics from a young age, I am so much attached to progress and I'm dedicated [. . .] [to] support women [. . .] and sometimes I feel that I'm doing it for myself and for my family and for my grandchildren—I have four grand-daughters—so they can live in a better society in this part of the world; so, I feel it is personal and I feel it is a continuation of the life I have chosen also.

LEILA NAFFA HAMARNEH
women's rights activist, member of Jordanian Communist Party, Amman

My father wasn't educated but he believed that education makes people rise in status. Therefore, he made sure to give us an education. [...] So, there was this idea, and there was the idea of work and the idea of the value you have in the society you work in. [...] And then I started looking around me, thinking how I could do something good for the community.

FATMA RAMADAN
trade unionist, Cairo, Egypt

Because that's that's what I am all about. [...]. It's part of my constitution. Yeah, that's my meaning in life.

LEILA ZAKHARIA
*development consultant, advocate for
Palestinian rights, Beirut, Lebanon*

I told you that I was born and raised in this house where there was interest in politics. There was a reason I grew to be who I am; this is how I was raised. You see? I feel that "it's not my own choice," I was born with it; it was "built in" rather than something I chose at some point in my life.

MANAR HUSSEIN ABDEL SATTAR
Revolutionary Socialist, Cairo, Egypt

When I was very young, I used to feel guilty about every single poor person [...] that I met. Finally, I resolved this dilemma by thinking [...], if you are privileged, if you do not want to be actually sucking poor people's blood, you have to give back. It's the only justification for accepting privilege in a sense.

LAILA SOUEIF
university professor and activist, Cairo, Egypt

BETWEEN 2013 AND 2014, I COLLECTED personal narratives of more than one hundred women activists of different generations residing in Egypt, Jordan, and Lebanon. Their stories form the basis of this book. The above quotes represent a sample of the responses that I received when I posed the question, "Why are you active in public life?" When I began to plan this book, the popular uprisings and mass protests that erupted across the Arab world, beginning in Tunisia in December 2010 often referred to as the "Arab Spring" in Western commentaries—were still ongoing. I was motivated to write against a prevalent discourse at the time—promoted by Western media, policy makers, NGOs, and think tanks, among others—that viewed women's participation in protests as new and exceptional. Such attitudes reflected an Orientalist epistemology, denying the possibility of women's agency within "Arab-Muslim culture," and viewing it, instead, as an expression of "Western" values of freedom and autonomy. The above quotes by women activists highlight that their public engagement long precede the Arab uprisings. Moreover, rather than viewing themselves as outside of "Arab-Muslim culture," these women emphasized their relationships to family, home, community, and nation. They narrated a situated and embodied geography, a geopolitics of intimacy and community, revealing the mutually constitutive relationships between women's activism, identities, subjectivities, and social relations, as well as place and space. *argument*

In this book, I argue that women's activism should be viewed as an embodied geopolitics. While the term *geopolitics* has predominantly been associated with the rationalization of dominant power and the efforts of powerful nations to control the globe, here, I build on work by scholars in the fields of critical geopolitics, postcolonial studies, feminist geopolitics, and feminist international relations (IR) that problematizes rather than normalizes oppression and inequalities of power across multiple scales and that is attentive to the spatialized dimensions of power and the role of power in constructing space, as well as the implications of this for ordinary women and men. A feminist geopolitics is concerned with the embodied dimensions of geopolitical processes, writing the experiences and agency of ordinary women (and men) into international politics. It reconceptualizes international politics to include the personal and the everyday as important sites in the exercise of and resistance to geopolitical power (Dowler and Sharp 2001: 169; Enloe 2014; Hyndman 2004; Pettman 1997; Sharp 2000; Tickner 1992). As Edward Said wrote, "Just as none of us is outside or beyond geography, none of us is completely free from the struggle over geography. That struggle is complex and interesting because it is not only about soldiers and cannons but also about ideas, about forms, about images and imaginings" (1993: 7).

This book treats women's narratives of their activism as forms of situated and embodied knowledge (Haraway 1988, Hyndman 2004) about the "struggle for geography" in the Middle East and North Africa (MENA) region. Viewing Middle East politics and international relations from the embodied perspectives of women activists reveals the particularly gendered ideas, forms, images, and imaginings that have informed and underpinned critical junctures in the region's contemporary history, from decolonization to the Arab uprisings. It demonstrates the crucial ways in which particular ideas of gender have underpinned the creation of regional order and the stability of postindependence regimes. It highlights the ways in which women's bodies have been the sites of geopolitical contestations, with devastating consequences for their security and bodily integrity. However, it also emphasizes the ways in which women activists have been active participants in the struggle for geography, contributing to the disruption of dominant geopolitical power as well as its reproduction. In addition, given that many of the assumptions underpinning the fields of feminist IR and feminist geopolitics continue to be based on experiences of state formation, militarization, and foreign policy making in the Global North, this book contributes to ongoing efforts to decolonize the field by highlighting the particular experiences of citizens of states in the MENA region and, specifically, the legacies of colonialism and the ongoing relevancy of neocolonialism and imperialism in shaping the embodied geopolitics of women's activism, as well as the politics of gender and sexuality more broadly. The remainder of this introduction theorizes women's activism as embodied geopolitics, contextualizes women's geopolitical agency in relation to the historical experiences of state building in the Middle East and North Africa, discusses this book's methodological approach to narratives, elaborates upon the choice of the country cases, and, finally, provides an outline of the book.

WOMEN'S ACTIVISM AS EMBODIED GEOPOLITICS

As Cynthia Enloe has famously argued, "the international is personal" and "the personal is international" (Enloe 2014: 351). Although feminist approaches have highlighted the gendered and embodied dimensions of geopolitics and international relations, the ways in which geopolitics shapes women's activism and what these reveal about international politics remain relatively understudied. Meanwhile, a substantial literature has documented women's organizations and movements in the Middle East and North Africa, their goals, strategies, philosophies/ideologies, and activities, but has tended to neglect the geopolitical consequences of women's activism. Moreover, there has been a tendency to view women's activism in terms of its *resistance* or *opposition* to dominant power at different scales and the forms of violence with which it is associated. I argue that women activists are illuminating subjects of research because their experiences necessarily straddle the private and the public; the personal and the political; and the local, the national, and even the international. This is particularly the case for many of the women whom I interviewed for this book. They have participated in struggles against colonialism, imperialism, war, and dictatorship; dealt with the aftermath of violence, conflict, and displacement; and simultaneously negotiated the politics of gender and sexuality in their homes, workplaces, communities, and beyond. Therefore, I argue that their embodied experiences and agency provide a window into the ways in which power relations at multiple scales intersect and play out, illuminating the complex and often contradictory ways in which gender is entangled in the construction and normalization of different geopolitical scales and wider relations of power. However, I do not conceptualize women's activism as necessarily resistance to or separate from geopolitical power; rather, I understand it as a crucial part of the circuits of gendered power that circulate at multiple scales, from the personal to the international—that is, as a form of embodied geopolitics.

This section theorizes women's activism as embodied geopolitics by elaborating how geopolitics shapes women's activism and how women's activism shapes geopolitics. In this regard, I emphasize the multiscalar and gendered nature of geopolitics and, hence, the geopolitical implications of activism that transforms or seeks to transform gender relations and norms. Here, I understand gender as discursively constructed and as embodied by living beings. In addition, I underline the need to dismantle the binary of resistance/compliance in understanding the relationship between women's activism and dominant geopolitical structures.

How does geopolitics shape women's activism? Women's activism occurs within geopolitical spaces and structures that provide opportunities, challenges, and limitations for women activists. For the most part, women's activism is located within the political boundaries of the state and is shaped by the respective state's policies and laws as well as significant national events, such as, wars, disasters, and economic crises. Women's activism may also be targeted at entities other than the nation state, such as the United Nations or the European Union. Rather than viewing the nation-state and other geographic scales as pregiven, feminist scholars have drawn attention to the ways in which these geopolitical constructs are dependent upon the production of gendered boundaries that distinguish the domestic from the foreign, the inside from the outside, order from chaos, us from them, and public from private (Dowler & Sharp 2001; Enloe 2014; Grewal and Kaplan 1994;

Peterson 1992b; Pettman 1996; Tickner 1992; Youngs 1996; Yuval-Davis 1997). These gendered boundaries are reproduced through a variety of state policies and laws, not only foreign policies but also laws governing marriage, divorce, and nationality, with differential implications for women's mobility (Yuval-Davis 1997). Moreover, such laws and policies serve to shape particular norms of femininity and masculinity that are essential to the reproduction of states and nations as well as practices of militarization and diplomacy (Enloe 2014, 1993, 2000, 2007; Parpart and Zalewski 2008; Peterson and Runyan 2010; Rai 2002). These gender norms, in turn, regulate women's behavior, including their activism.

Given the significance of gender to the operation of geopolitical power and the construction of dominant geopolitical categories, it follows that embodied geopolitics not only includes those activities targeting conventional sites of geopolitics, such as governments and international organizations, or "big geopolitical" themes, such as, war, foreign policy, or revolution, but also activism that transforms or seeks to transform gender norms and gender relations, including state laws and policies that regulate them. In this respect, the book documents activists' efforts to reform legislation and policies that enshrine gender discrimination as well as considering how their advocacy is "framed" (Benford and Snow 2000) in relation to dominant geopolitical constructs and power. This assessment is dependent upon an understanding of the specific geopolitical context of the MENA, as will be discussed in the next section.

The book also understands activism that targets conventional sites of geopolitics as also potentially transformative of gender relations and norms, even if this is not its stated aim. Activism entails embodied performances of gender norms that have implications for the organization and normalization of geopolitical power. As already noted, dominant geopolitical structures and processes depend upon the successful production of particular notions of femininities and masculinities. Drawing on Judith Butler's notion of the performativity of gender (1999: xxiv), gender is conceptualized as "always a doing, though not a doing by a subject who might be said to preexist the deed" (Butler 1999: 33). Just as ordinary men and women are constituted through hegemonic discourses of gender, so is hegemonic gender reproduced by ordinary women and men repeatedly performing the "correct" gender—through "the stylization of the body [...] bodily gestures, movements, and styles of various kinds" (Butler 1999: 179). By contrast, refusal by women and men to enact hegemonic gender exposes gender as "a politically tenuous construction" (Butler 1999: 179), which, in turn, threatens the successful reproduction of the geopolitical order that is dependent upon it. Hence, women's activism that "interrupts normative orders and activates competing ones through imagination, symbolism, and enactment" (Hasso and Salime 2016b: 4) should be considered in terms of a "corporeality of dissent" (Hafez 2019: 134).

In conceptualizing the relationship between women's activism and geopolitics, it is essential that women's activism should not be reduced to acts of resistance and transgression. Kimberly Hutchings (2013) warns against efforts to insist upon the existence of a "revolutionary subject" as a prerequisite for a feminist politics, arguing instead for a feminism that accepts pluralism. Meanwhile, women may also reinscribe power relations and uphold hegemonic gender norms (Abu-Lughod 1990; Kandiyoti 1988; Mahmood 2005). Moreover, given that women's activism may have effects at multiple geopolitical scales, from the personal to the international, it is impossible to understand it through a binary prism of resistance or compliance. Women's activism may resist *and* comply with dominant power structures at different geopolitical scales simultaneously. For example, women's use of motherhood and maternal politics to protest human rights abuses (among others, the Madres de Plaza de Mayo in Argentina) and militarism (among others, the Greenham Common base women) constitute the performance of their gender identity in accord with dominant notions of femininity. Yet, simultaneously, these women subvert this gender identity by transposing it from the private sphere to an overtly political space that challenges the legitimacy of the state's monopoly on violence.[1] This resignification may further expand the space for women's activism, creating incremental changes in gender norms rather than radical ruptures. Similarly, as this book reveals, much women's activism has taken the form of welfare and charitable work, which has been performative of dominant gender norms of female respectability as well as class privilege. Yet, in particular historical and geopolitical contexts, such as during the period of colonial rule and the geopolitical upheavals following the 1967 war, this work was resignified as part of political movements challenging the geopolitical order. While women's participation in such activities might be viewed as reproducing a gendered and classed public sphere, the resignification of their social activism as political/nationalist may simultaneously function to reconceptualize the political (Richter-Devroe 2012), with implications for geopolitical order.

This book demonstrates the need to go beyond conceptualizing women's activism as *either* resistance to *or* reproduction of the dominant geopolitical order, including the gender norms and gendered hierarchies that underpin it. It is necessary to be attentive to time and space at multiple scales in order to understand the geopolitical effects of women's agency. Women's activism may at once disrupt *and* reproduce the dominant (gendered) geopolitical order through their embodied performances of gender as well as the modes and discursive framing of the objectives of their activism. However, in order to assess the disruptive and reproductive effects of women's activism, it is necessary to understand the relationship between geopolitics and gender in the specific context of the MENA region, as the next section examines further.

CONTEXTUALIZING WOMEN'S ACTIVISM IN THE MIDDLE EAST AND NORTH AFRICA: THE LEGACIES OF COLONIALISM

In this section, I historicize the production of gender in the Middle East and North Africa in relation to experiences of colonialism, in order to understand the particular ways in which geopolitics is gendered, which, in turn, has implications for how we understand the geopolitical effects of women's activism. Feminist scholars of IR and critical geopolitics have shed light on the mutually constitutive relationship between, on the one hand, sovereignty and related concepts of state and nation and, on the other hand, gender relations, identities, and norms. However, they have tended to assume a Westphalian model of state sovereignty that corresponds with Western experiences of state formation. I draw on work from the field of postcolonial studies and Middle East studies, including Middle East gender studies, to discuss the specific experiences of state formation and its implications for gender. In the Middle East, like other parts of the world that were colonized, ideas of sovereignty and nationalism emerged in a context of European domination, while the state system was imposed by European colonial rule. Even the concept of the "Middle East" was a product of European imperialism. What, therefore, are the legacies of this for the production of gender in the Middle East and North Africa? As Maria Lugones argues, it is essential to historicize gender formation in relation to colonialism and the coloniality of power to understand the ways in which gender intersects with race, class, and sexuality and, thereby, to decenter patriarchy as a "binary, hierarchical, oppressive gender formation that rests on male supremacy" (2007: 187).

State formation under colonial rule differed significantly from European experiences of state formation, with important implications for the politics of gender. While European state building was predicated on the subordination of a private sphere—associated with women and femininity—to a public sphere—associated with men and masculinity (Pateman 1988; Peterson 1992b; True 2018), state formation under colonial rule was predicated on the construction of a racial hierarchy of colonizer-colonized—or what Partha Chatterjee calls the "rule of colonial difference" (1993: 10)—on the basis of which citizenship was denied to indigenous people of all genders. Yet gender—and sexuality—was integral to the construction of this racial difference and of the hierarchy of the colonizer over the colonized. European discourse portrayed the "Oriental woman" as wretched and oppressed, pointing to women's veiling and segregation not only as markers of women's sexual oppression but, simultaneously, of the "backwardness" and "barbarity" of "Oriental" society (Ahmed 1992: 144–68; Liddle and Rai 1998; Yegenoglu 1998), justifying colonial domination and violence in the name of what Gayatri Spivak has famously termed "white men saving brown women from brown men" (1988: 92). Hence, the "public sphere" under colonial rule was not a realm of citizenship but of racial subordination, discursively rationalized with reference to gender.

In light of the importance of gender to "the securing and maintenance of the imperial enterprise" (McClintock 1995: 6–7), women's bodies became an important terrain upon which anticolonial nationalist elites staked claims to sovereignty in resistance to European colonial rule (Bier 2011: 28; Kandiyoti 1991a, 1991b; Najmabadi 1991; Thompson 2000). In their struggle for national independence, modernizing nationalist elites opposed the racist "rule of colonial difference" by proclaiming the "universality of the modern regime of power" (Chatterjee 1993: 26) and sought to adopt European practices in the spheres of law, administration, economy, and society (Beinin 2001: 9; Watenpaugh 2006). As part of these efforts, polygamy, early and arranged marriages, gender segregation, and veiling became symbols of backwardness that had to be eliminated. Women's "liberation" was advocated as a prerequisite for building a modern society that, in turn, would be the basis for a modern sovereign state.[2] In response to the European construction of the "Oriental woman," they promoted a "new woman," who was educated and publicly visible, while also a good wife and mother practicing "modern" methods of child rearing and domesticity (Abu-Lughod 1998a; Badran 1995; Baron 2005; Joshi 2001; Kandiyoti 1991a, 1991b; Najmabadi 1991; Pollard

2005; Shakry 1998). Hence, the "new woman" was the symbol as well as the object of nationalist modernization efforts and struggles for self-rule.

While the right to self-rule over a modern sovereign state was based upon a demonstration of being "like Europe," simultaneously, the ability to claim such rights was predicated on the identification of a political community or "nation" that was different from Europe (Chatterjee 1993: 26; see also, Chakrabarty 1997; Rai 2002: 27–33). Toward this end, anticolonial nationalists constructed a boundary between an outer, material domain, in which the nationalists fought the colonizers, and an inner, spiritual domain of sovereignty, which included "language or religion or aspects of personal and family life," from which the colonizers were excluded (Chatterjee 1993: 26). In other words, the construction of a spatial division between an outer and inner sphere was performative of national sovereignty in a context of colonial domination. As Partha Chatterjee notes, "The more nationalism engaged in its contest with the colonial power in the outer domain of politics, the more it insisted on displaying the marks of 'essential' cultural difference so as to keep out the colonizer from that inner domain of national life and to proclaim its sovereignty over it" (Chatterjee 1993: 26).

A key site for the construction of cultural difference and, hence, the construction of national sovereignty, was (and remains) the female body. Within nationalist discourse, women were expected to be the bearers of cultural authenticity, representing the "essence" of the nation through their modest behavior and dress (Chatterjee 1989; Enloe 2014; Kandiyoti 1991a, 1991b; Najmabadi 1991; Yuval-Davis 1997; Yuval-Davis and Anthias 1989). Modesty was (and continues to be) a fluid and contingent notion, defined in opposition to what it is not— usually associated with the behavior of the culturally constructed "other." In the context of colonial domination, modest behavior was defined in opposition to what was perceived as the sartorial and behavioral choices of European women but also in opposition to the indigenous "other," such as religious and ethnic minorities (Kandiyoti 1991a, 1991b).[3] At its essence, modesty refers to a woman's sexual purity but also implies obedience to male authority (Najmabadi 1991; Parla 2001). "Immodest" behavior for women has often included activities that would oblige them to mix with unrelated men, such as political activism and actions that openly challenge male authority. Hence, while nationalist elites encouraged women to enter the public sphere, norms of modesty limited the types of public work and activism in which women could acceptably engage. As Afsaneh Najmabadi neatly summarizes, in discussing the case of Iran, women were expected to be "modern-yet-modest" (1991: 49).

The struggle for sovereignty did not end with formal decolonization but rather has continued throughout the postcolonial era. In the material domain of foreign policy, military affairs, the economy, and statecraft, countries of the MENA, and the Global South more broadly, continue to be dominated by the West. Western governments and international organizations limit the sovereignty of governments in the Global South, for example, through conditioning loans and aid on the basis of good governance, fiscal discipline, and human rights as well as through other types of liberal and coercive interventions (Doty 1996b; Duffield and Hewitt 2013; Jabri 2012).

State actors in the MENA continue to display what Chatterjee calls "the marks of 'essential' culture difference" in order to exclude the Global North "from that inner domain of national life and to proclaim its sovereignty over it" (1993: 26). For example, as Nadje Al-Ali observes in the context of postcolonial Egypt, "Nationalist elites and reformers adhere to notions of western modernity in the context of economic, political and social concerns all related to the 'outer' sphere. [. . .] Within the so-called 'inner' sphere of society, such norms and values related to women's 'proper' roles and behaviour, their duties and rights within the home and family and their relationship to men, an essential difference from Western culture was and continues to be upheld" (Al-Ali 2000: 225).

The postcolonial discourse of cultural difference and the ongoing construction of an inner and outer sphere produces what Roxanne Doty calls a "sovereignty effect" (Doty 1996a: 124), in a context of ongoing material violations of sovereignty. As Cynthia Weber argues, "Sovereignty should be understood as the discursive/cultural means by which a 'natural state' is produced and established as prediscursive" (Weber 1998: 92). The successful production of a "natural state," in turn, is essential to constructing the legitimacy of the state and the authority of respective ruling regimes. Yet, in the MENA, regimes face not insignificant challenges to construct the state as a "natural state" (Weber 1998: 92) due to the legacies of state formation under colonial domination. For the most part, state boundaries and institutions were largely imposed on the region by European powers, often against the wishes of indigenous actors (Owen 1991).[4] Consequently, state boundaries have been contested by non-state actors (Kurds, Palestinians) as well as suprastate actors (such as, pan-Arab nationalists), alongside irredentist claims by other states (Hinnebusch 2003: 64–86). Regimes have had to work hard to legitimize and normalize their authority as a requirement for successful state building (Hinnebusch 2003; Hudson 1977; Ayubi 1995; Owen 2000). Hence, given its significance to the construction of a "natural state," the delineation of an "inner sphere" over which the postcolonial state may exercise authority has been a highly (geo)politicized process. This, in turn, has implications for the production of gender norms as well as state laws and policies affecting gender relations in postindependence states, as the following section explores. Understanding the geopolitical logics underpinning the production of gender norms and relations is crucial to understanding women's activism as an embodied geopolitics.

The Geopolitics of Gender Norms and Women's Rights in Postindependence MENA States

The Middle East is generally regarded as one of the regions in the world with the greatest gender inequalities. This has served to justify various neocolonial interventions by Western governments to "save Muslim women" (Abu-Lughod 2013; Al-Ali and Pratt 2009b; Hunt and Rygiel 2006). Meanwhile, international agencies lay the blame for gender inequalities with "cultural attitudes" in the Arab world and charge the state with bringing about the necessary transformations through the education system and legal reforms (Hasso 2009). I argue that rather than viewing gender inequality as a stubborn residue of culture, it should be seen as performative of a cultural difference that serves to produce a "sovereignty effect" (Doty 1996a: 124), which, in turn, has played a crucial role in postindependence state building in the MENA region.

Women's bodies constitute the "finest scale of geopolitical space" (Giles and Hyndman 2004: 310), over which is waged "the struggle over geography"(Said 1993: 7). State laws and policies that control women's bodies and behavior construct gender hierarchies and fashion specific gender norms, which, in turn, serve to reproduce and naturalize the boundaries between "modernity" and "modesty," between the "inner" and "outer" domains, and between "us" and "them," in the service of state building and regime consolidation. In this section, I draw on scholarship from Middle East gender studies to discuss the various laws enacted by MENA states to control women's bodies, constructing "heteropatriarchy" and "heteropaternalism" (Arvin, Tuck and Morrill 2013; also, Lugones 2007, 2010) as the hegemonic cultural matrix (Butler 1999: 23–24) within which legitimate gender identities are produced, with various implications for women's activism. As discussed throughout this book, these laws have often been a major object of women's activism; however, they have also constructed norms of femininity in contradictory terms of modesty and modernity, which, in turn, have limited the autonomy of women activists.

Personal status laws—that is, laws that regulate marriage, divorce, inheritance, and child custody—have been a major target for women's activism over time and have been central to constructing and normalizing particular gender relations and identities, as well as national/cultural difference. These laws enshrine gender inequality within the home and are often predicated on a vision of domestic life in which the husband is the head of the family with responsibility for the financial maintenance of his wife, who, in return, is expected to obey her husband (Tucker 2008: 71–74; Welchman 2007: 89–109).[5] With the exception of Turkey, personal status laws remain the only laws in the Middle East not to have been completely secularized. As Nadia Hijab argues, the religious basis of personal status codes serves to signal "cultural authenticity" in resistance to the West (Hijab 1998), constructing an "inner domain of national life" (Chatterjee 1993: 26) over which the postcolonial state proclaims its sovereignty. Hence, as discussed in chapter 5, despite having signed the UN Convention on the Elimination of all forms of Discrimination against Women (CEDAW), almost all MENA governments retain reservations on those articles dealing with marriage and family life on the grounds of religion and culture.

However, the codification of family laws differs between countries and is reflective of respective elite approaches to establishing a "natural state" (Weber 1998: 92), shaped by the specific context of state formation under colonialism and decolonization, as well as the configuration of social forces comprising the anticolonial coalition. Suad Joseph compares women's rights and gender policies in two multiethnic and multireligious states: Iraq and Lebanon. In Iraq, a relatively progressive and unified personal status code, alongside state measures to increase women's participation in the workforce, served to weaken the power of tribes and other kin-based groups, thereby undermining potential competing centers of power and consolidating state power (Joseph 1991: 178–87). Meanwhile, Lebanon's sectarian personal status laws (whereby eighteen different personal status codes govern eighteen officially recognized religious sects) have been crucial to constructing and reproducing a political system based on power sharing between groups defined along religious and sectarian lines and "as a part of a strategy of maintaining the balance of sectarian power in the state" (Joseph 1991: 189). This has made it very challenging for women activists to overturn these laws, as explored in this book. Similarly, Mounira Charrad, comparing Morocco, Tunisia, and

Algeria at the moment of independence, argues that the development of personal status laws was part of elite strategies of regime consolidation, shaped by "the degree of autonomy of the state from—versus reliance upon—kin-based solidarities" (2001: 233). In essence, personal status laws, as well as other laws shaping gender relations, have served as mechanisms to naturalize the state by either incorporating or weakening the power of kin-based groups (see also Manea 2011; Al-Rasheed 2013).

Nationality laws also serve to construct a "natural state" and have also been a focus of women's rights activism. In most countries in the Middle East, only men have the right to pass on their nationality to their children and spouses. Denying a woman the right to pass on her nationality has material consequences in that the children of a foreign father may be denied access to free education, health care, and other socioeconomic and civil rights in the mother's country of citizenship (see Abou-Habib 2003; Amawi 2000; Joseph 2000a; Nassar 2010). This is particularly a problem in Jordan and Lebanon, where not insubstantial numbers of women are married to non-nationals who are often long-standing refugees or exiles from neighboring Arab countries. By limiting who may or may not be considered a citizen, the law strictly reinforces the boundary between the inside and the outside of the state. As Roxanne Doty argues, "When the criteria for differentiating the inside of states from the outside become blurred and ambiguous, the foundational premise of state sovereignty becomes shaky" (1996a: 122). In this regard, it is noteworthy that both the Lebanese and Jordanian governments frame their refusal to grant women citizens the right to pass on their nationality as a matter of national security and national interests (as discussed further in chapter 6). In effect, by not granting women an equal right to pass on their nationality, the law punishes any woman who marries outside her national grouping for blurring the boundaries of the state and failing in her expected role as the "biological and cultural reproducers of the nation" (Yuval-Davis 1997; Yuval-Davis and Anthias 1989).

The policing of women's sexuality is also central to producing the boundaries of the state and nation through the control of women's behavior. A number of laws seek to contain women's sexuality within heterosexual marriage, often in the name of protecting women's sexual purity. For example, a number of countries allow a rapist to be pardoned on condition of marrying his victim.[6] Until it was criminalized in 2007, the practice of Female genital mutilation (FGM)/female genital cutting (FGC) in Egypt was often justified on the basis of curbing women's sexuality. Similarly, laws that allow child marriage have been justified on the basis of ensuring that sexual relations between young men and women are confined to marriage. Meanwhile, in several MENA countries, the penalty for murder of a woman may be mitigated or even exonerated on the grounds that the crime was committed in a "fit of rage" as a result of the victim's sexual "misconduct" (Welchman and Hossain 2005). These are among "the mechanisms of surveillance deployed by the modern state [. . .] to secure the sign of the modern and/but chaste woman" (Parla 2001: 66). They amount to state-sanctioned violence against women, but are nonetheless often defended in the name of culture, tradition, and protecting public morality, as discussed further in chapter 5.

Even while MENA regimes have enshrined gender inequality as symbolic of the nation's cultural "essence," simultaneously they have implemented some version of state feminism—that is, "state programs that introduce important changes in the reproductive and productive roles of women" (Hatem 1992: 231). Of the country cases studied here, the regime of Gamal Abdel-Nasser (1956–1970) implemented the most ambitious state feminist program, introducing measures to encourage women into education and the workforce and granting women the vote. These policies were held up as a marker of the regime's success in modernizing the country, thereby contributing to regime legitimacy (Hatem 1992; Bier 2011). Postindependence regimes in Jordan and Lebanon also adopted state feminist policies, extending girls' education and incorporating women into some sectors of the workforce. As in Egypt, these policies were embedded within national modernization plans and signaled the modernist orientation of the Jordanian and Lebanese regimes. As chapter 1 reveals, these policies supported women's entrance into the workforce in unprecedented numbers, not only actively contributing to the modernization of their respective countries but also paving the way for their public activism. However, whereas state feminism in the 1950s and 1960s was embedded within populist social pacts, from the 1970s onward, state feminism became embedded within unpopular neoliberal projects seeking to dismantle the postindependence social pact. In this context, I argue in chapter 5 that state feminism became a tool for "genderwashing" neoliberal authoritarianism in the face of growing popular opposition. More recently, in the aftermath of the Arab uprisings, state feminism became embedded within highly repressive projects of authoritarian renewal, as discussed in chapter 7. The association of women's rights with the corruption and impoverishment brought about through neoliberal restructuring, dictatorship, and repression has contributed to marginalizing and even discrediting women's rights activism, as highlighted in chapters 4 and 6.

For opposition movements, contesting women's rights has been integral to contesting the authority of their respective regimes and envisioning a new political order. Since the 1970s, the most important political movements have been ideologically aligned with political Islam. In the post–Cold War period, international women's rights (specifically CEDAW) have emerged as an important site of opposition across the Middle East to the dominant global order, which many feel they "have no control over and that appears intent on marginalizing them and their values" (Tripp 2013:178). In response, they assert so-called authentic gender norms, which emphasize women's modesty and reject notions of gender equality, in order to differentiate the Middle East from the West. In this way, Islamists, like their respective regimes, reproduce the same divisions between "us" and "them" on the basis of cultural difference, signaled by women's bodies and behavior. However, while MENA regimes accept and adopt international women's rights that promote women's public participation, as performative of national modernity, Islamists reject *all* international women's rights as culturally inappropriate (as discussed further in chapter 5), and seek to Islamize the "outer" "material" domain, as signaled by calls for women's veiling and segregation as an expression of cultural authenticity (Abu-Lughod 1998a, 1998b).

Thus, state laws and policies targeting women's bodies should not be viewed as *reflective* of culture, tradition, or religion but rather as *performative* of national difference and state sovereignty. The shaping of women's rights underpins a particular gender order that serves to naturalize the state and legitimize regime authority, or to contest authority and reimagine the state. However, women's rights are not fixed across time and space. As explored throughout the book, there are differences between geopolitical contexts; also women's rights and gender norms have shifted over time, in relation to changes in the international and regional order, mediated by changing geopolitical ideologies of anticolonial nationalism, pan-Arabism, state-centrism, Islamism, and neoliberalism. Moreover, regimes may expand or withdraw women's rights and reshape gender relations as part of their strategies for maintaining power and authority in the face of domestic opposition and regional uncertainty. Finally, dominant gender relations and gender norms have been challenged (as well as upheld) through women's activism, with geopolitical implications, as discussed in the next section.

The Geopolitical Effects of Women's Activism in the MENA

As already discussed, I conceptualize women's activism as embodied geopolitics in terms of the degree to which it disrupts/transforms and/or upholds /reproduces dominant geopolitical structures and the gender relations and norms that underpin it. Hence, it has been essential, until now, to elaborate the ways in which gender relates to geopolitics in the MENA region; particularly the role of colonialism and anticolonialism in that regard. Throughout this book, I explore women's activism in terms of the discursive framing (Benford and Snow 2000) of activist demands alongside the embodied enactment of gender norms. I consider the degree to which the framing of demands and/or the enactment of particular gender norms challenges or reproduces dominant geopolitical structures. Specifically, I consider the degree to which women's activism disrupts or reproduces the boundaries between "inner" and "outer" domains, between modernity and modesty, and between "us" and "them," which underpin the production of a "sovereignty effect" and a "natural state," upon which regime authority depends.

For example, chapter 5 discusses the use of religious frameworks by secular women activists to advocate for reforms to personal status laws and measures to combat violence against women. While this discursive strategy has achieved some tangible success in reforming relevant laws and policies, simultaneously the association of women's rights with religion serves to reproduce an "inner" domain, thereby contributing to the naturalization of gender hierarchies on the basis of cultural difference. Hence, rather than viewing women's rights demands and discourses as necessarily oppositional, it is important to consider the more complex way in which they may both disrupt and reproduce geopolitical order and its gendered pillars. By contrast, in the 1950s and the revolutionary period ushered in by the 2011 uprisings, women were able to frame their gender demands in relation to the platforms of radical movements for social justice and political transformation that were challenging the geopolitical order. However, geopolitical transformations from the 1970s onward led to the separation of women's rights agendas from wider popular movements, while Western powers and regimes instrumentalized women's rights for their own geopolitical ends. In other words, the geopolitical effects of women's activism may change over time as a result of shifts in regional and/or international order.

In considering the ways in which women's enactment of gender norms may disrupt or reproduce dominant geopolitical structures, I examine the degree to which women's activism embodies or transgresses the norm of female respectability that is produced through and productive of the boundaries between the "inner" and "outer" domains, modernity and modesty, and "us" and "them." As in the case of discursive framing of activist demands, it is necessary to attend to the complex ways in which women's embodiment of gender norms relates to dominant geopolitical structures. As Najmabadi notes, "The boundary between modernity and modesty is of necessity a socially defined and fluid one, that leaves the woman herself in a perpetual state of uncertainty. The boundary becomes clear only in its transgression, which renders the transgressor an outcast" (1991: 66). Although all women who enter public space find themselves in a state of uncertainty with regard to the boundary between modernity and modesty, women activists are particularly conscious of the risks, since their ability to continue their public work may depend upon the avoidance of any perceived transgression. Hence, women activists may be mindful to comply with the norm of female respectability through "the stylization of the body [. . .] bodily gestures, movements, and styles of various kinds" (Butler 1999: 179).[7] For example, Abla Abu Elba, leader of the Jordanian leftist opposition party HASHD, and a former member of parliament, told me during our interview in 2014: "It's very important for a woman going into public service in particular in our Arab world that she presents herself in an appropriate manner. [. . .] In our parliament, they watch women, how they behave, what they wear, how they speak. How they laugh or behave around men and so on. I always wear long sleeves to the parliament. [. . .] I used to even watch the way I laughed and how often I smiled." Through her efforts to comply with the norm of female respectability, Abla illustrates the performativity of gender (Butler 1999: xxiv). Yet, the norm of female respectability is not only repressive but is also productive of women's agency. Abla's successful performance of female respectability enables her to continue her political work. In this way, through her embodiment of female respectability in parliament and other political spaces, Abla is able to contribute to shifting the boundary between modesty and modernity in a way that resignifies women's political work as respectable.

Not all women have complied with the norm of female respectability all of the time. Major national and regional crises have provided opportunities for women to transgress this norm and to produce a subversive construct of gender. Specifically, moments of geopolitical upheaval, such as in the wake of the 1967 war and the 2011 uprisings, reshaped women's subjectivities and opened up possibilities for women to challenge dominant gender norms, as demonstrated in chapters 2 and 6. In response, regimes have sought to reestablish gender hierarchies and discipline women's bodies as a means of reestablishing their authority and restabilizing geopolitical order. As such, women's bodies are often the battlefield between competing geopolitical projects, with negative repercussions for women's bodily integrity and personal freedoms, as explored further in chapters 3 and 6.

NARRATIVES OF WOMEN'S ACTIVISM

The choice to use personal narratives as the main sources for this study was motivated by the need to challenge orientalist, Eurocentric, and masculinist epistemologies that continue to dominate the study of the international relations of the MENA region. Feminist researchers, as well as historians of marginalized groups/classes, have long been champions of narratives/life stories/ oral history methodology as a way of bridging personal and public narratives, uncovering previously untold histories, and giving voice to those ignored by conventional scholarship (Armitage 2002; Gluck and Patai 1991; Thompson 1988).[8] In contrast to archival material, personal narratives/oral histories uncover the voices of those women whose activism would not necessarily be documented (for example, through personal memoirs). Similarly, the use of personal narratives helps to avoid overlooking small organizations that do not have resources to collect and catalog their archives or to make such archives available to other institutions.[9] In this respect, narrative approaches support a diversification of voices. More importantly, narratives reveal the embodied and subjective experiences of those who participated in organizations or in events that may otherwise seem familiar and well researched. While oral history, personal narratives, and life stories have been largely marginal to the study of the MENA, the uprisings of late 2010 onward and the critical role of non-elite participants in these struggles gave impetus to the collection of personal narratives and the creation of oral histories, with the aim of writing "ordinary people" and their perspectives into the records of significant regional affairs (for example, in Egypt, the Women and Memory Forum's "Archive of Women's Voices" and the American University in Cairo's "University in the Square" projects). I have been inspired by those studies as well as others that have centered women's personal narratives and life stories in the study of contemporary history and politics in the Arab world, bridging the personal and the political (in particular, Al-Ali 2000, 2007; Kassem 2011; Sayigh 2007).

The narrative approach adopted here does not treat personal narratives as objective sources that may present previously hidden histories. Some of the narratives that I have collected do indeed uncover stories that are marginalized, if not totally absent, in the existing scholarly literature on postindependence state building and geopolitics in the MENA. These include the important contribution of women's unpaid labor in the fields of social welfare and humanitarian work and the ways in which geopolitical upheavals, such as the 1967 war and the Arab Spring, reshaped subjectivities and provided openings for women to challenge dominant gender norms. However, I do not seek to establish a record of "what really happened" (Passerini 1979: 90). Instead, I approach personal narratives/life stories as revealing of the *meanings* of past events for different individuals and the motivations and intentions behind their past actions.

Personal narratives uncover the relationships between the self and memory, between the present and the past, between the individual and the collective, and between the individual and the wider sociopolitical context (Frisch 1990; Passerini 1979, 1987; Portelli 1991). I approach them as texts that "are not reducible to individual human beings. They derive their very meaning from being part of a larger whole, and without this dual perspective it is difficult, if not impossible, to access the meaning of what is being said" (Andrews 2007: 205). Hence, the meaning of personal narratives is not immediately comprehended from the narrative itself and entails in-depth knowledge of the larger whole within which the narrator is situated. In this respect, I rely on knowledge of the Middle East and North Africa acquired as a result of many years of studying, researching, and visiting the region, particularly Egypt, Jordan, and Lebanon, engaging in countless conversations with scholars, activists, and friends there, as well as consuming local media and popular culture. To deduce meaning from women's narratives, I have been attentive to the ways in which they might reproduce, disrupt, subvert, or resignify hegemonic narratives as well as how they might constitute particular kinds of subjectivity and identity that underpin activism. For example, Fahima Charafeddine, a Lebanese academic and director of the Committee for the Follow-up on Women's Issues in Beirut, as a girl living in a village in the south of Lebanon, benefitted from then president Fouad Shihab's modernization policies after 1958 in order to be able to finish her education. She told me, "During that time, education became widespread in Lebanon. [...] A secondary school was built in my village where I could study. The Lebanese University was established in 1964, which not only had Faculties for Law and

Sciences, but also Humanities and Arts. This made it easier for women to get their education. [...] The outposts that the university built in the different Lebanese governorates helped women get access to education. This is why 54 percent of Lebanese women have university degrees." I read Fahima's narrative as upholding a dominant narrative of the postindependence Lebanese state as an agent of modernization, of which female education is a key marker. In this sense, Fahima's narrative is similar to those of other women of her generation who have benefitted from state feminism in the early years of postindependence state building. Yet Fahima also goes on to question the achievements of state modernization, in light of the fact that, according to her, women do not study in order to get a good job, since "the image women have of work is still not linked to self-realization and self-worth." In this respect, Fahima simultaneously reproduces and disrupts the hegemonic narrative of state sovereignty underpinned by claims to modernity, as she highlights the failure of other women to sufficiently adopt modern behaviors of "self-realization." Implicitly, Fahima constitutes herself as a modern Lebanese citizen through her work in the Committee for the Follow-up of Women's Issues, as well as an agent of modernization vis-à-vis other women. In this way, she reveals the complex ways in which gender (and class and national identity) and the geopolitical are mutually constituted through both affirming and disrupting hegemonic narratives of state modernity and national sovereignty. In this sense, personal narratives disclose the ways in which gendered subjectivities are constituted in relation to the geopolitical as well as indicating the ways in which the geopolitical is gendered.

In seeking to understand the relationship between women's activism, gender, and the geopolitical, I draw on more than one hundred interviews conducted with women activists of different generations in Egypt, Jordan, and Lebanon, between 2013 and 2014.[10] Alongside this, during my fieldwork visits, I attended seminars and other events organized by or attended by women activists and collected literature produced by women's organizations.[11] This by no means provides an exhaustive account of women's activism. Indeed, given the extent of women's activities, this would be impossible within a single monograph. I focus on a sample of those women who engage intentionally in publicly oriented work (al-'amal al-'am) with the aim of contributing to the wider public good, and who also tend to be middle-class. This does not mean that I do not think that other types of activism, which may be hidden or less visible, and other groups of women are unimportant, but rather that studying such modes of activism and more marginalized social groups entails more extended periods in the field, which was not an option for me.[12] Practically, middle-class women's publicly oriented activism is more visible within civil society and, therefore, easier to study. Moreover, middle-class women have a historically important relationship to modernity within anticolonial and postcolonial geopolitical imaginaries. New constructs of gender in relation to modernity were primarily promoted and taken up by the emerging urban professional middle classes, or *effendiya*, who were the primary supporters of modernist projects and, in turn, deployed their commitment to modernity to differentiate themselves from traditional elites and lower classes (Watenpaugh 2006). Consequently, support for women's education and public visibility (within the limits of norms of female respectability) was not only integral to promoting national modernity but was also a marker of the modernity of the middle classes. It is through this historical lens of class, gender, nation, and modernity that we can understand the often quite detailed accounts provided by my interviewees of their own educational achievements and the achievements of their mothers as a narration of what Keith Watenpaugh terms "middle-class modernity" (2006). In this way, women's activism is not only performative (or disruptive) of the gendered boundaries that produce sovereignty and statehood but also of class differences that constitute the norms of female respectability.

Within the established parameters, I aimed to capture a diversity of activisms, which included not only women's rights activism but also advocacy of human rights and/or the rights of vulnerable groups, national and political causes, workplace rights, and democratic rights and freedoms, as well as poverty alleviation activities, service provision for marginalized and low-income groups, and charitable and humanitarian work, among others. I aimed to achieve diversity in terms of the types of women activists interviewed and was also concerned to seek out those individuals who are not usually cited in Western media and scholarship. The most important consideration was to capture women of different generations, since this was essential to exploring women's experiences of different historical periods and major geopolitical upheavals. Efforts were also made to interview women of different political-ideological backgrounds. The vast majority of women whom I interviewed could be described as pursuing their activism through a secular-oriented framework—for example, with reference to universal rights instruments.[13] Women adhering to political Islam formed a much smaller percentage of the sample of women that I interviewed. Partly this was due to problems of access. In Egypt, in the wake of the Raba'a and Nahda Square massacres, it was highly risky to be in contact with those associated with the Muslim Brotherhood.[14] In Lebanon, Hizbollah operates as a strict gatekeeper and I was only granted access to one female member.[15] In Jordan, it was relatively easy to gain access to members of the IAF. However, the time spent in the country was not sufficient to grow my networks among Islamist women. The smaller numbers of Islamist women also reflect their longer-term underrepresentation in public life, given that the growth in Islamist women's activism corresponds with the growth in political Islamist movements from the 1970s onward. Almost all women whom I interviewed were members of organizations or collective initiatives, rather than acting individually. For those women with long histories of activism, often their organizational affiliations have changed over time, reflecting personal changes in ideology and circumstances that have been shaped by geopolitical shifts, such as, the repression of leftist/nationalist movements in the 1970s and 1980s, as explored in chapter 3, and the rise of NGOs in the post–Cold War period, as discussed in chapter 4. Consequently, I also sought to capture these different trajectories.

In the process of conducting this research and presenting preliminary findings at different venues, I became aware of the degree to which the concept of women's activism is contested and the sensitivity surrounding who has the right or opportunity to represent the voices of women activists. After a lecture that I gave in Amman in May 2015, several audience members questioned my inclusion of narratives of certain women on the basis that they are not "real activists" because they are "only" involved in charitable work and/ or they are "too elitist," while others urged me to extend my sample to include more "nonpolitical" women, who would be "more representative" of "ordinary" Jordanian women. Similarly, in Egypt, one of my interviewees questioned what she viewed as my disproportionate focus on secular-oriented women activists rather than Islamist women, the latter being those she considered to be more representative of the majority of Egyptian women. Meanwhile, several women refused to self-identify as an "activist," unsure of whether they were sufficiently "active" to warrant the label or because they refused the hierarchies of activity implied by the label. The controversy over who constitutes an authentic woman activist must be understood as reflective of the contested meaning of the term *woman activist* in the context of the MENA. Social categories and practices are constructed in relation to concrete historical circumstances and dominant epistemologies, rather than existing in abstract terms (Mohanty 1991). As chapter 1 discusses, the category of "woman activist" can be traced to the anticolonial struggle, and its meaning has evolved over time in relation to shifting geopolitical dynamics. Contested notions of activism are themselves part of the story of women's activism in the MENA and reflect the geopolitical stakes in defining and representing women's activism, particularly in the post-9/11 era, in which women's agency and women's empowerment became securitized and instrumentalized by Western governments in the "war on terror" as well as the global expansion of neoliberalism (Abu-Lughod 2013; Al-Ali and Pratt 2009a, 2009b; Salime 2010). Undoubtedly, this wider geopolitical context shaped the ways in which my interviewees presented themselves to me and, in some cases, made potential interviewees wary of speaking to me; it may have been a reason why some women did not respond to my requests for an interview. I consider that the ways in which women have presented themselves, their lives, and their activism, including the editorial decisions that they have made in narrating their life stories, are integral to the production of an embodied and situated knowledge, shaped by the matrix of power relations at multiple scales within which they are positioned.

I conducted forty-six interviews in Egypt, twenty-six interviews in Jordan, and thirty-three interviews in Lebanon.[16] The differences in the number of interviews in each country were due to the differences in the relative volume of civil society activism in each country. With by far the largest total population and, at the time, emerging from a period of intense activism, Egypt was easily identified as having the largest number of potential interviewees. Although a much smaller country, Lebanon has a long history of civil society activism, enabled by its relatively free political and social environment, which also made it relatively easy to conduct interviews. While Jordan also has a long history of civil society activism and political opposition, constraints on political and civil freedoms meant that Jordan was the most challenging country in which to meet women activists. I identified potential interviewees based on my previous research visits to these countries, from earlier pilot studies, and through snowballing. At the time of the interviews, almost all of those interviewed agreed to be cited by name. I felt that this was an important aspect of my project so that women activists would be written into the archives of the history and politics of the region. However, at the time of finalizing the manuscript, the political situation in Egypt had deteriorated significantly and, therefore, I contacted all those who were cited with regard to their activism in the January 2011 revolution to ask whether they wanted to withdraw their consent to be cited by name. In a few cases, I made a unilateral decision to anonymize citations out of fears of safety for the interviewee.

The numbers of women interviewed were determined by the (limited) time and resources at my disposal. While I was very fortunate to have funding from the British Academy, the fieldwork budget did not allow me to stay more than four weeks in each of Jordan and Lebanon and five weeks in Egypt. Nonetheless, I was fortunate to be able to draw on many years of engagement with the region and networks of friends and acquaintances built over that time. I had hoped to organize appointments in advance of my arrival; however, in practice this was difficult to do, as most people preferred to wait until I was actually on the ground before confirming an appointment. Therefore, the first couple of days of each fieldwork visit were spent obtaining a sim card and local phone number, calling a list of names, and trying to pin people down to a particular date and time. Getting an appointment was the first hurdle. The second hurdle was to ensure that the potential interviewee kept the appointment. As I was dealing with very busy women, it was not unusual for individuals to cancel and reschedule—with all the knock-on effects that would have in terms of (re-)organizing my diary. As the days went by, I amassed more contacts and got more appointments, while experiencing more rescheduling, until by the last week, I was often conducting three or even four interviews per day. The whole process was nerve-wracking (would I get enough interviews before my departure date?) as well as mentally tiring, but also fascinating. I am very fortunate that so many women were willing to share their stories with me.

WHY EGYPT, JORDAN, AND LEBANON?

The choice of country cases for this book initially emerged from my ongoing research interests in Egypt and the Levant. Indeed, this book developed from a research project, started in 2007, examining women's activism in relation to the Arab-Israeli conflict, which focused on Egypt, Jordan, and Lebanon. In turn, this led me to become interested in the wider relationship between women's activism, gender, and the geopolitical. As frontline states in the Arab-Israeli conflict, the country cases studied here have allowed me to explore the embodied dimensions of "big geopolitical" issues of war and conflict and their aftermath. However, these country cases are also interesting because they represent different trajectories of state formation and regime building and different types of state-society relations and demographic makeup (although, that is not to claim that these are the *only* types of state formation and regime building in the region). These differences enabled me to study the ways in which different geopolitical contexts and processes may shape the constitution of gender and women's activism, and vice versa. Meanwhile, choosing countries with similar levels of women's legal rights enabled me to focus on tracing the significance of the geopolitical context (rather than the significance of gender laws) in shaping women's activism and gender norms. All three countries share similar levels of commitment to some form of state feminism, including being signatories of CEDAW, as a marker of national modernity, while maintaining gender inequalities in the "inner sphere" of family and nationality laws, as a marker of cultural difference.

The first country case, Egypt, has a long history of modern state formation dating back to the early nineteenth century, when Mohammed Ali, an Ottoman governor, began to modernize the country. Nevertheless, Egyptians struggled for a long time to achieve sovereignty over their state. First, they were ruled by Ottoman officials, and then, between 1882 and 1952, by the British. This led to various efforts at popular and armed revolt, which functioned to consolidate a modern Egyptian identity. However, it was not until an army coup on 23 July 1952, led by the Free Officers, that Egyptians finally achieved self-determination. Egypt's struggle against colonialism was translated into an anti-imperialist, pan-Arab foreign policy in the initial phase of postindependence state building. Under the regime of Gamal Abdel-Nasser, Egypt was part of the Non-Aligned Movement, and Nasser himself enjoyed region-wide popularity for his resistance to Western intervention. Domestically, the regime attempted to consolidate power through a highly centralized and interventionist state. This process of state building and regime consolidation was supported through wide-ranging social justice policies, of which state feminism was one example, alongside land reform, nationalization of industries, and the provision of universal health care and education. After the defeat of the 1967 war, Nasser's successors slowly began to roll back his populist policies both domestically and in foreign policy. President Anwar al-Sadat initiated Egypt's turn toward the West and the opening up of its economy to private and foreign investment as well as reconfiguring state feminism toward a more neoliberal orientation. These policies were continued under President Hosni Mubarak until he was overthrown in a popular uprising in 2011. Following a brief revolutionary period, the regime of Abdel-Fattah El-Sisi, who came to power following the ouster of the Muslim Brotherhood in 2013, has largely continued the policies of Mubarak, albeit accompanied with a much greater degree of political repression.

Jordan and Lebanon are examples of the challenges of state formation and regime consolidation in a context of colonially imposed borders. Both were created by European powers out of the remnants of the Ottoman Empire after the end of World War I. In the case of Jordan, a British-imposed monarchy has sought to unite disparate groups under its authority. In Lebanon, a sectarian pact between major confessional groups is the basis of the state. In both cases, gender has been a central mechanism for naturalizing the geopolitical order. Before 1922, present-day Lebanon was part of Ottoman Syria. It consisted of the province of Beirut, stretching from north of Jaffa (in present-day Israel-Palestine) to Latakia (in present-day Syria) and an autonomous district of Mount Lebanon. In 1922, following the dismantling of the Ottoman Empire, the French created the Mandate of Greater Lebanon, consisting of Mount Lebanon in addition to the coastal cities of Beirut, Tripoli, and Saida (Sidon) and their hinterlands and the Biqa' Valley, which had previously been part of the province of Damascus. While Maronite Christians were supportive of the Mandate and French protection, the borders and identity of the new Lebanese entity were contested by Sunni Muslims and Greek Orthodox Christians residing primarily in the coastal areas, who wished to remain part of Syria and were hostile to what they saw as the imposition of Maronite dominance with French backing (Khalidi 1979: 35). In an effort to settle this conflict and pave the way for Lebanese independence, two powerful politicians, Bishara al-Khuri, a Maronite Christian, and Riyad al-Sulh, a Sunni Muslim, reached an informal agreement, called the National Pact, in 1942, in which, "al-Khuri traded French protection for Christian political primacy and al-Sulh abandoned the idea of Muslim annexation to Syria in return for Muslim partnership in running the affairs of the country" (Traboulsi 2007: 105–6). This compromise gave rise to a unique system of government within the MENA: that of power-sharing on the basis of religious-sectarian affiliation. The stability of this system has depended upon "demographic balance" between the main religious sects making up Lebanon (Christian Maronite, Sunni Muslim, and Shi'a Muslim), foreign policy neutrality, and a relatively laissez-faire approach to national development. In moments of geopolitical upheaval, such as the post-1967 period and the post-2011 period, this system of compromise proved difficult to maintain. As already discussed, the sectarian political system has been buttressed by sectarian personal status laws, which function to reproduce and legitimize a political system based on sectarian power sharing at the expense of gender equality.

The Jordanian state has also faced challenges in asserting its sovereignty and creating a cohesive identity (Massad 2001). Prior to 1921, most of the territory of Transjordan was part of the Ottoman Empire; however, unlike other former provinces of the empire that were crafted into states after World War I, Jordan was sparsely populated, with no significant urban centers or sources of economic wealth (Robins 2004: 5–12). In 1921, the British established the Mandate of Transjordan (in what is present-day Jordan). They installed as its leader Amir (later King) Abdullah, born in Mecca (in present-day Saudi Arabia), as a sort of compensation for blocking the larger territorial ambitions of Abdullah and his brother, Faisal, who had led the Arab Revolt of 1916 against the Ottomans in return for a British promise of Arab sovereignty over Arab Ottoman provinces. Without any sort of popular base or natural constituency, the Amir was highly dependent upon the British financially and militarily in order to pacify and coopt the Bedouin tribes and consolidate his authority (Robins 2004; Tell 2013). This dependency continued after 1946, when Britain granted independence and the country became the Hashemite Kingdom of Jordan. Dependency upon the British was later replaced by dependency on the United States, which continues until today. The challenges to constructing a Jordanian national identity are linked to the large number of Jordanian citizens whose ancestry is traced beyond the borders of the current Jordanian state to other parts of the former Ottoman Empire and beyond. Not only does the Hashemite monarchy itself come from what is today part of modern-day Saudi Arabia (the Hijaz), but many of Transjordan's early civil servants came from Syria and Palestine, while large numbers of Circassians were displaced to the territory of Transjordan during the nineteenth century, and Armenian refugees arrived during the First World War, fleeing genocide. Following the Arab-Israeli war of 1948, Jordan annexed the West Bank and West Bank Palestinians were incorporated into the Jordanian state as citizens. Many of these became displaced persons during the war of 1967, after Israel occupied the West Bank and East Jerusalem. Today, it is estimated that up to one half of Jordan's citizens are of Palestinian origin. Since 1970, following the war between the Jordanian military and the Palestine Liberation Organization (PLO), the division between those deemed Jordanian-Jordanian (i.e., of East Bank origins) and Palestinian-Jordanian (i.e., of West Bank origins) has become a major division in Jordanian politics (as discussed further in chapter 3). The monarchy presents itself as the arbiter between the different groups that comprise Jordan and the guarantor of Jordan's progress and stability. In this respect, the extension of women's rights with regard to education and labor force participation constitutes a marker of the regime's modernity against the forces of "backwardness" (which, for the urban middle classes, would constitute the tribes and the Islamists), while the enshrining of gender inequality with regard to nationality laws and personal status laws are a marker of the regime's rootedness within tradition and respect for religion, thereby appealing to the tribes and the Islamists (Amawi 2000, Warrwick 2009, Jabiri 2016).

OUTLINE OF THE BOOK

Following this introduction, the book is divided into seven chapters and a conclusion. Each of the chapters discusses a significant geopolitical period in the histories of Egypt, Jordan, and Lebanon, from independence until the Arab uprisings. A large number of existing studies examine women's activism in the Middle East and North Africa region. However, these studies tend to be limited to specific time periods—such as, European colonial rule, the Palestinian revolution, or the Arab uprisings. By examining women's activism over several decades, the book historicizes the relationship between women's agency, gender, and the geopolitical, revealing how a particular configuration of space and power in a specific historical period, is not only contingent and temporary, but is naturalized through a specific gender order. As women's narratives reveal, gendered and spatialized relations of power are both constitutive of as well as constituted by women's activism over time. In this way, the book highlights the centrality of women's geopolitical agency and gender to understanding the contemporary politics and international relations of the Middle East.

Chapters 1–3 cover the period from decolonization until the end of the Cold War. Chapter 1 examines the role of women and gender in state building and regime consolidation in a regional context of threats to national sovereignty from geopolitical rivals and pan-Arab movements. While feminist scholarship has criticized the failure of postindependence states to grant equal citizenship rights to women, the chapter explores the degree to which women have contributed to normalizing state sovereignty and legitimizing regime authority through their embodiment of modernity and modesty, performative of female respectability, in their activism and professional lives. Yet not all women upheld dominant gender norms. The chapter also explores women's resignification of dominant gender norms as well as their transgression, particularly through their participation in anti-imperialist and pan-Arab movements. Chapter 2 investigates the impact of geopolitical crisis on gender norms and women's activism following the defeat of the Arab states in the 1967 war with Israel. In contrast to the majority of scholarship on this period, this chapter reveals the embodied dimensions of the defeat. While feminist scholarship has generally argued that war negatively impacts upon women, here I argue that the defeat also constituted an opportunity for women to expand their activism. Specifically, the breakdown of the gender order, caused by the weakening of Arab regimes in the aftermath of the war, provided opportunities for young women to transgress dominant gender norms through their participation in new sociopolitical movements in opposition to the status quo. While the weakening of regimes enabled the transgression of dominant gender norms, so the reinscribing of norms of female respectability were part of regime efforts to repress radical movements and reestablish regime authority, as revealed in chapter 3. Overall, this chapter highlights how political repression and violence, supported by the United States and its allies, closed down spaces for women's enactment of transgressive femininities, thereby challenging Western claims of bringing democracy and women's rights to the world. In response to political repression as well as to their experiences within political movements, women activists began to create their own organizations and initiatives with gender-specific demands.

Chapters 4 and 5 examine the first two decades following the Cold War, characterized by US military interventions and the spread of neoliberal economic reforms, which, in turn, contributed to growing inequalities and the strengthening of authoritarian rule in the MENA region. The chapters demonstrate the complex workings of women's activism and gender in relation to these structures and processes. Chapter 4 explores further how women activists pursued gender-specific agendas through the establishment of NGOs. While the existing literature casts NGOs as either part of neoliberal forms of governmentality or as offering alternatives to hegemonic geopolitical power relations, women's narratives challenge homogenizing accounts of NGOs and suggest that notions of resistance and compliance are partial and circumscribed when considered in relation to different scales of hegemonic power. Chapter 5 further explores these contradictory relations between gender and geopolitics in relation to the emergence of an international consensus around women's rights in the post–Cold War period. Discussing the ways in which women's rights activists, their respective regimes, and their Islamist detractors adopt, adapt, and resist international women's rights norms in each of Egypt, Jordan, and Lebanon, the chapter demonstrates the important role of women's rights discourses in shoring up hegemonic power on the national and international scales.

Chapters 6 and 7 investigate the period following the popular uprisings and mass protests that erupted across the region from late 2010 onward and highlight the ways in which, as Cynthia Enloe (2005) argues, gender is part of the "bigger picture" of geopolitical upheaval. Not only were women part of the protests, but many, particularly young women, also seized the moment of liminality to subvert and resignify female respectability in ways that legitimized their participation in the realm of politics while insisting that women's rights should be central to the political transformation. However, women faced a backlash, particularly in Egypt, where counterrevolutionary forces violently targeted women protesters, using rape and sexual violence to force women out of the public space as part of efforts to restabilize the geopolitical order. In Jordan and Lebanon, where there was no regime change and, therefore, the geopolitical stakes were not as high, sexual violence against women protesters did not occur. Nevertheless, resistance to demands for women's rights and gender equality were part of regime calculations in maintaining power and authority in a context of regional uncertainty and demands for political and social change. Chapter 7 explores an embodied geopolitics of fear unleashed by the 2011 uprisings and their violent aftermaths. It explores women's narratives of fears for their rights, safety, and personal freedoms, demonstrating how these have served to reproduce gendered and racialized boundaries between "us" and "them"—with the latter cast as political Islamists and refugees. In this regard, I argue that fears about women's rights and personal safety have underwritten the use of exclusionary and coercive measures, and even violence, in the name of protecting "us" from "them." They have contributed to strengthening counterrevolutionary projects of authoritarian restoration and militarization. This seemingly counterintuitive relationship between women's rights and authoritarianism can be understood as a legacy of the historical relationship of gender to modernity and sovereignty.

The book concludes by reflecting upon the implications of conceptualizing women's activism as embodied geopolitics for the field of Middle East politics and IR as well as the implications of understanding the geopolitics of gender for the wider field of feminist IR and feminist geopolitics.

ONE

Female Respectability and Embodied National Sovereignty

THIS CHAPTER EXAMINES the relationship between women's activism, gender, and state building in Egypt, Jordan, and Lebanon, from the moment of formal decolonization until the 1967 Arab-Israeli war. This was the period of what Malcolm Kerr (1971) called the Arab Cold War—geopolitical rivalries between pan-Arab republics, led by Egypt, and conservative monarchies, such as Jordan. Lebanon, where political elites were committed to foreign policy neutrality, found itself uncomfortably pulled in both directions, triggering a political crisis in 1958. Meanwhile, during this period, movements inspired by Gamal Abdel-Nasser's vision of pan-Arabism, freedom from imperialism, and modernization, challenged state sovereignty in Jordan and Lebanon.

Feminist scholarship on decolonization has tended to present women as either active and empowered participants in the anticolonial struggle (Badran 1995; Fleischmann 1999; Hasso 2005a; Jayawardena 1986) or victims of patriarchal nationalist leaders who denied them full rights once liberation was achieved (for example, Enloe 1989; Moghadam 1994; Yuval-Davis and Anthias 1989). This chapter aims to go beyond these seemingly contradictory conceptualizations of the relationship between decolonization and women's activism, arguing that anticolonial nationalism was simultaneously productive of women's activism while also contributing to the production of gendered inequalities in the postindependence state. Specifically, anticolonial nationalism mobilized women but on the basis of an emerging norm of "female respectability," which was constituted by as well as constitutive of national modernity and of national difference in resistance to the gendered and racialized "rule of colonial difference" (Chatterjee 1993: 10). Reformulated norms of female respectability were embedded within postcolonial state-building projects, enabling women's participation in national development on the condition that this would not challenge the gendered hierarchies underpinning the state.

Based on personal narratives, the chapter explores the ways in which different women embodied and/or resisted norms of female respectability in the early years of postindependence state building through their professional lives and respective activisms. Despite the apparent constraints of dominant notions of female respectability on women's agency, many women willingly embodied such norms to pursue professional ambitions and contribute to national development. In this way, they supported the naturalization of the dominant gender order, which, in turn, contributed to producing a "natural state" (Weber 1998: 92) that underpinned regime authority in a context of threats to sovereignty from regional rivals and pan-Arab movements. Meanwhile, some women sought to resignify female respectability through expanding women's roles within the existing gender order, while others transgressed dominant gender norms by participating in political activism. Specifically, anti-imperialist, pan-Arab, and other radical ideological movements provided a terrain for women to resist existing gendered hierarchies and dominant gender norms in Jordan and Lebanon. Hence, women's independent activism was a particular target of repression and control for postindependence regimes.

THE GEOPOLITICAL ORIGINS OF WOMEN'S ACTIVISM UNDER COLONIAL RULE

It is impossible to understand the significance, trajectory, and characteristics of women's activism in the Middle East without being attentive to the geopolitical context in which it emerged. While women (mainly of the peasant and working classes) have always participated in the economic, social, and cultural life of former Ottoman societies (Meriwether and Tucker 1999; Tucker 2008), the substantial public visibility of women—specifically those of the upper classes—was a modern phenomenon, linked to socioeconomic and political changes arising with European economic penetration and, later, colonial rule. The Europeans justified their domination of non-European societies on the basis of their supposed cultural superiority, or what Partha Chatterjee has called the "rule of colonial difference" (Chatterjee 1993). European discourse constructed the "Orient" as backward, irrational, and despotic, blaming Islam (Said 1978). Significantly, the situation of women, such as the existence of domestic seclusion (harem) and veiling, was held up as a marker of the region's backwardness (Ahmed 1992).

In response to European encroachment, Ottoman officials initiated modernizing reforms, such as, the introduction of European models of administration and education, contributing to the emergence of a new social strata of Western-style educated bureaucrats and professionals, who began to debate the role of Islam in public life (Badran 1995: 10–11; Hourani 1983) and, related to this, the "woman question"—that is, a set of debates about women's "proper" social roles as "mothers, managers of the domestic realm, as wives of men, and as citizens of the nation" (Abu-Lughod 1998a: 8; see also Baron 2005: 17–39). It is perhaps lawyer Qasim Amin who is best known for advocating the reform of women's situation with the publication of *Tahrir al-ma'ra* (The emancipation of woman) in 1899 and *Al-ma'ra al-jadida* (The new woman) in 1900, in which he insisted on an end to female seclusion and face veiling, the elimination of abuses of divorce and polygamy, and the establishment of women's education, as necessary for social and national regeneration (Badran 1995: 18–19; Hourani 1983). In fact, women writers such as, Zaynab Fawwaz and Bahithat al-Badiya (Malak Hifni Nassif) and educationalist Nabawiya Musa had already pioneered calls for women to be educated and allowed to play a role beyond the household (Badran 1995: 61–69). Similarly, in Beirut, which from the late nineteenth century was an important center for the Arab cultural and intellectual renaissance (*al-nahda*), the "woman question" was also taken up (Traboulsi 2007: 52–72). *Nahda* intellectuals, such as Butrus al-Bustani and Ahmad Faris al-Shidyaq, argued for the necessity of women's liberation for the progress of society (Traboulsi 2003: 15, 2007: 67). Women also contributed to these debates through an emerging women's press (Booth 2001; Fleischmann 1999: 101; Thompson 2000: 120).[1]

Public debates over the "woman question" alongside the growing anticolonial nationalist movements opened up new spaces for elite women, many of whom were the wives, daughters, or sisters of male nationalist leaders, to engage in public work. As philanthropists and educationalists, they created charitable associations and intellectual societies. In line with the broader aims of anticolonial nationalism, they sought to contribute to the struggle against national "backwardness" and for social progress, particularly through the provision of services and education to poor women (al-Tal 2014: 31–34; Badran 1995: 48–60; Fleischmann 1999; Thompson 2000: 96). In this way, through their associational work, women activists contributed to the erasure of the "marks of colonial difference" (Chatterjee 1993: 26) in welfare activities that sought "social uplift" but also by their embodiment of the "new woman." Yet, simultaneously, elite women's activism also reinscribed the class hierarchies within the nationalist movement (Bier 2011: 29–34; Thompson 2000).

Women's associational activities were generally encouraged by nationalist elites; however, they were expected to contribute to the national struggle without forgoing notions of modesty, docility, and respectability that marked the "essence" of the nation—that is, to be what Afsaneh Najmabadi has termed "modern-yet-modest" (1991: 49). Although such attitudes were contradictory, they were central to constructions of cultural difference from Europe, reflecting wider contradictions within anticolonial nationalism— which sought to be modern yet *different* from Europe (Chakrabarty 1997: 373). Notions of female modesty operated to exclude women from the sphere of formal politics. For example, in Egypt, a new constitution promulgated in 1923, following the awarding of nominal independence by the British, failed to grant women the right to vote, despite the important involvement of women in the 1919 uprising against the British (Badran 1995: 86–95). Meanwhile, in Lebanon, women activists were accused by conservatives and religious leaders of acting "contrary to religion" by calling for the right to vote (Thompson 2000: 143). However, rather than directly challenge norms of female respectability, women activists generally deferred to the gendered hierarchies of the nationalist movement, for example, by emphasizing the social and cultural aspects of women's mission, as well as through their choice of clothing (Badran 1995: 47–48, 58; Thompson 2000: 143). Likewise, in our interview, the late Marie Assaad, born in Cairo in 1932, in the then wealthy neighborhood of Faggala, insisted that women's activism during this period was not political: "When we think of active women like Huda Sha'rawi [founder of the Egyptian Feminist Union] and all, they were not really political. They were all volunteering to do something. For other people, for women, for poor women, for service. That was the expression of our participation in society." Marie herself was raised from an early age to take an interest in "the fate of the poor." During summer vacations from school, she would give literacy classes to underprivileged children living in her neighborhood. Marie was also a member of the Egyptian branch of the Young Women's Christian Association, which encouraged women's public participation through social work and youth activities. Yet, moments of political upheaval and crisis constituted opportunities for transgressing dominant norms of female respectability. During the 1919 uprising against the British, "gender rules were suspended" (Badran 1995: 74) and, for the first time, middle- and upper-class women participated in street demonstrations and other political actions, including organizing petitions, boycotts, and public debates (Badra 1995; see also Philipp 1978). In Lebanon, in the run-up to and during World War II, the participation of middle-class and upper-class Lebanese women in anti-French protests, which even included a collective unveiling by Muslim women, transgressed dominant gendered class norms, sometimes provoking hostile reactions (Thompson 2000: 184–96, 252–59).[2] In Jordan, during the 1947–48 Palestine war, the Society of the Jordanian Women's Union (Jami'iyat al-Ittihad al-Nisa'i al-Urdunni) trained women in first aid and nursing (not considered an appropriate activity for "respectable" women, since it would bring them into contact with men) to assist Jordanian soldiers and Palestinian refugees (al-Tal 2014: 157–58). Women created new organizations and initiatives, such as the Egyptian Feminist Union (EFU), Egypt's first independent feminist organization, founded in 1923, which not only provided welfare services to women and low-income groups, but also advocated for women's political rights, access to education, and changes to personal status laws (Badran 1995). However, these demands were framed in reference to gendered conceptions of citizenship, whereby reform of women's status was linked to their role as the mothers and nurturers of future citizens (Badran 1995: 128–33; Bier 2011: 33). While these moments of transgression did not dismantle the modesty-modernity boundary, they did enable a renegotiation thereof and a resignification of "female respectability."

However, following World War II, a new generation of women activists went much further in challenging dominant gender norms. These women were more radical in their ideological orientations and more diverse in their class-basis compared to the previous generation of women activists (Khater and Nelson 1988). For example, women members of the Egyptian communist movement, such as Inji Aflatoun and Latifa al-Zayyat, broke social taboos by mingling with men through their participation in political party work (Botman 1988: 118). They were primarily focused on mobilizing support for the struggle against the British but were also concerned to improve the situation of Egyptian women, linking the struggle against imperialism to the struggle against class and gender inequalities (Botman 1988; Khater and Nelson 1988). Meanwhile, in 1948, Doria Shafik founded the *Bint al-Nil* organization, which led an occupation of parliament in 1951 to demand Egyptian women's full political rights (Khater & Nelson 1988). However, all forms of independent women's activism were banned in Egypt and Jordan in the years following formal decolonization.

As this section has demonstrated, the origins of women's activism can be traced to the major geopolitical transformations from the end of the nineteenth century onward—namely European colonialism and growing indigenous resistance to it in the form of nationalist movements. Anticolonial nationalism sought to modernize society as proof of readiness for national independence and placed women at the heart of that project. While women from the working classes and peasantry had always contributed to economic, social, and cultural life, for the first time, women from the elite and emerging middle classes were able to enter public life through their participation in the nationalist movement. Norms of female respectability, however, prevented women from becoming involved in overtly political activities. As a result, women, with some exceptions, generally limited their activism to charitable and welfare activities, presenting these as a form of social activism in the service of the nation. The construction of the political/social distinction was constitutive of the norm of female respectability, which, in turn, was a marker of cultural difference from Europe. Therefore, despite insistence to the contrary, women's social activism was *geopolitical*, in that it was integral to the nationalist construction of the inner sphere of national sovereignty at the heart of the struggle that finally culminated in formal decolonization.

WOMEN'S ACTIVISM AND POSTINDEPENDENCE STATE BUILDING

The period from formal decolonization until 1967 was a time of regional upheaval and geopolitical contestations. The 1947 UN partition of Palestine triggered the first Arab-Israeli war, resulting in the defeat of the Arab forces and the Nakba, or "catastrophe" for the Palestinians. The loss of Palestine led to the political radicalization of a new generation of Palestinians as well as citizens of Egypt, Lebanon, and Jordan. New ideological parties emerged across the region espousing pan-Arab unity, anti-imperialism, anti-Zionism, and social justice, challenging the geopolitical order established by the European powers and their local allies. In Egypt, a group of army officers, calling themselves the Free Officers, launched a coup in July 1952, forcing King Faruq to abdicate, dissolving the government, and paving the way for a full withdrawal of British forces. The new regime, headed by the charismatic

Gamal Abdel-Nasser, set about building a new domestic order based on a coalition of popular forces and supplanting the class of wealthy business owners and landlords. Meanwhile, the regime sought to overturn Western influence in the region more broadly and became a leading member of the Non-Aligned Movement. Following the 1956 Tripartite Aggression by Britain, France, and Israel, Gamal Abdel-Nasser became a hero both at home and abroad, inspiring radical movements across the region, which resulted in the toppling of pro-Western regimes in Syria, Lebanon, Iraq, Yemen, Sudan, and Libya, and, if it were not for Western intervention, might have also overturned the Hashemite monarchy of Jordan. Pan-Arabism became a strong norm governing regional Arab politics (Barnett 1998). Even the pro-Western monarchies (Saudi Arabia, the Gulf states, and Jordan) were obliged to at least be seen to act in accordance with pan-Arabism or risk their citizens rising up against them. This section examines the ways in which norms of female respectability, produced through the anticolonial struggle, were deployed in postindependence state-building projects and anti-imperialist movements, and the ways in which women embodied, resisted, and renegotiated these norms through their activism and professional lives.

Gender and Geopolitical Order in Egypt

Under Nasser's leadership, Egypt would experience one of the most ambitious national modernization programs of all the Arab countries, including land redistribution, state-led industrialization, rural development, and expansion of free education and health care, which were accompanied by social benefits, including a minimum wage, reduced working hours, access to cheap credit and subsidized goods and services (Yapp 1996: 215–19; Vatikiotis 1991: 393–402). Urban middle and lower-middle classes experienced significant social mobility, as did peasants and workers in the formal sector, whose living standards improved until economic stagnation set in after 1965 (Waterbury 1983: 207–23). These measures not only boosted the popularity of the new regime but also helped to dismantle the power and wealth of the former elites.

An important component of the regime's state-building project was the implementation of a program of "state feminism" (Hatem 1992; Bier 2011). Important measures in this respect included the 1956 constitution, which granted women the right to vote and stand for office; the amendment of labor laws between 1958 and 1959 to provide maternity leave and workplace crèches for working mothers; a 1964 law guaranteeing jobs in the state sector for all university graduates irrespective of gender, and implementation of a state family planning program (Bier 2011; Hatem 1992: 232).[3] Other measures that greatly benefited women and girls included the introduction of free education. Between 1960 and 1976, female primary and secondary education enrolment increased threefold and female university enrolment increased by six times (see Hatem 1988: 413). Commitment to state feminism was part of the raft of social policies that built popular support for the regime, while serving as a means of mobilizing women's productive and reproductive capabilities in the service of the state's modernization policies (Hatem 1992). As Laura Bier argues, Nasserist state feminism represented a continuation of earlier nationalist projects to remake women but also transformed the "woman question" in a way that was "consistent with the dictates of a secular nation-state project and the notions of secular modernity that underpinned them" (Bier 2011: 16). State feminism signaled the progressive character of the regime, thereby contributing to the regime's legitimacy, particularly vis-à-vis its main political rival, the Muslim Brotherhood. Nasser ridiculed the Muslim Brotherhood's attitudes toward women's rights, characterizing them as reactionary and a threat to the gains of the Egyptian revolution (ERTU 1965).

Writer, literary critic, and political activist Farida El-Nakkash was one of many young women to benefit from the new regime's policies, graduating in English Literature from Cairo University in 1962, the same year in which the government announced that all university graduates would be guaranteed state employment. Farida worked for the state-owned Middle East News Agency as a journalist. She recalled: "When women began to get university education on a broader scale, they began to enter into all sorts of professions very actively. From time to time religious groups would say that a woman's natural place is in her home and that raising the children was her most important job, but the society in general was accepting of women entering the workforce." This shift in gender norms was also reflected in popular culture. Egyptian films in the 1960s promoted the idea of women working, such as the 1966 film *Mirati mudir 'am* (My wife, the general manager), staring popular Egyptian actress Shadia. As Laura Bier notes, "Female workers [. . .] were represented in state feminist discourse not only as necessary to the economic success of state socialist policies but also as a critical symbol of the regime's success in transforming Egypt into a modern socialist nation" (Bier 2011: 69).

The regime also sought to reshape gender relations within the private sphere as a means of facilitating women's participation in the workforce (Bier 2011). The notion of companionate marriage, which had first emerged earlier in the century as part of projects to modernize the family (Abu Lughod 1998b), was presented as the solution to resolving possible tensions between women's domestic and public roles (Bier 2011: 76). The notion of companionate marriage was strongly validated by Anissa Essam Hassouna, former executive director of the Sir Magdy Yacoub Foundation, who, in our interview, fondly remembered her own parents' relationship, emphasizing her father's support for her mother's work as a doctor and the cooperation between them. Among the many stories that Anissa told me about her parents, she was particularly proud that her father, Essam Hassouna, who had been minister of justice under Nasser, was responsible for canceling the compulsory enforcement of *bayt al-ta'a* (literally, "house of obedience"), that is, the right of husbands to seek a judicial ruling forcibly returning their wives to the marital home. Anissa recalled:

> I remember he used to tell us [. . .] that he got heavily attacked and all the men in the People's Assembly asked for his resignation [. . .]. And he gave a very famous speech, [. . .] "How dare you think that you can accept that your wife or daughters or mothers be brought by force to the beds of their husbands! This is against religion and against sharia!" And they all attacked him and he told us later that President Nasser talked to [then Speaker of the People's Assembly] Anwar al-Sadat and said, "What is this? Do you want the world to laugh at us? That the Egyptians treat women like this?"

Yet, as Laura Bier highlights, the cancellation of *bayt al-ta'a* did not remove the notion of wifely obedience from Egyptian law and, hence, did not challenge gender hierarchies within the private sphere. Indeed, despite ongoing lobbying by women activists, the Nasser regime resisted calls for more far-reaching reforms of personal status laws (Bier 2011: 112–20). Rather, the cancellation of *bayt al-ta'a* was more about promoting the regime's "vision of marriage based on cooperation and intimacy" (Bier 2011: 118). Anissa's narrative highlights that the cancellation of *bayt al-ta'a* was framed by the regime as in line with religious law, while necessary for protecting Egypt's modernizing image vis-à-vis the rest of the world—that is, simultaneously performative of cultural difference *and* national modernity.

It is argued that the disjuncture between state feminist measures to encourage women's contributions to the public sphere and their continued subordination within the "private sphere" reveals the limitations of Nasserist state feminism in transforming gender relations (see, for example, Hatem 1988). Similarly, writers have highlighted the apparent contradiction between the regime's state feminism and its suppression of feminist activism (Badran 1991: 217; Khater and Nelson 1988: 472–76), which effectively brought to an end women's independent organizing in Egypt until the 1980s, although women continued to be active in public work during this period, through the Arab Socialist Union and as champions of Nasser's state feminist policies, while women's voluntary and charitable activities continued, albeit under the direction of the Ministry of Social Affairs (Bier 2011; Howard-Merriam 1981).

Viewed through a critical geopolitical lens, attentive to the gendered constructions of public and private, or inner and outer spheres within anticolonial and postcolonial nationalisms, these apparent contradictions within Nasser's state feminist project are understandable. On the one hand, Egyptian officials sought to mobilize women's labor to develop Egypt's economy and to signal the state's modernity, thereby erasing the marks of "colonial difference" in the outer sphere (Chatterjee 1993: 26). Independent women's activism had no place within this state-directed vision of modernization. Meanwhile, the state sought to maintain gender inequality within the inner sphere as performative of "national difference" (Chatterjee 1993: 26). Within both inner and outer spheres, women were expected to be "modern-yet-modest," as signaled through their obedience to the gendered hierarchies of state building and national modernization. In other words, state feminism reformulated rather than undid the norm of female respectability.

For the most part, women did indeed respect these gendered hierarchies and boundaries, and the regime faced little opposition. When Doria Shafik staged a hunger strike in the Indian embassy against the regime's dictatorship, her comrades and others denounced her as a traitor to the revolution (Khater and Nelson 1988: 472). When state feminists tried to push the state's agenda further, by calling for reforms of the personal status laws, they did not seek to introduce complete gender equality within the family but rather to limit the most egregious forms of male power (Bier 2011: 112–20). Indeed, a great many women appreciated the gains made under the Nasser regime and actively supported it. As Farida El-Nakkash, who was part of the Arab Socialist Union and a great supporter of Nasser, commented:

[There was no feminist movement]. It was all within the Socialist Union and as part of Nasserism, which believed that the cause of women was a cause inseparable from that of other social causes. The belief was that when society changes, the cause of women would be automatically solved. I believed in the Nasserist idea, that women's issues could only be solved within the framework of social reform. I was interested in the progress of women's rights within the framework of Nasserism, that all the issues facing women would be solved as part of the progress made in social and economic reforms.

Through their compliance with the gendered hierarchies embedded within state feminism, women contributed to the (re)production and continued hegemony of the norm of female respectability. In turn, they contributed to legitimizing the new regime and its state feminist rhetoric. In this way, gains (albeit somewhat limited) in women's rights became entangled with authoritarian modernist projects, with longer-term implications for women's activism and their rights demands, as will be highlighted in later chapters.

Gender and Geopolitical Order in Jordan

In 1946, the British granted formal independence to what became the Kingdom of Jordan. Following the 1948 Arab-Israeli War and Jordan's annexation of the West Bank, the number of women's organizations in the kingdom grew substantially, largely because of the Palestinian women's organizations now within its borders but also due to the creation of new organizations established to assist Palestinian refugees (al-Tal 2014: 161–65). Most of these organizations continued the tradition of charitable and philanthropic work in the service of national uplift, including providing services for women and children, such as vocational training and literacy classes (al-Tal 2014: 164–65). However, new types of women's organizations emerged that were associated with the new, radical political movements, such as the communists, Arab nationalists, Ba'athists, and Jordanian and Palestinian nationalists, which grew in popularity in the wake of the Nakba ("the catastrophe," referring to the loss of Palestine in 1948). Many of these organizations sought to renegotiate or even transform dominant norms of female respectability.

The most important women's organization to emerge during this period was the Arab Women's Union, founded in 1954 under the leadership of Jordan's first female lawyer Emily Bisharat. The Union attracted thousands of members across the country and had close links with the new ideological parties (al-Tal 2014: 166–70). In a departure from previous women's activism, as Suhair Salti al-Tal documents, the Union not only provided social services and literacy classes for women but also launched a vigorous campaign for women's right to vote, as well as supporting Arab unity and nationalist causes (al-Tal 2014: 167). The Union also called for changes to family law, specifically to end polygamy and unilateral divorce, and for full equality of opportunities in higher education and employment and the expansion of education for girls in rural and desert areas (al-Tal 2014: 167–68). In 1955, the government granted educated women the right to vote, but women's rights activists continued lobbying for the right of *all* women to vote, collecting the thumb prints of hundreds of illiterate women to petition the government (al-Tal 2014: 168). A more radical women's organization, the Women's Awakening League, was established in Jerusalem in 1952 by women political activists from the Jordanian Communist Party, and extended to the East Bank under the name of the League for the Defense of Women's Rights in Jordan, led by Emily Naffa (al-Tal 2014: 171–72).[4] The organization, which issued a magazine called *Sawt al-Ma'ra al-Urdunniya* (The Voice of the Jordanian Woman) represented "a milestone in Jordanian women's activism, as it presented the first in-depth intellectual analysis of the 'woman question,' linking the emancipation of women to the emancipation of society as a whole, both in terms of class and colonialism" (al-Tal 2014: 172).

The general atmosphere of radical political movements and radical new feminist analyses, linking national liberation to women's emancipation, provided a fertile terrain for the emergence of new gender norms that challenged gendered hierarchies. Against the advice of her brother, Emily Naffa joined the Jordanian Communist Party and, in 1955, participated in mass protests in opposition to Jordan's participation in the Baghdad Pact—a regional defense pact created by Britain to contain Egypt's growing regional influence. Emily recalled that her father was initially angered by her political involvement: "Our neighbors put pressure on my father so I would not be a communist, because I organized demonstrations. They came to my father [who] was a merchant and he had a shop [and] they said to him, 'Look, you have to close your shop because your daughter Emily is organizing a demonstration. She will spoil the country, the city, blah, blah.' When I went back [home] he was there, ready for a big quarrel with me, 'Why did you go? Why you did that?,' etcetera. And we quarreled." However, Emily was defiant.

> I went to a friend and slept there to make him feel that he insulted me. And after two days [. . .] my father came [. . .] and he said, "Let's go home." I told him, "Are you ready to accept me to continue my work?" He said, "Yes. [. . .] They wanted to enter the Baghdad Pact [and] they stopped that due to your demonstration." I said, "Then you will back me, dad," and he said, "Yes, I will back you, you are doing marvelous work. Men can't do what you are doing." So, I went back, supported by my father, and I increased my work more and more.

As a result of the huge demonstrations, the pact was not signed, the government fell, the king dismissed Glubb Pasha as chief of the general staff, and new elections were called (Anderson 2005: 157–67; Robins 2004: 95). The elections coincided with the Tripartite Aggression against Egypt (or Suez Crisis) and there was huge public sympathy for Nasser. His speeches, broadcast on the Egyptian radio station Sawt al-'Arab, were popular in Jordan, his message of Arab unity and anti-imperialism resonating among the population (Anderson 2005: 159–61). In the elections, candidates associated with the radical nationalist and leftist parties of the Jordanian National Movement (JNM), some of which stood on a platform promising political rights for women, won a plurality of votes, leading the king to appoint Sulayman Nabulsi, leader of the center-left National Socialist Party, as prime minister (Anderson 2005: 174–76). The new government moved quickly to achieve one of the pillars of its nationalist platform by terminating the Anglo-Jordanian Treaty.

Tensions soon emerged between the government and the king. Matters came to a head in April 1957, leading the king to dissolve the government (Anderson 2005: 177–78). Simultaneously, an alleged coup against the king was aborted, providing a justification for the deployment of the army alongside pro-Hashemite tribal confederations to repress demonstrations and strikes in support of Nabulsi's government (Allinson 2015: 16970). Whether the planned coup was real or merely a ploy, the outcome was that the king and his supporters reasserted their control over the country and crushed the JNM (Anderson 2005: 183–87). In the context of the Cold War and fear of communist influence, the United States immediately demonstrated its support for the king, providing $10 million in aid and guaranteeing protection from the Soviet Union, thereby replacing Britain as the chief underwriter of the Hashemite Kingdom (Dann 1989: 65–66; Sharp 2016: 12) and providing crucial support for the regime's political crackdown (Anderson 2005: 184–87). The suppression of the leftist opposition also cemented Jordan's relationship with Saudi Arabia and placed it in the camp of conservative monarchies, against the radical republics led by Nasser (Dann 1989: 62–65; Kerr 1971). The episode illustrated that Arab nationalism "could be defeated by a combination of external support and royal dictatorship" (Hinnebusch 2003: 34).

Hundreds of political figures and activists were arrested and jailed, and others fled the country into exile. Martial law was introduced, and political parties, trade unions, and other civil society organizations, including the Arab Women's Union, were prohibited. Other women's organizations registered with the Ministry of Social Affairs were forbidden to carry out rights advocacy or political activities. Suhair al-Tal describes the period after 1957 as a "return to charitable work," with women's organizations focused on combating female illiteracy, providing vocational training to women and mother and child health care, and distributing donations among the poor (al-Tal 2014: 173–76). In this way, the regime sought to reinscribe female respectability as integral to the repression of radical political forces.

While the regime moved to repress the JNM, it took on board some of its modernizing agenda, including economic planning, infrastructural development, and expanded public sector capacity (Robins 2004: 111) alongside the promotion of women's public participation. Indeed, the Hashemite monarchy regarded itself as "forward thinking," bringing civilization to what it regarded as the previously untamed and undeveloped Transjordan, and the promotion of women's inclusion in the public sphere was considered (and remains) a marker of the regime's progressive image (Brand 1998). As in Egypt, women were encouraged to participate, but within the parameters of the regime's modernization project, an important aspect of which was the expansion of education, including girls' education, and encouragement of women's employment in some sectors of the economy, particularly teaching and nursing (Zahran 2011; Sawalha 2011). Laws were passed mandating paid maternity leave and workplace crèches (Sonbol 2003: 88–89). However, these reforms were not meant to threaten the gendered hierarchies of the inner sphere, and the law stipulated that a married woman must obtain her husband's permission to work (Sonbol 2003: 88–89).

As in the case of Egypt, women often responded positively to these measures and actively contributed their labor (both paid and unpaid) to Jordan's development. For example, Haifa Al-Bashir, born in Nablus (then still part of the British Mandate of Palestine) is very proud of her service to Jordan, having established the country's first nursing home for the elderly, the Golden Age Home, and won awards for her contributions to the fields of nursing, elder care, and mental health. She was initially encouraged to volunteer her time to promote nursing as a suitable profession for women by her late husband, physician Mohammed Al-Bashir, after he became minister of health in 1970:

> He persuaded me that the country is lacking nurses, because Jordanian people believed that nursing is not a suitable business for their girls, [. . .] because at that time [. . .] men and women [were not] working together, they were always separated [because of] custom, [. . .] and they used to import nurses from outside. They used really to suffer [because of], the language and the high cost of importing nurses, so he persuaded me to lend a hand in persuading Jordanian

girls to go into nursing. Really, we did a good job for around ten years, going around schools, [...] talking about nursing [...], and really, we made a good change in the mentality of the community. At the same time, we put another goal, to create auxiliary women for hospitals to help the staff in the nursing [...]. The third aim is to help the senior citizens. [...] We were visiting at that time the prime minister, Wasfi Al-Tal, [...] and he really encouraged me [and said] that I'm really doing a very good job for Jordan, but he said, "Don't forget the senior citizens," and we added this to our goals, and began initiating the first Golden Age Home in the country and it's still the best and the biggest.

After her husband was tragically killed in a helicopter crash, alongside the then wife of King Hussein, Queen Alia, Haifa singlehandedly raised six boys, who, as she proudly told me, are now "serving their country in different areas." Haifa's narrative frames her social reproductive labor both within and outside the home in terms of an active contribution to Jordan's progress that is respectful of the gendered hierarchies of both the inner and outer spheres. In this way, the activism of Haifa Al-Bashir, and many women like her who volunteer their time, has not only directly contributed to state building and development, but also to the reproduction of dominant norms of female respectability, which, in turn, have contributed to legitimizing the postindependence regime.

Another participant in the state's modernization project was Lamis Nasser, who was born in Jerusalem (also during time of the British Mandate of Palestine) and received a scholarship from the Jordanian Ministry of Education to study at the American University of Beirut. After she graduated in 1965, she taught in community colleges throughout Jordan, but then joined the diplomatic corps in 1969. In 1973, Lamis was the first married woman to be posted oversees to the Jordanian embassy in London, which created somewhat of a dilemma for the Ministry of Foreign Affairs. She recalled,

The administration, they said, "[...] this is the first time a married lady, [is stationed abroad] so, [...] we don't know how to give you all the benefits," because it is always said the wife [of the diplomat] gets this and this, [because it is assumed that] the diplomat is always a man, "and maybe according to the diplomatic charter we have to give you [the same benefits] because you are the diplomat but [...] we discussed this with the Awqaf [religious endowments] Ministry, [and] they said [that] legally they [women diplomats] deserve all of this, but religiously, or sharia-wise, [...] her husband [...] can't benefit from her to take air tickets, [or other benefits]." But I was happy that we were able to transfer, I mean I didn't mind. Sometimes [I think] we should have fought for it maybe.

Lamis's professional experience illustrates the tensions within postindependence state building, in that women's participation in the public sphere, whether through their voluntary or their paid work, was encouraged as part of the country's development, yet their public participation was expected to comply with, rather than challenge, the gendered hierarchies of the public and private spheres. In this case, the regime supported Lamis's appointment to the foreign service and her stationing abroad on the condition that she would not supplant her husband as the main breadwinner in the family. Lamis took up her post in the Jordanian embassy in London, while her husband, a gynecologist, joined her and continued his training at a London hospital.

Despite these challenges, Lamis told me: "I always considered the highlight of my career was the transfer to London, because I was thirty and I felt I was on top of the world." She then went on to reflect upon the degree to which, as a young woman, she willingly embodied the contradictions of state building: "Maybe because we were [brought up in that way], we always accepted the things [as they were], and I was always proud that I was chosen. [. . .] Sometimes, I look back and say, this was stupid, I should have had a row [. . .] but [. . .] there was some liberty." In embodying female respectability, Haifa and Lamis have contributed to the reproduction and normalization of the gendered boundaries between the inner and outer spheres and between modernity and modesty. In turn, the successful reproduction of these boundaries has contributed to the stability and authority of the Hashemite regime.

Gender and Geopolitical Order in Lebanon

Lebanon achieved independence from the French in 1943. Although more recent scholarship represents Lebanon's sectarian political system as a root of the conflicts and dysfunctions facing the country, it should be recalled that, in the period before the outbreak of the civil war in 1975, there was near unanimity among scholars that Lebanon was a successful model and unique in the Arab world for the degree of freedoms that it allowed and its recognition of religious pluralism, as well as its economic success.[5] It was one of the few countries in the region to have a competitive electoral system and a vibrant parliament. Political scientist Arend Lijphart included Lebanon as one of only two non-European countries (the other being Malaysia) in his model of "consociational democracies," characterized as successful elite cooperation in "culturally-fragmented" polities (1968). Lebanon was portrayed in scholarship as well as the country's own tourism marketing as an oasis of both political and economic freedom and cultural and religious coexistence; a country where "east meets west," a beacon of modernity and cosmopolitanism, where people could come to enjoy the beaches and mountain resorts, nightclubs and restaurants (Haugbolle 2010). Yet, as highlighted in the previous chapter, this model of religious pluralism and freedom was built upon gender inequality, enshrined within Lebanon's personal status codes.

This notion of Lebanese modernity constitutes an important basis for a unifying national identity, particularly among middle-class Lebanese citizens. Indeed, those women whom I interviewed that were born before Lebanon's independence tended to narrate their childhood, family background, and belonging in terms of key tropes of Lebanese national modernity: namely, educational achievement, openness to Europe, religious coexistence, and personal freedoms. For example, Nuha Nuwayri Salti, a physician and the founder of an outreach clinic in Shatila refugee camp, born in Beirut in 1941 to a Sunni Muslim merchant family, narrated themes of pluralism and cosmopolitanism through her memories of her childhood. Nuha grew up in her grandfather's house, in Ashrafiyyeh (East Beirut), an area that was more or less cleansed of non-Christians during the civil war of 1975–1990. Her father was an elected member of the Board of the Beirut Port, an important engine in Lebanon's economic growth through trade, and a friend of Maronite politician Kamil Shamun (before he became president). Central to her childhood memories was her education at the Lycée Française, her love of learning and intellectual exploration, and her educational success, most notably demonstrated by her admission to the American University of Beirut to study medicine. Through these memories, Nuha constructs herself and her family as agents in the building of a modern Lebanon. Against this backdrop, Lebanon's fifteen-year civil war is generally considered an aberration, or the result of external interference, whether from the Palestinians, Syria, Israel, or other regional and global powers (Haugbolle 2010: 13–20).

Lebanon, like other postindependence Arab countries, also encouraged women's education and entrance into certain sectors of the workforce as a marker of its modernity. New legislation—albeit not properly enforced—mandated employers to provide separate restrooms and eating areas for women, in addition to health coverage and special benefits for expectant and new mothers (Abisaab 2010: 120). While the early period of postindependence was characterized by laissez-faire economic policies, this changed after the crisis of 1958, under the presidency of Fuad Shihab. Shihab, aware of the socioeconomic and regional inequalities that had developed and the popular grievances that these had provoked, introduced more state planning and investment in infrastructure and social services, particularly in education (Traboulsi 2007: 138–41). As Fahima Charafeddine, born in south Lebanon, recalled in our interview: "During that time, education became widespread in Lebanon, new streets were paved to connect different parts of the country, and a village girl like me could come to Beirut and finish my education. Also, a secondary school was built in my village where I could also study. The Lebanese University was established in 1964, which didn't only have faculties for Law and Sciences, but also Humanities and Arts. This made it easier for women to get their education. I also think that outposts that the university built in the different Lebanese governorates helped women get access to education."

By 1972–1973, there were 2,486 elementary and secondary schools, in which girls made up 46 percent of all students, and fourteen institutions of higher education, in which girls made up 17 percent of all students (Shehadeh 1999a: 36). Fahima studied philosophy at the Lebanese University, after which, she joined the ranks of Lebanon's expanding civil service and worked as an educational advisor.

Although the Lebanese have highlighted women's public visibility as a marker of the country's progressive character, Jean Makdisi has termed Lebanese modernity a "mythology" (1996). Like other states in the region, the government has continued to enshrine gender inequality, particularly with regard to family law. Indeed, Elizabeth Thompson argues that Lebanon's famous National Pact, commonly represented as a historic act of cross-sectarian compromise paving the way for independence, was underpinned by a "gender pact," in which women were legally subordinated to their male kin, constituting a "crucial site of solidarity and compromise [between male political leaders] that muted class and religious tensions" (Thompson 2000: 287). The main source of gender inequality within Lebanese law is the eighteen different personal status codes, one for each of Lebanon's eighteen officially recognized sects. Sectarian personal status laws not only subject women to the control of the men of their extended kin groups (Joseph 2000a: 109) but also cement a relationship between citizens and their religious leader, "rather than the state" (as women's rights activist Linda Matar lamented in an interview in 2007). In this way, sectarian personal status laws, based on women's legal subordination, constitute a crucial mechanism in reproducing the primacy of sectarian affiliations, which form the basis for Lebanon's system of political power sharing, while sustaining the image of religious pluralism and freedom (Joseph 1991; Joseph 2000a).[6]

Another manifestation of the "Lebanese mythology of modernity" (Makdisi 1996) is women's low rates of participation in parliament, despite being granted the right to vote and to stand in elections in 1953, after a long campaign by women activists. Until 1991, no woman succeeded in being elected, with the exception of Myrna Bustani, "who was elected in 1963 to finish the term of her father, Emile Bustani, who had suffered a tragic death" (Shehadeh 1999a: 33). The Lebanese Council for Women (LCW), founded in 1952 as a cross-sectarian umbrella organization for all women's associations across the country (Stephan 2012), stood a candidate in every parliamentary election but failed to get any elected. This was partly a reflection of a continuing belief in the impropriety of women holding political office (Sharara 1978), but was also largely due to the nature of the political system itself. The voting system produced political loyalty along sectarian lines, thereby excluding independent women activists, the ideological parties that grew in popularity during the 1950s and 1960s, and others who drew on cross-sectarian support. Moreover, success in parliamentary elections depended upon wealth and local influence or the ability to bandwagon on those (Baaklini, Denoeux, and Springborg 1999: 88–90), and therefore Lebanon's elite families, who had vested interests in the system of power sharing along sectarian lines, stood in a favored position. Hence, the electoral system reproduced the sectarian loyalty that underpinned political power sharing, serving to further reinforce the gender hierarchies integral to building sectarian affiliations. This political system barely changed after the end of the civil war in 1990, and, consequently, the only women to win parliamentary seats until the parliamentary elections of 2018 were the wives, daughters, or sisters of male political leaders or members of prominent Lebanese families (for example, Bahia Hariri, Sethrida Geagea, and Nayla Moawad).[7] Meanwhile, political and religious leaders have been resistant to amendments to personal status laws (as explored further in chapters 5 and 6).

Lebanese women activists have adopted different and sometimes contradictory positions in relation to the sectarian political system and its gendered underpinnings. On the one hand, members of the LCW have sought to challenge the gender hierarchies produced through the political system by their insistence to stand in parliamentary elections. In addition, they have successfully lobbied for several legal reforms, including equality of inheritance for Christian women (1959), repealing the law obliging Lebanese women to renounce their nationality if they marry foreign men (1960), and abolishing the law that obliged women to obtain written permission from their husbands to be able to travel (1974). Nonetheless, the LCW also accommodated many aspects of Lebanon's sectarian system and its associated gender inequalities. Significantly, the Council has not broached the issue of abolishing the sectarian personal status laws, even when this became a demand of other social movements and political parties, as it did in the period preceding the 1975 civil war.

LCW members may have been unwilling to challenge the sectarian political system because many of them have been intimately linked to the elite families benefitting from this system. For example, Munira Solh (1911–2010), one of the founding members of the Council, as well as a member of the Mandate-era women's associations, came from the al-Solh family, an important Sunni Muslim merchant family that produced Lebanon's first prime minister and partner in the National Pact, Riyad al-Sulh, as well as several other prime ministers and politicians (Johnson 1986: 57–60). She married her cousin, Wahid al-Solh, who became a politician (and was assassinated in 1958 for his anti-Nasserist position). Her daughter, the late Sana al-Solh, proudly told me about the Wikipedia entry dedicated to her mother, who is considered to be a female pioneer. Munira graduated from the American Junior College for Women (later to become the Lebanese American University), worked as a school teacher in Iraq from 1933 to 1935, participated in the demonstrations against the French before independence, and dedicated her life to improving rights for women and helping society more broadly. She was the first Muslim woman to run for the Lebanese parliament (in 1960, then again in 1964 and 1968). Meanwhile, having a son with disabilities spurred her to found the Amal Institute for the Disabled in 1959, the first institute of its kind in Lebanon and the Arab World. She won national and international awards for her social work, especially her work for people with mental disabilities (Wikipedia 2016). Munira obliged her daughter Sana to participate in public work from a young age and Sana followed in her mother's footsteps, becoming a long-term and active member of the LCW, combining her social work for the Amal Institute with her support for women's rights.[8] Through their activities, Sana and her mother, and other members of the LCW, whose activities are predominantly focused on providing welfare and social services for underprivileged and vulnerable sectors of society, continued the work of the elite women's associations of the Mandate period, which mobilized women's motherly duties in the service of the national struggle and social progress under the banner of "patriotic motherhood" (Thompson 2000: 143). Members of the LCW embody a norm of female respectability that is constituted by and constitutive of gendered and class hierarchies underpinning the sectarian political system. Yet, simultaneously, members of the LCW have also renegotiated and modernized female respectability to include women's political participation and have challenged gendered hierarchies within the limits of the sectarian system. In this way, the LCW has contributed to the reproduction of the "mythology of modernity" that legitimizes the Lebanese state and its sectarian political system.

In contrast to the LCW, a new generation of women activists emerged in the postindependence period who were influenced by the leftist and radical nationalist political currents that were ascendant at the time. These women sought to build a mass women's movement, in contrast to the more welfare-oriented, elite women's associations of that time (LLWR 1987: 16; Aïssaoui 2002: 117). Linda Matar was far from the elite women's associations established during the French Mandate, having grown up in a working-class (Maronite) family and being obliged to leave school at the age of twelve in order to work to help her family financially. She told me how she first became mobilized into women's rights activism, sometime toward the end of the 1940s, when two women came to her door, asking her to sign a petition calling for women's political rights:

> So I said to the girls: "I will walk with you so that people will open their doors for you [...]." So, I walked with them and we went door-to-door collecting signatures. [...] I asked them who they were, those who made the petition [...]. They said they were from the Lebanese League for Women's Rights (*al-lajna lubnaniya li-l-huquq al-ma'ra*). [...] They said: "[...] We are an organization concerned with women's rights, the right of women to work in all fields, be they social, economic, cultural, or political." The word *political* wasn't used for organizations before. If you said "political" then it would be a party, because women had nothing to do with politics, even the law stated that [...]. So, I liked the organization and I established a branch for it in Ayn al-Rummaneh, and I was chosen as the head of that branch [...] The first responsibility I undertook in the LLWR was working with female workers, mobilizing female workers. I started visiting the factories; there were many factories in our area. [...] So, we continued doing our work and we demanded women's rights; other organizations emerged, and we worked together.

The LLWR carried out activities similar to those of the elite women's associations, in that they provided social services for women and children, as well as lobbying for the right to vote, but unlike existing women's associations at that time, the LLWR challenged the government by making specific social demands, such as opening public schools for girls and campaigning for health clinics for mothers and children, which were very few at the time (LLWR 1987:19–21). Moreover, unlike the paternalism of other women's organizations, members of the LLWR allied with other low-income sectors of the population in demanding electricity, clean water, housing, and other essential services and infrastructure, which the laissez-faire government of the time neglected to provide, and supported women factory workers striking for better pay and conditions (LLWR 1987: 21–23).[9] Meanwhile, they aligned their advocacy of women's rights and social justice more broadly with the anti-imperialist politics of the 1950s and 1960s, including opposition to the Baghdad Pact in 1955 and the Tripartite Aggression against Egypt (Suez Crisis) of 1956, and in solidarity with Algerian women in the war for independence from France, and with Palestinian women in their struggle for national self-determination (LLWR 1987: 23–25). Through their overt political activities, the women of the LLWR transgressed dominant norms of female respectability. Indeed, the Lebanese government refused to register the LLWR until 1969, on the grounds that it included politics as one of its spheres of activities.

Women were not only mobilized into public activism in relation to women's rights agendas. There were also young women who joined the leftist and radical nationalist ideological parties of the time. One of those was Iqbal Murad Doughan, who came from modest middle-class origins. Her father was a cleric, "but he was open-minded," and she and her brothers all succeeded at school thanks to scholarships and their own efforts. According to Iqbal:

> When I was growing up, it was the height of the political movement in the Arab region, especially in Lebanon. The communists were strong, the Syrian Nationalists were strong, the Ba'ath party was strong, the whole Arab nationalist movement [was strong]. All of them contacted me. I was very active as a young adult. I wanted to make my own choices; so, when I was twelve or thirteen years old, I joined the Arab Nationalist Movement because one of their main goals was revenge. "Unity, freedom and revenge." Not revenge in the literal sense of the word, but rather to free Palestine. And that was the reason I joined them. So I started to work in Tripoli and I was a very effective asset.

The Arab Nationalist Movement was created in 1951, initially by students at the American University in Beirut, and was part of the regional trend of radicalization of Arab politics in response to the loss of Palestine in the 1948 war. The Palestinian cause featured in the programs of most of the ideological parties of the time because it was seen as the most glaring example of the corruption of the pro-Western Arab elites and the need for a radical transformation and modernization of Arab societies and politics. The icon of this new politics was Egypt's Gamal Abdel-Nasser, whose popularity in Lebanon and other Arab countries, grew rapidly after the Suez Crisis of 1956. At the Arab University of Beirut, where she studied law, Iqbal became responsible for the ANM: "We were so committed that instead of wearing new clothes we donated the money for nationalist activities. For example, they had a newspaper called *Al-Hurriya* (Freedom) and I had to sell around ten issues of it every week. If I didn't sell them, I had to pay for them from my own pocket." In the decade before the outbreak of the civil war in 1975, the Arab Nationalist Movement (which in 1967 split into the Popular Front for the Liberation of Palestine and the Democratic Front for the Liberation of Palestine), the Lebanese Communist Party, the Progressive Socialist Party, and a number of other leftist groups formed the political wing of a growing social movement of workers, peasants, and students challenging the social injustices of Lebanon's oligarchic and monopolistic political economy (Farsoun 1973; Nasr 1978; Traboulsi 2007: 145–46, 161–70). Fahima Charafeddine was not a member of a political party during this period but, as a student at the Lebanese University, she identified with the radical political currents of the period: "We were the sixties generation, who started the student revolution. [. . .] I started to change what I believed in, in terms of believing in a sort of total change; a change that flips everything around, which was based predominantly on Marxist ideals. These ideals believed that if we change society, then people's conditions would change or that if we changed the political administration and gave it to the proletariat, then people's lives would change."

As in the case of Jordan, leftist and radical nationalist currents during this period supported women's public participation as part of their oppositional political agendas, and, after 1967, most of the political groups had their own women's committees. However, women discovered that the rhetorical support for women's inclusion rarely translated into full equality. For the most part, women were excluded from decision-making positions (Sharara 1978), the agendas of women's committees were controlled by male comrades, and women's issues were subordinated to national/political issues (Daou 2014: 30–33). Yet, as Yolla Sharara documents in her own reflections on political involvement in Lebanon during this period, these political movements were still significant for women: "To engage in politics, or to 'enter politics' as we put it, was not the done thing for young women. We entered despite the opposition of our frightened parents. [. . .] The world of politics had the taste of forbidden fruit. We were proud to have been admitted, proud to meet celebrated leaders in the corridors, and especially proud finally to be taken seriously (Sharara 1978).

More broadly, the proliferation of contentious social and political activism created a facilitating environment for challenging dominant gender norms (Abisaab 2010; Eggert 2018a). Indeed, women's experiences in political movements led them later to seek organizational autonomy to address gender-specific issues. For example, in 1976, members of the women's committee of the Organization of Communist Action created the Lebanese Women Democratic Gathering as an independent organization in order to be able to address issues of women's rights and equality without interference from male comrades (Aïssaoui 2002: 126–27; Daou 2014: 36–39).

CONCLUSION

This chapter has explored the relationship between women's activism, dominant gender norms, decolonization, and state building in the first few decades of independence. It has explored the emergence of a norm of female respectability in relation to struggles for decolonization and how this norm regulated women's activism in the early years of postindependence state building. The chapter began by tracing the emergence of this norm to the end of the nineteenth century, during which time growing European encroachment provoked public debates around the "woman question" in relation to national progress and calls for independence. Nationalist leaders advocated for a "new woman," who was expected to embody modernity through her increased public visibility while remaining modest as symbolic of the nation's cultural "essence." This norm of female respectability was constitutive of a boundary between the "outer sphere," in which nationalist leaders sought to be modern, like Europe, and a sovereign "inner sphere," in which cultural difference was constructed. In the postindependence period, postcolonial regimes refashioned the female respectability norm in the service of state building, introducing state feminist measures to signal the state's modernity and national progress, while maintaining personal status laws that enshrined gender inequality within the inner sphere as a marker of national difference. In the case of Lebanon, the existence of different personal status laws for each of the country's eighteen religious sects naturalized and reproduced a political system based on power sharing according to sectarian affiliation. In this way, the apparent contradiction between state feminist measures to increase women's public participation (in the outer sphere) and resistance to reforming laws that enshrine gender inequality in the family (or inner sphere) was performative of national sovereignty and integral to the construction of regime authority.

While the norm of female respectability operated to regulate women's behavior within certain parameters, simultaneously it was also productive of women's activism. In this sense, women were neither fully empowered agents nor victims of patriarchal nationalism. During the colonial period, women embodied the notion of the "new woman," who was "modern yet modest" (Najmabadi 1991: 49), by founding associations and conducting social welfare and philanthropic work as part of the struggle against European rule. In the postindependence period, many women continued this tradition of associational work, this time in support of national development. They also benefited from state feminism to enter education and the workforce in unprecedented numbers. Several women's organizations, such as the LCW in Lebanon and the AWU in Jordan (until its closure in 1956), attempted to resignify female respectability by combining social service provision and welfare activities with demands for women's political rights and participation. In this way, women renegotiated the modernity-modesty boundary and contributed to modifying gender norms over time. More significantly, I argue, women's embodiment of female respectability contributed to legitimizing the postcolonial state and regime authority in a regional context of geopolitical competition and threats to sovereignty from pan-Arab movements.

The significance of the reproduction of female respectability to regime stability and state building is illustrated by the lack of regime tolerance for women's political activism. In Egypt and Jordan (after 1956), women's independent activism was crushed. Meanwhile, in Lebanon, the government refused to register the LLWR, while the sectarian electoral system prevented independent women candidates from reaching parliament. However, radical political movements, which were stridently anti-imperialist and sought to overturn the vestiges of the colonial order, provided a fertile terrain for women to challenge dominant gender norms. Until now, relatively little attention has been paid to women in these movements (compared to women participating in women's organizations), given that their involvement was marginal, and the movements themselves subordinated the "woman question" to the "national question." Nonetheless, I argue that these women

deserve our attention for the remarkable role that they played. Their participation in radical movements disrupted the boundary between the inner and
outer spheres and modernity and modesty, threatening the successful reproduction of a national "sovereignty effect" (Doty 1996a: 124). In this way, these
women embodied resistance not only to dominant gender norms but also to
the construction of a "natural state" (Weber 1998: 92).

TWO

The 1967 Defeat and Its Aftermath

THE BREAKDOWN OF THE GENDER ORDER
AND THE EXPANSION OF WOMEN'S ACTIVISM

THIS CHAPTER INVESTIGATES the period following the defeat of the Arab armies in the 1967 war with Israel and its implications for gender norms and women's activism. The defeat created major geopolitical upheaval and social unrest in Egypt, Jordan, and Lebanon. The war led to the further expulsion of Palestinians from their lands, stoking growing disillusionment in the Arab states' ability to regain Palestine. While much historiography of the aftermath of the 1967 defeat, or "setback" (*naksa*), has focused on the decline of Arab nationalism and the rise of political Islam, in line with Sune Haugbolle (2017), I argue that the defeat gave further impetus to new left currents and other popular movements calling for radical sociopolitical and socioeconomic transformations in opposition to the geopolitical status quo. In Lebanon and Jordan, these new movements were allied with the Palestine Liberation Organization (PLO) and supported the armed struggle against Israel. In Egypt, the new popular movements centered on the student movement; nonetheless, the Palestinian question was an integral part of demands for greater democracy as well as calls for war against Israel to regain Arab lands.

In contrast to much of the existing scholarship on this period, I emphasize the gendered dimensions of the post-1967 crisis—specifically, the expansion in women's activism and challenges to dominant gender norms enabled by the weakening of postindependence regimes and the gender order on which they depended. The chapter begins by presenting women's personal narratives of the 1967 defeat, highlighting the intimate and subjective dimensions of the unfolding geopolitical crisis. It then goes on to discuss women's involvement in radical political and social movements, which grew in reaction to the defeat. While women's involvement in these movements was not new per se (as the previous chapter explored), what was different was the reemergence of antiregime movements in Egypt and Jordan, as well as the unprecedented mobilization of Palestinian refugee women by the Palestinian national movement in Jordan and Lebanon. The chapter considers the degree to which women were empowered to challenge norms of female respectability through their participation in these movements. The final section of the chapter focuses on the Lebanese civil war of 1975 to 1990 and the different ways in which women were active vis-à-vis the war—from humanitarian relief workers to members of political groups. While women's experiences of the war often present an alternative narrative to dominant "war stories" (Cooke 1999), nonetheless, I argue that we should avoid the danger of depoliticizing women's activism during this period.

THE 1967 DEFEAT AND ITS GEOPOLITICAL CONSEQUENCES

Against the backdrop of ongoing tensions between Israel and the frontline Arab states, growing inter-Arab rivalry, a permissive international context, and a series of miscalculations and brinkmanship, Israel went to war against Egypt, Jordan, and Syria in June 1967 (Louis and Shlaim 2009: 6–9). It took only six days for Israel to defeat the Arab armies, capturing the Sinai Peninsula from Egypt, the West Bank from Jordan, and the Golan Heights from Syria. The scale and speed of the defeat created massive shock among ordinary people, who had previously believed official media reports that the Arab armies were winning.

The defeat was a watershed moment for all those who lived through it. Nawla Darwiche, at the time in her late teens, recalled that, on hearing the news, "people were very depressed, very frustrated, [there was a] very humiliated feeling all over the country and especially for youth." Laila Soueif was only eleven years old yet recalled, "There was a feeling of absolute catastrophe, even [with] my parents; as I discovered later, they were very skeptical about Nasser and about all this dictatorship and so on. But we all felt it as a national catastrophe and as defeat of what was, after all, an attempt at building a modern Egyptian state, a modern independent Egyptian state." As Laila articulates, the defeat of 1967 was not only a military defeat but the defeat of the Nasserist project of national modernization, which had promised to liberate the Egyptian people from "political, economic and cultural backwardness to enlightenment and personal and collective development" (Meijer 2002: 13–14). Yet, despite the scale of the defeat, people rejected Nasser's resignation. Omaima Abu-Bakr, was ten years old when Nasser announced his resignation on television on 9 June:

> I remember that day, sitting on the sofa watching TV, watching Abdel-Nasser resign, and I remember my mother breaking down in tears crying, and my father was getting very, very upset, he was a heavy smoker, he gets up, he fetches his cigarettes, and starts yelling, "this is not right, this is not right, he is the best man in the world," talking about Nasser. Now my parents were not politicized at all, never, not part of political parties or political orientations, [. . .] just regular Egyptian citizens, and they were not Nasserites in the ideological sense, [. . .] but they were lovers and supporters of Nasser. [. . .] So I remember that day that there is a catastrophe, a national catastrophe.

Nawla Darwiche was among the millions of Egyptians who took to the streets, calling on Nasser to stay. She recalls that even her father, the late Youssef Darwiche, a communist who had been imprisoned and tortured by Nasser's regime, did not want Nasser to resign: "Nasser had a very high charisma, so on the ninth and tenth of June, there were very big demonstrations in Egypt, calling for Abdel-Nasser to return back [. . .]. It was the first time for me to go in a demonstration." Despite the widespread support for Nasser, people became disillusioned by the regime itself, which it blamed for the defeat. In February 1968, there was almost a week of demonstrations, led by workers and university students in Cairo and Alexandria, which resulted in 2 workers killed, 77 civilians and 146 policemen injured, and 635 people arrested in Cairo alone (Abdalla 1985: 150). The protests were initially sparked by the lenient sentences handed down in the trials of the army officers accused of negligence in the war. However, the demands of the students went further, including calls for greater political freedoms and democracy as well as the removal of intelligence and police from university campuses (Abdalla 1985: 151–53). In response to the protests, the regime ordered a retrial of the generals and promised some political liberalization of the system, while restrictions on freedoms on university campuses were lifted (Abdalla 1985: 158–59). However, following further student protests in November of that year, the regime reinstated its control over universities with the aim of stemming the student movement. Instead, the repressive measures laid the ground "for the emergence of a more militant student movement in the years that followed" (Abdalla 1985: 175).

Similarly, in Jordan, the swift defeat of the Arab armies in the 1967 war was not only a huge blow to the regime but also a huge shock to ordinary Jordanians. As Leila Naffa, sister of Emily, and also a member of the Jordanian Communist Party, told me, "Sometimes in Arabic we say facts are bitter, and we came to understand that our defeat was much, much more than we expected, and all our lives were changed [. . .]." Jordan lost a significant amount of its territory to Israel and the economic impact was huge, given that the West Bank represented some 40 percent of the Kingdom's GDP (Mutawi 1987: 169–71). Moreover, the humanitarian impact of the war was massive, as approximately three hundred thousand residents of the West Bank (who were Jordanian citizens) arrived to the East Bank in need of relief and assistance (Mutawi 1987: 169–71). Many of those displaced by the 1967 war were already refugees from the 1948 *Nakba*.[1] Among them was Muyassar al-Saadi, who was born in Haifa before 1948, expelled with her family to Jenin, on the West Bank, in 1948, and then displaced to the East Bank in 1967. At the time of the war, she was twenty years old and working for the UN Relief and Works Agency (UNRWA), the agency dedicated to assisting Palestinian refugees:

> I was working in the [Jenin] camp [. . .] and the war broke out in 1967. My first daughter was only two months old. [. . .] The first area the Jews entered was Jenin because it was on the armistice lines [. . .].[2] People thought this was just a phase; that they would run away from the Jews in the city and take refuge in the villages. But after that they occupied the whole West Bank. And when we came to Jordan, I didn't want to go because my father told us about the 1948 war and how people were scattered and suffered a lot, so I was against leaving, but my father-in-law, [. . .] had a wife and son so he was afraid for them, so he decided to go to Amman. Even when we came to Amman, we thought it would be a phase, that we would be back in a month or two, but we stayed. I started working for UNRWA in Jordan when I came here, in the camps [. . .]. I suffered through the 1967 war and through 1968 and I kept moving from one camp to another, so it was very hard. But thank God, I managed to overcome all these phases.

However, Palestinians were not mere victims in the 1967 war. The defeat led to the radicalization of the Palestinian national movement. No longer believing in the role of the Arab states in liberating Palestine and, inspired by anticolonial and anti-imperialist movements across the world, a new genera-tion of Palestinians advocated for armed struggle as the best strategy to unite the Palestinian people and liberate Palestine (Khalili 2007; Haugbolle 2017). In 1969, the radical Palestinian nationalist faction, Fateh, led by Yasser

Arafat, gained control of the PLO. This marked the beginning of what Palestinians call the Palestinian Revolution—a popular struggle against oppression and for the right of Palestinians to return to their homeland (Sayigh 2007: 148–97).

The Palestinian Revolution had its most profound impact on Lebanon, where Palestinian refugees lived in the worst conditions of all Palestinians living in the Arab states—mainly confined to camps, with few basic services and little infrastructure (Brynen 1990: 28). The origins of the camps dated back to the 1948 Arab-Israeli War, when more than one hundred thousand Palestinians fled to Lebanon as a result of the creation of the state of Israel (Sayigh 2007). Palestinians were granted refugee status but, unlike in Syria or Jordan, they were not allowed to work in the government or join the army, were obliged to obtain work permits, and were subject to discretionary regulations with regard to obtaining travel documents (Sayigh 2007: 115–17). After the creation of UNRWA in 1950, they were settled in refugee camps, where they had little choice but to become dependent on the UN agency for education, health, and even basic food rations (Peteet 1991: 24–26). Olfat Mahmoud, who grew up in Borj al-Barajneh camp, in the southern suburbs of Beirut, recalled the misery of the camps before 1969:

> There would be police outside and you are not allowed to leave the camp before 7 [a.m.] and after 7 [p.m.]. It's like, if you want to put a nail on your wall you needed to get permission from the government. Which takes lots of time. Women were not allowed to do, for example, housework during the daytime. Why? Because we had open sewage. So the police would march in the camp and they don't want to march in mud. So all women had to finish work before dawn. [...] This is my childhood, waking up very early. The houses in the camp were really shabby houses, very cold in winter, killing you in summer. [...] At first, people lived in tents. But then they replaced tents with mud houses and the roof was a metal roof with lots of holes. Like you would never sleep all night in winter. You would have all these buckets hanging.

Palestinians were closely monitored by the Lebanese authorities, who saw them as a threat to the sectarian balance underpinning the Lebanese political system (Sayigh 2007: 115). Palestinian camps were subject to strict surveillance by the authorities, particularly after the 1958 political crisis, and camp residents were routinely harassed by security services (Sayigh 2007: 143–45). Those Palestinians in Lebanon who were politically active were predominantly from among those who had been fortunate to obtain Lebanese citizenship and lived outside the camps.

Olfat recalled how happy people in the camps were when they heard that the PLO was coming to Lebanon: "Because we thought they were coming to save our lives; they are coming to help us." The signing of the Cairo Agreement in 1969, brokered by Gamal Abdel-Nasser between the PLO and the Lebanese government, radically changed the life of Palestinians by barring the Lebanese army from entering the camps and by handing over camp governance to the residents. Popular committees, consisting of representatives of Palestinian political parties, independents, and camp elders, functioned like a municipality, "maintaining services such as garbage collection, electricity, sewage, and water" (Peteet 1991: 28). In addition, the PLO brought with them "a wide-ranging infrastructural complex of health, welfare, cultural, educational, and recreational institutions and popular unions," while "PLO economic enterprises were a growing source of employment, particularly for women in the camps," thereby improving the quality of life for camp dwellers (Peteet 1991: 28).

The 1969 Cairo Agreement also gave the PLO the right to carry arms and launch attacks in specified areas of Lebanon. The Palestinian resistance movement established military bases on Lebanon's southern border with Israel. Meanwhile, Palestinian political factions began to recruit young men from refugee camps across the region to train them as fighters (*fedayeen*) for the armed struggle. According to Olfat:

> I remember it was night when someone would knock on your door, and say, "We need anything for the fighters." So, people would give them food from their own houses, like whatever you have in your house, they will give you a bag, and you will fill it with whatever you have, so people will donate it from their heart; they wanted to [do it] despite [that] they were poor, they wanted to help. And I remember those women knitting all those jumpers and scarfs and putting them in a bag and giving them to the people who collect items.

The Lebanese opposition movement, consisting of leftist and other progressive forces led by Kamel Jumblatt of the Progressive Socialist Party (PSP), as well as the Sunni Muslim public more broadly, supported the fedayeen. However, the Maronite Christian political parties and much of the Maronite public viewed the Palestinian presence as a threat to Lebanon's security and sovereignty. This political polarization led to episodes of violent conflict between the army, on the one side, and the fedayeen and the Lebanese opposition, on the other (Sayigh 1997: 190–91, 312–17). Meanwhile, Maronite parties began to arm their own militias, with the help of the Lebanese intelligence service (Khalidi 1979: 41; Sayigh 1997: 317).

The political crisis over the fedayeen intersected with the growing demands of the leftist and progressive forces for a reformulation of the sectarian distribution of political power and socioeconomic reforms, thereby cementing the alliance between the Lebanese opposition parties and the PLO (Traboulsi 2007: 154, 176; Khalidi 1979: 75–78). For example, Mona Saad remembers how her late father, Ma'ruf Saad, who was MP for Sidon and the leader of the leftist Popular Nasserite Organization, would assist the fedayeen:

> He would bring them, because he had parliamentary immunity, in his car, so no one can stop him, not the Lebanese army or the intelligence. [. . .] We would sleep at night and wake up in the morning and we would see men around the house, everywhere, with mattresses, in the house, they are sleeping. He would bring them at night and the next day they would take showers and eat and [. . .] in the afternoon he would tell us, "Could you go for a drive to Sur [Tyre]?" And we say yes. He put them in his car to transport them to the south, because the army couldn't stop his car.

The figure of Ma'ruf Saad is well-known among leftists and Palestinians in Lebanon, as his death, at the hands of the army, symbolizes the intersections of class and confessional politics that contributed to the outbreak of civil war in 1975 (Salem 2003: 100). In February of that year, Saad was leading a protest by fishermen in Sidon against a new fishing consortium of which former (Maronite) president and wealthy businessmen Kamil Shamun was a major shareholder. The army fired on the protesters, wounding Saad, who later died from his injuries. This triggered an uprising against the army, in which the fedayeen fought alongside armed progressive Lebanese forces, triggering, in turn, right-wing Maronite-sponsored counter-mobilizations in support of the army (Fisk 2002: 78; al-Haytham 1976: 4; Sayigh 1997: 360). Armed clashes escalated into all-out civil war after April, when the right-wing Maronite Phalangist militia gunned down Palestinians and leftist Lebanese on a bus in the Ayn al-Rummaneh suburb of Beirut (Traboulsi 2007: 187–204). Hence, even though Lebanon did not participate in the 1967 war, the defeat had the most destabilizing consequences for Lebanon out of all the Arab countries because of the polarization among the Lebanese with regard to the Palestinian presence and the inability of the sectarian political system and its ruling elites to respond to the demands of new sociopolitical movements.

WOMEN IN NEW RADICAL AND
REVOLUTIONARY MOVEMENTS

While historians and international relations scholars have discussed the political, economic, and military consequences of the 1967 defeat (Mutawi 1987; Louis and Shlaim 2012; Salibi 1993; Robins 2004; among others), the particular gendered consequences of the 1967 war have been largely neglected. What were the implications of these crises for gender relations and gender norms? In what ways did the defeat and its aftermath differentially affect men and women? Feminist scholars have mainly considered the gendered impacts of war and catastrophes in terms of the impact of nationalist and militaristic ideologies on gender norms as well as women's vulnerability to violence, particularly sexual violence (see Al-Ali and Pratt 2009a; Giles and Hyndman 2004; Jacobs et al. 2000; Meintjes et al 2001; Moser and Clark 2001). There has been less attention to women as political and social actors and their role in transforming gender norms in the wake of war. The scale of the political crisis, as well as the humanitarian crisis in the case of Jordan, created by the military defeat mobilized new generations of women into public activism. In some cases, women participated in "respectable female" activities, such as welfare provision, relief work, and other auxiliary activities, particularly in Jordan where the humanitarian need was greatest; however, these activities were often resignified as part of national struggles. In other cases, women transgressed dominant norms of female respectability through their participation in new popular movements and political groups that challenged regimes and even sought to overthrow the existing regional order.

Egypt

In Egypt, the political upheaval after 1967 developed into a sustained rebellion against the regime, which lasted until 1977. For the first time since the colonial period, independent activism reemerged and some women began participating in politically subversive and oppositional activities. According to Farida El-Nakkash: "I guess you could say that after 1967 [. . .] we lost hope in the idea that the system could be reformed. I was reading a lot about Marxism during that time and I converted from Nasserism to Marxism. Many secret organizations started being active after 1967. After the great disappointment and the defeat, and after the corruption within the army and public institutions was exposed, people lost all trust in Nasserism."

Farida's sister, Amina Al-Naccache enrolled in the Academy of Arts in 1968.[3] She told me,

> When I enrolled at the academy, there were already many seeds of leftist groups: the Communist Worker Party and other, small groups. So, I started reading the fliers they were handing out and so on. [...] So we used to take the fliers they would hand out and hold meetings. The Academy was in the Pyramids District and was surrounded by a lot of farmlands, in which we could do whatever we wanted, away from the government's watchful eye. So, we used to sit in the garden with some snacks and get the fliers and we'd read them together.

As the late Ahmad Abdalla's seminal work demonstrates, the Egyptian student movement played a key political role after 1967, organizing seminars and public meetings, wall magazines, sit-ins, and demonstrations critical of the government (Abdalla 1985). Leftist political groups were particularly influential in mobilizing and politicizing the student body. For example, Karima El-Hefnawy, entered university in autumn 1971 and began participating in student politics:

> During that time, there were secret socialist and leftist parties and we were active at the university [...]. There were two big student clubs in the 1970s that were leading the work and they were the Socialist Thought Society, which I joined. It was led by Ahmad Baha' Sha'ban, who is now the president of the Egyptian Socialist Party, of which I am the secretary. [...] At the same time, there was also the Nasserist Thought Society, whose most prominent member is probably Kamal Abu Eita, who is now the minister of labor, and Hamdeen Sabahi, the founder of the Egyptian Popular Current and who was also a presidential candidate.[4] The two clubs used to work together, because their goal was one. The Nasserists and the socialists were considered the leftists of the Egyptian community at the time. The clubs would host forums at the university, as well as political, cultural, and art weeks. We also organized peaceful demonstrations, in which all the students taking part were arrested more than once. I was arrested about five times and everyone would get arrested, released, and then carry on with what they were doing. At the same time, socialist parties were being formed, but they weren't public.

A resolution of the national question, namely an end to Israel's continued occupation of Arab land after 1967 was the spark to the movement. Another prominent student group was the Society of the Supporters of the Palestinian Revolution, established by students who had visited Palestinian camps and met with Palestinian groups in Jordan (Abdalla 1985: 176–77). However, student demands went further, linking the defeat to the lack of political freedoms in Egypt. Nadia Abdel Wahab El Afify entered the faculty of medicine at Cairo University in 1970 and recalled, "You know, we'd just come out of the Nasserist period, after the 1967 defeat and it was not possible for the regime to continue as it was because we felt that this regime was the reason behind the defeat and people needed some degree of democracy." In January 1972, thousands of students in various Egyptian universities rebelled against the regime, occupying university campuses for ten days and culminating in a sit-in in Tahrir Square on 25–26 January. They attracted support from among different sectors of the Egyptian population, sparking protests by workers and the unemployed in several cities across the country (Hussein 1972: 13), while four of the most influential professional unions—teachers, lawyers, engineers, and journalists—issued public statements praising the students' patriotism and supporting their demands (Abdalla 1985: 177–86).

In this turbulent atmosphere, young women felt empowered to transgress gendered norms of respectability. For example, Aida Seif El Dawla recalled:

> I remember I did things then, which now I am thinking about, I would never do them again, I mean thinking about them even is embarrassing, you know, like walking into lecture rooms and asking students to go out and to leave lectures and join the demonstration. This is something I would never do, it was so unlike me, [...] so I can't imagine how I did that then, and how come I was not aggressed or something. You just walked into a lecture room and [would say] "What the hell are you doing sitting in the lecture room? You should join the movement!" [...] And then you walk out, and it's so embarrassing to think about, especially that I had no position in those demonstrations, you know, it's not like I was the co-organizer.

Hala Shukrallah, a young activist campaigning for the release of arrested students, recalled a meeting with the Speaker of Parliament: "And it turned out that he knew my father very well so he started speaking very personally with me, "Oh Hala, I know you since you were a child." So I told him, "Please, be very professional." And he was very upset about it. I of course was very rude. But anyway, that was natural for the time."

Nadia Abdel Wahab recalled being arrested for her participation in student demonstrations, spending around two months in prison: "It wasn't common for girls back then to participate in students' movements or such events, as there were threats of arrest [...] and that was unacceptable in a middle-class conservative family. [...] People hadn't yet gotten used to the idea that girls could be subjected to that."[5]

Similar levels of student unrest continued into the following academic year and were met with repression, including the arrests of students and their sympathizers from among the professional unions (Abdalla 1985: 197–208). Freeing detained students became, in and of itself, an important objective of protests. Hala Shukrallah, who was propelled into activism by the arrest of her brothers, became one of the leaders of the movement of the families of the arrested, which mainly consisted of the mothers of prisoners. As mothers and sisters, the women of the prisoners' families' movement resignified their private roles in political ways. Hala recalled:

There were such a variety of activities; we used to go to different syndicates and sit and talk with leaders of syndicates. We went [. . .] inside the university and [the mothers] led a demonstration with the students [. . .]. We went to the parliament house and met with the leader of the parliament. [. . .] We used to go to the courthouse whenever there are students having their cases presented. [. . .] So while we were there, somebody got arrested, [. . .] and so I for some reason made a stand and I said we will not leave the courthouse until you bring her back, and so the captain, or general or whatever, [. . .] came and told me, "Go away from here, don't make any trouble." And I said, "No, we will sit here, and we will have a sit-in in the courthouse if you don't bring her back." So he told his soldiers, "Take her away!" So they started dragging me away and then the mothers started sort of pulling me away from the soldiers, [. . .] and so they pushed all the mothers into the box and we were all taken to the headquarters of the police, and interrogated, and so on. They made us stay for only one night and released us. [. . .] The students used to stay about seven or eight months [in prison], and they would be released, and once they are released, sometimes, some of the mothers even though their kids are released they would continue to be active until the kids of the other mothers were released.

These narratives demonstrate the significance of the student movement in politicizing and mobilizing women into public activism. Ideologically, the movement marginalized or subordinated gender issues to the national question; nevertheless, young women played roles similar to their male counterparts', for example, leading sit-ins and getting arrested (Hammad 2016). Through their participation in street demonstrations, speaking publicly against authority, disobeying parents, being recruited to underground political parties, and even getting arrested, they embodied new and radical gender constructs. In this way, the student movement provided a terrain for young, middle-class women to transgress dominant norms of gendered respectability and to resist gendered hierarchies within the private and public spheres.

Jordan

In Jordan, in the wake of the 1967 war, women's activism flourished and a new generation of women became politically mobilized for the first time since the introduction of martial law in 1957. There were two different factors propelling this development: first, the humanitarian implications of the war, which had led to hundreds of thousands of Palestinians being displaced from the West Bank, and, second, the weakening of the regime, which allowed space for the establishment of PLO bases and Palestinian parties and organizations in Jordan. Many women volunteered their time to provide relief and welfare services to the displaced (al-Tal 2014: 181–83). In addition, as interviews revealed, women were also mobilized by Palestinian parties and organizations.

Jordanian women's public activism in the wake of the 1967 war represented many continuities with pre-1967 women's charitable work. For example, Muyassar, herself displaced from the West Bank, began volunteering her time daily "in the service of women and children" in the camps: "I worked in refugee camps and lived the daily suffering of people. I saw how people stood in line to get food, I saw children without milk or food. [. . .] So my colleagues in nursing school and I would go to pharmacies, collecting medicines and milk for the children and so on; people used to sympathize a lot with the refugees who came from Palestine. [. . .] So, this is how we worked, on human impulse." Meanwhile, new organizations proliferated during this period (al-Tal 2014: 181–83), such as the Arab Women Organization founded by Emily and Leila Naffa. Leila recalled: "We started helping the new influx of refugees, even to start the camps and to help there, we spent hours helping. [. . .] It was a hard time, hard feelings inside, and that's why women were getting active to support the new influx of refugees, and that's how the Arab Women Organization that I work in now was established. The first center was in a new camp called Baqaa camp." For the first time, the General Union of Palestinian Women (GUPW, a body within the Palestine Liberation Organization, founded in 1965, to represent Palestinian women) was able to operate in Jordan. It provided literacy classes, first aid and civil defense instruction, and embroidery and sewing classes for Palestinian women living in the camps (Brand 1998: 123).

Although women's humanitarian and relief work appeared to be a continuation of traditional women's charitable and welfare work, in the aftermath of the 1967 war these activities became resignified. Pre-1967 welfare work was principally in the service of "national uplift," whereas, in the wake of the war, the plight of the Palestinian refugees/displaced persons symbolized the indignity of the defeat, and support for them was part of actions in solidarity with the newly emerging Palestinian Resistance Movement. For example, in addition to welfare work, the Arab Women Organization was also involved in organizing conferences and demonstrations against the Israeli occupation and in solidarity with the Palestinian cause (al-Tal 2014: 184). Meanwhile, Asma Khader, born in Jenin, but raised in Amman, was mobilized into public work with the Palestinian movement initially through the GUPW, providing relief and welfare to Palestinian refugees. She recalled, "When it comes to supporting the national movement [. . .], sometimes thousands of women were involved, and most of them, they took on the humanitarian work."

The huge popularity of the Palestinian fighters, or fedayeen, particularly following the Battle of Karameh in 1968, forced the Jordanian government, already weakened by the defeat, to relax its tight grip on political and civil life, creating an opening for all political and civil forces in Jordan (Brand 1995a: 161). In particular, leftist and radical nationalist parties once again flourished, for the first time since the introduction of martial law in 1957, and the Palestinian resistance "became the 'backbone' of the Jordanian opposition, whose programs and activities became 'Palestinianized'" (Hasso 2005a: 30). Indeed, the fedayeen received significant support across multiple sectors of Jordanian society, not only those of Palestinian origin or progressive Jordanian political parties, but also among progressive forces in professional associations and women's organizations (Abu Odeh 1999: 175; al-Tal 2014: 184).

The weakening of the regime and the reemergence of radical political movements provided an opportunity for women to challenge gendered hierarchies and transgress dominant gender norms that previously limited middle-class women's public participation to charitable and welfare activities. Leila Naffa remembers the atmosphere at university at that time "was very liberal," with many students involved in political activities, including young women: "The fedayeen [. . .] were everywhere in Amman while I was in the university, and we were very active; girls, especially those of Palestinian origin, many, many girls were involved in politics, so it was not an extraordinary thing. I was among the majority in the mainstream; most of the university students, boys and girls, were so much involved in politics at that time."

Asma Khader became active in the General Union of Palestinian Students and, in 1968, was elected to the students' union executive committee. Meanwhile, for the first time in Jordan's history, significant numbers of women joined political groups, particularly the Palestinian political factions. For example, Abla Abu Elba, born in Qalqilya, on the West Bank, arrived in

Amman in 1967 and first worked with the GUPW before going on to join the Democratic Front for the Liberation of Palestine (DFLP)—one of the leftist factions within the PLO. I also met Jordanian-Jordanian women who joined the DFLP during this period (see also Hasso 2005a).

However, women faced contradictory attitudes within radical political movements. The rhetoric of movement leaders encouraged women to participate in the national struggle; however, they did not address gender inequality within the private sphere (Hasso 2000). Julie Peteet's seminal study on the Palestinian resistance movement in Lebanon found there was no coherent policy regarding the question of gender inequality and no attempts to transform gender norms beyond calls for women's participation in the national struggle (Peteet 1991). Several of my interviewees confirmed the degree to which gender inequalities existed within the Palestinian movement. For example, when I asked Asma whether it was common for women to be involved in public work during that period, she told me:

> When it comes to national issues, even the conservatives, conservative families, were participating, but it was not accepted for them to participate on a daily basis; it's just on the main occasions, for example demonstrations against something, but it was not in the [PLO] institutions. Very few numbers of women were able to join the institutions, the unions, the organizations, the societies. [. . .] Of course, women's participation in economic life as well was very, very limited. Most of the activists came from the educational sector, [. . .] because women were working mostly in this area, those [. . .] who were able to complete their education, like lawyers, very few lawyers at that time, in fact, [. . .] or even doctors, the very few women who studied medicine [. . .], they came and they were more ready to be active in society.

Moreover, male activists would demonstrate double standards toward their female comrades. Writer and activist Suhair Salti al-Tal, whose father was a Marxist, was one of several young Jordanian-Jordanian women who joined the Democratic Front for the Liberation of Palestine after 1967. She recounted to me that "when it came to dealing with women, there were two types: [. . .] If it was his sister, he would make her stay home; if she was a comrade in the party, then he would say, 'You're free and you can sleep with me,' and whatnot. [. . .] So that made me pull away from them. I believed that you should be progressive in all aspects, applying progressive measures to yourself first of all."

Despite these limitations, leftist and nationalist groups successfully mobilized young women into political activism on an unprecedented scale.

Moreover, for the first time, there emerged mass women's organizing among Palestinian refugee women, who, until then, had been mainly addressed as recipients of middle-class charity. In particular, various factions of the PLO actively recruited young women in the camps, directly challenging existing gender norms. Nadia Shamroukh remembered being in sixth grade when her teacher asked for volunteers to join the Zahrat, a youth wing of Fateh for girls:

> I was the first one to raise my hand. I did not tell my parents. I went to the [fedayeen] camp with my teacher. She told me to tell my parents, but I refused. I just wanted to go and register. [...] They told me I had to ask my parents and come back. I asked my parents, but they refused. [...] At the time my brother [...] yelled at me and said, "You are a girl and I will not allow it." The next day [...] I learned that other girls started to register. They told their parents and started to register and went to the camp. [...] I went home very depressed and I remember that I refused to eat. [...] I did not want to study either. [...] That went on for three days. On the third day, my mother complained [...] [and] she told my brother and father. So my father asked if I wanted to go to the camp and I said, "More than anything," so he allowed it. [...] I put on my shoes while he was still talking and ran to the camp. [...] I went to the camp every day. [...] The two years I spent in the camp, 1968–1970, [...] changed my personality completely. Completely. They played a role in my whole life in two things: That I am strong and that I am exactly like a boy. This is the feeling I got, actually, I was better than boys. This is how I felt and I continue to feel that way. I have felt that way my whole life within my family. That I am not weak.

Nadia's story and the narratives of other women illustrate the significance of the 1967 defeat and the strengthening of the Palestinian Resistance Movement in mobilizing women, particularly refugee women, into public activism. More broadly, the weakening of the Jordanian regime in the wake of the military defeat contributed to the destabilizing of dominant gender norms. Irrespective of the Palestinian movement's failure to articulate a coherent agenda for gender equality, it enabled many young women to embody new gender constructs through their participation in the movement. Meanwhile, other women continued a tradition of welfare and charitable activities but resignified this in the service of the national struggle.

Lebanon

In Lebanon, the arrival of the PLO transformed the agency of Palestinian camp women who, until 1969, were largely regarded as recipients of charity and welfare activities by middle-class Palestinian and Lebanese women living outside the camps. A Palestinian Women's Union existed in Lebanon after 1948, consisting of elite women who carried out relief work for Palestinian refugees as well as representing Palestinian women in international conferences. With the arrival of the PLO in Lebanon, the General Union of Palestinian Women (GUPW) displaced the Palestinian Women's Union as the representative of Palestinian women (Peteet 1991: 61–64).

As in Jordan, camp women were mobilized for the national struggle through the GUPW as well as the different political factions operating in the camps (Peteet 1991: 37). Amne Suliemane (born in Shatila camp, Beirut, and, at the time of our interview, was president of the Lebanese branch of the GUPW) was initially organized while at school, through the General Union of Palestinian Students, to dig shelters and visit the fighters on the frontline. Then she was recruited to the GUPW by Fateh women activists Jihan El Hilo, Shadia El Hilo, Shadyah Habashna, Um Jihad, and Salwa Abu Khadra.[6] Samira Salah, originally a member of the Arab Nationalist Movement in Syria and then, after 1967, a member of the central committee of the Popular Front for the Liberation of Palestine (PFLP), came to Lebanon in 1971 and was responsible for organizing women in Ayn Helweh and other camps in the south of Lebanon. Like Nadia Shamroukh in Jordan, Haifa Jammal, born in Bourj al-Shammali Camp, near Tyre, was mobilized at a young age after the PFLP arrived at her camp:

> They announced that they will make a training course about how to use weapons, how to become strong, make exercises and lectures about Palestinian issues and the Palestinian cause, and they announced a special course for girls, from twelve years old until thirty years old. And I was ten years old at the time. I would like to be a part of this, [so] I went to their office and asked them to register my name, and they said, "No, you are still young, you have to be a minimum of twelve years old." At that time, my teacher [. . .] had a good position in the PFLP, [so] I asked him to help me [. . .] and my cousin Fayza [. . .]. And we were the two youngest girls.

Within the Palestinian national movement, women were mainly concentrated in "mass work" (i.e., working among the people to raise political awareness and mobilize support for the Palestinian resistance) and social services (Peteet 1991: 115–19, 147–48). During the Lebanese civil war, the GUPW played a particularly important role in providing humanitarian relief for injured and displaced Palestinians. As Amne recalls:

It was a difficult time where the women's union worked a lot through its committees all over Lebanon and our headquarters was like a very active cell. Women were providing people with food, and [providing food to the] fighters also. We were helping people, first-aiding people. We made a list of our blood groupings, you know, in order to give blood at any time if someone needs blood for the wounded people. It happened that Tal al-Zaatar camp fell [in 1976] and it was really a catastrophe. There were thirty to thirty-five thousand people displaced. We worked in the places where displaced people were living, especially in Beirut.

While the GUPW's relief and humanitarian work has been viewed as complying with traditional gender norms of caring and nurturing (for example, see the discussion in Peteet 1991: 165–74), in the context of the Palestinian Revolution, this work took on a new meaning. For example, Olfat Mahmoud volunteered in first aid and nursing activities because she had a strong desire to do something for the Palestinian cause:

So within the student union I was active. I did lots of activities. I also did a first aid course, and I started to help in emergency [relief], then I did nursing after I finished my high school. It was heavy fighting, and I could not go to my university; lots of things [were happening], so I joined the nursing college. And I started to be active, from this point of view, like I have in all wars. I was involved; I was working as a nurse in an ambulance car; this is where I felt I can support my people.

Similarly, Samira Salah would organize women from the camps to cook for the fighters and recalled this as an important activity, rather than merely an extension of women's traditional activities:

I can't forget those days. [...] Even during the civil war, we would go to the south and take hot meals to the fighters there, because they couldn't cook, [...] so every week we would go to one place. [...] We were a group of women; [...] we would cook, bring the meals to them, sleep in the base, and then come back the next day. There was an unforgettably warm relationship amongst us and everyone still knows me to this day because of that. So, I can say that, thanks to God, I did something with my life.

Women were also involved in nontraditional work through the political factions. Haifa Jammal narrated her involvement in the PFLP training course as a personally empowering experience: "We stayed more than one year to make exercises [...] to become strong, and through this course I really became very active, because they also give us lectures about the history of

Palestine, about [...] communism, about the Soviet Union, about Lenin, about Marx, Guevara, and since then I am active." Haifa recalls that they also received some training in using Kalashnikovs but "only at the end of the course." As Julie Peteet notes, many Palestinian women received military training, even those in the GUPW, yet the number of Palestinian women who actually fought in combat was very small (see also, Eggert 2018b). Instead, military training for women performed a symbolic role in impressing upon the Palestinian community the extent of the crisis that they faced in Lebanon (Peteet 1991: 149–52).

The PLO also mobilized Palestinian women outside of the camps who came from more middle-class backgrounds, where public work was acceptable but political activism was usually frowned upon. For example, Leila Zakharia grew up in a middle-class, secular, anti-sectarian environment in Ras Beirut, born to a Palestinian Greek Orthodox father and Lebanese protestant mother. Leila was politicized by the 1967 defeat but did not begin attending political meetings until about ten years later. She was unable to tell people about her political involvement because her parents would have "cut [her] into forty thousand pieces if they knew [...] so it was always in the shadows for me." By contrast, Wafa Ali Al-Yassir, who was born to Palestinian parents in Lebanon but had never lived in a camp, was encouraged by her father to become active:

> I started to be active with the [Palestinian student] union, but I was young at
> that time, and then, I don't know how, I joined one of the Palestinian politi-
> cal factions, and I started to be very active when I was a student in the school.
> I was active and everything, demonstrating, collecting money and clothes
> and sending them to the south for the people who were really suffering from
> the Israeli bombardment of the villages in the south, [...] and I was reading
> and I was of course getting a political education and even military training
> and everything. I was so ambitious and I was so active and full of energy at
> that time that I wanted to do something for my country.

Souad Amin Jarar grew up in Saudi Arabia to wealthy Palestinian parents with Jordanian citizenship, and moved to Beirut in 1978 to attend the American University of Beirut (AUB). She became active in support of the Palestinian movement and fondly remembered this period as "maybe [...] the first time I really enjoyed being a Palestinian. "We used to do so many things on a voluntary basis. I used to go to the camps, help kids, help women, teach, we used to go of course to demonstrations. The political situation was completely different; we felt at that time that we are part of whatever was going on."

As mentioned above, the Palestinian movement did not have a coherent policy on gender. Women were mobilized on a scale previously unseen in the Palestinian refugee camps; however, gender-specific demands were not part of the national agenda, and the issue of women's subordination within the private sphere was not directly addressed (Peteet 1991: 165). Moreover, there was often a contradiction between the extent of women's contributions to the national struggle and their inclusion within decision-making structures, as highlighted by Samira Salah:

> From the very beginning it was our belief that Palestine couldn't be liberated just by the men, but that all the Palestinian people, men and women, must fight this battle together. This was the slogan of the PFLP: "Men and women, side by side, in the war of liberation" and this was the basis for our work in the PFLP. It must be noted that throughout all the stages of the Palestinian struggle that women were active in all the political parties and organizations and were also leaders in all areas: in the field, within civil society, in law, education, health services—women had a huge role in all of these. Unfortunately, the recognition that women received for their contributions did not correspond to their efforts. It's this sort of thing that is hurtful, that even the leftist parties [...] were depreciating the value of the services rendered by women. So, in the top leadership positions of all political parties [...] the highest percentage of women in the top positions was fifteen percent.

Despite the limitations and contradictions, the Palestinian movement provided a legitimate framework for women to renegotiate and resist norms of female respectability. The degree to which young Palestinian women challenged dominant gender norms during this period is apparent in the opposition of parents, particularly mothers, to their daughters' political involvement. For example, when I asked Haifa Jammal about her parents' attitudes toward her activism, she told me, "My father was always encouraging me, but my mother was always worried about me [because] she didn't like me to be active; she preferred that [...] I help her with housework and to focus on my education and not to enter into politics, but [...] I was very strong in my family. [...] When I believed in what I wanted to do, I would argue with them and most of the time I succeeded to convince them." Similarly, Wafa Al-Yassir told me, "My father was very supportive [of my activism], but my mother was not supportive because she was afraid. I was a female and, you know, there is this traditional attitude towards females that you have to be nice, you have to grow up as a woman and get married and all this; so, I refused all this traditional way of thinking and tried to find for myself something else."

As Julie Peteet notes, the Palestinian Revolution did not completely dissolve existing gender ideologies, but it opened up "a moment of experimentation with new forms of social relations" (1991: 208). However, this revolutionary moment would end in 1982, with the forced withdrawal of the PLO from Lebanon, following Israel's invasion and ten-week-long siege of Beirut. The PLO's departure from Lebanon marked the end of the Palestinian Revolution and a new, more dangerous, phase in the Palestinians' struggle for survival in Lebanon, with implications for women's activism, as discussed further in the next chapter.

The Lebanese Civil War, Women's Activism, and Gender Norms

Between 1975 and 1990, Lebanon was ravaged by civil war, the culmination of growing tensions between, on the one hand, the Palestinian resistance movement and their Lebanese allies, who sought to transform the Lebanese political system, and, on the other hand, the right-wing Maronite Christian parties and militias, who sought to maintain the political status quo. Among the women that I interviewed, the war was remembered overwhelmingly as a time of hardship, pain, fear, and despair. Yet, their memories also demonstrate a period in which gender norms were in flux and many women were mobilized into public work as a direct consequence of the war.

The lasting impression that I had after interviewing more than twenty women in Lebanon who remembered the war was that the personal experiences of Lebanon's civil war differed greatly depending on geographical residence, confessional belonging, and Lebanese or Palestinian nationality. The war did not cover the whole of Lebanon simultaneously but was rather a series of episodes of fighting in different locations. As Malcolm Yapp states, "After 1976 the history of Lebanon is a history of the separate developments of various regions. Within the territories controlled by the different communities there was often something approaching normal life, but on the borderlands and especially in West Beirut and in the south there was conflict, violence and even anarchy" (Yapp 1996: 271).

The first phase of the war, in 1975–1976, was more or less a clear-cut battle between the Maronite militias (the Lebanese Front), on one side, and the fedayeen fighting alongside the leftist forces (Lebanese National Movement), on the other. During this period, Maronite militias ethnically cleansed East Beirut, carrying out the massacres of Karantina and the Tal al-Zaatar

Palestinian refugee camp. In retaliation for Karantina, Palestinian fighters killed more than six hundred civilians in the predominantly Christian town of Damour. This phase of the war came to an end with the intervention of Syria on the side of the Maronites. The second phase of the war, between 1977 and 1982, is characterized by Syrian-Israeli rivalry to control Lebanon as leverage within the broader Arab-Israeli conflict. During this period, Israel bombed Palestinian refugee camps in Southern Lebanon and then, in 1978, invaded and occupied the area. In 1982, Israel carried out a much more substantial invasion, reaching Beirut, which it bombed and laid siege to throughout the summer. After the forced withdrawal of the PLO in August of that year, Israeli forces oversaw the massacres of the Sabra and Shatila refugee camps by the right-wing Maronite Phalange militia, during which hundreds of camp residents, mainly Palestinians but also some Lebanese, were murdered.[7] The third and final phase of the war, between 1982 and 1990, consisted of Lebanese resistance to Israeli occupation of Southern Lebanon, alongside increasing inter- and intra-sectarian conflict, as different militias battled for control of territory and wealth (Traboulsi 2007: 187–239). For Palestinians, this period is remembered as one of the most horrific periods of the war because of the "War of the Camps," during which the Syrian-backed Amal militia attacked and besieged Palestinian refugee camps, leading to massive destruction, hunger, and thousands of deaths.

Despite a significant number of books written about the Lebanese Civil War, women and gender are conspicuous by their near absence, except to refer to war casualties. The marginalization of women in scholarship on the war is reflective of the masculinist geopolitical lens through which Lebanon is studied. In addition, feminist researchers themselves have marginalized this period, since the Lebanese women's movement largely abandoned the struggle for women's rights (see for example, Stephan 2012). Indeed, the Lebanese Council for Women suspended its activities during this period, while the Lebanese League for Women's Rights stopped its preparations for the 1975 UN Women's Conference in order to put "the nation first" (LLWR 1987). As Fahima Charafeddine summed up in our interview, the civil war "changed the focus [of the women's movement]: social demands took a backseat and the role of women changed; from activists demanding their rights to aid workers helping the injured of the war." Indeed, I came across many examples of women who had volunteered in field hospitals to help the wounded and to provide support for those displaced by the war.

Miriam Cooke (1999) is one of very few writers to examine the war from women's perspectives through the medium of novels. She argues that Lebanese women's voices have provided a counternarrative to the war story, with its usual focus on political and military elites. Cooke argues that Lebanese women writers such as Hanan al-Shaykh, Emily Nasrallah, and Huda Barakat, among others, "questioned the binary epistemology that organizes war into neat dichotomies like friend and foe, victory and defeat, front and home front [. . .] and the 'lie' that men go to war to protect their women" (Cooke 1999: 76). They reimagined Lebanese nationalism not in terms of the militaristic and destructive nationalism that fueled the civil war but rather a more maternal and nurturing nationalism that emphasized loyalty to the land (Cooke 1999; see also Cooke 1996). In this way, women writers transformed themselves from victims of war into agents of peace.

Several of the women whom I interviewed indeed narrated a counternarrative that emphasized their participation in the civil resistance to war. For example, Linda Matar recalled how the outbreak of the war changed the priorities of the LLWR:

> We were busy preparing for the international year of women, and then came the civil war on April 13, [1975]. We stopped and we said that our country is our first priority. If there's no country, then there are no rights, not for women, not for men, not for anyone. We started struggling to stop the civil war. There was a lot of destruction but we kept working. We didn't stay home, despite all the shelling. We were on the streets. Nobody from the League left the country. We worked every day until at some point my neighbors told me that they thought I must have been paid since I was going out under the shelling. That was how much I loved my country; no matter what happened in my country I would never leave it.

Indeed, the only time that Linda left Lebanon during the war was to participate in an international speaking tour to raise awareness of Israel's devastating invasion and siege of Beirut in the summer of 1982.

After 1982, Lebanese civilians became increasingly frustrated with the militias and their violence, and different sectors of the population, including women, began organizing regular street protests (Hanf 1993: 639). These occurred across the country, with the biggest held in Beirut, where some sixty thousand demonstrators from East and West Beirut marched toward the Museum checkpoint chanting "East and West united" and "national unity," much to the anger of the militias (Hanf 1993: 639–40). Joumana Merhy, a member of the Lebanese Women Democratic Gathering, recalled:

During this time, there was a strong popular movement to stop the war, which had become a suicide war that was only bringing more death and destruction. A group of civil society activists started a peaceful movement to stop the civil war in Lebanon and this was one of the great things that we [the Lebanese Women Democratic Gathering] took part in. We would try to mobilize the people about the importance of ending the war and organize strikes and sit-ins simultaneously in both areas; eastern and western, Muslim and Christian, to demand civil peace in Lebanon. Until one day we decided we were going to march onto the [militia] check points and we walked towards them without fear, even though there were bullets flying over our heads, but we were determined and we made a human chain with people from both sides holding hands and saying that we didn't want Beirut to be divided into two cities anymore. That day was one that I can never ever forget. Even after it got dark and it was time for us to go back to our houses, we found it difficult to let go of the hands of each other, although we didn't know each other, because they were from a part of town where we weren't allowed to be. I think when we talk about the civil peace, I can say it was the civil society organizations that made it happen.

Another women's initiative that emerged to challenge the sectarian and masculinist logics of war was the Lebanese Association of Women Researchers (Bahithat), founded in 1987. The organization brought together women from different areas and of different backgrounds and gave them a voice at a time when Beirut, and Lebanon more generally, was divided among the militia. They continue to work today, producing publications and holding conferences on different topics. Their only rule is to not discuss religion or politics among themselves.[8]

Resistance to the war also took more mundane forms. Several women stressed that they stayed in Lebanon throughout the civil war, despite the difficulties of everyday life. Women mentioned the hardship of having no water, no electricity, and no food, and the anxieties caused by violence and destruction, while trying to care for their families as well as working outside the home. Lamia Rustum Shehadeh describes women's lives as an "accordion day": "They [women] had to fulfill all household chores and adapt themselves to all external duties such as taking children to school and be ready to bring them back at short notice due to shelling or intra-communal fighting, taking them for recreation, shopping for food, providing gas, water and candles, and health services, and, last but not least, going to work" (Shehadeh 1999c: 51). In this context, the commitment to stay in Lebanon, against the odds, could be considered a form of resistance, not dissimilar to the Palestinian philosophy of *sumud*, or "steadfastness" (see, for example, Peteet 1991: 153).

While a narrative centering women's resistance to war counterbalances the many studies that focus solely on the actions of predominantly male political and military elites, nevertheless, the association of women with peace is, as feminist scholars have highlighted, problematic in the way that it essentializes women (Elshtain 1982) and arguably reverses rather than dismantles the gendered epistemology of war. Associating women with peace displaces them from the sphere of parties, militias, and ideologies, and depoliticizes their agency. Yet, as in the case of Palestinian women previously discussed, some Lebanese women were also linked to militias/armed groups. Joumana Merhy left home at the age of seventeen to join the Lebanese National Resistance Front against Israel, as a member of a leftist party. As a student in the mid-1980s, Rima Fakhry became involved with the Hizbollah student affairs society, impressed by the armed resistance against Israel. Much of women's work in this regard was in the form of social work and nursing and administrative work, such as secretaries, clerks, and telephone operators; however, some women were involved in combat operations (see Eggert 2018b, Shehadeh 1999: 149–61, Sharara 1978).

Women who participated in political or military activities complicate the notion of a woman's counternarrative to the war story. They challenge the dominant, masculinist war story, not by positioning themselves beyond political and military spheres but by criticizing the marginalization of women's contributions to these spheres. For example, echoing the words of Samira Salah of the PFLP (see previous section), Joumana Merhy told me, "Women's work and their contribution remained in the shadows, because what was always in the forefront was the men's contribution on the battlefields and their fight against the Israeli invaders. The logistics support was provided by the women, such as, food, nursing, even cleaning the weapons. We would work all night cleaning the weapons. The fighters would come back and sleep and we would help with the cleaning." Moreover, the particularly gendered consequences of the war served to politicize and resignify women's productive and reproductive roles. Joumana remembers the period after 1982 as a time of shifting gender norms, "because after the Israeli invasion, many women joined the workforce." The Lebanese Democratic Women Gathering (LDWG) worked to support these women, by raising awareness of labor laws and workers' rights and encouraging women to join labor unions. Joumana's memories of this period suggest a growing politicization of women's roles as providers for their families: "There was a lot of activism at that time and women had a strong stance on these issues, such as the rise in living expenses, school fees, and oil prices. One incident I remember is during an open union strike that lasted seven days, where we organized daily women's demonstrations to demand higher wages and the increase in the subsidization of flour and fuels."

Women's political involvement also led many to question gendered hierarchies and to formulate gender-specific demands. The LDWG was established by women who were already active in the leftist-democratic milieu of the period and felt that neither the parties and organizations of the political opposition movement nor the existing women's organizations were adequately addressing questions of women's liberation and equality (Aïssaoui 2002: 126–27). Joumana Merhy explained her reasons for joining the LDWG in 1984:

> We saw how it was always the men in the forefront and the women were always way behind in importance, how women were viewed as inferior in society, within the party and even in the student movements and at the university. This is what drove me to women's rights activism. Because we lived through all the moments in which women were being discriminated against. We lived through times where the women contributed maybe even more than that of men, but they were still viewed as less important. Our main concern was to raise awareness among women about their own rights and in the society as a whole about women's rights and also, how to protect women from exploitation.

CONCLUSION

This chapter has contributed to existing scholarship on the aftermath of the 1967 war by examining the gendered dimensions of the geopolitical upheavals that unfolded. While existing feminist scholarship tends to focus on the negative consequences of war and the challenges facing women in its aftermath, this chapter has demonstrated the degree to which the post-1967 crisis weakened the gender order established with decolonization and provided new opportunities for women to expand their activism. In particular, the chapter focused on women's involvement in the radical social and political movements that emerged in reaction to the military defeat at the hands of Israel and in opposition to the postindependence Arab regimes who were responsible. While these movements prioritized political-national questions over issues of women's rights and gender equality and, moreover, excluded women from decision-making, reflecting and reproducing existing gendered hierarchies, nonetheless, women, particularly Palestinian refugees, entered these movements in unprecedented numbers. Feminist scholarship of this period has tended to ignore women's activism within these movements (the exceptions being Eggert 2018a, 2018b; Hasso 2005a; Peteet 1991) often because it did not prioritize gender issues; thus, this chapter has sought to highlight the significance of this activism in terms of its embodied resistance to dominant norms of female respectability. Such activism contributed to further undoing the gender order upon which regime authority was built, suggesting the intimate relationship between disruption of the existing geopolitical order and disruption of the existing gender order.

Not all women participated in political parties and movements and not all women's activisms directly challenged dominant gender norms. Many women in Jordan and Lebanon engaged in welfare and humanitarian work that sought to address the human consequences of war (both the 1967 war and the Lebanese Civil War), such as nursing the injured and supporting those displaced. Moreover, women provided "traditional" reproductive labor (cooking, knitting sweaters, cleaning) in support of armed groups. In Egypt, women mobilized as mothers and sisters to free imprisoned student activists. While this type of women's work has been largely ignored in scholarship or considered simply a continuation of women's charitable and welfare activities and an extension of the gendered division of domestic labor, in the context of the post-1967 upheavals, many women whom I interviewed considered their activities to make an important contribution to the political/national struggles of that period. In other words, disruption of the geopolitical order enabled the resignification of female respectability to include public work in the service of political and national struggles. In turn, by extending their domestic roles into the political sphere, women exposed the boundary between private and public, "inner" and "outer" spheres, modernity and modesty, as well as the "natural state" that depends upon it, as a (geo-)"politically tenuous construct" (to paraphrase Butler 1999: 179). Given the mutually constitutive relationship between geopolitical and gender order, it follows that women's bodies and women's activism became a target of efforts to reestablish regime authority, as the next chapter explores.

THREE

The Gendered Effects of Political Repression and Violence in the 1970s and 1980s

IN RESPONSE TO THE WAVE of radical and revolutionary movements and political currents that emerged after the 1967 defeat, a range of reactionary forces rallied to reestablish the geopolitical order in their favor. However, this was not a case of returning to the status quo ante of the postindependence period but rather a counterrevolution against what Vijay Prashad (2007) calls the "Third World project"—that is, a collective project for political independence, a rejection of foreign domination, and a redistribution of global wealth. These were not only the ideological goals of the progressive and radical movements that emerged after 1967 but also part of the Arab socialist project of Gamal Abdel-Nasser alongside other Arab nationalist leaders in the initial decades after independence. This counterrevolution was spearheaded by regional actors with the assistance of the United States and its allies, seeking to extend their influence across the Middle East region in the context of Cold War global rivalries. It entailed shifts in foreign as well as domestic policies, with implications for women and gender norms.

While scholars of the region's history and international relations have examined the changing regional order in the wake of the 1967 defeat and the significance of Cold War dynamics (Halliday 2005; Hinnebusch 2003; Khalidi 2009; Sayigh and Shlaim 1997), little attention has been paid to how these geopolitical transformations were experienced by ordinary men and women, let alone their impact on gender relations, gender norms, or women's activism. Yet, as already discussed, gendered bodies are central to the (re)production of borders, territories, sovereignty, and national identity, which, in turn, are constitutive of regime authority, foreign policy making, war making, and constructions of state security, with repercussions for human security (Dixon and Marston 2011; Smith 2001; Smith, Swanson, and Gökarıksel 2016).

The chapter begins by exploring events in Egypt, where President Anwar al-Sadat, who replaced Gamal Abdel-Nasser after his death in 1970, initiated a reversal in Nasserist policies, dismantling the populist social pact, reorienting Egypt's foreign alliances toward the United States, and signing a bilateral peace deal with Israel, the latter of which had dangerous implications for the Palestinians and other Arab states. In response to popular opposition to his policies, Sadat clamped down on the student movement and other political activists. The chapter then goes on to examine Jordan. There, the regime, with the support of its Western allies, launched a military attack on the Palestinian fedayeen, leading to their expulsion to Lebanon. This was accompanied by a wider regime crackdown on the Jordanian political opposition and a reinforcement of martial law. The final section of the chapter considers the Lebanese case. There, right-wing Maronite forces clashed with the PLO and its leftist and nationalist allies, thereby contributing to the outbreak of the Lebanese Civil War in 1975 (as examined in the previous chapter). The war entered a new phase in 1982, with the US-sanctioned Israeli invasion, which led to the expulsion of the fedayeen from Lebanon and a deterioration in the security of Palestinians in Lebanon.

In all three cases, the chapter highlights the varied implications of changes to regional order and the dismantling of the postindependence social pact for gender norms and women's activism. US intervention in the Middle East region enabled repressive and reactionary forces to violently suppress revolutionary and radical movements, thereby removing an important arena for women's transgressive gender performances. The reinscribing of female respectability norms was both a consequence as well as an instrument of political repression. Simultaneously, the weakening of radical political movements led to new forms of women's activism that prioritized gender-specific demands. In this way, the chapter explores how geopolitical transformations lead to changes in the modes of women's activism as well as shifts in gender norms.

EGYPT: THE GENDERED EFFECTS OF DISMANTLING ARAB SOCIALISM

Building Sadat's Authority

Upon the death of Gamal Abdel-Nasser in 1970, his vice-president, Anwar al-Sadat, was named president. He faced a number of challenges, not least of which were an ongoing war with Israel, severe economic problems, social unrest, and the difficulty of following in the footsteps of his highly charismatic and much-loved predecessor (Cook 2011: 113–19). In order to build his authority and eliminate rival centers of political power, within a year of taking office Sadat launched the "corrective revolution," purging Nasser's supporters from the administration. Meanwhile, reflecting the increased general religiosity in the wake of the 1967 defeat, he began to "infuse his government with an Islamic persona" (Al-Arian 2014: 86), adopting more religious language and symbols, and presenting himself as the "believer-president" (Al-Arian 2014: 86–90; Ayubi 1991: 75; Esposito 1984: 236–37). He inserted a new article into the 1971 constitution (Article 2), stating that: "the principles of sharia are a major source of legislation," and Article 11, guaranteeing women's equality provided that it "did not infringe on the rules of Islamic sharia" (cited in Hatem 1992: 241). Such policies marked a clear break from the more secular language of the Nasser regime.

Sadat also initiated a rapprochement with the Muslim Brotherhood, hundreds of whom had been imprisoned under Nasser, allowing them to reestablish their organization and circulate their publications, hoping that the Brotherhood and other Islamist groups would provide a counterbalance to Nasserist and leftist political groups (Ayubi 1991: 56–57; Gerges 2012). In particular, with the tacit support of the authorities, the Islamist movement was allowed to promote Islamic cultural and religious activities on university campuses, such as, study circles, public lectures, conferences, and summer camps (Abdalla 1985: 226; Al-Arian 2014: 129–33). However, as Nazih Ayubi argued, "The Islamist movement took on an independent life and logic of its own," growing sufficiently in strength to harass Christian students and secular-oriented students and faculty (1991: 56). Aida Seif El Dawla, then a student at the Qasr al-Aini teaching hospital, recalled the ideological divisions on campus at this time: "So those final years in university, there were the Islamists on the one hand and the Nasserists on the other hand. And the confrontations were violent, [. . .] students got beaten up."

An essential part of reshaping campus culture centered around the female body. Islamist groups promoted female veiling, with student vendors selling modest female dress (Al-Arian 2014: 133). Aida remembered the point at which Islamist students took over the student union, and Islamic dress, an innovation by the Islamic movement rather than a return to traditional Egyptian garb, began to be advertised at reduced cost: "And it was during that time [. . .] [that] I got to know a couple of young women, both of them were veiled and we got on well and so [...] they started saying, 'Why don't you put [on] the veil?'" Aida did not accept this invitation; however, female veiling became widespread on university campuses. While several authors have explored the reasons why women chose to wear the veil from the 1970s onward, including socioeconomic need, growing religiosity, and cultural identity (El Guindi 1981; MacLeod 1991; Zuhur 1992), it is also important to recognize that Islamist movements promoted veiling and norms of female modesty as an important part of extending their political influence. On university campuses, the promotion of the veil and more modest female behavior, including the establishment of segregated public transportation for female students, were part of efforts "to enforce public morality by decreasing interaction between male and female students" (Al-Arian 2014: 133–34) and functioned to differentiate Islamists from their political rivals in the student movement—that is leftists and Nasserists—as well as from the increasingly authoritarian and pro-Western regime of Sadat. Moreover, Islamists deployed notions of female respectability against women activists in order to delegitimize their participation in the student movement. According to Aida: "Of course, we as women, we did not get beaten up. I didn't, at least. But we received a lot of abuse. [...] You know, calling us "bitches" and "whores" and that 'we are after husbands' and that's why we are involved in politics and stuff like that. So I was happy to graduate."

Reorienting Egyptian Foreign Policy

Sadat prioritized the recovery of the Sinai Peninsula above all else. It was a question at the heart of national sovereignty and the regime's legitimacy. Indeed, the occupation of the Sinai Peninsula was a major issue driving the student protests of 1972–73, attracting sympathy among the wider public and intelligentsia (Abdalla 1985: 186). Sadat sought to enlist the help of the United States to pressure Israel to reach a negotiated settlement, but to no avail. Therefore, in October 1973, Egypt, in coordination with Syria and supported by the Saudi oil embargo, launched a military attack on the Israeli occupied lands (Hinnebusch 2003: 173–75). The war failed to liberate any part of the territories controlled by Israel; nonetheless, Egyptians viewed it as a victory because Egyptian troops had managed to overrun Israel's fortifications on the east bank of the Suez Canal (the Bar Lev Line), inflicting a blow against perceptions of Israel's invincibility. Meanwhile, the huge financial costs incurred by the US and other Western countries as a result of the oil embargo succeeded in persuading the US administration to intervene to support a negotiated settlement (Hinnebusch 2003: 175). As Raymond Hinnebusch argues, the 1973 war gave the Arab states increased leverage over Israel to achieve the settlement that they wanted, so long as they remained united (2003: 175–76).

Yet Sadat decided to pursue a separate peace deal with Israel at the expense of wider Arab interests, leading to the Camp David Accords of 1978 and the signing of a peace treaty with Israel in 1979, in which the latter returned the Sinai Peninsula in return for full normalization of Egypt-Israel relations (Hinnebusch 2003: 178–79). Egypt was rewarded by a generous package of US aid, while Western governments hailed Sadat as a courageous leader willing to make the difficult decisions necessary for peacemaking. Since 1979, the West has viewed the Egypt-Israel peace treaty as the cornerstone of regional stability and the guarantor of Western strategic interests. However, across the Arab world, Egypt's peace treaty was vilified for abandoning Palestinian rights, sparking protests in Beirut, Amman, and other Arab capitals, in which several of my interviewees participated at the time. Egypt was expelled from the Arab League, and its headquarters in Cairo were closed.

Meanwhile, Sadat also faced domestic opposition to the peace treaty from across the political spectrum, from leftists to Islamists. Farida El-Nakkash, a member of the leftist National Progressive Unionist Party, otherwise known as the Tagammu' Party, which was one of three parties licensed after the introduction of a multiparty system, explained her party's opposition to the treaty: "The most important thing that the Camp David Accords achieved was that it divided the Arab cause. The Palestinian cause, the occupied Egyptian lands, and the occupied Syrian lands all became separate causes, which is why we referred to it as the 'separate peace' and we were against it, because we wanted a peace that would benefit all affected parties, in which the Arabs would get back what is rightfully theirs and we would recognize the State of Israel as part of the region, but with fair conditions."[1] Sadat cracked down on his critics and became increasingly intolerant of dissent. Various public figures, including writers, journalists, political activists, and religious figures were imprisoned after 1977, culminating in the detention of over one thousand public figures in September 1981. Farida El-Nakkash was imprisoned twice: for two months in 1979 and eleven months in 1981–82 for her opposition to the peace treaty (Booth 1987). Sadat introduced various measures to criminalize dissent, including a law banning parties that opposed peace with Israel, marking a dramatic reversal of the controlled political liberalization experiment introduced by Sadat earlier in his rule (Baaklini et al. 1999: 228; Brownlee 2011–12).

Egypt's policy had "profoundly damaging consequences" for the Arab region, tipping the balance of power hugely to the benefit of Israel (Hinnebusch 2003: 179). With Israel's southern border secured, its forces were freed up to launch a massive invasion of Lebanon in 1982 with the aim of expelling the fedayeen and pushing back Syrian forces (Hinnebusch 2003: 184–88), terrorizing civilians over several weeks, as discussed later in this chapter. Therefore, while the agreement with Israel enabled the return of the Sinai Peninsula to Egypt, the term *peace treaty* is a misnomer, coming at the expense of the rights and security of Palestinians and Lebanese and political and civil freedoms of Egyptians.

Dismantling the Political Economy of Nasserism

Sadat's signing of a peace treaty with Israel in 1979 represented a culmination in the process of reorienting Egypt's foreign alliances toward the Western camp. This shift was enabled not only through diplomacy but also through transformations in domestic policies—specifically the introduction of the "Open Door" or Infitah economic policy. Sadat capitalized on his 1973 "victory" to introduce this major policy shift, which aimed at dismantling the state-directed economy of the Nasser regime through enticing foreign investment, ending state monopoly over foreign trade, and lifting restrictions on private trade in foreign currency.[2] Sadat hoped that attracting Western capital and increasing trade relations would facilitate Egypt's alliance with the West, which in turn would attract more foreign capital and aid to Egypt (Waterbury 1983: 123–28; Weinbaum 1985).

Infitah policies had far reaching social effects, benefitting a class of rentiers, middle men, and landlords at the expense of the working and middle classes and peasantry, who had been the main social base of the Nasser regime (Waterbury 1983: 173–87; Zaalouk 1989). Whereas under Nasser's state-led modernization, the route to social mobility and prestige was through education and a public sector career, under Sadat, new opportunities for social mobility opened up that did not necessitate education, such as, speculation, migration, and employment "directly or indirectly, in the service of foreigners" (Amin 2000: 15–16). As a result of underfunding of the state sector, wages for civil servants, public sector workers, and others on fixed incomes began to stagnate (Amin 2000: 17; Tucker 1978; Aulas 1978). By the beginning of the 1980s, a plumber could earn more than a university professor (Waterbury 1983: 432).

The effects of Infitah had gendered consequences. For the middle-class women whom I interviewed, many of whom pursued professional careers in the public sector, the impact of Infitah was narrated in terms of a resulting loss of status. University professor Iman Ezzeldin expressed unreserved contempt for Sadat and the way in which he undermined the possibility of social mobility through educational achievement: "I hated Sadat, I really hated him, because he ruined, from my point of view, he ruined the society, with this Infitah, you know, this policy of people sitting in cafes and making business and making deals, these rich people from very . . . uneducated—I don't care if they are from which part of society but I care about education because to put money in the hands of uneducated people, from my point of view this is a disaster. This is what happened to the Egyptian society since Sadat."

While previously the public sector had been viewed as the engine of national development and progress, as well as a respectable route for middle-class women to enter the workforce, under Sadat, the public sector became corrupted by encroaching marketization. At the upper echelons, huge sums of money were involved (Waterbury 1983: 255–57). However, petty corruption came to be practiced at all levels of the public sector as a means to supplement wages that were declining in relation to the private sector, with negative implications for the quality of public services. After graduating from Cairo University, Nadia Abdel Wahab went to work as a doctor in a village in Gharbiyya governorate and tried to resist this corruption:

When doctors went to these villages they turned into con men. They tried to increase their earnings so they take the medicine provided by the unit which should be given to people for free and when someone came for a paid "private" examination, as the government started giving permissions for such "private" work, those patients got the medicine provided by the unit, which is not supposed to be given to private patients, and all the villagers knew that if they came for a private examination, they would get the good medicine or the expensive medicine or the medicine that would work best. So, I tried not to do that.

The corruption of the public sector, which was the largest employer of women, and the erosion in the pay and conditions of public sector workers, contributed toward a reconfiguration of the norm of female respectability. In a marked departure from the Nasserist era, women's participation in the workforce was no longer held up as a symbol of national modernity. Instead, there emerged public debates questioning the desirability of women working, and the government even "offered numerous incentives [to women] to take a leave of absence without pay to raise their children and/or to work on a part-time basis" (Hatem 1992: 235). Such attitudes were supported by the growing Islamist movement, which emphasized women's primary roles as mothers and wives. However, for lower-middle-class and working-class women, the economic transformations after 1974 and the dismantling of the Nasserist social pact meant that women's employment became even more necessary for family survival. Arlene MacLeod's ethnography of lower-middle-class women in Cairo in the 1980s, many of whom were employed in the public sector, found that women adopted the headscarf (hijab) as a means of signaling their "respectability" in the face of conservative attitudes toward women's working (MacLeod 1991). By the 2000s, the hijab had become ubiquitous among Egyptian women of all classes, with the exception of Christians and the majority of secular-oriented women activists whom I interviewed, as a means of performing female respectability in public spaces.

Paradoxically, while Sadat's policies helped to encourage conservative attitudes toward women's working, he oversaw amendments to the personal status laws that aimed at improving women's rights with regard to divorce. The amendments, which came to be known disparagingly as "Jehan's Laws," in reference to the First Lady, included a stipulation that husbands must inform their wives if they take a second wife; that wives had the right to seek divorce on the basis of their husband's taking a second wife; and that a divorced wife had the right to remain in the family home until her children had grown up (Hatem 1992: 242). In addition, a presidential decree reserved thirty seats in the People's Assembly for women and introduced a quota of 20 percent of seats for women in local councils (Hatem 1992: 243), while the Egyptian government ratified the Convention on the Elimination of All Forms of Discrimination against Women (CEDAW).[3]

The apparent paradox in Sadat's policies toward women may be understood through a prism of critical geopolitics. On the domestic level, Sadat hoped that women's rights reforms would bolster support for his regime among the middle classes in a context of increasing opposition to his economic and foreign policies and, in particular, vis-à-vis an increasingly popular Islamist movement. Simultaneously, on the international level, the reforms signaled Egypt's "liberalism" to a Western audience, which Sadat viewed as an important source of economic aid and investment to Egypt (Hatem 1992:

242). Yet Sadat's state feminism failed to garner him the domestic support for which he had hoped. While Nasserist state feminism was articulated with (populist) objectives of social justice, pan-Arabism, and anti-imperialism, Sadat rearticulated state feminism with largely unpopular polices of Infitah, a separate peace with Israel, and growing political repression. This provided an opportunity for the Islamist movement to discredit women's rights through their association with corruption, injustice, and subordination to Western geopolitical interests and cultural values. The Islamists mobilized public opinion against the First Lady, accusing her of imitating the West, and alleging that the changes were against sharia. Meanwhile, secular groups, including leftists, opposed the reforms because of the authoritarian way in which the amendments were passed during a period in which Sadat was repressing critical voices and antigovernment activists (Hatem 1992: 242–43). Women activists were divided over the amendments, with the Progressive Women's Union, affiliated with the leftist Tagammu' Party, opposing the amendments on the grounds that they were passed unconstitutionally, while independent feminist Nawal El-Saadawi and a coalition of other women campaigned to retain the law because they saw it as a positive step for women (Al-Ali 2000: 74–76; Hatem 1992: 243). The articulation of state feminism with authoritarianism and corruption under Sadat, and, later, under the regime of Hosni Mubarak, would come to haunt women activists in the aftermath of the Egyptian uprising in 2011, as discussed in chapter 6.

Political Repression

As already mentioned, Sadat's policies were largely unpopular and were met with a growing number of strikes and protests by workers and students. Between 1975 and 1976, there was a wave of industrial unrest in opposition to the reversal of Nasserist social gains (Beinin 2001: 156–57). Popular resistance to Infitah culminated in the 1977 "bread uprising," often referred to as the "bread riots" in Western media. The protests were triggered by a government announcement of the removal of subsidies on several basic commodities, including sugar, bread, and rice, in line with IMF loan conditionalities, leading to a doubling of prices over night. On 17 January, workers walked out of their factories, and were later joined by thousands of students, civil servants, and ordinary people, who marched on downtown Cairo. Magda Adli, at that time a student of medicine at Al-Azhar University, recalled, "On that day we were having a conference at the university on democratic freedoms. We canceled the conference as soon as we heard the news that morning and we joined the people's protests." Demonstrations occurred throughout Egypt. In Cairo, protesters converged on Sadat's office at Abdin Palace, shouting slogans criticizing him and his economic policies, as well as the lack of political freedoms (Kandil 2012: 169). Security forces battled through the night to disperse the protests (Hirst 1977), and calm was not restored until the government rescinded the decision and the army was called onto the streets (Kandil 2012: 169). All in all, 160 demonstrators were killed and 800 injured (Kandil 2012: 169).

Sadat was clearly shaken by the extent of the protests, calling them the "uprising of thieves." He accused communists of attempting to overthrow the regime and ordered the arrests of thousands of leftist activists (Hirst 1977; Stevens 1978). Amina Al-Naccache, a founding member of the Tagammu' Party, helped to establish a committee to defend the detainees. She recounted that:

> when the riots on the 17 and 18 of January 1977 happened and the [Tagammu']
> Party was accused of inciting them, most of the party leaders were arrested,
> including my husband, Salah, although he wasn't a member of the party, but
> everyone from the left was accused of inciting it. Of course, this was something that shook the chair from under Sadat and made him feel that despite
> his victory in October [1973], he didn't have popular support. Because his
> internal policies were not in the interest of the masses of Egyptians. They only
> benefitted the wealthy and the businessmen and so on.

Many of those arrested were released without charge, but not before having spent up to six months in administrative detention (Stevens 1978). Student activist Magda Adli was one of several people who spent more than a year in prison following the uprising: "So, I was arrested as soon as the university opened again. [...] I was arrested at university and I was charged with attempts to overthrow the regime and joining a secret organization and all the rest of the list of accusations by the state security that is still used until now. I spent fourteen or fifteen months in jail. [...] So, that was a year lost from university."

US aid to Egypt was immediately increased in response to the uprising in order to shore up Sadat's presidency and protect prospects for a peace settlement between Israel and Egypt (Brownlee 2012: 25–26). Alarmed by the extent of the 1977 uprising, Sadat concluded that the security apparatus must be strengthened (Kandil 2012: 170). Between 1977 and 1980–81, the fastest growing parts of the state in terms of personnel were related to "law and order, 'sovereignty,' and other control and 'repressive organs,'" (Ayubi 1995: 300) with expenditure on law and order increasing by 263 percent between 1976 and 1980/81 (Ayubi 1995: 301). Since then, billions of dollars in US aid to Egypt have contributed to funding a large security apparatus and maintaining regime stability (Brownlee 2012).

The wide-scale clampdown on activists and the growth of the Egyptian security state following the 1977 uprising decimated popular resistance to Sadat and heralded the end of the secular student movement as a force within Egyptian politics. While Sadat's repression of political activists was not gender specific, it did have gendered implications. The disappearance of radical, secular political movements, which had been dominant on university campuses in the first decade following the 1967 defeat, and the simultaneous increasing influence of the Islamist movement, closed down opportunities for women to publicly perform gender in radical and subversive ways. Secular-oriented women were squeezed out of the sphere of contentious political activism through intimidation and harassment. As Magda told me: "I was one of those who was sentenced to three years, but I didn't do the rest of the time. I was under surveillance by the state security all the time, even when I was doing my exams, and every new case that state security had against political activists or socialists or whomever, I was wanted for interrogation. [. . .] So, I was playing cat and mouse with the state security all the time."

In the wake of Sadat's assassination in October 1981, emergency law was imposed, considerably narrowing political freedoms and giving the security apparatus the power to stop peaceful protests and other types of gatherings, such as party rallies and strikes. The Tagammu' Party, despite its earlier criticisms of Sadat's policies, became a docile opposition, not wishing to risk its status as a legal political party. While the party leadership considered this to be in line with their reformist rather than revolutionary strategy, it clearly frustrated younger activists, who had hoped that the party would become a focus for leftist oppositional activity. In the absence of organized political and social movements (with the exception of the Islamists and some underground leftist groups), many women activists began to focus their activism on building civil society organizations or became active in professional syndicates. One of the most prominent organizations to emerge in this period (still existing today, albeit somewhat reduced in its willingness to challenge the regime) was the Egyptian Organization for Human Rights, founded in 1985, which aimed to advocate respect for human rights as laid down in the various UN human rights covenants and the Egyptian constitution and to defend those whose human rights had been violated (Pratt 2002: 26). Azza Kamel was among the founding members and recalled:

> The Egyptian Organization was founded by some of the most important people in Egypt. It had people of all walks of life: young men and women, people from my generation and the older generation. People had big expectations for it, because we didn't have any other human rights organizations. We started on a voluntary basis and with very limited resources. I remember that the first thing we did for the organization was that a group of artists organized a gallery showing of their work and the money raised went to the Organization. It was very well received; everybody wanted to be a part of it and help out because it was something new in Egypt. The political parties were very weak. Political life in Egypt was crippled and the political parties couldn't do anything at all. That's why this organization acted as a substitute for political parties and movements.

The Reemergence of Independent Women's Activism

Perhaps a paradoxical effect of the repression of political parties and groups was the reemergence, for the first time since the 1950s, of independent women's organizations promoting gender-specific agendas (Al-Ali 2000). Experiences of repression provoked reflection and reconsideration of existing political trends and ideologies, opening the way for, in particular, a renewed approach to the "woman question." For example, Farida El-Nakkash recalled, "In prison, my eyes were opened to the reality of the situation concerning [poor] women [. . .] I realized that it was imperative for women to work harder to better the reality of other women." Therefore, after her release from prison in 1981, Farida became the driving force behind the development of the Tagammu' Party's women's bureau into a semiautonomous organization, the Progressive Women's Union (PWU). The PWU, like earlier women's organizations in the Arab world, combined the provision of social services to low-income women with advocacy of women's rights. Its ideological outlook was influenced by Nasser-era state feminism, with a focus on "modernizing women" through supporting their participation in the workplace as well as advocating for amendments to the personal status law (see also, Al-Ali 2000: 151–66). In 1984, Farida stood for the Tagammu' Party in parliamentary elections in Mansoura, as she described, on a "program geared toward women's rights—that is, personal status issues, the extreme shortage in bakeries, and day care centers. All these services that should be available to women, especially women who work outside the house, [and which] weren't available."

Meanwhile, several women activists who had participated in the student movement began meeting in 1984 to consider the relationship between women's rights and the leftist agenda. As Aida Seif El Dawla explained:

> During the university years, the women on the left, we all [believed the slogan] that things would get better for everyone once socialism had been achieved. [...] By '83, '84, many of us had already got married, and of course got married to comrades or leftist activists and realized what nonsense was that now. Because if it's true, if you marry a leftist or a comrade, then you should have a small, in-house example of how relations should be like between men and women. But that was not the case at all. It was a shared experience, for several of us so we started this group and then, eventually it became the New Women Foundation.

The group initially studied the history of the Egyptian women's movement, of other women's movements and feminism and, in 1986, began issuing a newsletter (Al-Ali 2000: 186–87). Their approach to women's rights differed from the PWU in that they were particularly interested in gender relations within the domestic sphere.[4]

The emergence of these new trends, centered on a gender-specific agenda and prioritizing gender over other kinds of social inequalities and injustice, demonstrated the resilience of women's activism in the face of political repression. The following chapters will explore how this would operate to isolate women's rights struggles from other sociopolitical struggles and a wider social base, making them vulnerable to attack by conservative forces and/or co-option by the regime.

JORDAN: "BLACK SEPTEMBER" AND THE DEFEAT OF THE FEDAYEEN

As discussed in the previous chapter, the 1967 defeat greatly weakened the Jordanian regime, while empowering the PLO and the Jordanian political opposition. With the Palestinian fedayeen openly challenging Jordanian sovereignty, the situation became intolerable for the regime. In September 1970, the PFLP hijacked a number of European and US commercial planes, three of which were flown to Jordan, where fifty-four passengers were taken hostage. This triggered an armed conflict between the Jordanian army and the fedayeen, which came to be known as Black September, lasting until July 1971, when the PLO was finally expelled from Jordan (Sayigh 1997: 262–81; Abu-Odeh 1999: 174–89; Salibi 2006: 236–41).

The events of Black September remain a taboo topic in Jordan, and almost none of my interviewees were willing to speak about their experiences. Yet this was surely a very difficult period, as indicated by Samar Dudin, the daughter of West Bank parents forced to flee to Amman after the 1967 war, and who was living at the time in Jebel Lweibdeh, a middle-class neighborhood in central Amman:

> I remember how my mom used to hide my dad [who was a political activist] and how my brother Sakher had to drink more water than all of us because he was a little bit sick and we had to not drink to make sure he drinks. [. . .] I remember how Talal, who was the son of our neighbor who's from Karak, the first week when there was a ceasefire, he came and he brought water to all the houses, and he gave every house chicken to cook, because people had months without any meat. [. . .] And then I remember the tears of the people in the neighborhood because there were Palestinian rebels and Jordanian [soldiers] who were shooting next door, very young people were shot. I don't know, there was a lot of turmoil.

Fighting was particularly intense in Amman, a stronghold of the fedayeen, where the army faced fierce resistance. There were large numbers of civilian casualties, with some three thousand people killed and ten thousand wounded, mainly residents of the Palestinian refugee camps (cited in Hasso 2005a: 32). The country was placed under military rule and road blocks were set up in Amman and around the country. Water, electricity, and telephones were cut. Palestinian fighters and activists were hunted down by the authorities. A report at the time described Amman "like a funeral corpse": "Every 20 meters a soldier with an M-16. Constant patrols in the streets by trucks armed with 50mm machine guns. [. . .] During the day, people went about their business but everyone was tense. [. . .] The town closed up tight by 7pm. [. . .] People are very scared. [. . .] The damage to the city is just incredible. [. . .] *Not one* building that we could see in the downtown area had been left untouched" (MERIP 1971: 1–2; emphasis in the original). Given the strategic importance of Jordan to US interests in the region, the United States moved the Sixth Fleet further east, placed units in West Germany on high alert, requested that the Soviet Union rein in the Syrians, who had sent troops to back up the fedayeen, and even devised a plan for Israeli military intervention (Quandt 1978: 110–17). This was backed up by new deliveries of arms and funding to the Jordanian regime (Joyce 2008: 65).

The events of 1970–71 are referred to either as Black September or as the civil war. Both terms are rather unsatisfactory; the events were not limited to September 1970 (see Sayigh 1997: 274–81). Meanwhile, the term *civil war*, implying a war between Jordanian-Jordanians and Palestinian-Jordanians, is also rejected by a number of people (for example, Abu Odeh 1999: 183). Samar characterized the war as: "really between those who are with King Hussein, meaning his approach to solving the Palestinian question, I guess. And those who were with the PLO, wanting to [. . .] liberate Palestine through military attack."

The military defeat of the fedayeen in 1971 forced many of the fighters to leave Jordan, with most moving to Lebanon, while all PLO institutions, including the GUPW, were closed. Meanwhile, the regime rounded up political activists and anyone suspected of being allied with the Palestinian Resistance Movement. Fedayeen supporters were purged from the public sector and security services (Abu Odeh 1999: 190). According to Emily Naffa, by 1975, there were six hundred members of the Jordanian Communist Party in the notorious desert prison of Al-Jafr. Suhair al-Tal recalled that "everyone was shocked, wondering what had happened. I remember three of my friends, one killed himself, another one withdrew from public life completely and started a chicken farm, and a third one who was the closest to me went to London, [. . .] so I was left alone."

Women activists were also targeted by the regime. Unlike their male colleagues, they were not imprisoned. However, they faced other types of harassment. Abla Abu Elba, who continued her political work underground after 1970, told me that "the women were dismissed from their jobs. I was personally fired from my job and wasn't allowed to travel for seventeen years. I was a teacher and I was dismissed, and thirteen of my family members were punished because of me. Great difficulties faced those who were involved in politics and worked with the opposition Jordanian national movement, whether Jordanian or Palestinian."

The events of 1970–71 created new divisions within Jordanian society along the axis of Jordanian-Jordanian (i.e., a Jordanian originating from the East Bank) and Palestinian-Jordanian (i.e., a Jordanian originating from the West Bank). The regime abandoned the pan-Jordanian, hybrid identity that the Hashemite monarchy had sought to create since 1950 (Brand 1995b: 50) and, instead, began to sponsor the "Bedouinization" of Jordanian national culture (Massad 2001: 250–58; Layne 1989), to the exclusion of Palestinian-Jordanians. Meanwhile, the events strengthened a particular Transjordanian, hardline nationalist narrative that portrayed the Palestinians as ungrateful and disloyal to the state (Brand 1995b: 53). These divisions were (and continue to be) exploited by the regime to suppress political dissent. Adma Al-Zuriekat, from Karak, was a student at Jordan University in the 1980s and recalled: "The Jordanian regime would infiltrate the universities. [...] They would try to use the East Bankers, the Jordanian-Jordanian youths, to oppose students who thought about [political] issues. They would feed them ideas that these people were against the country and the regime. That they want to cause problems like what happened in 1970. [...] They would incite the East Bankers against anyone thinking of reform in the country. [...] They would use them to suppress protests."

The suppression of political dissent and the Bedouinization of Jordanian identity had gendered implications for women activists. Indeed, the restoration of the pre-1967 gender order was integral to rebuilding regime authority. After 1970, there was a conservative backlash against the comparatively progressive gender norms associated with the Palestinian and leftist factions (Brand 1998: 124; Massad 2001: 210). As in Egypt, the regime encouraged the Muslim Brotherhood as a counterbalance to leftist and Arab nationalist forces (Brand 1995a: 163), leading to increased Brotherhood activities in student unions, professional unions, and trade unions (Gharaybah 1997: 181). Women experienced growing pressure to abandon subversive gender performances and comply with dominant gender norms. According to Leila Naffa, "People left [the political parties] and changed to the old traditional way and traditionally women don't mingle with politics."

Nadia Shamroukh's story vividly illustrates how control over women's bodies was constitutive of the post-1970 political repression. Nadia recalls that after the departure of the PLO, her family expected her to "go back to being a normal girl": "I did not know how to deal with my surroundings because I was no longer the girl that they wanted. [Previously] they had allowed me to join the [training] camp [for the youth] and were okay with that. [...] I carried weapons and we would hold parades in the refugee camp. [...] They praised me and thought I was strong and what not. But now they wanted me to return to normal. They wanted me to return to life as usual, which was difficult." Nadia insisted on continuing her political activism through underground channels. However, women like her were obliged to modify their public behavior in order to avoid accusations of immorality (Hasso 2005a: 113–14). Nadia explained: "[At college] I was introduced to the cultural and political life and got involved. I was always very careful to ensure that my parents never found out and to not begin a relationship with a guy because that would be my weak point." Specifically, the notion of "honor" was used as a political-moral weapon against women activists (Brand 1998:

124). In this respect, families became key actors in policing female behavior. Nadia recounted:

> So after I finished the first year, [...] [my family] discovered my involvement in political issues. [...] I got home and [...] as soon as I walked in the door [my brother] hit me. [...] My uncle, father, and mother were all sitting there. They let him hit me. [...] He asked me about my things one by one. I told him they were fliers for parties like the Communist Party, Democratic Popular Party, Fatah, and others. He [said] that if these books were discovered in our house, he would be sentenced to fifteen years in prison. I very simply and innocently said, without thinking: "They will imprison me, not you." [...] That is when he beat me to the point my eye was black and blue [...]. For me to say that it does not concern them and I would be the one they imprison not them, that I saw nothing wrong with going to prison [...] was seen as flagrant rudeness, because I'm a girl. [...] [My brother] said I was prohibited from letting my hair show or wearing jeans and [...] I had to wear the *jilbab* [a full-length, loose-fitting dress]. This was in 1975 or 1976. The spread of religion had started. He said I could not go to college the way I was dressed.

However, Nadia was defiant: "Anyway, college started so I wore a skirt and shirt and left the house. [...] and when I came home, he [my brother] was having lunch. [...] He looked at me and did not say anything. My mother said, "That's enough." [...] He understood that there was no way I would wear what he wanted. He never mentioned it again to this day."

Efforts to Reestablish Independent Women's Activism

As in Egypt, the period after 1970 witnessed the emergence of new activities and initiatives prioritizing an agenda for women's rights, for the first time since the closure of the Arab Women's Union in 1957. The most significant of these was the establishment of the Women's Union in Jordan (*al-ittihad al-nisa'i fi-l-urdunn*) (WUJ) in 1974. The Union emerged as a result of efforts by a group of women, among them Emily Naffa, to use the preparations for the forthcoming UN Women's Conference in Nairobi in 1975 to launch a new campaign for women's rights, lobbying government specifically for the right to vote (al-Tal 2014: 194–96). Similar to the motivations of Sadat to reform the personal status laws, Laurie Brand argues, the Jordanian government's decision to grant women's suffrage two decades after women first began their campaign and to allow the registration of the WUJ was motivated by the regime's desire to project a modern image internationally, particularly in light of the imminent UN Women's Conference (Brand 1998: 130).

The aims of the WUJ were similar to those of the Arab Women's Union of the 1950s, combining women's charitable and welfare activities with advocacy of women's rights and Arab nationalist causes (al-Tal 2014: 197). The Union was very active, establishing branches throughout Jordan and opening centers in refugee camps, rural areas, and poor neighborhoods to train women in vocational skills, combat illiteracy, support mothers and children, and provide nurseries (al-Tal 2014: 197–98). It held weekly seminars, fundraising dinners, and annual charity bazaars; advocated changes to laws concerning women workers; undertook studies on the situation of women; participated in regional and international women's conferences; and advocated for the rights of Palestinians. By 1981, its membership had grown to some three thousand (al-Tal 2014: 198–205).

However, the WUJ became a target of regime harassment. A former member told me, "The intelligence would tell people that we're a communist organization and tell the fathers not to allow their daughters to go to the Union." Unlike other civil society organizations, the WUJ was particularly vulnerable to repression because it had the audacity to express opinions on matters of national security and foreign policy. Specifically, the authorities accused the WUJ of taking positions in regional and international conferences that were in conflict with official Jordanian positions, leading the Interior Ministry to dissolve the WUJ, on the grounds that it was undertaking activities "beyond its remit" (al-Tal 2014: 205–7). Despite a court ruling that overturned the decision, the Union's activities remained frozen (al-Tal 2014: 207–12) and would not restart until after the onset of political liberalization in the 1990s (as discussed in chapter 4).

Simultaneously, in a bid to undermine the Union, in 1981, the minister of social affairs, In'am al-Mufti (Jordan's first woman minister), created a rival organization called the General Federation of Jordanian Women (GFJW) to bring together women's organizations under the tutelage of the ministry. The GFJW became the official representative of women in Jordan, with a membership comprised of mainly women's charitable organizations. Its program complied with state feminism, listing its goals as training women in vocational skills, educating women whether "homemakers, wives, mothers, or leaders" to play their role "fully" in society (al-Tal 2014: 219). As Brand argues, the closure of the WUJ alongside the government's creation of a new women's union "suggests a state apparatus heavily involved in the demobilization of women or obstruction of their efforts at independent organizing" (Brand 1998: 129). Indeed, the creation of the Federation marked the beginning of regime efforts to coopt and direct the women's movement, a process that became more pronounced in the 1990s, as discussed in later chapters.

Hence, by the 1980s, mass organizing of women was either frozen or state directed, despite efforts by some leftist activists to create independent women's organizations, such as the MAJD-affiliated League of Democratic Women (RAND) and the Popular Committee of Women (al-Tal 2014: 238–49). Nevertheless, during this period there was a growing interest in studying legal reforms for women's rights, possibly motivated by the UN Decade for Women (1975–1985) and the adoption of CEDAW in 1979 (Gallagher 2000: 212). In 1981, a group of female lawyers who were WUJ members created the Woman's Committee in the Bar Association, whose activities included highlighting discrimination in Jordanian law, advocating for legal reforms, and raising awareness of women's legal rights (al-Tal 2014: 252–53). Among this group was Asma Khader, who by this time had graduated with a law degree from Damascus University and was addressing issues of public freedoms, human rights, and women's rights. Asma became chair of the Woman's Committee and in 1982 was appointed to be rapporteur for the Women's Affairs Committee of the Arab Lawyers' Union. She recalled: "It was a new committee. [...] There was a group of women lawyers from different countries [...], specifically from Egypt, Morocco, Lebanon, Syria, and we together focused on women and law, on the need for legal literacy programs, legal education, legal amendments, reforms, and even legal aid and counseling for women, [...]. And we recommended that each bar association should have a women's committee, and [...] I think the women's movement benefitted from women lawyers who have this experience."

Another organization that focused on women's legal rights was the Arab University Women Graduates' Club (*nadi al-jami'at*) (founded in 1978). The club organized seminars and workshops on different issues affecting women and the family (al-Tal 2014: 254–55). Lamis Nasser, a member, recalled, "We were interested very much in the laws [and] one time we made [a paper] about the personal status law." They chose Toujan al-Faisal, who would later go on to become the first woman MP in Jordan, as the spokesperson for the Club because, as Lamis remembers, "she was the most courageous amongst us."

Initiatives such as the Woman's Committee in the Bar Association and the Arab University Women Graduates' Club were significant in presenting an agenda for women's rights independent of the state and of political groups.

This distinguished these initiatives from the General Federation of Jordanian Women, whose aims did not address the issue of discriminatory legislation, as well as the Women's Union in Jordan, where, according to Suhair al-Tal, the organization's priorities were subject to the considerations of the political parties represented there. Suhair became a member of the Union toward the end of the 1970s and sat on the administrative committee as an independent. She explained:

> The leadership of the Union was divided between FATAH, the Democratic Front, the Communist Party, the Popular Front, and the Ba'th Party. Each one of them would come carrying the instructions of her respective party for the issue at hand. [...] I felt that we were practicing the patriarchal partisan mentality through women. Instead of men penetrating the circles of women, because they weren't able to do that, they would send the female members in the parties to operate within the circles of women in favor of the political movement. On the one hand, that is not wrong, but not when it's done at the expense of the women's cause, starting from the issues of violence, divorce, early marriage, the poverty and unemployment facing women, the difference in wages, and things like that. These issues were not addressed at all except on International Women's Day and such occasions. When we discussed them with the parties, they would say we should focus on the national cause.

As in Egypt, independent initiatives to promote women's rights emerged in the wake of political repression. This led to a process of disengaging women's rights from popular struggles—a trend that became further consolidated after the end of the Cold War—as explored in the following chapters—and was exacerbated by the ongoing repression of leftist and nationalist political forces, which also became increasingly isolated from popular struggles. This became apparent when, in 1989, protests broke out around the country, beginning in the regime strongholds of Maan, Karak, and Tafileh, triggered by the government's announcement of IMF-imposed austerity measures. Rather than leading these protests, oppositional political activists in Amman looked on as events unfolded in other parts of the country (Hasso 2005a: 180). Similarly, women's rights activists did not visibly participate in this uprising and women's specific concerns were not included in the protesters' demands, which were for an end to austerity and corruption and for the resignation of the prime minister and changes to the electoral law (Amawi 1992: 27). This is in stark contrast to the 1950s and post-1967 period, when outbreaks of political upheaval and contestations over Jordan's geopolitical alignments provided opportunities for middle-class women to transgress dominant gender norms through their support for political struggles, while women's rights were part of the agendas of leftist and nationalist political movements during these periods, even if the "woman question" was subordinated to the "national question."

LEBANON: THE ISRAELI INVASION AND ITS AFTERMATH

As mentioned above, the Egypt-Israel peace treaty had terrible consequences for the Arab world, and specifically for progressive forces in Lebanon and, most of all, for the Palestinians. Egypt's pursuit of a separate peace "generated deepened insecurity throughout the Arab world that intensified the retreat to state-centric self-help by the Arab states, notably Syria" (Hinnebusch 2003: 179). Syria abandoned pan-Arabism for the sake of state survival, and sought to impose its domination over Lebanese warring parties, preventing a victory by the PLO and its Lebanese allies in order to preclude Israeli intervention (Traboulsi 2007: 194). Meanwhile, emboldened by the removal of its arch military rival, Egypt, from the equation of the Arab-Israeli conflict, Israel launched a military offensive against the PLO, invading the south of Lebanon up to the Litani River, in 1978, and then, in 1982, progressing to Beirut and besieging the city for weeks.

The invasion and siege of Beirut in the summer of 1982 had terrible humanitarian consequences. It was the one episode in the fifteen-year long civil war that almost all my interviewees mentioned. For almost three months, Israel bombed the city, including hospitals and residential buildings, while its use of air-burst and white phosphorous artillery shells and cluster bombs pushed up the mortality rate among the wounded to double the normal levels in war (Sayigh 1997: 530, 535–37). Racha Salah, daughter of Samira Salah, recalled: "I don't know if I would ever be as scared as that time in my life [. . .] not knowing where the bombs will come."

In this context, many women participated in relief activities. Souad Amin Jarar told me: "Now if I think about it, oh my God, we were really courageous, not to care about the bombardment or anything and just move from one place to another, because we felt, yes, it's your duty and this is the time that you can help, and so on. It was a very, very tough experience." Electricity and water were cut and there were limited food and medical supplies, making day-to-day living almost impossible. Joumana Merhy remembered this period as "the most difficult time. We had to build makeshift field hospitals in every neighborhood because all the roads were blocked and if someone was injured there was no way to get them to a hospital." Leila Zakharia explained: "We used to do these collective cooking things because there was no food, so you had to search for whatever was available, to cook it together, and eat together, and then everybody dispersed and went to their homes or wherever they were living. Some of them were squatting or living in someone else's home."

Finally, following a US-brokered agreement on 23 August, the siege came to an end. However, in return, the PLO was forced to leave Lebanon. After months of valiant resistance, West Beirut fell to the Israelis. Leila Zakharia remembers that the mood in the city transformed almost overnight: "The Israelis entered and started checking all the houses, everywhere, barging into apartment buildings, checking everyone, and then of course the atmosphere changed [. . .]. People who were in solidarity and protected you, they switched because they were afraid [. . .]. Yeah, it changed completely. Completely." Over the following days (until 18 September), the Israeli army facilitated the massacre, by a Maronite militia, the Lebanese Forces, of Palestinians and some Lebanese in the camps of Sabra and Shatila, amounting to more than a thousand murdered and hundreds disappeared (al-Hout 2004). The international outcry as well as Israeli public opinion forced the Israelis to withdraw from Beirut by the end of September.

The Palestinian Camps

The departure of the PLO had devastating consequences for those left behind. When I asked Leila Zakharia how she felt at this time, she told me, "I was extremely shocked, I felt that I was being amputated because the Palestinian movement was leaving. What will I become? What will my identity be? Of course, it was pretty hard." Souad Jarar also remembers, "The people were really [. . .] down, especially in the camps." As Julie Peteet observed, "A community that had felt itself proud, increasingly self-sufficient, and protected was now vulnerable, humiliated, and anxious as to its fate" (Peteet 1991: 212). The PLO's withdrawal meant an end to all the welfare institutions and social services that supported Palestinians in the camps, with particular implications for women, who disproportionately bore the burden of ensuring family survival. These conditions were exacerbated by the almost continual aggressions suffered by Palestinians after 1982. The Lebanese army and Maronite militias conducted a campaign of terror against

Palestinians, randomly arresting, disappearing, and even murdering them (Stork 1983: 5). In the south, which remained under Israeli occupation until 1985, Israel continued attacking the camps and many Palestinians were arrested and held in the infamous Ansar prison.[5]

The withdrawal of Israeli forces did not bring an end to the terror waged against the Palestinians. Between 1985 and 1988, in what became known as the War of the Camps, the Shi'a group, Amal, backed by Syria, attempted to eradicate any remaining Palestinian fighters by attacking and besieging refugee camps in Beirut and the south. Haifa Jammal, living in Burj al-Shamali, in the south, recalled:

> All the time, they were bombing the camp. It was similar to the Israeli invasion for us. [But] [. . .] we know each other very well. They know me. They know that I am active. [. . .] Some people from Amal, [. . .] they know me personally. [. . .] They bombed Rashidiyyeh camp, and they increased their pressure on the other camps. They arrested most of the men over sixteen years old, until sixty years old, put them in jails and tortured them. They also came to the houses at midnight to search if there are weapons or someone. It was really a difficult time for us.

During this period, Palestinian women in the camps played a key role in the civil defense of their communities. Amne Suliemane, then a member of the Shatila Camp Committee for the General Union of Palestinian Women, was commended by several of my interviewees for her role in organizing relief during the War of the Camps. When recounting her memories of this period, Amne was modest and did not distinguish herself:

> In 1985, you know, we were besieged in Shatila camp and it was a very bitter experience. We were taking care of women and children in the camp and it was besieged for three years. [. . .] The camp is so small and it was destroyed three times, and we were rebuilding it. Imagine through a siege you are building. Many people were killed, many people were wounded, and a great number of people went missing, and this was all after [we had already suffered] the Israeli invasion of Lebanon, and it was bitter. [. . .] People ate cats at that time, because it was besieged for a long time. [. . .] many women, mothers, lost three or four persons in the Camp Wars. It was very ugly and barbarous.

Olfat Mahmoud, who was living in Burj al-Barajneh camp during this period, and working as a nurse, also retains terrible memories:

> I was a very skilled nurse, [but] what to do under such circumstances, when you have no operating room, no doctors, when you have no facilities? By the

end of the war, we used to boil water and salt to clean the wounds and I had to do lots of women's deliveries, it was like—it was impossible. And when you have casualties and lots of casualties coming to the emergency room [and] I would decide which one you will work with and which we will ignore. It is a horrible feeling. [...] It's like, who am I to decide who will die and who will not? But we didn't have enough resources. [...] That was terrible. So after this war, I quit nursing, in spite that I loved it, but [...] that was too much for me.

Although Palestinian women continued to be active, in light of the dangers, many, particularly those living outside the camps, withdrew from working with the Palestinian political factions (see also Peteet 1991: 216–17). Moreover, the withdrawal of the PLO deprived women of an infrastructure for mass mobilization. Increasingly the old paradigm returned, in which camp women (and, also men) were viewed by those outside the camps as recipients of charity and aid, rather than as agents of a national struggle. Wafa Al-Yassir had already become disillusioned with the behavior of the Palestinian leadership in Lebanon. However, following the Israeli invasion, Wafa abandoned politics and turned toward social activism: "I started to be involved and be interested in the socioeconomic issues related to my people. But I benefitted from my political background and [...] invested all I had learned [...] in my work in the Palestinian community. [...] Something came to my mind that [...] nobody is doing something for the people on the ground, so, [...] we started thinking of programs to be implemented for the people in the camps."

Meanwhile, the weakening of the PLO in the camps left an ideological and organizational vacuum, which enabled the growth of Islamist groups (Knudsen 2005). As a result, the relatively liberal gender norms cultivated during the years of the Palestinian Revolution slowly disappeared. Leila Ali, who grew up in Shatila camp, told me: "I have to say before [...] '82, the Palestinian community was really open [...] in the Lebanon camps, so we were doing almost all community activities together, boys and girls, the activities were mixed. We were doing voluntary work for cleaning the camps, for instance, camping, we have been doing cultural activities, also, exhibitions, performances, Palestinian dancing, such kind of things. [...] Almost all families they had boys and girls together and they have been active at the community or the political level." Hence, the forced withdrawal of the PLO from Lebanon, in line with the foreign policy goals of the US and its allies, paved the way for the spread of more conservative gender norms within the Palestinian camps.

In 1989, a meeting of Lebanese parliamentarians in the Saudi Arabian city of Ta'if began a process of reconciliation that would pave the way for the end of violent conflict and the rebuilding of the Lebanese state. Rather than viewing the Ta'if Agreement, as it became known, as a peace settlement, it is perhaps more accurate to consider it a "pact" (Krayem 1997) among local elites and regional and international powers, ending the ambitions of radical geopolitical and social transformations that had initially fueled the civil war. The basis for this pact was the amendment of the confessional power-sharing system in place since Lebanon's independence. Instead of a 6:5 ratio (Christian to Muslim), parliamentary seats would henceforth be distributed according to a fifty-fifty split, with increased representation for Shi'a Muslims and reduced powers for the (Christian Maronite) president (Traboulsi 2007: 244–46). In other words, the almost fifteen-year-long war, initially fought for the deconfessionalization of Lebanon's political system, resulted in the maintenance of that sectarian system, albeit with some modifications. Meanwhile, the leftist and radical nationalist forces of the Lebanese National Front that had led the fight against confessionalism found themselves greatly enfeebled. Their involvement in the war had pushed these parties to sacrifice their political and social reform agendas for tactical military gains and some had even participated in sectarian violence, leading them to lose popular support (Khayat 2012: 91–92).

The responsibility for overseeing the Ta'if Agreement was granted to Syria, with the blessing of the United States and the rest of the international community (Traboulsi 2007: 251). Syria would maintain a continued security presence ostensibly to assist the Lebanese army in regaining control of the country. Yet Syria's interpretation of "security" went beyond military affairs to include significant intervention in Lebanese politics (Traboulsi 2007: 252–52). Many of my interviewees described the Syrian presence in negative terms. Ferial Abu Hamdan, a community activist in the Chouf Mountains, told me, "When the Syrian army came, I was very happy. Initially, they were really very good. We felt that, 'oh my God, it is now normal, nobody is carrying guns in the streets.'" However, Ferial soon changed her mind, after witnessing an elderly man in the street being beaten by a Syrian soldier: "I wanted to [get out of] my car and to stop him, and I remember my husband wouldn't let me, 'because he will shoot you,' he told me. So, I started being afraid of them [. . .] and I felt that, oh my God, [. . .] they didn't come to let us live in peace; no, they want to control everything we do."

Nonetheless, the compromises at the heart of the Ta'if Agreement were accepted by many Lebanese as necessary to bring an end to years of violence and deprivation. By the end of the war, Lebanon's physical infrastructure was destroyed, a quarter of the population was displaced and living in substandard housing, unemployment was around 40 percent, and per capita income was $500 compared to $1,800 before the war (Kubursi 1999: Sbaiti 1994). Under the former prime minister, the late Rafiq al-Hariri, the Lebanese government embarked on an ambitious program to stabilize and reconstruct the country. Several of my interviewees spoke positively about al-Hariri, who was assassinated in 2005, provoking mass demonstrations that finally forced Syria to withdraw (as discussed in the following chapter). Former political activist Iqbal Doughan told me: "Rafiq al-Hariri used to say that whatever Israel destroyed, we would build again. [. . .] And we should educate our children. He sent thirty-six thousand students, [. . .] to teach them in the best universities without having to worry about money [. . .]. He lifted a whole community upwards." However, al-Hariri's reconstruction program entailed a strengthening of the free market, leading to growing corruption and socioeconomic inequalities, alongside the repression of popular movements, especially the labor unions, who led the opposition to neoliberal economic reforms (Baumann 2016; Leenders 2012; Perthes 1997; Young 1998). Mona Saad was among the few of my interviewees to criticize al-Hariri's policies: "It was all reform for the private pockets of investors; nothing for the people at all. [. . .] Not a factory was opened in the age of rebuilding Lebanon, a factory to employ people, and prevent youth from migrating [. . .]. This never happened at all."

Meanwhile, the Ta'if Agreement failed to recognize women's extensive contributions to humanitarian relief, their involvement in political groups, and their important role in resistance to violence and sectarianism. On the contrary, women's rights were implicitly part of the compromise underpinning the postwar pact. As Donna Pankhurst argues in relation to other postwar contexts, "The ideological rhetoric is often about 'restoring' or 'returning to' something associated with the status quo before the war." (2004: 19). In the case of Lebanon, the sectarian personal status laws, integral to the reproduction of the sectarian political regime, remained unchanged after 1989 and attempts to reform them through a proposed civil marriage law in 1998 (that would have allowed for interfaith marriage) were rejected by then prime minister Hariri and religious leaders on the basis that it would encroach on the powers of religious authorities and threaten the political settlement based on religious coexistence (Zalzal 1997; Zuhur 2002: 195–98).

CONCLUSION

By the end of the 1980s, as a result of repression and violence, leftist and radical nationalist movements were greatly weakened, while pro-imperialist, pro-market, and reactionary forces dominated. Norms of pan-Arab solidarity were replaced by those of state survival and self-help (Barnett 1998: 161–212), and populist social pacts were replaced by neoliberal policies to the benefit of local elites and a new parasitic business class, along with their foreign allies. The fall of the Soviet Union at the end of the 1980s set the stage for the further expansion of US hegemony and market forces. The geopolitical order forged earlier that century through anticolonial struggle, what Vijay Prashad (2007) has called the "Third World project," was largely dismantled.

The narratives of women activists highlight how this geopolitical transformation was dependent upon and constitutive of particular gender norms and gender relations. Although the radical political and social movements that flourished in the post-1967 era did not prioritize gender justice or women's rights within their programs, their challenge to the geopolitical order facilitated the transgression of dominant gender norms by women activists. Women's participation and leadership in contentious politics and their defiance of gendered hierarchies, through street protests, sit-ins, and even participation in armed groups, in the case of Lebanon, broke down the modesty-modernity boundary underpinning norms of female respectability. By contrast, the repression of radical movements, with the complicity if not active help of the United States and its regional allies, pushed women out of contentious political activism and deprived them of spaces for performing alternative norms of femininity. Simultaneously, regime policies in Egypt and Jordan encouraged the spread of even more conservative gender norms through the encouragement of Islamist groups and other reactionary forces to counterbalance progressive movements. In Lebanon, gender norms were challenged and gendered hierarchies were destabilized in a context of war. However, at war's end, this transformation in gender roles, relations, and norms was not reflected in the postwar settlement, while the progressive forces that had been supportive of women's mobilization were defeated. In this way, the reinscribing of norms of female respectability was integral to rebuilding geopolitical order during this period.

The role of the United States, and Western governments more broadly, in the defeat of radical and revolutionary forces through their support for political repression, militarism, and right-wing groups, highlights the historically devastating role of imperialism with regard to women's rights and security, as well as the security of their families. The US-brokered so-called peace treaty between Egypt and Israel represents a particularly destructive episode for the Lebanese and Palestinians. Women's voices in this chapter provide a counternarrative to Western self-representations as the historical force of progress and the "savior" of women in the Arab world; rather than advancing women's empowerment and gender equality, Western intervention in the Arab world after 1967 contributed to undermining the possibilities for transgressive gender performances and empowering conservative forces.

Finally, the narratives presented here shed light on the crucial relationship between geopolitical transformations and changes in the modes of women's activism. However, this relationship is not straightforward. While political repression and violence led to the disappearance of certain forms of contentious political activism and a reinscribing of female respectability norms, women continued to be active, but in new ways. The demise of leftist and radical nationalist groups and their associated ideologies provoked many women activists to formulate a new sociopolitical agenda that prioritized women's rights and needs and created spaces for new women's organizations to emerge. Yet this also marked the beginning of a trend in which women's rights activism became isolated from other social and political struggles. The following chapters further explore the complex relationship between geopolitical shifts in the post–Cold War period, various kinds of women's activism, and gender norms, highlighting the different and sometimes contradictory ways in which women's activism has become articulated with hegemonic power at global, regional, and national scales.

FOUR

_____

The Political Economy and Geopolitics of Women's Activism after the Cold War

THIS CHAPTER INVESTIGATES the implications of the end of the Cold War for women's activism in each of my country cases. The fall of the Soviet Union opened the way for the region's increased integration into the global capitalist economy and the expansion of US influence, resulting in the increasing dependency of Arab states upon the United States (Halliday 2005: 130–64; Hinnebusch 2003: 204–39; Ismael and Ismael 1994). In this regard, the Gulf War of 1990–91 was a watershed moment, in that the United States was able to coopt pivotal Arab states—namely, Egypt, Syria, and Saudi Arabia—to join a Western-led international military coalition against a fellow Arab state, Iraq, in response to the latter's occupation of Kuwait (Hinnebusch 2003: 212–13, 215–18). As the US military prepared for war, President George H. W. Bush proclaimed the beginning of a "New World Order," in which democracy, freedom, rights, and free markets would spread across the globe to the benefit of all (1998). Yet, rather than bringing peace, prosperity, and freedom to the region, US hegemony brought insecurity and dispossession, not least to the people of Iraq, who, after 1991, were subjected to comprehensive sanctions with severe humanitarian consequences, and to the Palestinians, who faced increasing Israeli colonization of their land under the banner of a US-brokered peace process. Meanwhile, economic liberalization, which in some countries preceded the end of the Cold War but was greatly intensified thereafter, led to a concentration of wealth and power in the hands of a small circle of politicians, businessmen, and military and security officials close to their respective ruling regimes, thus dismantling the postindependence social pact that had provided some semblance of a social safety net (Hinnebusch 2003: 231). By the early 2000s, it was clear that the US-engineered regional order lacked popular legitimacy and was dependent upon US military coercion and political repression by regional allies (Hinnebusch 2003: 239).

While much of the existing literature on the post–Cold War era focuses on the responses of political, military, and economic elites to geopolitical and political-economic changes, this chapter sheds light on the responses of women activists to these changes and assesses the degree to which their activism challenged the post–Cold War international order. In this respect I contribute to the literature that examines women's activism in relation to global processes and structures (Eschle and Maiguashca 2010; Moghadam 2005; Naples and Desai 2002). I emphasize the significance of the *respective geopolitical contexts* as well as *individual activist trajectories* in mediating between global processes and local activism in the countries studied here.

The chapter identifies two main trends in women's activism in Egypt, Jordan, and Lebanon during this period: first, the proliferation of non-governmental organizations (NGOs), largely funded by Western donors seeking to strengthen civil society as a means of supporting political liberalization and/or mitigating the negative social consequences of economic restructuring; and, second, the emergence of protest movements, particularly after 2000, largely in opposition to the consequences of US hegemony and the associated spread of free markets. The chapter begins by exploring the rise of NGOs and assesses debates concerning "NGO-ization" in light of the narratives of the women that I interviewed. In the existing literature, there is a tendency to view NGOs either as "an extension of existing neoliberal forms of government" in support of the geopolitical order or "as offering alternatives to existing geopolitical power relations" (Jeffrey 2013: 388). The chapter attempts to go beyond these binaries by differentiating among NGOs and between different geopolitical scales, from the personal to the international. I argue that, overall, women's NGO activism produces contradictory and ambiguous effects that cannot be reduced to either neoliberal forms of government or an "anti-geopolitics."

The second part of the chapter examines the rise of new protest movements after 2000 in opposition to Israel's ongoing colonization and violence in Palestine, US-led military intervention, neoliberal economic reforms, and growing authoritarianism. Unlike much of the existing literature on these movements, the chapter draws on women's narratives to highlight women's leadership roles and the gendered dimensions of their participation. It highlights a paradox in this regard: while these movements challenged major dimensions of the geopolitical status quo at the national, regional, and international levels, they were less willing to challenge dominant gender norms. Indeed, norms of female respectability were often reinscribed by these movements even though women's participation in these contentious movements was transgressive of dominant gender norms. The disconnect between women's leadership roles within social movements and movement dynamics that often reinscribed female respectability can be understood in a context of the weakness of leftist and radical political forces and the isolation of women's rights agendas from popular movements in the post–Cold War period.

MAPPING WOMEN'S ACTIVISM AFTER THE END OF THE COLD WAR: THE GROWTH OF NGOS

The growth in women's NGOs is the defining feature of women's post–Cold War activism. The 1990s witnessed a rapid growth in the number of NGOs in Egypt, Jordan, and Lebanon, as well as more widely across the region (Ben Néfissa et al. 2005; Carapico 2000; Wiktorowicz 2000). Many of the women whom I interviewed established or joined NGOs after 1990. These new organizations included those working not only on women's issues, but also human rights, democracy promotion, development, and training and education.

Many scholars, activists, and practitioners, particularly in the West, have celebrated the rise of NGOs as a core part of civil society (for example, Falk 1999; Fisher 1998; Jeffrey 2007; Keck and Sikkink 1998; O'Brian et al. 2000), which, in turn, they view as essential to resisting authoritarianism and strengthening democracy (see Diamond 1999; O'Donnell et al. 1986). NGOs are viewed as playing an important role in the global diffusion of norms of human rights and gender equality (Bunch 1990; Keck and Sikkink 1998; Risse, Ropp, and Sikkink 1999; True and Mintrom 2001; Joachim 2003; in the case of the Arab world, see Ibrahim 1995; Norton 1995, 1996). In particular, women's rights organizations are lauded for using CEDAW and other international instruments as tools to pressure their respective governments to adopt legal reforms in line with gender equality, in what Margaret Keck and Kathryn Sikkink call a "boomerang effect" (1998).

There have also been considerable criticisms of NGOs globally. They have been viewed as intrinsically linked to the emergence of neoliberal economics and structural adjustment programs (Hewitt de Alcantera 1998; Beckman

1993). Authors argue that NGOs have become subcontractors for the state in providing essential social services, cushioning the negative social effects of neoliberalism, and becoming its "community face" (Petras 1997). They are charged with demobilizing popular movements and depoliticizing issues of poverty, dispossession, inequality, and injustices in the Global South (Petras 1997; Choudry and Kapoor 2013). Others have drawn attention to the increasing dependency of NGOs on Global North government funding, arguing that it makes them beholden to these governments' policy agendas and priorities rather than local needs (Hulme and Edwards 1997; Wallace 2004).

In the Arab world, there have been similar criticisms coming from leftist and progressive quarters—specifically, that NGO-ization has led to the demobilization of popular movements and the depoliticization of social change (see Carapico 2000; Hammami 1995; Hanafi and Tabar 2006; Jad 2007; Langohr 2004). Some of the women whom I interviewed echoed these concerns. For example, Egyptian-Lebanese filmmaker Arab Loutfi, coming from a leftist background, was a founding member of the New Woman group during the 1980s but left because of differences over whether to accept donor funding. According to her:

> Ninety percent of those who have worked in that system [that is, within NGOs] they became very corrupt—moneywise, politically, socially, even those who didn't really gain so much money but they changed all their attitude toward the struggle. They became much more into the system. Not only the Egyptian system, the international system. They became part of the imperialist regime. [...] It fragmented the movement and [...] it did something very dangerous. [...] Some activists [...] afterwards they become like employees. It becomes their livelihood. Bit by bit you just corrupt the relation with the struggle itself.

Leftist political activist Abla Abu Elba views the funding of NGOs as a mechanism for mitigating rather than transforming the social problems facing ordinary women:

> International organizations have been [...] fund[ing] several women's organizations in order to reduce the intensity of social problems [...] in the name of "women's empowerment," "democracy," "peace" and so on. The titles are beautiful and tempting, and I definitely support them, but the mechanism has been incorrect and yielded no positive results. For example, how can we empower women under a dictatorship? [...] How can we reinforce something and its opposite? Most of these women's organizations [...] have isolated themselves from ordinary women. The only concern for many of them is

how to get funding, and how to speak in the global language of the United Nations and so on [. . .]. This isolation of the women's organizations from their social base has changed the image of the Arab feminist movement. [. . .] A lot of dispute arose between [women's] organizations over this matter [of funding], while we're in need of unity amongst the feminist movement for the sake of poor women.

Beyond leftist circles, the growth in NGOs in the Arab world after 1990 has sparked substantial controversy. The issue that provokes the fiercest debates concerns NGO relationships with Western governments and donors, principally as recipients of donor funding but also through sharing information (such as reports on human rights violations) and promoting concepts and agendas that are deemed "foreign." While Western scholars have celebrated the ability of local NGOs to use transnational links to pressure their respective governments to adopt liberal norms (i.e., the "boomerang effect" described by Margaret Keck and Kathryn Sikkink in 1998), regimes and many non-regime actors in the Arab region view such links with suspicion, if not outright hostility. The public debate over NGOs has been particularly heated in Egypt, where strong feelings of Egyptian nationalism among the intelligentsia have worked in tandem with regime campaigns questioning the loyalty of foreign-funded NGOs (for example, see Pratt 2004, 2005, 2006). This perception of NGOs' transnational links is shaped by historical experiences of colonialism and neocolonialism and can also be considered as a reaction against Western discourses of (post)colonial difference, in which violations of women's rights and human rights serve to construct non-Western countries as "backward" and to justify violations of state sovereignty. Reports disseminated by local human rights NGOs are often a source for Western media and diplomats and can lead to uncomfortable questioning of regime policies, if not outright diplomatic pressure. Consequently, a common accusation levied against human rights NGOs is that of "tarnishing the reputation" of the country (for example, see Pratt 2005).

Governments in the Arab world (and beyond) have used these perceived threats to the nation-state and fears of Western domination to discredit the work of those NGOs that openly challenge regime policies and to legitimize restrictions against them (Pratt 2004, 2005, 2006). In this regard, human rights NGOs have been particular targets because of the ways in which they criticize their respective regimes with regard to the actions of the police and other national security forces, including practices of torture, arbitrary detention, and state violence. Governments have also targeted NGOs who work on ostensibly technical issues that touch on a regime's ability to control political processes, such as, the Egyptian regime's targeting of foreign democracy promotion NGOs in December 2011 (for further details of this case, see Carapico 2014: 1–2). Nonstate actors—principal among them Islamists, but also conservative nationalists—have also targeted women's rights NGOs, claiming that these organizations import Western agendas that undermine the family and, hence, the nation (see the next chapter for further discussion). In Egypt and Jordan, regimes have implemented a series of measures to curb the autonomy of NGOs and push back against donor-funded civil society promotion (for further details, see Pratt 2004, 2007; Wiktorowicz 2000; Carapico 2014: 150–98). Advocacy NGOs have tried to circumvent these obstacles by registering as civil companies, private law offices, or private clinics (where appropriate). However, over time, the Egyptian and Jordanian regimes have succeeded in closing these loopholes (Amnesty International 2017; Carapico 2014: 176–79; HRW 2016). By contrast, in Lebanon, elite fragmentation and competition has created spaces for NGOs to operate largely without official restrictions and there has been less controversy surrounding the work of NGOs as they are often regarded either as a counterbalance to the sectarian state or as compensation for state weakness and failure, particularly with regard to the provision of social services.

Here, I explore the narratives of women NGO activists in Egypt, Jordan, and Lebanon and highlight the importance of going beyond a binary perception of NGOs and their effects—whether as agents of democracy and liberal norms or of neoliberalism and imperialism. The following discussion not only highlights the need to avoid homogenizing and essentializing NGOs (as also argued, for example, by Bernal and Grewal 2014) but also emphasizes the significance of understanding women's agency in relation to particular geopolitical-personal conjunctures.

UNDERSTANDING THE RISE OF WOMEN'S NGO ACTIVISM: BEYOND BINARY ACCOUNTS OF NEOLIBERALIZATION VERSUS DEMOCRATIZATION

The following discussion highlights the differences among NGOs by contextualizing them in relation to historical trends in women's activism, specifically: longer-term trends of women's associational activities, dating back to the turn of the twentieth century; women's involvement in radical social and political movements, dating back to the earlier twentieth century but more recently to the aftermath of the 1967 war; and generational differences among women and more recent trends in young women's activism. I draw attention to the ways in which global processes of neoliberalization and Western democracy promotion efforts intersect with national histories of repression and authoritarianism, modernist projects of female respectability, and the personal trajectories of women activists.

Women's NGO Activism as a Continuation of Women's Voluntary Activities

Similar to other NGOs in the Global South, many NGOs in Egypt, Jordan, and Lebanon seek to mitigate the negative social consequences of structural adjustment policies and neoliberal economic reforms, rather than mobilizing people to resist these (Hewitt de Alcántara 1998; Petras 1997; Choudry and Kapoor 2013). They work within the parameters set by the regime and the dominant structures of the global political economy, rather than seeking to challenge or resist these. Moreover, in many cases, they have adopted and adapted neoliberal paradigms into their activities. However, my interviews suggested that a preponderance of NGOs that emerged in the post–Cold War period represent a continuation of a longer tradition of middle-class women's voluntary associational activities going back to the beginning of the twentieth century. Their activities aim to serve society and contribute to "national uplift" and state modernizing agendas, often through providing social services and welfare. For example, in Lebanon, many women's NGOs formed after 1990 work at the local community level, contributing to the social reconstruction of the country following the civil war and meeting basic needs not provided by the government (Nauphal 1997). May Makarem Hilal helped to found a women's organization in her village of Qarnayel, in the Mount Lebanon region:

> As you know, the war caused a lot of chaos and many people were displaced and some were killed. We started with founding a society in Qarnayel that would cater to the needs of the inhabitants of the village of Qarnayel, regardless of political affiliation or religious sect. We wanted to found a society to help all the people of Qarnayel; Druze, Christians, all sects. [. . .] We had two objectives: one was to provide care and social services and the other was to bring the people together, to create a sense of closeness and remove causes of conflict, so that we can all go back to living together happily and peacefully.

In Jordan, Muyassar al-Saadi established the Families Development Association in 1999 after winning a UN prize for her poverty alleviation work with the Jordanian Women's Union. In the 1970s, Muyassar was involved in political work through the Palestinian national movement, but, in a context where political parties were all forced underground, she decided to leave politics, explaining that: "doing social and humanitarian work to help people is also a form of struggle; it's no less important than politics, because it's politics too; when you work with people to improve their lives, I think it's more important." Similar to the women's organizations of the 1940s and 1950s, the Association offers services for women and their families, particularly those on low incomes, such as, vocational training, preschool centers, and legal counseling for families in the low-income neighborhoods of East Amman. One of the most successful programs is the Izdihar ("Flourishing") program, which not only trains young women in vocational skills but helps to place them in jobs through contacts with the private sector. Hence, the Families Development Association works within a modernist paradigm of incorporating women into education and employment as well as a neoliberal paradigm of empowerment through access to the market. Queen Rania is honorary president, and the association has received funding from local government and ministries as well as foreign diplomatic missions and international NGOs.

While such organizations work in tandem with neoliberalization, they are not fully professionalized, since the notion of volunteerism is central to this work. For example, Lubna Dawany, a Jordanian lawyer, began to volunteer her time, from the late 1980s, as she explains,

> giving support and giving time for ladies around me that I feel they need help. And then, the idea came of having an organization. So I felt that was perfect, that was a message from God that, yes, He's blessing me in serving people, [...] to share some of my life and some of the things that I have to support these women and the girls that need some kind of support. So, I was one of the founders for Mizan, a group for human rights. In the same year, I was one of the founders for Sisterhood is Global Institute, SIGI.

Through her work, Lubna helps women prisoners, some of whom are foreign domestic workers imprisoned without charge or Jordanian women held in "protective custody" because they risk being killed by their families in so-called crimes of honor. She also volunteers with the Families Development Association, seeking to empower young women by speaking to families and persuading them to allow their daughters to participate in the Izdihar program. Despite facing obstacles at the social level as well as increasing official bureaucratic red tape surrounding NGO work, Lubna perseveres, "believing in serving our society, believing in serving women in general, and Jordanian women and girls in particular; I'm going full force, no matter what."

Access to donor funding as well as growing awareness of international women's rights conventions in the post–Cold War era have led women to diversify beyond their traditional welfare activities. May Makarem Hilal told me how the Qarnayel association began to expand its work: "[We] started cooperating with other organizations such as the Lebanese Council for Women and taking part in events and activities. I became a member of the National Committee for the Follow-up of Women's Issues after the Beijing conference. Through my work there I became more active in the field of women's rights and other issues of national interest." Rather than simply being a conduit for neoliberalism, this type of women's NGO activism has actively appropriated international agendas and funding to enable the continuation of a longer tradition of women's voluntary activism that seeks the social "uplift" and modernization of the nation. Through this type of NGO activism, women not only perform crucial reproductive work for the nation but also embody norms of female respectability that reproduce the modesty-modernity boundary, stabilizing the inner/outer boundary of the nation in the face of globalization and Western imperialism.

Former Politically Active Women and NGO Activism: Bargaining with the Geopolitical Order

Several of those NGOs founded from the 1980s onward were established by women (and men) coming out of leftist/radical nationalist movements (see also Karam 2005; Larzillière 2016; Pratt 2002). As discussed, one of the main criticisms leveled at NGO-ization, particularly from among leftist activists, is that NGOs constitute an extension of neoliberal forms of government, leading to the depoliticization of social movements and the undermining of struggles for sociopolitical transformation, as well as a conduit for Western influence and imperialism. Yet former female political activists have attempted to embed their NGO activism within progressive frameworks of opposing authoritarianism, sectarianism, and imperialism, and supporting women's rights and human rights, in line with their leftist political outlooks. There are several examples where NGOs led by former political activists have been at the forefront of national campaigns and issued public statements aimed at expanding democratic rights and freedoms. For example, in Egypt, several human rights and women's rights NGOs joined forces to lead an important campaign in 1998–99 opposing efforts by the regime of Hosni Mubarak to introduce new restrictions on freedom of association (Pratt 2004). In the 2000s, some human rights NGOs (Nadim Center for the Rehabilitation of Victims of Violence and Torture, Hisham Mubarak Law Center, and the Egyptian Center for Economic and Social Rights) were involved with a series of conferences that sought to build a popular movement against dictatorship, imperialism, and neoliberalism, while the New Woman Foundation worked to support women workers who were involved in important strikes and protests (discussed later in this chapter) (Pratt 2012b). Moreover, individuals from those organizations were also part of post-2000 protest movements. After the Egyptian uprising of January 2011, many more NGOs attempted to link their work to the revolutionary struggles that were unfolding. Likewise, in Lebanon, in 1997, NGOs spearheaded campaigns to hold municipal elections, after the parliament voted to postpone them (Karam 2005). After 2011, a coalition of Lebanese NGOs and civil society groups also campaigned to reform the electoral law as a means of breaking the sectarian political status quo. Meanwhile, the Jordanian Women's Union is perhaps unique among NGOs in Jordan in taking political positions, often contrary to the government. As Afaf Jabiri told me:

> The main issue for us [in the JWU] is related to Palestine and at a certain stage to Iraq. Between the 1990s and 2003, we did so much work about Iraq [. . .]; either we were working with Iraqi refugees in Jordan or we were working in Iraq. I've been to Iraq several times as part of campaigns to break the siege against Iraq. [. . .] [We are also concerned with] the corruption in the country, the economic situation, issues related to freedom of speech, [Jordan's] relationship with the United States and Europe, [. . .] privatization, [. . .] internal or regional or international political issues. [. . .] We do have our policy paper every three years where we say what we think of everything going on and we debate these things.

Moreover, the narratives of former female political activists reveal that rather than NGOs contributing to the demobilization of existing social and political movements, in fact they emerged as *a response to* the failures and/or repression of previously existing political organizations and parties. The beginnings of this trend can be traced back to the 1970s and 1980s, as discussed in the previous chapter. For example, in Lebanon, the rise of

Palestinian NGOs was closely linked to the PLO's expulsion in 1982, which severely weakened collective political structures and rendered Palestinian refugees extremely vulnerable. In the absence of the PLO, NGOs came to replace the parties in terms of providing social services and governance in the camps (Roberts 2010: 8). With the end of the civil war, the precarious situation of Palestinians became even clearer. Former DFLP member Haifa Jammal explained to me why she began working in NGOs:

After 1991, after the civil war stopped [...] and the Lebanese government became strong, [...] we realized that in this country we don't have [rights] [...] we didn't realize it before, because when the PLO was strong [...] and the Lebanese government was weak, we could work everywhere; and also, there were hundreds of job opportunities with the PLO, and with the Palestinian political factions. So, we didn't feel there is a problem called "the right to work." [...] But after [the civil war ended], we realized that we don't have rights in this country and if we graduate, for example, and want to be a lawyer or a doctor, we can't work, because we don't have the right to work. After that, in 2001, they [the Lebanese government] issued a new law to prevent us from enjoying the right to own property and [later] also [restricting] the right to movement in Nahr El-Bared [refugee camp].[1] In the south, we can't bring in building materials [into the camp] even to repair or fix our houses, [...] then I started to focus more on this kind of work [i.e., rights advocacy].

The PLO's expulsion also contributed to the transformation of the PLO-affiliated General Union of Palestinian Women (GUPW). Rather than mobilizing Palestinian refugee women to participate in the national struggle, these days the GUPW operates more like an NGO than a social movement, providing a large number of social services to different sectors of Palestinian refugees—children, youth, people with disabilities, orphans, widows, the poor, as well as women. As head of the GUPW Lebanese branch, Amne Suleimane, told me, "We are working on all these issues in order to empower our people and try to solve some of their problems, because we can't pretend that we solve all problems of the Palestinians in Lebanon. In general, our people in Lebanon have so many problems: in health issues ... educational levels and we have the problem of the future [...], [that] people, after sixty-five years, you know, do not find any horizon in front of them. Israel is still turning its back to all UN resolutions. They don't want to discuss the refugee issues." In Amne's narrative, the language of "liberation" and collective mobilization has been replaced by that of "empowerment" to enable individuals and families to cope with the desperate situation of Palestinians in Lebanon.

Indeed, Laleh Khalili argues that the rise of NGOs in the Palestinian refugee camps in Lebanon has contributed to the emergence of a "tragic discourse" in which NGOs display Palestinian suffering to appeal to transnational publics, thereby erasing Palestinian agency (2007: 33–36).

Although the GUPW no longer plays a mobilizing role, this does not mean that the GUPW's work is totally depoliticized. Its efforts and activities aimed at sustaining a Palestinian existence in Lebanon can also be considered a deeply geopolitical act in view of local, regional, and international actors who deny the existence of Palestinians as a national group, let alone as refugees entitled to rights (for further details on the status of Palestinians in Lebanon, see Peteet 2005; Roberts 2010; Suleiman 1997). In addition to Israel's ongoing refusal to allow the return of the Palestinian refugees, Lebanese politicians have, since the end of the civil war, united around a series of measures to restrict the rights of Palestinian refugees living in Lebanon, justified, disingenuously, in the name of preventing *tawtin*, or "naturalization" of the refugees in Lebanon and safeguarding the Palestinians' right of return (Peteet 2005: 174–76). Palestinians in Lebanon also wish to safeguard their right of return but do not see the granting of social and economic rights as threatening their national rights. Rather, they see that Lebanese politicians' use of the issue of *tawtin* is for their own political and sectarian ends (Peteet 1996, 2005: 173–74). In a context in which collective Palestinian political structures within Lebanon are effectively nonexistent and Palestinian refugees are socially and politically marginalized both within Lebanon and within the wider Palestinian national movement, GUPW and other local NGOs, such as Association Najdeh and the Women's Humanitarian Organization, as well as some foreign NGOs, such as Norwegian People's Aid,[2] have played a key role in creating campaigning networks to defend Palestinian social and economic rights in Lebanon (e.g., the Palestinian Right to Work Coalition), as well as continuing to raise the right of return. Hence, in this case, NGOs play a central role in articulating an "anti-geopolitics" (Routledge 2003) or "alter-geopolitics" (Koopman 2011).

In other cases, many women activists turned away from political parties, even those of the left, as a result of experiences of gender discrimination. For example, Nawla Darwiche, who had previously been a member of the Egyptian Communist Party and then later the Hizb al-Sha'b al-Ishtiraki (People's Socialist Party) recalled her work within political parties in the following terms: "My experience [. . .] is that women are used as secretaries in the political parties [. . .]; they are used to type things, make photocopies, etcetera." Meanwhile, Joumana Merhy, who was a member of a leftist political party in Lebanon from 1983 until 2003, told me:

> I think that it was the immense masculine culture that I experienced in political parties that drove me to become such an active proponent of women's rights. [...] A political party that doesn't believe in equality is an oppressive and totalitarian party, not a democratic party. [...] At the time being, I am not part of any political party, but I do campaign on some political issues, but always outside the framework of a political party. Many women are politically active without being part of a party, because there isn't a single party that supports women's rights.

Similarly, Nadia Shamroukh, who was a member of a leftist Palestinian party, finally resigned in 1997 and, since then, has focused her public activism on the Jordanian Women's Union: "I stopped because working with Palestinian organizations and parties in Jordan became useless. There was no response whatsoever; not to your needs as a woman or political needs. It was difficult. I thought for a very long time about leaving."

Although she did not abandon party politics, Farida El-Nakkash, an active member of the Egyptian Tagammu' Party since its founding in the 1970s, and also responsible for establishing the party-affiliated Progressive Women's Union, became disillusioned with her party's position on gender issues:

> We in the women's movement realized [...] that there were contradictions within the progressive parties; extreme contradictions when it came to the subject of women. For example, Khaled Mohieddin, the [former] president of our party, stood in parliament in the year 2000 and defended a man's right to forbid his wife to travel. [...] So, we realized that we've been tricked and we felt like our existence within this organization was just for show, because when it came down to the sensitive issues, the president of our party took a very backward stance on women's rights matters.

Against this back-drop, NGOs have provided institutional platforms from which women activists have been able to formulate independent agendas for women's rights. For example, Farida created a coalition of NGOs working on women's issues, called the Forum for Women in Development. In a 2008 interview, she recognized the limitations of previous leftist ideologies, which subsumed the woman question to the question of socioeconomic transformation: "It is not enough to say the development of society will eventually liberate women. Women themselves need to be actively involved. This is the aim of the Forum."

Not only did political parties fail to advocate for women's rights but, in the case of the Jordanian Women's Union, political party interference also prevented advocacy for women's rights. According to Nadia Shamroukh, secretary general at the time of our interview, "The party members [...] who were in the Union [...] they joined the Union to issue a [political] statement; that was their role, which is not the role of the Union. It's a women's union. [...] They wanted politics more than women's rights. That is the last thing the parties were thinking about. For me, the women's cause is a national cause, [...] and liberating women cannot happen without liberating the country, but liberating countries does not mean forgetting women and leaving them to be oppressed." Consequently, throughout the 1990s, a group of members, including Nadia, struggled to rid the organization of political party involvement and put forward an independent gender-based agenda. This process was facilitated by the professionalization of the Union—which, at the time, was contentious.

One of the ways in which former women political activists seek to resist NGO-ization is through a very selective approach to accepting donor funding. For example, Afaf Jabiri of the JWU explained to me the principles guiding the JWU's acceptance of foreign funding: "[JWU] needs to sustain its grassroots programs. [...] So we have to kind of adhere [to] some kind of professional work in order to get funding. But the Union all the time has conditioned the funding, not the other way around. [...] We have our priorities, our strategies, and whatever fits with that strategy, we apply for. So, it's very clear and everybody knows. It made the Jordanian Women's Union very distinctive from other unions [and organizations]."

Other women also mentioned the rejection of any sort of conditionalities as well as the need to distance themselves from certain donor agencies because of the foreign policies of their respective governments. In this regard, several NGO activists mentioned USAID as one of the donors whose funding they refuse to accept (see also Al-Ali 2000: 200–205; Pratt 2006). Some organizations refuse all foreign funding (for example, the Lebanese League for Women's Rights) or try to reduce dependency on foreign funding by not being totally professionalized and still being led by volunteers (for example, the Nadim Center for the Rehabilitation of Victims of Violence and Torture, the Lebanese Democratic Women Gathering).

Although women activists exercise agency to resist the depoliticizing effects of NGO-ization and embed their activism within an "anti-geopolitics," many of my interviewees acknowledged the difficulties of resisting NGO-ization as a whole. On the one hand, donor funding enables groups to expand and diversify their activities and to contribute to what they see as important social change. Yet, to successfully attract external funding, organizations must be able to comply with particular ways of working—presenting their work in terms of discrete projects, writing funding proposals in fluent English, and meeting donor requirements for monitoring and reporting. Many women complained about the heavy burden of this professionalization and recognized the ways in which competition for funding led to a fragmentation of the women's movement as well as the undermining of future sustainability as a younger generation of women expect to find a full-time, paid position in the NGO sector rather than working as volunteers. In this respect, former political activists pursue what Sonia Alvarez has called a "hybrid strategy" (1999: 182) in that they remain committed to movement goals or, at least, the goals of previously existing movements, while complying with professionalized models of working in order to be able to attract funding. Essentially, former political activists bargain with the international system: subjecting themselves to processes of neoliberalization in order to create some space for agency that challenges the direct and structural violence of imperialism, authoritarianism, and gender inequalities.

Younger Women's Social Entrepreneurialism and the Micropolitics of Gender

While older generations of women NGO activists were either former members of political parties and movements or volunteers in charitable associations, younger generations of women activists are often "professional" activists. Because of regime repression, they have not been exposed to oppositional movements (except for Islamists) and/or are turned off politics because of the corruption of the political system and, in the case of Lebanon, the dominance of sectarian parties. Moreover, their formative years have seen the dismantling of the postindependence social pact; therefore, they are not necessarily as invested in notions of contributing to "national uplift" as previous generations, while their subjectivities have been shaped by neoliberal governmentalities. They tend to demonstrate social entrepreneurial attitudes to sociopolitical questions and are often motivated to work for or create NGOs to implement new methods and best practices from the field of international development. For example, Ghida Anani began working with the Lebanese Council for Resisting Violence against Women (LECORVAW) in 2002, as a paid employee within the organization, and left in 2005 to join KAFA: Enough Violence, established by Zoya Rouhana, following divisions within LECORVAW. In 2011, she left KAFA and established ABAAD and introduced a novel approach to the work of combatting violence against women: "I [...] found that [...] it needs to have a strong gender lens in the sense that you can't work on addressing violence against women without working also with the second part of the equation, which is the men who are responsible for the behavior; that is part of the problem and should be part and core maybe of the solution. [This] was a little bit a different approach or a different perspective from the organizations which I've been [previously] part of." ABAAD established the first men's center in the region "providing rehabilitation services for men engaged in violent behaviors," and it also works on "the policy development level, on national strategies, [...] family [violence] prevention for boys and girls to be able to raise a new generation of nonviolent men and also women non-tolerant to violence in a relationship." Ghida differentiates her organization from a previous generation of women activists: "It's no longer just about being on the street and shouting." Rather, Ghida's narrative emphasizes the need to study what has worked and did not work in the past, bringing "expertise and scientific knowledge" to bear on the work. ABAAD's approach to working with men has won the organization a lot of attention from Western donors and, at the time of writing, the organization has grown significantly since its establishment in 2011. Through Ghida's emphasis on professionalism, the disavowal of collective action, and focus on technical approaches, ABAAD adheres to a depoliticized, neoliberal model of NGO work. Yet, like former political activists, Ghida insists on maintaining the organization's autonomy by refusing any sort of grant conditionalities from foreign donors.

Similar to Ghida, Samar Muhareb in Jordan also positions her organization as different from existing women's organizations. Like Ghida, Samar had previous professional experience of NGO work before cofounding Arab Renaissance for Democracy and Development (ARDD) in 2008. Samar is a lawyer by profession but has worked in the field of development and human rights, previously with Oxfam. Initially ARDD provided legal aid services to poor and marginalized communities, including women and refugees, but it has grown rapidly to also provide other services, such as capacity building and training. The organization emphasizes empowerment and participation of marginalized communities, as well as investing in institution-building through adopting appropriate procedures and governance within ARDD, which has enabled the organization to grow. In 2015, ARDD had a professional staff of approximately seventy people. As well as working at the grassroots throughout Jordan, ARDD engages with government officials to advocate for legal reforms. Samar won the Takreem Arab World Young Entrepreneur Award in 2011 and was one of a handful of women honored by the King and Queen in 2015 for their leading roles in Jordan's development. Samar differentiates ARDD from many other civil society, including women's, organizations, by emphasizing the importance of building institutions on the basis of procedures and structures, rather than around individual leaders, as happens not only in Jordan but also in Egypt and Lebanon (see also Al-Attiyat 2003; Joseph 1997; Al-Ali 2000). In this respect, ARDD, like many other women's NGOs in Jordan, works within the existing parameters of the geopolitical order and neoliberal political economy; however, through the active embrace of professionalism and other neoliberal modes of work, Samar, and other younger women, attempt to challenge the monopoly of older women activists over the field of activism.

Generational differences among women are an important factor propelling the proliferation of NGOs and NGO-ization within the field of gender activism. Young women activists often express dissatisfaction with the agendas and ways of working of older women. As highlighted above, younger generations of women have established NGOs to pursue alternative approaches to women's rights than those pursued by older generations of activists. In particular, they are often much more concerned with the micropolitics of gender, rather than focusing on reforming state structures and laws. For example, in Egypt, Mozn Hassan founded Nazra for Feminist Studies in 2008 after failing to find a space for her concerns within existing women's organizations. She told me:

> I always had this perspective that the older women are more conservative than our generation, and they were more into laws and policies, and I felt like feminism is about communities and grassroots and things like this. After that I changed my mind, but at that time I felt like I don't want to work on a campaign to reform the nationality law. [...] I felt like sexuality is something important. [...] It is a big question [...] to live in a conservative society like this and a big question for [...] a feminist, and I saw [...] almost all of the feminists or those rights groups are ignoring this issue, and sometimes some of the groups are labeling women who are open-minded, that "they're not part of us."

In Jordan, Randa Naffa cofounded an NGO called SADAQA in 2011, after her personal experience of trying to balance work and motherhood. Randa and her colleagues lobby companies to comply with Article 72 of the Jordanian Labor Law, which mandates that companies with twenty or more female employees provide workplace crèches. Randa's aunts are the high-profile and long-standing women's rights and political activists Emily and Leila Naffa, who founded the Arab Women Organization in 1970. Randa herself volunteered with the Arab Women Organization when she was younger and then went on to do an MA in gender studies in the UK. According to Randa:

> I never felt a strong association with an issue until I had my son. I was working at an international organization and my mother was looking after him. To breastfeed him, I had to go home or my sister would bring him to me. It was very tiring as well as not fair for my mother, who also has her own life. I ended up in hospital due to exhaustion. At that point, I decided with a friend to work on advocating for Article 72 [of the labor law]. [...] In the past, there were more important issues for the women's movement, such as political participation and the nationality law. Women's economic participation was not high and, therefore, not seen as an important issue. But things have changed now because of economic development and there needs to be new priorities.

In Lebanon, the desire to promote an agenda different from existing women's organizations motivated a group of queer feminists who came together around 2007 and later went on to found Nasawiya. However, unlike many other younger women's organizations, Nasawiya also set out to resist NGO-ization. According to one of the founders, Lynn Darwich:

> At the beginning when we were trying to conceptualize that group, [...] first of all it was a membership-, and it still is a membership-based organization, so [...] we didn't have staff and a project manager, and project coordinators, where we are focused on one project, you know, [and you] fundraise, you implement, you evaluate, you report. We didn't have that kind of structure. It was an open space that members could come into, bring in projects of their own [...] and [...] form their teams and [...] work on making them happen; so, it had more of a free-flowing kind of atmosphere. [...] [Also] our vision at the beginning was a lot more radical, in the sense that we didn't want to work with the existing system, we wanted to create alternatives; we weren't very sure what those alternatives looked like, but we knew that our space, was an alternative space, right? [...] So, we put a lot of value in that, [and] a lot of value in writing [...] and, you know, trying to understand the complexities of our lives and politics.

However, the experience of Nasawiya also illustrates the difficulties of resisting NGO-ization and building alternatives. Speaking to me in the autumn of 2013, Lynn reflected on the current situation within Nasawiya: "[B]ut [. . .] if you look where Nasawiya is now, I think it drifted a lot from that initial vision. I think sometimes you fall in the trap when you say, 'Oh, we don't believe in structures and we don't believe in hierarchies,' and we end up creating a lot of invisible hierarchies, and these are very dangerous. [. . .] [And] the moment you have some sort of tension, it explodes and it's very hard to pick up the pieces. So, Nasawiya now is in a very rough spot in that sense."

During my research, groups such as Nasawiya were the exception rather than the norm.[3] In the case of Egypt and Jordan, this could be explained by the strict rules governing associational work, which make it difficult for groups to legally operate outside of a formalized, NGO structure. However, some young (middle-class) women, may also prefer working within NGOs that operate within dominant geopolitical structures rather than trying to resist them. For example, a young Lebanese woman who works for a UN agency and volunteers for several humanitarian and developmental NGOs differentiated between "old" women's organizations, which are "too rigid" in their approach, "such as just calling for a women's quota in parliament," versus "new" NGOs, such as Women in Front, which are trying to work within the political limitations of the sectarian system by focusing on increasing the number of women candidates and working with political parties.[4] In her mind, calls for a quota were fruitless because the confessional political system, political rivalries, and geopolitical dynamics prevent the current government from accepting such a reform (see chapter 6 for further discussion of the challenges facing women's political participation in Lebanon).

As Sheila Carapico argues, NGO activists "make creative use of resources within the parameters of constraints" (Carapico 2014: 200). I found that there were differences among NGO activists in terms of how and for what purposes they creatively use the resources made available through NGO-ization. NGO activists position themselves differently in relation to the geopolitical order, with some attempting to use the resources made available through NGO-ization to challenge it, while others work within dominant geopolitical structures. Moreover, women's NGO activism may contribute to reproducing dominant geopolitical structures at the national and global scales while resisting or trying to transform structures at the interpersonal scale through challenges to gendered hierarchies, which may, over time, contribute to wider incremental change. Overall, it is crucial to historicize and contextualize the growth of NGOs in relation to longer-term histories of women's activism within the region, regime repression of political opposition groups and movements, and the specific ways in which these trends have been strength-ened or reshaped by Western imperialism and the spread of neoliberalism, rather than analyzing NGOs as *either* conduits for neoliberalism and imperi-alism *or* as agents of democratization and human rights. In other words, inter-secting and sometimes contradictory processes at the international, national, and personal scales shape the modalities of women's activism.

WOMEN'S PARTICIPATION IN NEW PROTEST
MOVEMENTS AFTER 2000

While NGO-ization has continued to dominate the post–Cold War era, nonetheless, a very important development, particularly after 2000, was the rise of new protest movements, in which women played a visible role. These included movements in solidarity with the Palestinians and against the war and occupation of Iraq, as well as in resistance to neoliberal restructuring and authoritarianism. If NGO-ization functioned for the most part within the limits of the post–Cold War geopolitical order, protest movements can be understood, for the most part, as resistance to this order. Nonetheless, the picture is more complex than this. While NGOs largely embraced women's rights agendas, protest movements eschewed transforming dominant gender norms even though women were visible in leadership positions. Moreover, protests in Egypt and Jordan were clearly in opposition to US imperialism and neoliberalism; however, in Lebanon, in the context of the War on Terror and US ambitions to remake the region, anti-Syrian protests aligned with US foreign policy rather than resisting it. For this reason, the following sections map women's involvement in post-2000 protests in Egypt and Jordan sepa-rately from their involvement in protests in Lebanon. The final section con-siders the gendered dynamics and geopolitical effects of movements in all three countries.

Mapping Protest Movements in Egypt and Jordan after 2000

Egypt has received the lion's share of attention concerning the emergence of new protest movements after 2000. These included the Palestine solidarity movement, pro-democracy movement Kefaya, and the proliferation of work-ers' strikes (Beinin and Duboc 2013; El-Mahdi 2009; El-Mahdi and Marfleet 2009; Vairel 2013). Several authors as well as movement participants point to a decade-long evolution of networks and repertoires that underpin the mass mobilization that culminated in the 25 January 2011 uprising against the regime of Hosni Mubarak (Abdelrahman 2015; El-Mahdi 2009; Povey 2015; Sowers and Toensing 2012; Tohamy 2016). Jordan also witnessed large-scale protests and activism in solidarity with Palestine and against the Iraq War, bringing together a range of political activists, from Islamist to leftist, as well as independents (Schwedler 2003; Schwedler and Fayyaz 2010). In addition, there was a significant wave of labor activism from the mid-2000s onward (Ababneh 2016; Adely 2012). Yet, until now, very little attention has been given to the role of women within these movements or their gendered dimensions.

Cairo University professor Laila Soueif was one of several women who pointed to the movement in solidarity with the Second Palestinian Intifada as a major catalyst for independent activism throughout the first decade of the twenty-first century:

To me, this whole—the movement, which had its highest point in the 25 January revolution, started around 2000, actually with the first groups of solidarity with the Palestinian Intifada. I think the main thing was that people suddenly [. . .] decided, "Okay, this is it, I want to back the Palestinian Intifada. I want to organize and start collecting help and getting it to Gaza. I'm going to do that and I'm not going to try and hide that I'm doing that, and the government can do what it likes. I'm not going to try and get a government permit to do that, I'm just going to do it." [. . .] I think that's why we suddenly had all this movement, because everyone realized that they could just do that and not waste time and energy and effort in trying to get around a bureaucratic maze, which tells you what you're allowed to do and what you're not allowed to do. [. . .] There were lots of initiatives at that time. [. . .] We discovered that there was a portion of the street at least that was with us, it wasn't just an elitist thing. From that moment, there was always attempts at doing different things in different places.

One of the earliest initiatives that came out of the pro-Palestine protests in 2000 was the creation of the Egyptian Popular Committee for Solidarity with the Palestinians (EPCSP). The Committee was innovative because of its loose organizational structure and its cross-ideological, cross-generational cooperation, which became common to other initiatives and movements emerging after 2000 (Abdelrahman 2013). It was founded by a diversity of activists, which included leftists, Nasserists, Islamists, and independents, and political and NGO activists. Women, many of whom who had participated in the 1970s student movement, as well as the iconic activist for peasants' rights, the late Shahenda Maklad, played visible leadership roles.

Magda Adli, who was arrested for her participation in the 1977 "bread uprising," was one of the founders of the EPCSP. She explained to me,

> Since 2000, [when] the Second Palestinian Intifada took place, [...] the whole [Egyptian] people showed solidarity. I can't forget that. We formed committees and this was the first big thing to be formed during Mubarak's rule. We formed a committee called the Popular Committee for Supporting the Palestinian People. It started in Cairo and in a very short period of time it was present in all the Egyptian governorates. [...] We collected signatures to denounce the aggression and to reiterate the right of return for the refugees and to stop the building of settlements [...] and we collected around three or four million signatures in two months. The other part was the humanitarian support; we sent convoys of medicine and basic nutritional supplies; the poorest people in the countryside would donate everything they had, so much that there was a woman who had only a duck and she donated it. She gave it to us alive; the duck was alive and quacking. She insisted that we take the duck to Palestine. We said it wouldn't work, she said, "Then sell it and use the money to buy medicine." That was the public sentiment amongst the Egyptians back then. This committee kept working for years, we would send flour, sugar, rice, medicine, medical supplies, ambulances, so there was an unbelievable public support indeed.

The activist networks established in solidarity with the Palestinians paved the way for mobilizations against the 2003 Iraq War. When George Bush gave his ultimatum to the Iraqi regime in February 2003, many of those already involved in the EPCSP made a public call for people to assemble in Tahrir Square as soon as the United States attacked Iraq. The response surprised many. Heba Ali Hilmi, a member of the Revolutionary Socialists, who, at the time was teaching at the College of Fine Arts in Cairo, went down to Tahrir Square: "This was the first time in my life that I saw Tahrir Square full of people. Not as much as it was on January 25th [2011], but there were at least forty thousand people there. I had distributed the invitation at the faculty and to the students and I got in trouble for that." Despite the square being surrounded by security forces, the demonstrations were peaceful. Protesters managed to stay in the square into the evening and slogans against Mubarak were heard (Schemm 2003). In light of the surprising success of 20 March, many protesters decided to return the next day. As Heba recalls: "[However] The events of March 21st were nasty. It was a street war. People were being arrested. Anybody who was coming to Tahrir Square got arrested. [. . .] It was awful. But that day, the picture of Mubarak at Abdel-Monem Riad Square was ripped up and the same scenes that we saw there were similar to the ones that would happen in El-Mahalla [factory strikes] in 2008. But it was the first time something like this happens."

One important initiative that came directly from the antiwar mobilizations was the 9 March Movement for the Independence of the Universities. It was founded in 2004, emerging out of weekly antiwar rallies held by Cairo University staff and students. Like the EPCSP, the 9 March Movement was a loose network of individuals. As Revolutionary Socialist Manar Abdel Sattar explained:

> [We] decided to do something about the independence of the university, in the sense of stopping security from controlling the recruitment process, as anyone who wished to be hired by the university must get a security clearance first. Of course, they controlled the research, especially in "social sciences," there were taboos not to be touched upon and so on. For example, it was not allowed to have a guest lecturer from outside the university, and if you wanted to do that you needed security clearance, and even if it was by someone from the university itself, they could stop it. And of course, their control over the Students' Union elections. [. . .] [So] the movement started against the war on Iraq and then it turned into a group focused only on the independence of the university, in the sense of academic freedoms, and we continued like that, we held a number of conferences, there was the annual March 9th conference, every year.

The creation of the 9 March Movement was significant because historically university professors had tended to be politically quiescent. As Laila Soueif, one of the movement's leaders, told me: "The interesting thing was how many people who had [previously] kept themselves well away from the political-type movements, were willing to invest in backing us; maybe not to invest in actually attending all our meetings but in backing us, in signing our petitions and so on." For example, Ayn Shams University professor Iman Ezzeldin, who had never previously been involved in activism, joined the 9 March Movement about a year after its founding, provoked by an assault on one of her colleagues by a policeman on campus. She attended the monthly meetings at the Cairo University Staff Club and participated in many demonstrations against university administrations around the country and against the Ministry of Higher Education. The movement was successful in achieving one of its objectives, when in 2009 it obtained a supreme court ruling outlawing the presence of state security on university campuses (see also Abdelrahman 2015: 39–42, for more details on the 9 March Movement).

The 9 March Movement was part of a growing wave of demands for political and social change; the Movement for Change, or Kefaya (meaning "enough" in Arabic), was probably the most high-profile of these. It was founded in 2004 by a small group of veteran activists from different political and ideological backgrounds, many of whom were already working together through the EPCSC and anti-war activism (El-Mahdi 2009: 1018). Leftist political activist Rabab El-Mahdi recalls: "There was a feeling after the second Iraq War, [...] this regime was not in control as we thought it was, and that there is a lot of potential on the ground to topple down the regime [...] [and] that's what prompted the whole Kefaya thing." Initially, the group's main objective was to oppose the extension of President Mubarak's mandate for another term and the "inheritance" of the presidency by his son Gamal, who was already being groomed for the post. The group held its first demonstration in December 2004, attended by a few hundred people, and then, over the course of the next year or so, managed to mobilize new faces and young people beyond the existing activist community (El-Mahdi 2009). What was distinct about Kefaya, compared to previous mobilizations, was that it articulated demands for domestic political change and, significantly, that it crossed a long-established red line by criticizing the president and his son. As Karima El-Hefnawy, a former student activist from the 1970s and one of the founders of Kefaya, explained: "We believed that the only way we can solve any of the issues, whether social justice, justice for Palestine, our freedom of will, and preserve our natural resources, was by overthrowing the oppressive regimes, because these regimes are the ones that are standing in the way of people's rights and work to serve the interests of the United States and Israel."

Many of the women whom I interviewed participated in Kefaya or in one of the many initiatives that flourished in the wake of Kefaya, including the various initiatives "for change" among different sectors of society: Writers for Change, Youth for Change, Engineers for Democracy, among others (Abdelrahman 2013: 575). Rabab El-Mahdi recalled the excitement and energy resulting from the Kefaya movement: "Despite the fact that Kefaya demonstrations were small, there *were* demonstrations; we could stand, even I know it's on the Bar Association's stairs, but still, you know; and there was a community of activists being formed; we had this email group list called Taqaddum ["progress"] for the leftists, we had "Youth for Change" and Kefaya email groups that were forums for discussions, blogging was coming out, so [...] things were opening up in a way that I hadn't seen throughout the previous twenty years in Cairo."

Although Kefaya did not achieve its objectives and soon dissipated after 2005, it played a significant role in creating a spirit of dissent, which touched even usually quiet quarters. For example, Ghada Shahbender, previously an apolitical mother of four, told me, in an interview in 2008, how the sexual attacks on women by regime-hired thugs during Kefaya protests in 2005 outraged her and led her to create, first, the White Ribbon Apology Campaign and, then, "Shayfeen.com," (meaning, "We're watching you")—a movement to monitor and hold the government to account. Kefaya also contributed to politicizing a new generation of youth. An active blogosphere emerged, which continued even after the downturn in Kefaya and street demonstrations, where young Egyptians began writing freely about politics, oppositional activities, and publicizing police brutality (Lynch 2007; Radsch 2008), as well as writing about social and personal issues not broached by the mass media (Otterman 2007). Despite the difficulties of translating online dissent into offline action, blogging and social media more broadly played a role in raising awareness, arguably contributing to the mobilization of offline activism against the police murder of Khaled Said in the summer of 2010 and, later, in support of demonstrations on 25 January 2011 (Alaimo 2015).

In Jordan, despite the presence of large-scale Palestine solidarity and anti-war activism bringing together a range of political actors from Islamist to leftist, as well as independents (Kilani 2003; Schwedler 2003; Schwedler and Fayyaz 2010), these protests and initiatives, for reasons that are beyond the scope of this chapter, did not develop into an effective political reform movement until 2011. Nonetheless, similarly to Egypt, a community of bloggers emerged from the mid-2000s "as the leading edge of a new engagement with politics by Arab citizens" (Lynch 2007). According to cofounder of online magazine *7iber.com*, Lina Ejeilat, blogging operated as "some kind of alternative media, [...] a space where we were trying to get certain voices and ideas across that maybe we're not able to [...] in other media outlets," such as discussions of taboo social issues, human rights, women's rights, as well as politics.

Women were also involved in the large waves of workers' strikes that hit Egypt and Jordan after the mid-2000s, in response to the intensification of neoliberal economic restructuring. In Egypt, strikes began in the textile industry but spread to other sectors of the economy, including both blue-collar and white-collar workers. In December 2007, eight thousand real estate tax collectors organized a sit-in outside the cabinet offices in Cairo, camping out on the streets for eleven days, demanding better wages and paving the way for Egypt's first independent union since 1952 (Lachapelle 2012).

In 2008, university professors, doctors, and nurses, all normally quiescent sectors, went on strike demanding better wages and working conditions. According to labor historian, Joel Beinin, some two million Egyptian workers participated in 2,623 protests, strikes, and other forms of collective action between 1998 and 2008 (Beinin and Hamalawy 2007; Solidarity Center 2010; Beinin 2012). Jordan also saw a growth in worker strikes. The day-wage laborers' movement was one of the first groups of workers to organize and protest the use of temporary contracts to hire civil servants, beginning in 2006 (Ababneh 2016). After 2008, there were important strikes and protests by port workers, phosphate workers, and day laborers in the public sector, who were protesting against poor wages, job losses, job insecurity, and loss of benefits, as a result of privatization and public sector retrenchment (Adely 2012; Ababneh 2016). In 2010, teachers organized a series of protests and strikes to demand higher wages and the right to form a union. These economic protests and strikes increased after January 2011 as part of the Hirak al-Sha'bi al-Urdunni—the Jordanian popular movement (Adely 2012).

Lebanon: The Uprising against Syrian Occupation

In Lebanon, the post-2000 wave of contentious politics was mainly centered on opposition to Syria's continuing presence in the country after the end of the civil war, and the growth in political repression and corruption linked to it (El-Husseini 2012). As mentioned previously, the Ta'if Accords, signed in 1990, which brought an end to the Lebanese Civil War, gave Syria a significant political and military role in Lebanon. This was opposed mainly by the Christian parties, who were marginalized by the Ta'if accords, but also increasingly by leftists as a result of increasing human rights abuses and limits on civil liberties, "leading many to fear that Lebanon was becoming more like Syria in its lack of respect for human rights" (El-Husseini 2012: 134–35).

Mirna Shidrawi, like several other young Lebanese, first became involved in anti-Syrian protests as a student at the American University of Beirut (AUB), from 1997 to 2001, through an independent leftist group called Bila Hudud (No Frontiers). No Frontiers and other student leftist groups emerged toward the end of the 1990s as a secular alternative to the Hariri neoliberal project (El-Khoury 2008) and in the wake of the slow demise of the "old" or "classic" Lebanese left after the civil war (Haugbolle 2010: 210). Mirna recalls: "Back then [...] the Hariri clan was pro-Syrian, [Walid] Jumblatt was pro-Syrian. There was only the Christians that were against them. [...] We worked a lot with the Christian factions to support them in their cause against the Syrians. That started developing. [...] We had a group in AUB and then there was another group similar to us, a leftist independent group in LAU [Lebanese American University] and USJ [Université Saint Joseph] [...] I was very active there alongside a bunch of other friends from AUB, both females and males."

Another important vector of activism during this period was around solidarity with the Palestinians and against the Iraq war. Bernadette Daou, living in East Beirut, attended USJ, where Christian Maronite parties were dominant. However, she was uncomfortable with these parties and joined the Communist Students:

> From 2001 till 2004, we had two main events that we organized; sit-ins and demonstrations. The first was in 2002. It was the Jenin massacre and the siege of Ramallah. We organized a permanent sit-in for a month and a half. Different independent leftist groups from AUB, LAU, Communist Students [participated together] [...] and this sit-in was a success because it was recruiting people and making noise about the issue, and also the people from the Eastern side [that is, predominantly Christian East Beirut] which were the Aouniyyeh [supporters of Michel Aoun] were also participating. [...] And [the second event] in 2003, we had an anti-war campaign. The campaign here was named "No War, No Dictatorship," because these groups of the left were involved against imperialism and globalization, but at the same time against dictatorship, against the Syrian hegemony. [...] And this was a, it was a big and hard discussion in the classic [old] left, and we succeeded to split from the big meetings and to organize our own meetings. [...] We actually succeeded to recruit all people on the left or secular people that are not necessarily affiliated to or [...] oppose the classic left. So, it was mainly young groups, young people from universities, and independent political groups.

The different groups making up the "new" left attempted to unite in a common platform "to try to make a leftist alternative in the country," as Mirna explained. This resulted in the creation of the Democratic Left Movement (DLM) in 2004. In addition to being against the Syrian presence, the movement's position was pro-Palestine, anti-US intervention, pro-democracy, pro–social justice, and anti-sectarianism (Quilty 2005). Despite the DLM's desire to embrace a pluralism of leftist opinions, not all leftist activists joined, including Bernadette. Controversially, the DLM allied itself with sectarian parties, namely, the Qornet Shahwan Gathering (a group of moderate Christian parties under the informal leadership of Maronite Patriarch Nasrallah Sfeir) and Jumblatt's Democratic Gathering Bloc, in opposition to Syria. This unprecedented cross-sectarian coalition was provoked by Syria's attempts to override the Lebanese constitution and extend the presidential term of pro-Syrian politician Emile Lahoud in the summer of 2004. In this regard, they found common ground with the US administration of George Bush, who had identified Syria as part of the "axis of evil" and an obstacle to US ambitions to reshape the Middle East after 9/11. In December of that year, the DLM, Qornet Shahwan, and the Democratic Gathering Bloc held a joint meeting and issued the Bristol Declaration, which condemned Syrian interference in Lebanese affairs (Lebanon Opposition 2004, Haugbolle 2010: 77–78). However, not all Lebanese parties agreed with these sentiments—specifically the Shiʻa parties of Amal and Hizbollah, which continued to support Syria's presence.

In February 2005, former prime minister Rafiq al-Hariri, who, by then, had also joined the anti-Syrian opposition, was assassinated, leading to spontaneous outpourings of grief among ordinary Lebanese, which quickly developed into a popular movement against Syria's presence in the country. Mirna recalled:

> I used to finish work every day and go down to the open sit-in. [. . .] Every time we used to call for a demonstration [. . .] the number of people was increasing and people broke their silence and fear. In one of the demonstrations, the demonstrators started giving roses to the Lebanese army to allow them to go into the demonstration area. It was lovely to see that in Lebanon people stood up against the tyranny and expressed their political opinions with no fear and no shame. I felt back then, that the feeling of apathy, which is common for most of the Lebanese, especially after the civil war, wasn't there anymore. Everybody wanted change and everyone had a political opinion that they are ready to fight for.

While initial demonstrations were spontaneous, later demonstrations, particularly the "'one million person" demonstration in downtown Beirut on March 14, were organized by political parties, albeit supported by a wide spectrum of civil society groups opposing the authoritarianism of Syrian hegemony (Safa 2006: 31). The slogan of the demonstrations, which Lebanese called their "independence intifada" and the international press dubbed the "Cedar Revolution," was "truth, freedom, and independence," reflecting widespread hopes that Lebanon was turning a new page, going beyond the sectarianism that continued to haunt the state and society (Haugbolle 2010: 196–203). However, a significant proportion of the Lebanese population, namely, supporters of Amal and Hizbollah, representing the Shiʻa community, were not behind the anti-Syrian movement, as demonstrated by a massive counter-rally organized in downtown Beirut on 8 March. The divisions between the anti-Syrian and pro-Syrian blocs were not solely about the role of Syria within Lebanon but also about respective visions for the future of Lebanon and its foreign relations (Shehadi 2007).

As a result of the mass protests, the Syrian government withdrew from Lebanon leading many to hope for wider sociopolitical transformation. Mirna Shidrawi told me:

> It was a beautiful phase in 2005 when we demonstrated and everyone was using the Lebanese flag and everyone was united for one cause. Not everybody. It's a bit of a generalization to say everybody because there was a big faction against our effort. [. . .]. But we felt free and, yeah, I think that was the problem. We all thought that this revolution is going to change the world. We thought that we're going to have a state with secular laws. We thought that we're going to have civil marriage in Lebanon. That's how silly we were back then. This is what we should have done at the end of the civil war and not now. And this is what the whole of Lebanon is united to do. And then [. . .] zero political voice, we cannot change anything.

The opposition that had helped to mobilize and lead the Lebanese people, which came to be known as the March 14 bloc, was dominated by sectarian parties, which had no interest in changing the fundamental rules of the game— notwithstanding the participation of the Democratic Left Movement. Politics after Syria's withdrawal exhibited many continuities with the past (Kurtulus 2009) and became even more fiercely polarized between the anti-Syrian March 14 coalition and the pro-Syrian March 8 coalition. The US supported the March 14 coalition as part of its project to remake the Middle East and eliminate rivals. In 2006, the US backed Israel's war on Hizbollah, which lasted several weeks, causing large numbers of casualties and significant destruction. While the US and its allies had hoped to weaken the organization, instead Hizbollah's ability to withstand Israel's onslaught propelled its domestic and even regional popularity, leading to further tensions between it and the March 14 coalition, which spilled over into armed conflict in 2008. Following this, many younger activists became disillusioned and demobilized or shifted their focus away from political change to focus on social change, including women's rights.

Gendered Dimensions of Women's Involvement in Protest Movements

While several authors have written about the emergence of protest movements after 2000 and their political significance, particularly in the Egyptian case, there has been very little written about the gendered dimensions of these movements. Yet, as revealed by my interviews, women played an important leadership role in protests and strikes. However, they were mobilized not according to their gender identity, but as citizens or members of national, class, or ideological groupings. In some cases, activists from women's rights NGOs joined these popular movements, seeing the struggle against authoritarianism as part of the struggle for women's rights. Nevertheless, gender-based demands were not part of the demands of these new social movements. Nor did social movement activists include gender justice as part of their critique of authoritarian regimes and foreign occupation. On the contrary, notions of women's rights and equality were sometimes criticized for being part of imperialist and neoliberal agendas, particularly in light of the Bush administration's post-9/11 claims to be "liberating" women in the Middle East through military interventions in Afghanistan and Iraq (Pratt 2012b).

The failure of popular and political reform movements to include women's rights demands can be seen partly as the outcome of the isolation of women's rights activists from wider political struggles as a result of years of NGO-ization and decades of political repression, in addition to the particular ways in which women's rights agendas became co-opted by imperialism and authoritarian regimes (as discussed in the next chapter). This divergence between women's rights NGOs and other social and political struggles was tangible in the Cairo Conferences against Imperialism, Zionism, and Dictatorship, which were a series of international conferences held more or less annually between 2002 and 2009, the central organizing committee of which was made up of leftists, radical nationalists, and Islamists (see Pratt 2012b for further details). The conferences included a Women's Forum, at which representatives of the different political organizations on the conference organizing committee spoke. Rather than highlighting issues of gender inequality or calling for greater women's rights, almost all women speakers at the Cairo conferences erased gender differences as a source of subordination and instead valorized these differences as a source of agency in resisting imperialism, Zionism, dictatorship, and neoliberalism (Pratt 2012b). Very few women's rights advocates participated in the Cairo conferences, and those who did were mainly former leftist political activists.

Despite the lack of a clearly articulated gender agenda, gender was an important dimension structuring these movements and their dynamics. This is not only because women were part of these movements but also because the visible presence of women in protests openly opposing dominant structures of geopolitical power also directly challenged dominant norms of female respectability. Yet movement dynamics also tended to reinscribe female respectability norms. In Egypt, the involvement of predominantly middle-class women (university lecturers, journalists, lawyers, and doctors, among others) in Kefaya demonstrations was encouraged in order to signal the respectability of these movements, thereby subverting regime attempts to label them as "terrorists" and "crazed thugs" (Amar 2011: 308–9). However, in turn, the regime weaponized female respectability against the movement by deploying plainclothes policemen and regime-hired thugs to assault, molest, and grope female protesters and journalists, as part of a strategy for repressing anti-regime demonstrations during the referendum on a constitutional amendment in 2005 (Amar 2011: 309; HRW 2005). The regime's use of sexual violence in this way, in public and broad daylight, was particularly shocking and provoked an outcry among many Egyptians as well as internationally. Yet protests against the sexual assault of women often framed women protesters as repositories of collective morality, rather than rights-bearing citizens. For example, one banner read, 'Violating the dignity of women is like violating that of our country' (BBC 2005). In our interview, Rabab El-Mahdi related her frustrations over an ongoing struggle within Kefaya over "the idea of the female body as an extension of the male 'honor' [which] was used both by the state and Kefaya [...] and this drove me absolutely crazy in the sense that I was fighting on both [fronts]."

Female bodies were also weaponized in the Cedar Revolution in ways that reinscribed female respectability norms as well as racialized notions of Lebanese citizenship. Women, particularly young, cosmopolitan-looking women (read: emancipated and progressive) were highly visible in Western media coverage of the protests (for example, see the covers of the *Economist, Newsweek,* and the *Weekly Standard* in March 2005). The media focus on these young and stylish women functioned to signify the progressive and cosmopolitan character of the anti-Syria protests. The progressiveness of the protests was implicitly constructed in opposition to a more "backward" other—that is, Syria and its Lebanese Shi'a allies—with some of the slogans being explicitly sectarian (Haugbolle 2010: 214–16). Indeed, several women that I interviewed, despite being critical of the Syrian occupation, stated that they did not participate in the anti-Syria demonstrations because of the racist and sectarian slogans that were raised. Simultaneously, women protesters were instructed not to camp out in Martyrs' Square, unlike their male counterparts, "after fierce rumors were spread by the pro-Syrian Lebanese forces that meant to tarnish the image of this intifada and shake its popular support," as Mirna Shidrawi explained to me.

Important gender dynamics were also present in workers' strikes and protests. In 2006–2008, Egyptian workers' protests were remarkable for the role that women played in organizing and leading them. In many cases, women camped out or slept inside their factories as part of worker occupations and strikes (Alexander and Kubaisy 2008; Duboc 2013). A famous slogan attributed to the Mahalla strikes was "Where are the men? Here are the women!" aimed at shaming men into joining the strikes (Duboc 2013). In Jordan too, women were visible in workers' protests. Women played an organizing role in the day-waged workers' movement and even organized an overnight sit-in outside the Royal Court (Ababneh 2016). As Sara Ababneh notes, it is surprising that so many women from "conservative backgrounds" participated in the movement (Ababneh 2016).

In Egypt, women were both praised for their roles in the strikes and discredited as "promiscuous" for spending the night with male colleagues in factory sit-ins (Duboc 2013: 46). Jordanian women also faced criticisms for their involvement in strikes and protests. Adma Al-Zuriekat, a teacher and leftist political activist from Karak (approximately 130 kilometers south of Amman), was active in the struggle by Jordanian teachers for recognition of an independent union and better pay and conditions. Adma succeeded in being the only woman elected to the National Committee for Reviving the Teachers' Association, representing teachers' grievances to the government in 2010. She told me about the various pressures she faced because of her involvement, some of which targeted her specifically as a woman: "A lot of people started to talk to my husband saying: 'She's a woman. What is she doing? [...] This is not acceptable. Why is she the only woman doing this? Are there no men left? Why does she go out and leave her house and daughters? Go help your girls study; that is better. Cook for your husband.'"

In all the cases above, the notion of female respectability was weaponized both to legitimize protests and to undermine them, obliging women to renegotiate gender norms in order to secure their participation in these movements. Women deployed different approaches in this regard. For example, in the case of Egyptian workers' strikes and the Jordanian day-wage labor movement, women were careful to frame their activism as *with* rather than *against* gendered hierarchies. Marie Duboc highlights how women workers underlined male leadership of strikes while emphasizing solidarity across gender lines in their struggle for justice in the workplace (Duboc 2013). Similarly, in Jordan, Sara Ababneh argues that women's participation was facilitated by the personal relationships built by the movement's founder, Muhammad Sneid, with the husbands, fathers, and brothers of the women participants (2016). Another important strategy was the framing of the movement's goals as apolitical and limited only to demanding economic rights and a decent standard of living (Ababneh 2016). Adma Al-Zuriekat also highlighted the significance of depoliticizing the movement to ensure women's participation: "The idea of union work was hard for women to understand because the union was linked to politics, and women fear politics. [. . .] When [. . .] did the female teachers' sector move? When there was an economic demand. When there was a demand for increased wages. Women [. . .] felt that it was important for their homes and children so they moved. It was not [for] the idea of the union." In both the Egyptian and Jordanian cases, women participants in socioeconomic struggles resolved tensions surrounding their inclusion in protest movements by framing their participation as an extension of their "private" identities as mothers and wives in the service of their families; in other words, *resignifying* rather than *resisting* dominant norms of female respectability.

Women in the Kefaya movement attempted to resist the female respectability frame through which assaults on female protesters were constructed. They released a statement that condemned the regime's use of sexual violence, linking it to more widespread state violence against Egyptian citizens (anonymous statement 2005). Several rallies were held to protest what had happened, including a well-attended one held under the slogan, *"al-sharia lina"* ("the street is ours"). An informal group called Women for Democracy came together, which attempted to link regime violence and authoritarianism to the issue of violence against women; however, it only met for a few months before dissolving (El-Mahdi 2010: 385–86). In an article, activist and academic Rabab El-Mahdi argues that the group was unable to transcend divisions between those seeking to embed women's rights within a universalist discourse and those seeking to embed it within a "culturally" relevant discourse, which tended to mirror the division between secular and Islamist women activists (see the next chapter for a further discussion of this divide), as well as the division between NGO versus political activists (El-Mahdi 2010: 386–93). These divisions are explored further in the next chapter.

CONCLUSION

Narratives reveal the contradictory and heterogeneous ways in which women's activism is positioned in relation to post–Cold War hegemonic power structures, which cannot be reduced to either resistance or compliance. For the most part, NGOs tend to work *in tandem with* rather than directly challenging structures of neoliberalism, imperialism, and regime authority, while raising gender-specific demands and issues. Yet not all NGOs are the same. This chapter challenged homogenizing accounts of NGOs, highlighting the crucial distinctions between them as a result of the differences among women NGO activists in ideological-political backgrounds and generation. In contrast to many NGOs, those organizations created by former political activists have sought to resist and transform hegemonic power relations at multiple scales, while simultaneously being disciplined by neoliberal processes of NGO-ization. Hence, the chapter argues that resistance and compliance are often partial and circumscribed when considered in relation to different scales of hegemonic power.

Meanwhile, for the most part, protest movements have directly challenged neoliberalism, US hegemony, and authoritarianism. However, the geopolitical effects of different protest movements are also mediated by their specific geopolitical context. Whereas in Egypt and Jordan, protest movements emerged in resistance to the political-economic and geostrategic dimensions of US hegemony, the relationship between protest movements and post–Cold War hegemonic power was more complex in Lebanon, where the objectives of anti-Syrian protests converged with US ambitions to overthrow the Syrian regime, deemed part of the "axis of evil," and remake the Middle East in the post-2003 period. While these protest movements did not put forward any gender-specific demands, there were significant gendered dimensions to the dynamics of these movements. Women were highly visible, playing an important leadership role, thereby, transgressing norms of female respectability. This was weaponized both to legitimize and delegitimize these movements, leading to a reinscription, rather than disruption, of the modernity-modesty boundary that has historically structured women's involvement in political and social movements.

The embodied experiences of women activists suggest the somewhat contradictory reworkings of gender in relation to the post–Cold War international order and political economy. While during the Cold War period, women's rights and radical gender performances were articulated with anti-imperialism and postcolonial ambitions for development and sovereignty (what Vijay Prashad (2007) terms the "Third World Project"), by contrast, in the post–Cold War period, movements resisting imperialism and neoliberalism marginalized or eschewed women's rights and reinscribed female respectability norms. The next chapter investigates further the post–Cold War international women's rights discourse and its relationship to geopolitical order.

FIVE

Women's Rights as Geopolitical Discourse

THE STRUGGLE OVER GEOGRAPHY IN
THE POST–COLD WAR PERIOD

Personally, when I was called upon to be a member in the preparation team for the Beijing conference, I wasn't interested in
women's rights issues [. . .]. But after the committee [. . .] was
assembled, [. . .] I realized that there wasn't any information
about women's right in Lebanon. If you look at the situation of
women in Lebanon, you'd say that Lebanese women have all their
rights, but when I was working on the report I discovered that
not only do women not have a role in political decision-making,
but not even in any decision-making processes. It was then that
I saw that fighting for women's rights should be a priority. So,
I started writing about women's rights issues and later became
an expert on the subject with the UNDP. [. . .] That is why the
Beijing conference was so important. It changed the priorities of
women and gave political participation special importance, as a
means to change the situation of women in Lebanon.

FAHIMA CHARAFEDDINE
*on preparing for the 1995 UN Women's Conference in Beijing as a
representative of the Cultural Council of South Lebanon*

[Prior to 1990,] all our direction in this organization was for economic empowerment, which means that we provide vocational
training for poor women. [. . .] We used to move from one village
to another for illiteracy classes, and for the vocational training,
but after 1990 we started to speak about [. . .] exposing women
to public life and to politics, and started to talk about a quota,
and we started to talk about international conventions, to apply
them in Jordan, so [there was a] whole shift, a redirection of the
organization, and now [. . .] after twenty years [. . .] our organization, we went as far as to monitor governments, whether they
employ the international conventions that they ratify or not; so
we moved a very big step forward.

LEILA NAFFA HAMARNEH
*of the Arab Women Organization on the changes
after the Cold War*

AS PREVIOUS CHAPTERS HAVE HIGHLIGHTED, from the 1980s onward, as a result of geopolitical transformations at the national and international levels, women activists began to promote gender-specific agendas, including legal reforms to women's rights. This chapter explores further the relationship between women's rights and geopolitical reordering in the post–Cold War period. Specifically, it explores the ways in which women's rights are constitutive of post–Cold War order. Existing literature generally highlights the emergence of a new consensus around international women's rights norms following the fall of the Soviet Union, and investigates the role of women's rights organizations in the global diffusion of these norms, the degree of commitment by governments to an international gender equality regime, and contestations over women's rights between conservative and liberal actors in the international system. By contrast, a postcolonial feminist literature is critical of the ways in which international women's rights norms reproduce racialized global hierarchies through the construction of the victimized "Third World woman."

To further unpack these dichotomous theorizings of international women's rights norms in the post–Cold War period, I use Gearoid Ó Tuathail's concept of "geo-power" (1996b)—that is, the writing of global space—to understand the construction of international women's rights norms as a geopolitical discourse that is integral to what Edward Said termed "the struggle over geography" (1993: 7). Building on Said, Ó Tuathail describes, "the struggle over geography" as "a conflict between competing images and imaginings, a contest of power and resistance that involves not only struggles to represent the materiality of physical geographic objects and boundaries but also the equally powerful and, in a different manner, the equally material force of discursive borders between an idealized Self and a demonized Other, between 'us' and 'them' [. . .] between different ways of envisioning the world" (Ó Tuathail 1996b: 14–15).

Viewing women's rights norms as an important site of struggle over geography, this chapter explores how women's rights activists, their respective regimes, and their Islamist detractors adopt, adapt, and resist international women's rights norms in each of Egypt, Jordan, and Lebanon, and, more significantly, highlights the implications of this at various geopolitical scales. The chapter begins by discussing the emergence of an international women's rights discourse and its relationship to the emergence of a US-dominated global order in the post–Cold War period. Next, I examine how the Egyptian, Jordanian, and Lebanese regimes have taken up gender equality norms. While the failure of Arab states to fully adopt global gender norms, by placing reservations on some articles of CEDAW, is often discussed, less attention has been paid to the ways in which regimes have actually deployed women's rights norms to shore up their authority at the state level, in a context in which the postindependence social pact is being dismantled. The chapter then discusses the ways in which secular-oriented women activists have adopted international women's rights norms as a means of transforming gender relations within their respective national contexts. This section focuses on the process of "vernacularization" (the adaption of international norms to local contexts), highlighting the pragmatism of this approach but also its performative effects in terms of reiterating the inner/outer binary that underpins the gendered hierarchies of the postcolonial state. The final section discusses Islamist opposition to international women's rights norms. Overall, the chapter highlights how, in practice, there is much convergence between Islamists, secular women's rights activists, and their respective regimes in terms of how women's rights are deployed to construct the "discursive borders between an idealized Self and a demonized Other, between 'us' and 'them' [. . .] between different ways of envisioning the world" (Ó Tuathail 1996b: 15).

INTERNATIONAL WOMEN'S RIGHTS DISCOURSE IN THE POST–COLD WAR ERA

Feminist international relations scholars have generally attributed the growing awareness of international women's rights conventions and increased attention to gender issues in the post–Cold War period to the growth in transnational women's activism and networks (Bunch 1990; Chen 1995; Keck and Sikkink 1998; Moghadam 2005; True and Mintrom 2001; Zwingel 2016). The conclusion of the Cold War has been viewed as positive for the advancement of women's rights in that it ended the ideological divisions that had prevented the emergence of a unified position among women activists globally (Chen 1995). A series of international conferences organized by the UN throughout the 1990s, beginning with the UN Conference on Environment and Development, in Rio in 1992, and ending with the UN Women's Conference, in Beijing in 1995, were characterized by increased bridge-building among women activists from different parts of the world and increased cooperation between governments and NGOs (Chen 1995).

The post–Cold War consensus over women's rights stands in contrast to the Cold War period, throughout which, the US and Soviet Union competed with one another to dominate the international women's rights agenda. The US promoted a "depoliticized" agenda that focused on women's legal equality. Meanwhile, the Soviet Union's discourse, which linked the woman question to problems of capitalism, colonialism, war, and imperialism, resonated with many women activists in the Global South (Ghodsee 2010: 6; Prashad 2007: 51–61), including with women activists in Egypt, Jordan, and Lebanon.[1] Women's conferences during this period witnessed sharp divisions between East and West and also between the Global South (or "Third World") and the United States and its allies, particularly with regard to supporting Palestinian women and opposing Zionism (Chen 1995; Ghodsee 2010; Moghadam 2005: 85). Indeed, in a 2007 interview, Emily Naffa recounted how she faced efforts at the 1985 Nairobi women's conference to prevent her from speaking out about Israeli violence committed against Palestinian women.

While many have celebrated the increased cooperation and bridge building of the post–Cold War period, postcolonial feminists in particular have been critical of the ways in which this supposed global consensus over women's rights masks differences among women and works in tandem with dominant global structures and hierarchies. Gayatri Spivak (1996) criticized the Beijing conference and other UN conferences as "global theatre" in support of the interests of the United States and global capitalism, marginalizing the exploitation of poor women and their struggles against it. Meanwhile, Diane Otto (1996) has argued that the prevailing use of gender equality language in the 1995 UN Women's conference affirmed the status quo by calling only for the extension of women's rights within the existing structures, thereby marginalizing the possibilities for more radical sociopolitical transformations. Under the administration of Bill Clinton, US support for women's rights was announced alongside promoting democracy and free markets and framed in terms of advancing US strategic interests (Garner 2013). After 9/11, George W. Bush made women's empowerment, alongside the spread of democracy and free markets, a key pillar in the "war on terror" (Salime 2010) and used the language of women's rights to justify military interventions and occupation in Afghanistan and Iraq (Abu-Lughod 2013; Al-Ali and Pratt 2009b; Pratt 2013c).

Yet the notion that women's rights are a neocolonial imposition was strongly opposed by the secular women activists that I interviewed, many of whom view such criticism as a wholesale attempt to deny women's rights (see also,

Abu-Odeh 2015). For example, when I asked Farida El-Nakkash about the association of women's liberation with the US-led occupations of Afghanistan and Iraq, she stated, "I make a distinction between imperialism and American and European civilization. American and European civilization has many positive values: freedom, equality, fraternity, justice, human dignity, and respect for women's rights. These have become universal values that should not be associated with imperialism. Imperialism is a process of political, economic, and social exploitation. Its connection to women's rights was accidental. We must not—and this is my personal opinion—connect the two, because the concept of women's rights is universal." How can we get beyond this apparent disconnect between postcolonial feminist scholars, many of whom are based in institutions in the Global North, and feminists/women's rights activists on the ground in the Global South/Arab world? One way is to view international women's rights not merely as a set of norms and practices that impact upon gender relations but, as suggested above, as a geopolitical discourse with differential and contradictory effects at different scales, from the interpersonal to the global. Therefore, the view of international women's rights largely depends on where one is positioned as well as how one views sociopolitical transformation. The rest of the chapter will focus on the geopolitical effects of international women's rights and the ways in which they have been adopted, adapted, and resisted in each of Egypt, Jordan, and Lebanon. It will argue that struggles over women's rights have been constituted by and are constitutive of geopolitical struggles in the post–Cold War period.

STATE FEMINISM IN THE POST–COLD WAR PERIOD: MAINSTREAMING GENDER INTO NEOLIBERAL AUTHORITARIANISM

Over the past few decades, almost all Arab regimes have signaled some form of commitment to international women's rights norms. This section argues that compliance with the "international gender equality regime" (Kardam 2004) has sought to buttress regime authority in a context of increasingly unpopular domestic policies. As the previous chapter demonstrated, neoliberal restructuring, increasing corruption, and authoritarianism, in addition to US foreign policies in the wider Arab region, provoked popular struggles and opposition movements against incumbent regimes in the run-up to the 2011 uprisings.

Regimes have signaled their compliance with international women's rights norms primarily by signing the Convention on the Elimination of all forms of Discrimination against Women (CEDAW). All Arab states except Sudan have ratified CEDAW. Of the countries studied here, Egypt was the first Arab state to do so, in 1981, with Jordan ratifying in 1992 and Lebanon in 1997. However, all three states (as well as other Arab governments) have made exceptions to those CEDAW articles relating to equality in marriage, divorce, and nationality, on the basis of safeguarding national "culture" and "traditions," arguing that equality in these matters would contradict personal status laws, which are based on religion (Mayer 1997).

In addition, regimes have demonstrated a commitment to gender mainstreaming through the establishment of National Women's Machineries (NWMs), first advocated by the UN's International Women's Conference in 1975 and then emphasized in the 1995 Beijing Platform for Action, according to which, "A national machinery for the advancement of women is the central policy-coordinating unit inside government. Its main task is to support government-wide mainstreaming of a gender-equality perspective in all policy areas" (UN Fourth World Conference on Women, 1995). NWMs are generally considered important mechanisms for the institutionalization of gender equality norms within government (Khafagy 2012, Rai 2003b). In the Arab world, the First Lady or female royalty tends to head up these units. External encouragement (rather than internal demand) typically initiates their establishment, and they are buttressed with financial support from UN agencies and other foreign donors. Jordan established the Jordanian National Commission for Women (JNCW) in 1992 as a semi-governmental entity under the leadership of Princess Basma bint Talal (the aunt of current King Abdallah II), in preparation for the Beijing conference. Lebanon established the National Commission for Lebanese Women (NCLW) in 1996 in response to the Beijing conference recommendations, and it is always headed by the wife of the Lebanese president, with the prime minister's and speaker of parliament's wives serving as the organization's vice presidents (thereby reflecting Lebanon's institutionalized confessional balance). In 2000, the Egyptian National Council for Women (NCW) was established under the leadership of former First Lady Suzanne Mubarak, reporting directly to the president.[2] In addition to National Women's Machineries, First Ladies and female royalty have played an increasingly public role since the early 2000s supporting women's rights issues (as discussed further below).

As they are headed by First Ladies or female royalty, NWMs have a national platform to highlight issues of women's rights and participation that would not necessarily be available to nongovernmental organizations. In Egypt, the successful passage, in 2000, of the *khulaʿ* law (i.e., amendments to the personal status laws allowing women to seek a divorce on condition of relinquishing their financial rights in marriage), after several years of campaigning by women activists and despite resistance from parliamentarians, was due in large part to the role of Suzanne Mubarak. Her support was also considered crucial to the introduction of several other reforms introduced after 2000: the creation of a new family courts system and a family security fund to collect alimony payments from husbands, the granting of the right for Egyptian women to pass their nationality to their children, raising the age of child custody for mothers to fifteen, raising the minimum age of marriage to eighteen, criminalizing FGM, and the introduction of a gender quota in parliament and a law to combat human trafficking (National Council for Women 2015). However, after 2011, Suzanne Mubarak's strong association with women's rights backfired, as these laws were attacked as part of dismantling the former regime.

Since the 1990s, there has also been an increased focus on gender issues and women's rights in Jordan. The JNCW was not necessarily the initiator of women's rights reforms, but it has played a role in attempting to coordinate between women NGO activists and government in this regard (Al-Atiyat 2012: 146–49, 159–60; Brand 1998). Similarly, other members of the royal family have played a prominent role in publicly raising and supporting the expansion of women's rights. In 2000, the royal family helped to break a significant social taboo by supporting a campaign for the cancellation of the so-called honor crimes article in the penal code (Article 340), but parliament successfully resisted this move.[3] In 2002, Queen Rania, during the Arab Women's Summit in Amman, announced a raft of temporary laws that included increasing the minimum age of marriage to eighteen, granting women the right of *khulaʿ* divorce, forcing a judge to inform a wife if her husband takes a second wife, permitting women to pass on her nationality to her children, granting a woman's right to obtain a passport without permission from a male relative, and an amendment to Article 340, dropping the impunity clause for so-called honor crimes (although parliament approved none of these).[4] In 2003, a quota for women in parliament was introduced and, in 2007, this was extended to municipalities; in 2007, the government published CEDAW in the Official Gazette and established a family shelter for victims of domestic abuse; in 2008, the law was amended to improve the ways in which the police, courts, and medical services deal with domestic violence cases; and in 2009, parliament passed a law outlawing human trafficking. In 2014, the government went some way to meet women activists' demands with regard to the rights of children whose mothers are married to foreigners by granting special provisions for the children (see chapter 6 for further discussion); and, in 2017, parliament canceled a legal provision that had allowed rapists to marry their victims to avoid prosecution.[5] In Lebanon, political crises and sectarian competition have prevented any substantial progress in women's rights, and the NCLW has focused mainly on CEDAW reporting and supporting women's political participation. Nevertheless, the government enacted a Family Violence Law in 2014 (see chapter 6 for further discussion) and, in 2017, also canceled the legal provision allowing rapists to marry their victims.

State compliance with international women's rights norms is generally viewed as a positive step for women's status and is understood to be the result of states' participation in an international gender-equality regime alongside pressure from local women activists (Kardam 2004; Zwingel 2012: 117). In other words, state adoption of women's rights norms is primarily understood through a liberal framework. Yet state compliance with international women's rights norms may produce other effects. For example, Frances Hasso argues that the expansion of women's rights, particularly in the realm of personal status issues, is underpinned and shaped by a logic of governmentality that seeks to "reconstitute norms of behavior" and expand state power over the most intimate of aspects of life (2010: 168). Meanwhile, Dana Olwan (forthcoming) highlights the ways the state may appropriate the expansion of women's rights for its own purposes at the expense of the most marginalized victims of rights violations. Here, I am concerned with the ways in which the women's rights discourse contributes to the (re)production of geopolitical power at multiple scales, from the personal to the international.

On the one hand, state compliance with the international gender-equality regime projects a "modern" image to the international community (Merry 2003: 962) and particularly to Western allies. On the other hand, state reservations on particular CEDAW articles in the name of "culture" and "religion" are performative of national/cultural difference, and constitutive of the so-called inner sphere of national sovereignty (Chatterjee 1993). This apparently contradictory attitude toward women's rights can be seen as continuous with a longer history of state feminism in Egypt, Jordan, and Lebanon, which has endorsed gender equality in the public sphere while protecting gender inequality in the private sphere, thereby reproducing the inner/outer boundary that underpins regime authority and constructs gendered hierarchies. However, while state feminism was originally rooted in state-led development projects and populist social contracts that characterized the early years of postindependence state building, state feminism in the post–Cold War period is embedded in projects of neoliberal restructuring and the dismantling of the postindependence social pact, alongside growing authoritarianism and corruption.

Against this backdrop, regime commitment to international women's rights and, in particular, the prominent role of First Ladies and female royalty in this regard, may be seen as a form of "genderwashing."[6] The term *genderwashing*, like *greenwashing* and *pinkwashing*, is derived from the term *whitewashing*—that is, efforts to hide from public view certain facts that would reflect poorly on an organization, group, or individual. These terms are often used to criticize "cause marketing" by large corporations. For example, *pinkwashing* or *greenwashing* are terms that refer to the ways in which corporations position themselves as leaders in the battle against breast cancer or environmental degradation, respectively, while simultaneously engaging in practices that contribute to these same social problems (Beder 2002; Lubitow and Davis 2011). In this way, "cause marketing" obscures the structural bases of environmental problems or the environmental sources of health problems and co-opts or diverts social activism away from addressing these core issues (Lubitow and Davis 2011). Cause marketing is also a form of reputation management that can offset negative perceptions of a company's involvement in human rights violations or other negative practices (Beder 2002). States also engage in similar kinds of whitewashing activities. Much attention has been drawn to the Israeli government's pinkwashing: its marketing of Israel to Western markets as a "gay-friendly" holiday destination as "a deliberate strategy to conceal the continuing violations of Palestinians' human rights behind an image of modernity signified by Israeli gay life" (Schulman 2011). This is in a context in which, as Jasbir Puar has argued, acceptance of gay rights has become "a barometer by which the right to and capacity for national sovereignty is evaluated" (2013: 336; also 2007, 2011). The use of gay rights as a marker of modernity and a measure of the right to national sovereignty is similar to the ways in which the situation of women in the Middle East has historically been used, both by colonial powers and anticolonial movements, as a measure of the right to and capacity for national sovereignty. In this way, genderwashing (like pinkwashing in the case of Israel) is a geopolitical practice.

Hence, I use the term *genderwashing* to refer to a regime's self-representation as committed to women's rights in order to mask negative practices, such as neoliberal restructuring and growing authoritarianism. For example, as mentioned above, Queen Rania announced several improvements to women's legal rights during the Arab Women's Summit in Amman in 2002. However, these reforms were part of a wider package of temporary laws that were introduced in the absence of parliament, which had been suspended in the previous year under the banner of protecting stability and fighting terrorism. Women's rights amendments were also introduced as part of the controversial Jordan First campaign, launched by the King in 2002 to encourage unity among Jordanians and define national priorities. The political opposition criticized the campaign as a ploy to delegitimize political dissent as implicitly treasonous, while promoting neoliberal norms (Schwedler 2012: 263–65).

Simultaneously, the commitment to women's rights signifies that a regime is "modern" and "progressive," particularly vis-à-vis "regressive" Islamist movements. This helps to strengthen alliances with the West in the context of the "war on terror," as well as to garner the support of secular-oriented constituencies at home. As part of the Jordan First campaign, committees were established to examine different issues, including one to study the introduction of a women's quota in parliament. While the quota achieved was far less than activists hoped for, the committee at least responded to a long-standing demand among women activists and signaled the regime's commitment to advancing women's rights (Al-Atiyat 2012; Pietrobelli 2013). The insertion of the gender quota into this campaign functioned to project a positive image of the regime despite the narrowing of civil and political freedoms and growing impoverishment due to neoliberal economic reforms. In effect, by implementing women's rights reforms, regimes appear to respond to pressures to democratize without threatening the political basis of regime power and authoritarianism (Ottaway 2004).

Their promotion of women's rights also attracts important material resources for regimes at the expense of independent women's activism. In all three countries studied here, activists expressed concerns that respective national machineries were siphoning donor funds away from independent civil society organizations. Indeed, NWMs in Egypt, Jordan, and Lebanon have attracted large amounts of funding from major international donors, such as USAID, the EU, UN agencies, and the World Bank (Khattab 2010: 91; Tadros 2010: 231–32; Brand 1998: 140–44). These funds have been augmented since the onset of the "war on terror," with women's empowerment being one of the four pillars funded by the US Middle East Partnership Initiative (MEPI) to combat Islamist extremism in the Middle East after 9/11 (Salime 2010). Hence,

NWMs can be important sources of rent for their respective regimes as well as potential mechanisms for patronage (for the case of Cameroon, see Adams 2007), enabling the cooption of women's organizations and individual women activists into new networks of patron-client relations.

Activists are also critical of the effectiveness of national machineries in advancing gender equality. The approach of NWMs in Egypt, Jordan, and Lebanon is one of working within dominant structures of power, including gender relations, rather than challenging them (Brand 1998: 163–64; Tadros 2010; Khattab 2010). Since NWMs are regime-sanctioned entities, under the leadership of regime-associated figures, they avoid any measures that may overtly challenge the positions of their respective regimes or antagonize religious leaders. For example, they discuss domestic violence without discussing the personal status laws that subordinate women within the private sphere (Khattab 2010: 162–65) or the police violence to which women protesters are subjected (Tadros 2010: 233–34). In this way, they appear to acknowledge feminist goals yet they are involved in a "displacement of feminism as a political movement," to borrow from Angela McRobbie's critique of postfeminism (2004: 258).

The adoption of global gender equality norms by the Egyptian, Jordanian, and Lebanese regimes has had some positive impacts in terms of legislative and policy changes (although it is unclear how these policies have impacted upon different groups of women). However, assessing the adoption of global gender equality norms should not only focus on the implications for gender relations but also the effects at other geopolitical scales. Perhaps the most significant implication has been in relation to the ways in which regimes have adopted and adapted international women's rights norms in ways that signal a commitment to modernity and progress without disturbing the gendered boundaries and hierarchies that underpin regime authority and national sovereignty. In this sense, state commitment to women's rights norms should not be understood within a liberal framework, but rather within a critical geopolitical framework that reveals the role of women's rights in genderwashing authoritarianism, securitization, and neoliberal restructuring in the post–Cold War period.

SECULAR WOMEN'S RIGHTS ACTIVISTS AND INTERNATIONAL WOMEN'S RIGHTS NORMS

As highlighted at the beginning of the chapter, many secular women activists have enthusiastically adopted international women's rights norms. This section looks in more detail at how they have deployed these norms in their respective activities, drawing on the concept of "vernacularization." In particular, it focuses on activism to combat violence against women and reform personal status laws.

Several women activists in Egypt, Jordan, and Lebanon told me that the preparations for the UN International Conference on Population and Development (ICPD) in Cairo in 1994 and the UN Women's Conference in Beijing in 1995 were an important catalyst for working on the issue of violence against women. Prior to this, the issue had been largely considered taboo, and many activists reported expressions of both denial at the extent of the problem and hostility toward addressing it. In 1997, Zoya Rouhana cofounded the first Lebanese organization dedicated to combating violence against women, the Lebanese Council to Resist Violence Against Women (LECORVAW), following her involvement in the Arab Women's Court—a hearing of testimonies from women survivors of domestic violence, held in preparation for the Beijing conference. She told me, "At that time, there was a total resistance, that 'this is not our problem.' [. . .] [An] article was written in a magazine, that accused the writer [of an article about violence against women] of being a Zionist because we were 'destroying the Lebanese society, the image of the Lebanese society.'"

Meanwhile, in Egypt, the New Woman Foundation together with El-Nadeem Center for the Rehabilitation of Victims of Violence and Torture, and the Appropriate Communications Techniques for Development Center (ACT) conducted a study on the prevalence of violence against women in Egypt, the findings of which they presented at the Beijing conference. However, in response, the official Egyptian delegation, headed by former First Lady Suzanne Mubarak, denied any existence of the problem (Al-Ali 2000: 169–71). It was not only the government that refused to address the issue but even some women activists, who believed it to be a diversion away from women's more important economic concerns (Al-Ali 2000: 169–71). Likewise, in Jordan, when the JWU began a hotline and shelter for women survivors of gender-based violence, some of the Union's own members were against it, because, as Nadia Shamroukh told me, "They did not consider them important issues."

While Western feminism has long conceptualized violence against women as a key mechanism in securing male domination over women (Brownmiller 1975; Kelly and Radford 1996), postcolonial feminists have highlighted how "violence against women" has been framed in colonial discourse as a marker of the "barbarism" of colonized peoples and a justification for neocolonial projects of exploitation and dispossession. Historically, colonial authorities criminalized some types of violence, such as *sati* in India and female circumcision in Sudan and Kenya, under the banner of "civilizing the natives" (Spivak 1988; Boddy 2007; Thomas 2000). Despite formal decolonization, such civilizational discourses continue to circulate and serve to justify Western intervention in the Global South, including military intervention, such as in the case of the US-led War on Terror (Abu-Lughod 2013). Western feminists have often been complicit in reproducing this civilizational discourse, framing the issue of violence against women as a marker of the backwardness of the Global South and the "superiority of Western civilization (Kapur 2002: 12; Liddle and Rai 1988; Mohanty 1991), pointing to Islam or indigenous traditions as the main culprit, rather than examining the structural conditions that (re-)produce gender inequalities and violence (Abu Lughod 2013; Al-Ali and Pratt 2009b; Shalhoub-Kevorkian 2007).

In reaction to a neocolonial discourse that deploys the issue of violence against women to culturally denigrate (formally) colonized peoples, Islamist and other conservative nationalist political actors have defended certain forms of violence, such as so-called honor crimes and female genital mutilation/cutting (FGM/FGC). They have framed this violence as religiously sanctioned and/or necessary for the maintenance of the social-moral order and the defense of national values in the face of cultural imperialism (Husseini 2009; Seif El Dawla 1999). Others have not necessarily defended violence against women but have opposed its open discussion, which they view as inviting unwelcome external interference (Seif El-Dawla 1999). In both cases, women activists are criticized for encouraging Western interference by raising the issue of violence against women. The refusal to acknowledge violence against women as a problem operates to protect the "inner sphere" from foreign intervention as part of safeguarding national sovereignty.

Navigating between, on the one hand, Western discourses that characterize violence against women in the Middle East as a marker of backwardness and, on the other hand, local discourses that seek to deny or minimize the problem, or even to justify it in the name of protecting national sovereignty, women's rights activists have sought to legitimize their efforts to eliminate violence against women through what Sally Engle Merry (2006) has termed "vernacularization." Rather than conceptualizing the diffusion of international women's rights norms as a top-down process, from the international to the local, vernacularization highlights how women activists in different contexts appropriate women's rights norms and adapt them to their local contexts in ways that will resonate (Levitt and Merry 2009; Merry 2006). Vernacularization differs between countries, depending on their individual histories and cultures, and even between organizations in the same country, depending upon their respective power bases, networks of supporters, ideological orientation, organizational structure, and external relations (Levitt and Merry 2009: 455–57).

One can identify several different ways in which secular women activists vernacularize the international agenda to combat violence against women. First, they emphasize that violence against women is an actual problem in women's lives and not the construction of a Western or Zionist agenda. For example, Zoya Rouhana told me:

> The life testimonies that we presented in our two or three years of existence, either through TV or newspapers, these were the most effective tool, to prove that this problem exists in our society and unfortunately, we had to have balance between the different cases. I mean, you can't only take Christians and present them because they will think that we are against the Christians, I mean, the same thing happens with the Muslims. [. . .] This is how we started and we grew. [. . .] I think we were able to present the problem of violence against women as a social problem, as a local problem.

Many women activists have also rejected foreign funding as a way of demonstrating that this is a local rather than a foreign issue. The late Marie Assaad, one of the pioneers advocating against the practice of FGM/FGC in Egypt, and founder of the FGM Taskforce, established in the wake of the ICPD, told me, "The funding agency wanted to give us money, and I told them, 'I'm not building an empire. It's a movement and it has to be of the people.'"[7]

A common vernacularization strategy is to draw on religion to argue that violence against women is not religiously permitted or to demonstrate that proposed legislative reforms are in line with Islam and do not violate sharia. For example, in the struggle against FGM/FCM in Egypt, an important strategy of campaigners has been to collect fatwas that state that the practice is not a religious requirement and has no textual basis within Islam (Khafagi 2001; Van Raemdonck 2013). Meanwhile, in Lebanon, ABAAD works with religious leaders as part of its campaigning against violence against women. A (male) counselor at ABAAD, told me:

> Last year, in the fifteen days of activism campaign, we made the 'We Believe' campaign, which engaged leaders of the four main religions. The campaign

focused on violence against women. Previously, at a regional workshop where we discussed religion and gender equality, a common denominator that all religious leaders were against was violence against women, although there is still no agreement over the issue of rape within marriage. We have made a manual for engaging religious leaders. This is very controversial amongst civil society actors. But the worlds of religion and gender equality are not opposite. There is no need to choose. We can combine both. It is good to get the support of religious leaders.

Indeed, increasingly since the end of the Cold War, secular women's rights activists, as well as their respective governments, draw on religion to justify women's rights demands more broadly (Abu Lughod 2013). For example, in Egypt, in the 1990s, several women activists successfully lobbied for a "new marriage contract" that would enable women to stipulate conditions, such as the right to unilateral divorce and the right to work and travel. The idea emerged out of preparations for the ICPD conference. Among the key figures promoting the idea was Hoda Elsadda, cofounder of Women and Memory Forum, who told me, "Our marriage certificate [at the time] did not allow for women to state conditions [. . .] even though we did a lot of historical research and we discovered [. . .] that there were precedents in history about women putting conditions in a marriage contract, and this was allowed, and, you know, marriage in Islam is a civil contract, [. . .] and we thought we can build on that."

Another important campaign in Egypt was to amend the law to allow a woman's right to unilateral divorce, which relied heavily on demonstrating the compatibility of the law with sharia. In particular, the law was presented as a type of *khula*ʿ—that is, a mutual divorce initiated by the wife in return for the wife paying some compensation to the husband (Esposito and DeLong-Bas 2001: 32). Campaigners proposed that a woman should be granted the right to initiate divorce in return for relinquishing her financial rights in marriage. The *khula*ʿ law, which was supported by First Lady Suzanne Mubarak and passed in 2000, despite much opposition in parliament, has been celebrated by many secular women's rights activists as giving women the option to divorce their husbands without having to endure lengthy court proceedings to establish proof of fault before a judge. Despite the permissibility of *khula*ʿ in Islam, it has been criticized by most Islamists, as well as other conservatives, as being against Islam, threatening the family, and undermining the social and moral fabric of the nation. Interestingly, some secular women activists have also criticized the reform as not addressing the needs of poor women, who cannot afford to relinquish their financial rights. In Jordan, a similar law was introduced in the absence of parliament in 2001 (see Warrick 2009: 116–18).

In Lebanon, religious leaders of all sects and confessions have consistently blocked attempts to amend the personal status laws. In 2009, a small group of secular women activists, led by former president of the Lebanese Council of Women and lawyer Iqbal Murad Doughan, thus took a pragmatic approach to legal reform by lobbying the Sunni religious authorities to amend the age of child custody for divorced Sunni women. Under previous laws, women retained custody of boys only until seven years of age and of girls only until nine years of age, after which time they would revert to the father or the father's family. Dima Dabbous Sensing, then a professor of women's studies at the Lebanese American University, was motivated to join the group of women, "to really try to do something about the mothers who are about to lose their daughters and sons when they're divorced." A group of around forty women met with the Islamic Legislative Authority, asking custody to be raised to fourteen years of age for girls and thirteen for boys. The ILA agreed to thirteen for girls and twelve for boys. As Dima Dabbous explained to me:

This [age of custody] is not a Quranic issue. This is just a sexist old way of letting men decide when to give up custody. [. . .] But once you're learned in the Quran and the Sunna, you know that the root of this practice is cultural and not religious, but they hide it behind religious quotes to intimidate you. That's what they do. Now I know this because I educated myself. So, if somebody tells me that in Islam, you have to do it this way, I'll say "really? Where in Islam?" [. . .] And I think you can solve a lot of problems in the Arab world when it comes to women's activism by being educated, by knowing what's religious, what is the result of jurisprudence, and what is truly culture masking as religion.

As Peggy Levitt and Sally Merry have argued, vernacularization presents activists with two particular dilemmas. First, there are "resonance dilemmas," in that rights ideas need to resonate at the local/national level but also must reflect universal principles to be legitimate as human rights. Second, there are "advocacy dilemmas," in that framing rights in ways that are compatible with existing ideas renders them more acceptable but also represents less of a challenge to the status quo (2009: 457–48). The vernacularization of women's rights through reference to religion constitutes a pragmatic approach to dealing with the power of religious authorities and the influence of religious conservatism in society, as well as a strategic way to present the women's rights agenda as indigenous rather than a "Western imposition." Moreover, as illustrated here, it has produced some tangible results.[8] Yet some secular-oriented activists and scholars have opposed using Islam as a reference for women's rights on the grounds that it subjects rights to cultural relativism and reinforces rather than challenges patriarchy (Moghissi 1999; Mojab 2001; Sholkamy 2011; Tadros 2011).[9] There are concerns that Western donors are driving engagement with religion in the fields of development and rights as part of post-9/11 counter-extremism policies, with the effect of sidelining activists working within secular-oriented and universal-rights frameworks and empowering "moderate" religious actors (Sholkamy 2011; Tadros 2011; Youssry 2011).

Beyond debates over the most effective strategies for advancing women's rights, it is also important to highlight the geopolitical effects of framing women's rights, particularly issues pertaining to the "inner sphere," in terms of religion. In this way, secular women's rights activists contribute to reproducing the inner sphere as the repository of "authentic" culture (see also, Al-Ali 2000: 223–27) and, thereby, reproducing the boundary between the inner and outer spheres that underpins rather than dismantles the gendered hierarchies of the nation-state. In turn, the reiteration of the inner/outer boundary contributes toward reproducing national difference and state sovereignty, normalizing the authority of their respective regimes in a context of authoritarianism and neoliberal restructuring. Hence, women activists' vernacularization strategies may reinforce rather than challenge their respective regimes' genderwashing practices.

ISLAMIST RESISTANCE TO
THE POST–COLD WAR ORDER

While the end of the Cold War melted the divisions between East and West and the Global North and the Global South with regard to women's rights agendas, it also ushered in new divisions, which were particularly apparent in intergovernmental women's conferences as well as follow-up events. These differences centered primarily on issues of women's reproductive freedoms and sexual rights, with the Vatican and several Catholic-majority and Muslim-majority countries, in addition to conservative-religious NGOs, opposing what they regarded as efforts to undermine the family, promote homosexuality, and violate cultural and religious specificities (Chappel 2006).

Opposition to international women's rights norms within Arab countries has been led by Islamists and has centered on resistance to the incorporation of CEDAW into local legislation. Islamist women themselves have become highly visible in these campaigns (see also, Pruzan-Jørgensen 2012), in line with the growing visibility of women within the region's Islamist movements (Abdel-Latif 2008; Deeb 2006; Abu Hanieh 2008). Rather than rejecting the notion of women's rights per se, Islamists oppose CEDAW on the basis of cultural specificity. For example, in the words of Islamic Action Front (IAF) Shura Council member and former parliamentarian Hayat Musimi (Jordan):

> There is the problem of international agreements related to women, which, in my opinion and the opinion of the party, is an attempt to impose a social and cultural vision on a different society. I mean, in the end, we are a society that is different from the society that drafted the agreement. That is why the culture and religion of this different society should be taken into account. That is why we reject the CEDAW agreement for many reasons, [. . .] and we consider that in the Jordanian constitution and in Islam, which the constitution is based on, women get their rights but it must be implemented correctly.

Islamist opposition to CEDAW is underpinned by the construction of cultural/national difference between the Arab/Muslim world and the West, which, in turn, depends upon the delineation of an inner sphere, in which women's rights are governed by religion. Hayat went on to explain: "We oppose tampering with religious laws governing women because they are religious. [. . .] As for the civil laws concerning women [. . .], women give as much as men do, so she must receive what men do in civil laws. The social security law, health insurance, and income tax. Women pay for these as much as men do, so she must receive what he does. That is why, in civil laws, we demand equality. In civil laws, we want complete equality but in religious laws, they are the way God intended."

The demarcation of a culturally authentic inner sphere, characterized by gender inequality, versus a secularized outer sphere, characterized by gender equality, is performative of the inside/outside boundary that underpins national difference and state sovereignty, in much the same way that regimes make exceptions to particular CEDAW articles in the name of religion and culture, and many secular women's rights activists frame women's rights in the private sphere with reference to religion, as discussed above. However, despite this convergence between Islamists, women rights activists, and their respective regimes, Islamists refuse CEDAW in its entirety, constructing it as an existential threat to the family and the gender order. As Leila Naffa, head of the Arab Women Organization described to me:

> They have a booklet about CEDAW. On the cover they put the picture like this: a mother, who is not with a scarf and wearing jeans, because they consider that this is the way of Westerners, is turning her face away from her family, [...] so the man [...] is taking responsibility for the children, and the liberated woman is leaving, and they put a crack, which means divorce. It's either that they tell the men that they should divorce women without scarves, or they are telling the ordinary people if you don't put a scarf [...] and if you don't abide by your husband's orders, you will be like this woman; you will crack the family.

Moreover, Islamists not only construct CEDAW as a cultural and social threat, but also frequently attack women's rights activists, often using mosque sermons to denounce them. As Leila Naffa told me: "They [the Islamists] go and educate their women [...] that CEDAW is a nasty thing, it is for lesbians, [...] when they use the term gender they don't put it in its proper context, they say this is for bad women; they use the word *sharamit* ['whores'], you know the ugliest word in Arabic, for women who fight for women's rights, so there is [...] no possibility for working together when it comes to women's issues." Similarly, Dima Tahboub of the IAF argued that there was no prospect for cooperation between Islamist women and secular-oriented women. She views secular women's rights agendas as epistemologically oppositional to Islamic agendas: "You know that as an Islamic movement our platform is governed by Islamic sharia, so I think that what they [secular women's rights activists] are doing is not a matter of a personal choice it's a matter of opposing Islam. This is why there aren't any meeting points. While their agenda is not purely secular, our agenda is purely Islamic; so here it's a matter of principles, [...] not matters of just feminist competition to show who's more powerful or who is stronger."

This oppositional stance between Islamist and secular women activists belies the fact that, in practice, Islamist women activists have adopted methods and programs that are very similar to those of secular women activists. Not only is there some convergence in how Islamist and secular women's rights activists address personal status issues, in addition, as Islah Jad's work on Hamas women (2005), Aitemad Muhanna's work on Ennahda women

(2015b), and Zakia Salime's work on Moroccan women activists (2011) all illustrate, Islamist women have learned from the secular women's movement. I also found evidence of this in Jordan and Egypt. For example, the IAF Women's Sector, according to Dima Tahboub, trains women in leadership skills, such as "courses in public speaking, in dealing with the media, in giving lectures and so on. So, this making a leader out of a woman is one of our political priorities, part of our social priorities." Similarly, following the 25 January 2011 Revolution, an initiative called Daughters of Egypt was founded by Egyptian Muslim Sister Naglaa El Shaker.[10] It was meant to raise political awareness among women, especially "women from less educated backgrounds and poorer areas. We would talk to them about the importance of the political process and explain parliamentary elections." Such projects resemble those organized by secular women's organizations to train women in political participation and leadership. Moreover, despite the IAF rejection of a gender quota for Jordanian parliamentary elections, the IAF women's section lobbied for a quota for internal elections as a temporary measure after only one woman (Dima Tahboub) was elected in previous Shura Council elections. Dima justified this measure using arguments similar to those of secular women activists: "If people are not going to be convinced to elect us for our potential and our work, we need a transitional stage [. . .]; we need to empower women [. . .] if it's the quota, let it be the quota until we reach a stage where people would nominate a woman, and men, specifically, would nominate a woman and would elect her to that post."

Although Islamist women activists propose that their vision of women's rights is culturally appropriate, they also differentiate themselves from what they deem to be "traditional" or "tribal" mentalities. Indeed, as Lila Abu-Lughod has argued, Islamist support for women's rights is rooted in the modernist ideas that emerged in the Middle East toward the end of the nineteenth century, which have equally shaped secular discourses about the "woman question" (Abu-Lughod 1998b). Similarly, Mervat Hatem observes that both Islamist and secular discourses on gender share "a common national history" and both seek "to reconcile cultural nationalism with the pursuit of the universal project of modernity and the role that gender plays in it" (1998: 85–86). For example, Dima Tahboub told me about one of the campaigns of the IAF Women's Section to "empower" women by ensuring that women inherit their share according to Islamic law: "I'm not aware if you know that some women are prevented in the Jordanian society out of customs and traditions from taking their inheritance. Islamically, they should be empowered, and we've taken on this issue to revive people's attention that Islam does not prevent women from taking their share of inheritance, [...] but certain people, let's say in tribal societies, [...] prevent women from taking their inheritance. So, we took on this issue."

The campaign to ensure that women obtain their share of inheritance in line with sharia is, for Dima and other Islamist women, a tool of ("authentic") modernization against "tribal" or "traditional" mentalities that stand in the way of women being able to claim their rights. Such a campaign shares a similar epistemology to secular campaigns for women's rights in that they are predicated upon a binary of modern/traditional, whereby women's rights are deemed modern, while opposition to women's rights is traditional and, therefore, undesirable for society.

Yet, despite the shared foundations and imbrications of religion and secularism in women's activism (see also Hafez 2011b), there remain sharp divisions between Islamist and secular-oriented activists over women's rights. Such conflicts are integral to what Edward Said termed "the struggle over geography" (1993: 7). Islamist opposition to CEDAW and international women's rights norms and their construction of "authentic" women's rights rooted in Islam is a process of boundary making, between the Self and the Other, between "us" and "them." By positioning themselves as protectors of the inner sphere from Western cultural invasion, Islamists construct their political authority vis-à-vis those who support international women's rights norms—namely, their respective regimes as well as secular women's rights activists. This is not a struggle over the nature of women's rights per se, but rather a struggle for political authority and influence within the current geopolitical order.

CONCLUSION

This chapter demonstrates the differential and contradictory effects of the promotion of women's rights norms at different geopolitical scales. The emergence of a post–Cold War international consensus around women's rights norms, particularly manifested at the 1995 Beijing UN Women's Conference, was welcomed by many of my interviewees as positive for women's ability to promote women's rights and improve women's situation within their respective societies. This is particularly salient in a context in which popular struggles have ignored or even eschewed women's rights (as the previous chapter highlighted) and regimes fail to uphold gender equality within the family on the basis of respect for religion. Women activists have successfully adapted international women's rights norms to their local contexts by using religious frameworks to combat violence against women and advocate for reforms to personal status laws. Within liberal frameworks, such a strategy is viewed as a positive way to globally diffuse women's rights norms. Yet, simultaneously, such an approach serves to reproduce the boundary between an inner sphere, governed by culture and religion, versus an outer sphere, in which cultural difference should be erased—a boundary, as this book has argued, that is integral to the naturalization of gender hierarchies rather than their dismantling.

More importantly, the chapter highlights the ways in which the relationship between gender and geopolitics was reformulated in the post–Cold War period. Whereas during the Cold War, specifically during the heyday of the Third World Project and the building of a pan-Arab regional order, modernist notions of women's rights were advocated by radical movements resisting imperialism and calling for social justice, in the post–Cold War period, modernist notions of women's rights have been articulated with projects of empire, securitization, and neoliberal restructuring, and have served to genderwash authoritarianism and imperialism. Meanwhile, anti-imperialist positions have been mainly voiced by Islamists, who condemn international women's rights norms. I argue that international women's rights norms should not be viewed as essentially supportive of imperialism; rather, this relationship is historically contingent upon changes to geopolitical order in the post–Cold War period. As the next chapter reveals, the association of women's rights with imperialism and authoritarianism rendered women activists and women's rights extremely vulnerable in the wake of the Arab uprisings of 2010–11.

SIX

The Struggle over Gender at the Heart
of the Arab Uprisings

AT THE TIME OF WRITING, several books and articles have been written telling the stories of the Arab uprisings.[1] For the most part, these accounts have been gender blind in their analysis of causes, assessment of consequences, and examination of patterns of mobilization and repression (among many others, see Abdelrahman 2015; Achcar 2013; Bayat 2013a, 2013c; Dabashi 2012; Gelvin 2012; Hinnebusch 2015a, 2015b; Korany and El-Mahdi 2013; Lynch 2013; Marfleet 2016; McMahon 2017; Noueihed and Warren 2013; Said 2015). By contrast, feminist scholars have foregrounded the gendered dimensions of these political upheavals, examining not only women's involvement in the uprisings but also the struggles over women's citizenship rights, political representation, and, in particular, their bodies (for example, Abouelnaga 2016; Agosti 2018; Al-Ali 2012, 2014; Allam 2017, El Said, Meari, and Pratt 2015; Elsadda 2011; Hafez 2019; Khalil 2015; Hasso and Salime 2016; Olimat 2013).

This chapter builds on existing feminist scholarship on the Arab uprisings, exploring the significance of gender to the political transformations after 2010 through women activists' own narratives, centering on their embodied experiences. However, the chapter considers these experiences in relation to different geopolitical contexts (Egypt, Jordan, and Lebanon), each with their own specific histories of the relationship between gender and power. In this way, it places gender at the heart of a geopolitical analysis and geopolitics at the heart of a gendered analysis of the Arab uprisings. On the one hand, the post-2010 political upheavals made the gendered boundaries of the inner/outer sphere, underpinned by the binary of modesty/modernity, more fluid and contestable, opening up spaces for men and women to transgress and transform gender norms. On the other hand, rival political actors sought to restabilize gendered boundaries as part of (re-)establishing geopolitical order and asserting their respective claims to political power. The regulation of women's bodies was integral to these efforts, with harmful consequences for women's bodily integrity (Agosti 2018; Al-Ali 2012; El Said et al. 2015; Hasso and Salime 2016; Hafez 2014, 2019). To borrow and adapt a phrase from Cynthia Enloe, gender is, therefore, integral to "the bigger picture" (2005) of political transitions.

Given the extent of popular mobilization and political upheavals, the chapter focuses largely on Egypt. I define the eighteen-day sit-in in Tahrir Square, which led to the ouster of former president Hosni Mubarak, as an *uprising*; while the aftermath of the eighteen days ushered in a revolutionary moment that comprised a battle for power between revolutionary and counterrevolutionary, as well as "post-revolutionary" forces (namely, the Islamists). In Jordan and Lebanon, large protests for sociopolitical change did not develop into wider anti-regime uprisings, and, consequently, these countries did not experience the same level of violent contestation between different political trends as in Egypt. Nevertheless, the general mood of the region's uprisings provoked broader calls for change, particularly in respect to women's rights, while the control over women's bodies has been central to efforts by the Jordanian and Lebanese regimes to maintain their authority and grip on power. We cannot fully understand the geopolitical dynamics of the uprisings, and the processes of revolution and reaction that they unleashed, without paying attention to the ways in which gender norms were deployed, subverted, and transgressed, as well as forcefully policed and reinscribed. The chapter begins by exploring women's shifting subjectivities and modalities of agency after 2010, highlighting the ways in which women's activism unsettled the modesty-modernity boundary, thereby threatening the successful reproduction of the inner and outer spheres, which is crucial to the construction of national difference, state sovereignty, and regime authority. The chapter then proceeds to investigate the centrality of women's rights and bodily integrity to the (re)imagining of the geopolitical order.

THE EIGHTEEN DAYS OF TAHRIR SQUARE

Salma Shukrallah, a leftist political activist, neatly summarized the lead-up to the 25 January 2011 demonstration:

In retrospect, now I can say that there had been a lot of—there was so much networking for like ten years that managed to organize and mobilize on the same day, but at the time I didn't see that it was going to be big. I remember [. . .] I went to a meeting a couple of days earlier. There were representatives from the different groups [. . .], every single group that had been working on any case, basically, were in the meeting. We planned the points of departure. At the time, the [We Are All] Khaled Said [Facebook] page made the call and stated the points of departure. I went and didn't think it was going to be that big. The demonstration I went to wasn't that big. It was an average demonstration. By the time I got to Tahrir, then I realized how big it is. Because it had departed from all the different places, and then converged on Tahrir. This is when we knew it was going to be big. I still thought it will be something like the Iraq [war] demonstrations, but of course this time it was much more powerful because it was actually against the regime. It was the first thing against the Egyptian regime that is that big.

Almost all of the women I interviewed participated in some way in the 25 January uprising. Among other activities, they joined the sit-in in Tahrir; mobilized friends and family to participate; collected food, medicines, and other provisions to distribute to the protesters; and volunteered in field hospitals. These contributions were basically a continuation of Egyptian women's long involvement in civil society and political and social movements, as discussed in previous chapters. Yet what was notable in 2011 were the numbers of women who were mobilized on the streets for the first time. When I asked Dina Wahba what she thought when she heard that there was going to be a demonstration on 25 January 2011, she told me:

I didn't think twice, I knew I was going, although I would never participate in the political process before. That was my first time. [. . .] I wanted to participate in the first protest for Khaled [Said], but I got sick and I couldn't go, and I was really sad that I couldn't go. [. . .] My friend [. . .] was against going to the protest. I remember she asked me why [I was going]. And I couldn't answer, and not because I couldn't find a reason, but because I couldn't list all the reasons! I was speechless. [. . .] I mean it became so horrendous that you can't ask why, and I didn't know exactly why. [. . .] It was everything, and especially after what happened with [. . .] the [bombing of the] Two Saints Church, [. . .] that's it; it was this feeling of sadness and helplessness; that is enough. I remember on that day, I had work, [. . .] so I decided to go after work, and my friends went since the morning, and I told my parents that I was going, and my mum was freaking out, kept calling me the whole day.

Amal Elmohandes did not attend the demonstration on 25 January, although her sister and some of her friends did, and she was not even initially sympathetic to the protests, being more concerned about having to take her father to the hospital:

> Toward the end of the street where we live, [there was] a demonstration, and I was actually quite angry. I was like "What? What the hell are you doing here? I need to take my father to hospital. You're blocking all the streets!" So anyway, we went to hospital and [...] we ended up spending the night at the hospital and of course that was when the curfew was announced and actually, a lot of people were shot and injured. They came into the ER at that hospital. And then a couple of days later, a cousin of mine, [...] he came to visit him and we started to chatting about what was happening and I was telling him it's horrible and its chaotic everywhere and then he started talking to me, explaining to me what was happening. [...] I used to volunteer with, like, charity organizations, but I was never involved in anything political. So when I listened to what he had to say I decided, okay, maybe I should go and check it out for myself. So, I started going to the Square on my own. And then it hit me that what was happening was something amazing, and I started going down ever since, either helping the people who joined the sit-ins there, take them food, write just blogs or notes about what I see. Because a lot of people were attacking what was happening in the Square.

Despite the large numbers of women who participated in the eighteen days, they did not organize *as women*. Indeed, there was hostility in the Square to people organizing as anything but Egyptians, including a ban on individuals speaking in the name of their respective political parties or groups. Tahrir Square was awash with Egyptian flags. People painted their faces in the colors of the Egyptian flag; wore wrist bands, scarves, and caps adorned with the Egyptian flag. The eighteen days of protest in Tahrir Square was not only a movement to unseat a dictator but also a celebration of Egypt.

Mozn Hassan, founder and director of Nazra for Feminist Studies, focused her efforts during the eighteen days with the Front to Defend Egyptian Protesters, an already-existing initiative to monitor violations against protesters. I asked her whether there were opportunities during this time to engage people in discussions about women's rights and feminism. She replied, "No, I was more overwhelmed in the eighteen days, [...] asking myself what will happen after Mubarak will leave and, I don't know, I didn't want to. [...] I saw the gender part and I have been discussing with my friends all of these gender issues, but I didn't have a round table in the Square talking about feminism, no."

Although women did not raise specific demands for women's rights as part of the anti-Mubarak protests, their participation in a political protest movement was necessarily a gendered act in that it transgressed dominant norms that disapproved of women's presence in political protest spaces. Women negotiated their inclusion in the protests in various ways. They resignified socially acceptable private roles as public contributions to the uprising. For example, many women volunteered to bring food, medicine, and other supplies to protesters in Tahrir, as well as caring for the wounded in the field hospitals. Women also supported the protests by blogging, tweeting, and taking photographs of events to share on social media. Many women also openly transgressed norms of female modesty and docility by being on the frontlines of protests, exposed to tear gas and police violence; mobilizing friends, family, and colleagues; leading the chants of slogans; and even, in some cases, camping overnight in the square. Several young women mentioned that they participated without their parents' knowledge or despite their opposition. For the most part, Sally Zohney would return home by the curfew time (8 p.m.). However, one day, she told her mother that she was unable to get home in time and would be sleeping at a "friend's house."

Actually, I slept in a tent in Tahrir. I think my marriage would not be a happier day. I was over the moon, "I am sleeping in Tahrir!" And I feel so bad for people like my brother, who never had that memory, who never lived the experience. [. . .] And I think there were times where there was this "don't ask, don't tell policy" with my parents: they wouldn't ask me where I am directly, I wouldn't tell them where I am, but then they'd just call, "Are you okay? Don't be late. Take care of the curfews. At what time?" Bla bla bla. So, this was how it worked over the eighteen days.

Overwhelmingly, the women that I interviewed remembered Tahrir Square during the eighteen days as a space of freedom, equality, and solidarity. Many told me that it was the first time they felt that their presence in public spaces was valued. Revolutionary Socialist Manar Abdel Sattar echoed the words of many when she told me, "Tahrir Square was nice, the way people dealt with each other, how a woman could smoke on the street and it would be okay and you wouldn't be harassed." These memories of the eighteen days narrated to me at the end of 2013 and beginning of 2014 expressed some of the sense of loss many women felt in the context of deep polarization within the country, ever-increasing political repression, and especially the closing down of public spaces, in which women had battled so hard to maintain their presence (as discussed further below).

In Jordan and Lebanon, protests were smaller but, as in Egypt, women were visible among them. Throughout 2011 and 2012, street protests, sit-ins, and strikes became weekly occurrences in Jordan and can be considered a continuation of the wave of strikes and protests in preceding years. Undoubtedly, the uprisings in other countries gave further momentum to already-existing movements for socioeconomic and political reforms, as well as politicizing a younger generation of men and women, previously unaffiliated with any parties or organizations. For example, Rania Al Jaabari, a writer and a journalist, was already skirting the edges of social movements for political reform prior to 2011 but became more politicized and hopeful of change when she heard that Ben Ali had fled Tunisia.

> I then felt there was something different. I started to read analyses, [whereas] I didn't read analyses before that. [. . .] I had Egyptian friends on Facebook and I started to see the calls for the January 25th revolution. I would say that if the Egyptian revolution came to pass, then this is true. [. . .] So, my friend told the editor-in-chief there would be a demonstration by the Muslim Brotherhood outside a mosque across from the Fourth Circle, and at the same time there would be a demonstration by the leftists in front of the Egyptian embassy. He looked at me and said: "Rania will cover the Egyptian Embassy demonstration from this day until Mubarak is deposed." So, we had this sense, we believed things were going in that direction. I wasn't a good analyst, and perhaps I'm still not a good one, but I got really happy in front of the Egyptian Embassy. I think I did all the coverage in front of the Egyptian embassy [. . .] until Mubarak was deposed, I did the coverage on the day Mubarak was deposed, and I wrote the article in the sense that we've risen.

The Egyptian and Tunisian uprisings gave hopes for change and emboldened people to push the boundaries of political expression. Lina Ejeilat, cofounder and editor of independent e-zine *7iber.com*, which began in 2007, told me that before 2011 they did not have a big audience, but with the outbreak of the Arab uprisings, "you know, it was just so exciting; [we were publishing pieces by] young people talking about what it meant to them or, you know, just what they thought should happen, you know, talking about, criticizing things in Jordan and the army and the intelligence and interference in political life and things like that, you know. And I think the more we published these pieces, then that would attract even more, you know, people who just wanted to get their voice out. So that was a really exciting time."

Dina Batshon, who at the time of our interview was working for community development NGO Ruwwad, was also not previously involved in any organized activism. She joined the demonstrations in solidarity with the Egyptian uprising outside the Egyptian embassy in Amman and then began attending demonstrations on a regular basis:

> Some of your friends would tell you to join or you would find an event on Facebook [. . .] and it would be a different topic each time and according to whether you thought there would be a big number at the demonstration or not, you would go. [. . .] Many of them started downtown, so you would join in these, [. . .] then some of them moved to Fourth Circle.[2] These were a bit smaller numbers but they were a bit more specific about the cause, I think. Each one would have a specific title and would have people chanting about that issue. I also joined these.

In particular, unaffiliated youth were inspired by what had happened in Egypt and used social media to organize an open-ended sit-in on 24 March in Gamal Abdel-Nasser Square, otherwise known as al-Dakhliyeh circle, because of it being the location of the Ministry of the Interior. The aims of the sit-in were for political and economic reforms, as well as an end to state security interference (ICG 2012a: 16). Rania Al Jaabari was among the hundreds who attended the sit-in on 24 March, which she described to me as including a diversity of people: "journalists and participants, young and old, Islamists and leftists, Christians and Muslims":

> In the first hours of [. . .] the sit-in we were chanting slogans against hunger and poverty and we chanted songs shared by all groups of society and by all Arabs. The song I remember everyone sang together was Mawtini."[3] [. . .] There was no slogan for toppling the regime but the youth dreamed about it. They had a dream to expand the movement until it reached that stage but the first slogans were against hunger and poverty. What scared the regime and the intelligence apparatus was that the slogans started to escalate. [. . .] Let's say we were two hundred, we chanted the slogan: "The people want Al-Raggad to step down." Al-Raggad was the head of the intelligence apparatus back then. [. . .] The next day, the sit-in was dispersed. I remember the bitter feeling of injustice I had, [which] stayed with me for a week.

On 25 March, Lina Ejeilat attended in order to cover the sit-in and witnessed the events leading up to the dispersal:

You had this small group of people who were throwing rocks at the protestors and the police was just, like, creating this barrier between the two groups but [. . .] not like arresting people who were throwing rocks. They just said: "we have to be balanced, we can't take sides." [. . .] Anyway, that went on for hours then it actually started getting pretty tense. [. . .] And they [the people throwing rocks] came because somebody told them that there's this group, [. . .] chanting unacceptable slogans about Jordan or against the king or against, you know, the country. And then that gave the police an excuse to kind of step in [. . .] and the wrap at the end of the day was essentially that it was clashes between pro-government and anti-government groups. [. . .] [And] after the protests were dispersed and everything, there were some people literally celebrating on Dakhliyeh circle the fact that they were able to "cleanse" the circle from the "traitors," you know.

As a result of the attacks on the sit-in, one person was killed and many were injured (*Jadaliyya Reports* 2011). In the aftermath, rumors were spread that the protest was organized by Palestinian-Jordanians seeking to take over the country, thereby provoking memories of the war of 1970–71 and stirring up hostility toward the protests among Jordanian-Jordanian nationalists, leading many Palestinian Jordanians to retreat from further protest activities (Christophersen 2013: 56).

At the time of my visit to Jordan in May 2014, protests had become far fewer and were mainly focused in particular sectors, rather than mobilizing a broad movement. Various coalitions and initiatives founded in 2011 to propose specific political reforms, such as, the National Front for Reform, were no longer active. On the political front, several people expressed frustration that the protests had not led to substantial political reforms. Commentators put forward various reasons for this, including divisions within the protest movement in terms of objectives (ICG 2012a) and the regime's ability to manage the protests by providing a semblance of top-down reform, such as dismissing the government, pledging to fight corruption, initiating constitutional reforms, and promising to create jobs, without actually threatening regime security or restructuring the economy (Abu-Rish 2012).

As in Egypt, women did not participate in these protests, strikes, and other forms of public dissent specifically as *women*. None of the demands of the protests included demands for women's rights (although some women attempted to insert their specific demands into protests, as discussed further below). Moreover, except for the Jordanian Women's Union, which participated in protests and calls for reform, and even opened its offices to treat those wounded during the Dakhliyeh sit-in, established women's rights

NGOs were not a visible part of protests or other pro-reform initiatives. Nevertheless, as in Egypt, women's presence in the protests was significant in terms of transgressing dominant gender norms of female respectability.

People in Lebanon also took inspiration from events in Egypt and Tunisia. Bernadette Daou had abandoned activism following her disillusionment with the May 2008 events in Beirut.[4] However, she was reenergized by the uprisings of 2011:

> I was participating in all the demonstrations in front of embassies in support and solidarity with the Tunisian and Egyptian revolutions. So, in the same time, after one of the sit-ins in solidarity with the Egyptians, some groups, amongst them the group that I was a member of, which [later] became the Socialist Forum, organized a meeting to gather activists to work on toppling the Lebanese sectarian regime. [. . .] I went to the second meeting because I heard that there were like two hundred activists that we don't know in the meeting, so I was very excited to know who those people are. So, I saw that there is really mobilization.

Activists organized three large demonstrations, calling for the "fall of the sectarian regime" (Azzi 2011). In contrast to Egypt and Jordan, demands included an issue central to gender relations—that is, the end to sectarian family laws (Azzi 2011), which, as previously discussed, many activists and scholars viewed as a lynchpin of Lebanon's confessional political system. Women's rights and feminist organizations were also involved in mobilizing for the protests (Azzi 2011).

As in Jordan, protests in Lebanon also dissipated, partly because of the failure to address the roots of sectarian divisions within the country (Mikdashi 2013) but mainly because of the increasing political polarization caused by the conflict in neighboring Syria (as discussed in the next chapter). Nevertheless, mobilizations in Jordan and Lebanon illustrated the desires for sociopolitical change, particularly among young people. The uprisings in Tunisia and Egypt gave hope to a new generation of both men and women that it was possible to demand change. Moreover, increasing numbers of women were motivated to speak out on issues that directly affected them as women. A good example of this is the Facebook group, the Uprising of Women in the Arab World, founded in 2011. Lebanese activist Diala Haidar, a cofounder, told me:

> After the start of the Arab spring [. . .], we felt that it is the right moment in history to shed light on all the problems that women are suffering from in

the region, especially that women participated in the revolutions in all the countries, and paid the price just like men, whether being detained or killed or harassed, even raped like what happened in Egypt. [. . .] We asked women to participate by sending us photos holding a banner and stating why they support an uprising of women in the Arab world. And the campaign went viral because there was such a genuine need for a platform to address all the problems that women are facing in the region.

The campaign of the Uprising of Women in the Arab World is one example of how the Arab uprisings opened spaces for women, particularly young women, to articulate their demands for equality, inclusion, and respect. The rest of the chapter highlights new modalities of women's activism and considers their geopolitical implications.

WOMEN'S STRUGGLES FOR POLITICAL INCLUSION AND WOMEN'S RIGHTS IN POST-MUBARAK EGYPT

Despite their high visibility during the eighteen-day uprising, women protesters soon faced serious attempts after Mubarak's departure to exclude them from the political transition and the public sphere more broadly. A committee established by SCAF in February 2011 to revise some articles of the constitution in preparation for elections did not include a single woman (ECWR 2011a). The women's parliamentary quota established in 2010 under Mubarak was canceled. Instead, it was mandated that every electoral list had to contain at least one woman but not necessarily in a winnable seat (IFES 2011). A total of 376 women ran in parliamentary elections in November–December 2011—making up about 24 percent of all candidates and 43 percent of all party lists (ECWR 2012). Most parties placed women lower down their lists so that, in the end, only nine women won seats, and three were appointed by SCAF, representing less than 2 percent of parliamentary seats (EISA 2012). Of the nine women who won seats, five were members of Islamist parties who, in line with their respective parties, supported a conservative gender agenda. Many observers compared the results negatively to the previous Mubarak parliament, where, thanks to the quota, women occupied sixty-five seats or 13 percent of the total, interpreting Egypt's election results as an indication of how women were faring poorly in post-Mubarak Egypt (Coleman 2012; Garcia-Navarro 2012). In addition, with Islamist candidates winning 70 percent of seats, many began to worry that women's rights were seriously in peril. Islamists dominated the Constituent Assembly formed to draft a new constitution. Only six out of one hundred members were women, some of whom withdrew along with other secular-oriented forces in protest of what they regarded as the Islamists' insistence to impose their worldview (for example, see El-Tibi 2012).

Scholarship on women and political transitions generally argues that the strength of the women's movement prior to the transition determines the degree to which women are included in transition institutions and how many of their demands are recognized (Brand 1998; Waylen 1994, 2007). Arguably, after decades of state feminism and NGO-ization, Egypt's women's rights advocates were ill-equipped to adequately mobilize for women's inclusion in the post-Mubarak transition. However, women's exclusion should be understood not only in relation to the balance of forces at that moment, but also as crucial to the efforts of rival political actors to (re)establish political order and assert authority following the toppling of Mubarak's regime.

For its part, SCAF sought to quash the revolutionary movement and return Egypt to what it considered normalcy, violently targeting ongoing protests and singling out women for particularly humiliating forms of violence. On 9 March 2011, SCAF broke up a peaceful sit-in in Tahrir Square, allowing thugs to beat protesters and arresting many, including eighteen women, taking them to the Egyptian Museum, where they were beaten and tortured (Amnesty International 2011a). Of the eighteen women arrested, seventeen were transferred to a women's prison, where they were beaten, tortured, strip-searched in front of male soldiers, and forced to undergo so-called virginity tests (Amnesty International 2011b). The use of sexualized torture was justified in terms of the women's transgression of dominant gender norms. A senior Egyptian general (Abdel Fatah Al-Sisi, who would become Egypt's president in 2014) told CNN, "The girls who were detained were not like your daughter or mine. . . . These were girls who had camped out in tents with male protesters in Tahrir Square" (Amin 2011). In other words, "proper" Egyptian girls do not participate in political protests, which involve mixing with members of the opposite sex. Moreover, the general explained that the virginity tests were necessary to prevent female protesters from accusing the military of rape (Amin 2011), thereby casting female protesters as a threat to Egypt's most important national institution. In this way, the justifications for so-called virginity testing sought to discredit political protests more broadly as threats to Egypt's social and moral order and national security.

On 8 March 2011, another group of women protesters were attacked in Tahrir Square, this time by unknown groups of men. The women were marching in celebration of International Women's Day. Salma Nagy recalled:

> That was a bad day, because we went there, a very small number, and then quite the crowd mobilized in front of us to counter chant what we were saying, to [. . .] attack everything we were saying, to make it seem as if this is all anti-religion what we were saying, what we were asking for. And the turnout was very small. The turnout was disappointing. I tried to persuade a lot of people to come. Many people didn't think that this was the time, and many people didn't think that they wanted to go to a protest on a Tuesday in the middle of the day in Tahrir, [as] there were too many protests already going on. [. . .] And I was there, I went there with my mother,[5] and I had friends there. [. . .] I barely escaped the harassment, it happened in front of me and I was pulled by a friend of mine at the last minute. Yeah, that was a depressing day.

The targeting of the women's day march indicated opposition not only to women protesters but also to demands for women's rights in the post-Mubarak transition. Indeed, a backlash against women's rights began to be expressed by a range of political actors, including Islamists and the nominally secular-liberal Wafd and Nasserist parties, with calls for the repeal of legislation passed under Mubarak: namely, the *khula'* (divorce) law, the right of a mother to custody of her children until the age of fifteen, the criminalization of FGM/FGC, and the minimum age of eighteen for marriage, among others (Elsadda 2011: 86–87). Similar to what happened in Iraq after the fall of Saddam Hussein (Al-Ali and Pratt 2009b), calls for a rollback of women's rights were not only the expression of conservative ideologies but also served to mark a break with the former regime. The body of women's rights laws under attack were those specifically sponsored by the National Council for Women (NCW), under the leadership of Suzanne Mubarak, called Suzanne's Laws by their opponents. More broadly, as discussed in the previous chapters, in the post–Cold War period women's rights had become imbricated in processes of neoliberal restructuring, authoritarian survival, and imperialism. Indeed, as women's rights activist Hoda Elsadda argued in 2011, there was "a prevalent public perception that associates women's rights activists and their activities with the ex-First Lady, Suzanne Mubarak, and her entourage—that is, with corrupt regime politics in collusion with imperialist agendas" (2011: 86).

The conflict over women's rights became clear in relation to the drafting of the 2012 constitution. During the constitution drafting process, women's rights groups lobbied specifically for the inclusion of articles guaranteeing equality and non-discrimination between women and men in all areas (Working Group on Women and the Constitution 2011). Maissan Hassan, from the Women and Memory Forum, participated in the Women and Constitution Study Group and described what happened when they went to meet the women members of the constituent assembly who were representing the Freedom and Justice Party (FJP) (the main Islamist party, affiliated with the Muslim Brotherhood):

> They told us bluntly that they will not include an article on equality between men and women. It will not happen [. . .] because of sharia, but three things [specifically]: interfaith marriage, because Muslim women aren't allowed to marry non-Muslim men; inheritance; and the right to divorce. And they told us that it's not going to happen. So, the reaction was that they knew that we existed, they invited us, and we went there, and it was a decision that we will talk to them and say [what] we believe, but the reaction was, "Lower your expectations; it's not going to happen." [. . .] It was one of the very difficult days because you felt that that's it.

The insistence of the FJP members to reject the inclusion of a gender-equality article on the basis of sharia was not merely a reflection of their Islamist ideology but part of the (geo)political struggle in the post-Mubarak period. By insisting that personal status matters be governed by sharia, the FJP members ensured the reproduction of the "inner sphere" as the cultural essence of the nation, and, in turn, constructed the FJP as the protector or guarantor of this sphere of national sovereignty vis-à-vis their political rivals. In this way, the determining of personal status issues was part of a strategy of building the FJP's authority.

WOMEN'S STRUGGLES FOR POLITICAL INCLUSION AND RIGHTS IN JORDAN AND LEBANON

As in the case of Egypt, women in Jordan were largely excluded from the political reform process that the regime initiated in response to the protest movement. In March 2011, the government formed the National Dialogue Committee to propose amendments to the electoral and political parties laws (ICG 2012a: 3). Of the fifty-three members, only four were women, while no women were appointed to a royal committee created to propose amendments to the constitution (al-Maaitah et al 2013: 25). Women's rights groups were disappointed that no women were included in the newly created Independent Electoral Commission, in 2012 (Husseini 2012a) (although former head of the Jordanian National Commission for Women Asma Khader was appointed to the Electoral Commission in 2014).

Women were not only excluded from emerging political institutions but they also faced political resistance to their rights demands. The electoral law for the 2013 elections failed to increase women's representation in parliament, despite calls from women activists for a quota of 30 percent, in line with international recommendations (Husseini 2012a). Similarly, an amended electoral law in March 2016 also failed to meet activists' demands for an increased women's quota (Staton 2016a). As in Egypt, women's rights activists lobbied the constitutional amendments committee for the inclusion of gender equality in relation to the article on nondiscrimination. Leila Naffa, head of the Arab Women Organization told me:

> What happened is that we were very active, we went into the streets and we made our lobbying, we selected a troika from women's movements to try to change Article 6 in the constitution, but we failed; we couldn't do it. [...] And honestly speaking, the people who were formed to change the constitution accepted it, [...] but [...] when it went [...] to the [Royal] Court, it was taken out, and they replaced it with something reactionary; they started to speak about the family. [...] So, we felt that the blow was hitting us in the struggle, and from that point we feel that we are standing still.

The rejection of gender equality in the Jordanian constitution can be seen as part of regime efforts to reestablish political order in the wake of large and ongoing protests demanding political and economic reforms throughout 2011 and 2012. Reflecting on the lack of progress in women's rights after 2011, Asma Khader, then head of the JNCW, stated, "It seems the government is succumbing to the conservatives who want to limit women's role to staying at home" (quoted in Husseini 2013). Khader's statement suggests the way in which gender issues have been part of the regime's appeasement of key constituencies, specifically the Islamists, who constitute the largest political opposition, and the tribes, who constitute a main pillar of support for the regime. As already discussed, the Islamists reject any plans to implement CEDAW, which they view as a threat to religion and Jordanian culture. Meanwhile, tribal leaders reject any measure that would pave the way for granting a woman's right to pass on her nationality to her children and foreign spouse, claiming that such a move would enable the naturalization of

Palestinians and other nationalities, making Jordanian-Jordanians a minority in their own country (as discussed further below).

In Lebanon, protests did not lead to any political reforms; rather, political reforms stalled due to the Syrian conflict, which exacerbated the existing political polarization and paralyzed government (ICG 2015). Iqbal Doughan, director of the Working Women's League, complained to me in 2013 that politicians were using the unstable security and political situation as an excuse not to address women's rights demands, claiming, "now is not the time." This paralysis contributed to postponing a long-awaited law against domestic violence, which had been awaiting parliamentary approval since 2010 (see below for further discussion). In addition, the postponement of a new electoral law also prevented progress in increasing women's representation in parliament, which is among the lowest in the region. In our interview in the autumn of 2013, Nada Anid, cofounder of the NGO Women in Front, established in 2012, told me about their efforts to encourage women to stand in elections and build their capacity. Women in Front was also one of the women's groups concerned with introducing a women's quota in parliament:

> We strongly believe that we need a quota, and we are working with [an expert on electoral law] on how to implement a quota. [. . .] We are working on the basis of a system of proportional representation. We could also call it "temporary measures." But we need a law to put it into practice. There needs to be a national will for it. [. . .] Last year, we approached the parties to ask them if they were putting forward women candidates. However, the problem is that when we speak to them about the quota, they say, "We don't even have an electoral law yet. So how can we discuss the quota?"

Finally, in June 2017, following a postponement of parliamentary elections three times, a new electoral law was agreed, with elections scheduled for May 2018. Disappointingly, the law did not include a women's parliamentary quota (el-Khoury 2017). The rejection of a women's quota in parliament ensures not only that male politicians keep their seats but, more importantly, that each sect maintains its share of political power, making it very difficult for independent candidates, let alone female candidates, to win a seat. As Ferial Abu Hamdan, a community activist and former municipal counselor, explained to me: "In the Chouf area [where Ferial lives], [. . .] we have two seats [for Druze] because [. . .] in Lebanon, [. . .] we have a quota for every sect, so how can we have another quota for women? [. . .] It's very complicated. [. . .] If I wanted to register [to stand as a candidate in the parliamentary elections], I would be instead of Waleed Jumblatt or Marwan Hamadeh?"[6] The low level of women's representation in formal political institutions and the failure of amended constitutions and new legislation to meet the expectations of women activists in the wake of the Arab uprisings was hugely frustrating. The cases of Lebanon and Jordan illustrate how regime efforts to preserve the gender order, despite lobbying by women activists, has served to maintain the political status quo in the face of popular demands for political change. In the case of Jordan, the regime refused to support gender equality to appease the most powerful constituencies demanding political and economic change. In Lebanon, demands for a women's quota have been sacrificed to maintain the sectarian balance of power.

WOMEN'S BODIES AS SITES OF GEOPOLITICAL STRUGGLE IN EGYPT

Within the literature on women and political transitions, there is a tendency to focus on the sphere of formal political institutions, in terms of assessing women's presence or absence within them, the degree to which they represent women's interests and protect women's rights, and whether women are able to influence them (Alvarez 1990; Brand 1998; O'Rourke 2013; Waylen 1994, 2007). This literature tends to ignore the performative effects of women's activism in spaces beyond formal institutions, which are also (geo)politically significant. As discussed in relation to previous periods, women's involvement in protests and other political spaces unsettles the modesty-modernity boundary that has underpinned gendered hierarchies and is constitutive of national difference, thereby threatening the successful reproduction of a "natural state" (Weber 1998: 92) and, in turn, the maintenance of regime authority. Hence, in a context of political transition, women's insistence on challenging dominant gender norms should be considered in terms of its wider geopolitical effects and its relationship to building an alternative geopolitical order.

In Egypt, women were very visible in ongoing protests against the rule of the SCAF between March 2011 and June 2012. These included weekly Friday demonstrations in Tahrir Square through the spring and summer, the Mohammed Mahmoud Street clashes in November, and the cabinet sit-in in December 2011. Women's mass participation in protests, despite high levels of violence perpetrated by the security forces, operated to claim public spaces as legitimate spaces not only for women protesters but also for demands for gender justice, even while formal political institutions were excluding women and women's rights. Indeed, there emerged unprecedented mass women's activism for gender issues outside the established spaces of women's rights NGOs (see also Salime 2012; Muhanna-Matar 2014, which highlight similar trends in Morocco and Tunisia). A key object of women's organizing was that of women's bodily integrity.

The first major women-led protest came about in response to several incidents of violence perpetrated by the military against women participating in anti-SCAF protests in December 2011. In particular, there was widespread outrage after a video of soldiers dragging a woman protester across the street, beating her, and stripping her to her bra, went viral (Associated Press in Cairo 2011). Thousands of women, of different ages and from different walks of life, as well as men, marched in downtown Cairo to condemn SCAF violence against women protesters, under the slogan "Egypt's women are a red line" (Langohr 2011; Shukrallah 2011). Highlighting the significance of the December 2011 protest, Nagwan El Ashwal, who became active through her participation in the uprising, told me, "This is when I saw that women can really lead and that the youth really have new values."

The other significant dimension of the December 2011 women-led protest against military violence was that it occurred in the middle of a brutal crackdown by the military on the ongoing protests in front of the cabinet offices, which resulted in more than ten killed and eight hundred wounded. While clashes between protesters and soldiers were happening in front of the cabinet offices, close to Tahrir, women and men were protesting violence against women. One young woman told me, "The men were telling us not to go to Tahrir because it was too dangerous. I was with a friend [. . .] and she said to me, 'Let's make a human shield.' So, we made a woman-only human shield. All the women held hands and walked together towards Mohammed Mahmoud Street [off Tahrir Square]. When the men saw us, they followed us because they said that they couldn't stand by whilst the women were acting."[7] In this way, women physically inserted their bodies and their antiviolence demands into the middle of the revolutionary movement and its agenda. They actively sustained the public space of Tahrir and its environs as a space of protest but also transformed it into a legitimate space for raising feminist demands, in contrast to the negative experience of the Women's Day march several months previously. While the slogan "Egypt's women are a red line" in resistance to SCAF violence, constructed women protesters as objects of protection, thereby reinscribing norms of female respectability, simultaneously, through their presence in protest spaces, women resignified these hegemonic norms to include their participation in political protests.

The women's demonstrations against SCAF violence were the start of a number of women-led demonstrations not only protesting violence against women, but also promoting women's rights and representation in the constitutional process. In contrast to the previous year, the 2012 International Women's Day march was lively and well attended and presented a list of demands for women's rights to parliament. Activist Sally Zohney, who participated in anti-SCAF protests throughout 2011, also joined the women-led marches: "I remember my first women's march, it was amazing. A crowd full of women who are angry, [. . .] and who are ordinary women, they are not activists."

An important new actor in this regard was Baheya Ya Masr, a movement formed in March 2012 to publicly raise women's rights demands (Baheya Ya Masr n.d.). Baheya Ya Masr introduced a new paradigm for women's organizing, characterized by its open and fluid structures, in contrast with the existing women's rights NGOs. It reflected a growing feminist consciousness that emerged in direct resistance to the threats to women's rights posed by the Islamist-dominated parliament from the end of 2011. Salma Nagy, one of the founders, recalls:

> "The activities of the movement were more [informal] in terms of organizing marches, [. . .] that sort of thing and then at other points we were very much involved in lobbying for candidates in the different committees that were formed, specifically the constitutional committee. [. . .] We created a list of a hundred names of women from all walks of life that could represent women in the committee that was formed in 2012, and then in 2013 [. . .] and basically to get some gender balance in decision-making places [. . .] and also with initiatives that had to do with sexual harassment. [. . .] So it was quite active at the time, mainly in 2012 and early 2013.

Moreover, in contrast to existing women's rights NGOs, the Baheya Ya Masr movement did not frame their demands in terms of international women's rights conventions but rather in relation to the Egyptian context specifically. In this respect, the movement was innovative in its use of Egyptian popular culture and history. Salma Nagy told me, "The movement basically aimed to create awareness about women's rights, and aimed most of all to look at and borrow from the heritage of Egyptian women, and to basically say we're not just starting; there is a long history of very prominent Egyptian women in all fields and it's not that we're redefining the role of women in 2012."

In demonstrations organized by Baheya, protesters held up banners and placards depicting icons of Egyptian popular culture, including renowned singer Um Kulthoum, and famous actors Souad Hosny and Faten Hamama, as well as women from Egypt's history, such as ancient Egyptian queen Nefertiti and Sally Zahran, one of the most famous woman martyrs of the eighteen days (Gulhane and Omar 2013; Sami 2015). As Hala Sami argues, Baheya Ya Masr "has appropriated these metaphors of the nation, thereby clearly locating itself within the nation, yet has re-signified them beyond hegemonic nationalist discourse by representing women as agential in claiming rights and resisting despotism. Moreover, the movement has also imbued these national icons with the legitimacy of the 25 January Revolution" (Sami 2015: 94–95). The insertion of the images of women representing "authentic" Egyptian culture into street protests demanding women's rights functioned simultaneously to legitimize protests as respectable spaces for women and to resignify female respectability as including participation in political protests, thereby subverting Islamist discourses that were criticizing women's participation in protest demonstrations.

Another important space for women's activism that emerged in the post-Mubarak period, in contrast to the period before 2011, was political parties. As discussed in previous chapters, the sphere of politics has been generally viewed as inappropriate for "respectable" women, although women have a long history of joining political parties and movements, particularly during periods of political contestation and geopolitical instability. However, as also discussed, many women who had joined parties abandoned them from the late 1970s onward, partly due to regime repression but also because the parties failed to address women's rights issues. The only political movements in which women's visibility increased after the 1980s were those of the Islamist parties.

The post-Mubarak period experienced a flourishing of political parties and a noticeable increase in the number of women, including young women, not only joining parties but actively participating in all aspects of organizing and decision-making. Moreover, in contrast to previous periods, many of those women who joined parties, particularly leftist and liberal parties, were women's rights activists. Hala Shukrallah, one of the early members of the New Woman study group that later became the New Woman Foundation, became the first woman to head an Egyptian political party when she was elected president of the Dastour Party in early 2014 (she stepped down in 2015). In particular, a significant number of high-profile women's rights activists were concentrated in the Egyptian Social Democratic Party (ESDP), among them, Hoda Elsadda, founder of the Women and Memory Forum, who became vice president of the party, and Nadia Abdel Wahab, a founding member of the New Woman Foundation and, at the time of our interview, member of the party's High Committee, political office, executive office, and the Women's Secretariat. According to Hoda Elsadda, at the time of our interview, women had achieved 30 percent of the leadership positions in the party, which compared very favorably with other parties at the time.

Women in the ESDP actively challenged the existing model of women's involvement in Egyptian political parties, which had previously centered on the women's committees. As Maha El Said, a Cairo University professor who had not been involved in political parties before 2011, discovered, there was a widespread idea that women's committees were supposed to engage in charitable activities: "I was facilitating a workshop for all the different women's committees around the country for the [Egyptian] Social Democratic Party. [. . .] We were trying to have them write an action plan for the year, and activities that they could work on that would promote women, promote their work, and promote the [Egyptian] Social Democratic Party. They were talking about things like 'We can bring women in and teach them how to knit and then they can sell those knittings,' or 'We can have a charity,' whatever." Nadia Abdelwahab also found that she had to directly challenge the idea that women's committees "do charity": "[I told the women at the meeting] that our approach as the Egyptian [Social] Democratic Party must be something completely different; we're supposed to be seeking to change women and make them a part of a democratic movement or a movement for the future, and [. . .] that was the beginning of the change that happened in our approach in the women's committee, as it was called back then."

Women in the ESDP not only worked in the women's committees but were actively involved in shaping the party's program and structures. Dina Wahba, who joined the ESDP because of "the presence of very strong women activists and feminist leaders," told me about the first few months of establishing the party, during which time she was head of the women's committee and found herself battling with the party leadership to include women on all decision-making bodies and to mainstream gender throughout the party program: "I was twenty-four, very new to political life, and I would have huge fights with party leaders, basically older men, very experienced, and I didn't know how I got the courage. I think it was [because it was] the aftermath of the revolution."

Significantly, the post-Mubarak period was not only one of backlash and exclusion for women. The uprising created an environment in which women felt empowered to subvert and resignify existing gender norms of respectability, modesty, and docility through their participation in political protests, protest spaces, and political parties. In this respect, women's activism in the post-Mubarak period has parallels with women's activism in the post-1967 period, during which time women also transgressed dominant gender norms through their participation in political movements and protests. However, in contrast to the post-1967 period, women in post-2011 Egypt successfully inserted women's rights demands into the public and political spaces of the uprising, linking women's rights demands to the broader goals of the revolution, thereby contributing to imagining an alternative geopolitical order.

RE-DISCIPLINING GENDER: SEXUAL VIOLENCE AGAINST WOMEN IN EGYPT

When I asked Mozn Hassan, founder and director of Nazra for Feminist Studies, what had been the most important issue in the post-Mubarak era, she replied, "sexual violence": "I think it's the harshest thing I have ever felt, and it affected me, on different levels. [. . .] It's tough for me personally because [. . .] I felt like 'that's it; if we lose this struggle, we will not exist.' Violence is the thing that [pushed] women out of the public space [. . .] and any policies or regulations or quotas or movements couldn't do a thing."

While violence against women and sexual harassment in Egypt long predate the 2011 revolution and have been taken up by women's rights activists since the 1990s (as discussed previously), violence against women in public spaces, particularly sexualized violence, grew at a shocking rate in the post-Mubarak period. An identifiable pattern of sexual violence began to emerge from June 2012 onward, coinciding with the presidency of Mohammed Morsi, in which an individual woman protester would be surrounded by a large group of men, separating her from her friends, whereupon they would strip her and repeatedly abuse or rape her. The similarity among these attacks, based on testimonies, suggests that they were organized and systematic. One report presented over 250 cases of sexual assault and rape that took place between November 2012 and January 2013 (El-Nadim Center, Nazra, and New Woman Foundation 2013). In the period of the 30 June 2013 protests against Mohammed Morsi, at least ninety-one women were victims of sex attacks (HRW 2013a). The brutality of the attacks was unprecedented, with women being repeatedly beaten, stripped, molested, and penetrated by fingers and even sharp objects.

In 2013, Deniz Kandiyoti wrote that violence against women in post-uprising contexts signaled that "patriarchy-as-usual is no longer fully secure and requires higher levels of coercion." In other words, the levels of violence against women were a direct reaction against the breakdown in previously hegemonic gender norms. If we understand the performativity of female respectability as significant for the building or undermining of geopolitical order, public violence against women may serve to (re)establish not only particular gender norms but also political order and authority in a context of upheaval and instability. While there is no direct evidence that the Muslim Brotherhood was behind the sex attacks, it and other Islamist groups created a permissive environment for sexual violence through their failure to unambiguously condemn it. Instead, they opportunistically blamed the political opposition groups who were organizing the demonstrations for failing "to secure their rallies against acts of rape," and even blamed the women themselves, "who insist on demonstrating with men in unsecure areas" (El-Din 2013). Moreover, the Muslim Brotherhood government rejected a UN Declaration to Eliminate Violence against Women, which included several articles guaranteeing women's rights to bodily and sexual autonomy, arguing that the declaration's content contradicted "Muslim values" and undermined the Egyptian family, to the outrage of Egyptian women activists (Elsadda 2013).

In direct response to the increasing levels of sexual violence against women protesters, and the failure, if not complicity, of the authorities in this regard, hundreds of women and men began to organize from June 2012 onward to directly resist sexual violence against women (Langohr 2013). Initially, activists organized protests in Tahrir and other public spaces, aiming to "break the silence" around the discussion of sexual violence and sexual harassment (Trew 2012), but these were also attacked by unknown assailants. Consequently, several youth-led initiatives emerged to directly intervene to prevent sexual harassment and violence in public spaces. In November 2012, OpAntiSH (Operation Anti-Sexual Harassment) and Tahrir Bodyguards were formed, primarily to intervene to secure protest spaces but also to rescue women and provide medical, psychological, and legal support to victims and document attacks (Langohr 2013). Like other youth initiatives after 2011, anti–sexual harassment groups were based on cross-gender alliances; however, OpAntiSH distinguished itself because women were also part of the rescue teams (Langohr 2013), thereby challenging what Iris Marion Young calls the "logic of masculinist protection" (2003). Meanwhile, Shoft Taharrosh and Basma Imprint Movement worked to prevent sexual harassment and assault in other public spaces while also providing awareness and education on the issue. This mode of direct action was highly innovative in the Egyptian context, constituting a break with previous forms of anti–sexual harassment/violence work, which predominantly took the form of lobbying for relevant state measures, particularly legislative changes (see also Skalli 2014; Tadros 2014).

In addition to organized resistance, women survivors of violence themselves broke the taboo and stigma of the female body as shameful by speaking publicly about their rapes (Abouelnaga 2015: 50). Samira Ibrahim, the woman who brought a court case against the doctor who performed "virginity testing" on women prisoners, was a pioneer in this respect (Seikaly 2013). Others provided testimonies to newspapers and rights organizations and even interviews on primetime TV programs, detailing their experiences and directly resisting their victimization and stigmatization. According to Mozn Hassan, who was heavily involved in the anti–sexual violence movement through her work at Nazra, the TV appearances made an important shift in public awareness of the problem: "What Yassmine [El Baramawy] did and Hania Moheeb, it turned things [around]. We had been talking from November [2012] to January [2013] [about sexual violence against women protesters], but when Yassmine and Hania came out publicly, it affected [things so] much."

By speaking openly about their experiences, women challenged conservative nationalist and Islamist discourses that reduce women's bodies to repositories of collective honor and shame, blaming the victim for her violation (Abouelnaga 2015: 39). It was not the first time women had spoken publicly of sexual assaults or campaigned to end sexual violence.[8] Nevertheless, this was the first time a grassroots movement developed in which demands for women's bodily integrity were central. Hind Ahmad Zaki and Dalia Abdel Hamid, women human rights defenders and researchers, argue that these anti–sexual harassment groups constituted "an entry point for feminist consciousness of thousands of women and men" and "also raised the issue of feminist values of solidarity" (Ahmad Zaki and Abdel Hamid 2014). Moreover, unlike some previous NGO campaigns against sexual harassment

(Amar 2011), the post-2011 anti–sexual violence movement reframed sexual violence not as a question of morality but as a threat to women's rights to bodily integrity and to their ability to participate in public and political life. In so doing, they successfully inserted the question of violence against women onto the agenda for revolutionary change; contributed to dismantling the boundary between the inner and outer spheres; and, thereby, challenged the authority of those actors seeking to claim sovereignty over the inner sphere through the control of women's bodies.

DEMANDING GENDER EQUALITY, CHALLENGING THE GEOPOLITICAL ORDER IN JORDAN AND LEBANON

Neither Jordan nor Lebanon experienced the types of revolutionary struggles that helped to unleash mass women's activism in Egypt, yet there has clearly been a new impetus for demanding women's rights as a result of the Arab uprisings. Increasingly, women have taken their demands to the street and launched public campaigns. Moreover, they have focused on specific issues of gender inequality that touch on fundamental pillars of geopolitical order in Jordan and Lebanon: a woman's right to pass on her nationality and the criminalization of domestic violence, including rape within marriage. As discussed in the introduction, nationality laws that deny a woman's right to pass on her nationality not only violate women's equal citizenship rights, but also serve to fix the boundaries between the inside and the outside of the nation, as crucial to the successful construction of state sovereignty. In the Jordanian and Lebanese contexts, this issue is tied up with the politicized issue of demographic balance and regime maintenance. Meanwhile, the issue of domestic violence is intertwined with the gender inequalities enshrined in personal status laws, which, in the Lebanese context, are at the heart of the power of religious leaders and the reproduction of the sectarian system.

In Jordan, the late Nimeh Habashna was persistent in her efforts to insert women's rights demands into the weekly protests for political reforms and social justice throughout 2011. Nimeh, who sadly passed away in 2015, was active around a particular right's issue that affected her personally: the right of Jordanian women married to foreigners to pass on their nationality to their children and husbands. For many women and their families who are affected by this issue, it is not simply a question of gender inequality; it also has serious socioeconomic impacts. As mothers of children who are treated like foreigners, they must pay for their children's education, for health care, and for residency permits, constituting a considerable economic burden for many families (Abuqudairi 2014). Nimeh began raising this issue by setting up a Facebook group in 2008, but it was a struggle to build a campaign, as many women were afraid to speak out. In 2011, she joined the anti-government protests in Amman and saw a unique opportunity to raise the profile of her campaign. Nimeh told me:

> In 2011 in Jordan [there] started the Arab Spring, and everyone was coming to the streets. I was thinking, why should I stay online all this time? It's time to go to the street. [. . .] I wanted to go to make my campaign. I named my campaign "My mother is Jordanian and her nationality is a right for me." [. . .] Some people told me, "Why you didn't start from the women themselves? [from the angle of] 'I am a Jordanian woman and I have the right to give my nationality to my children.'" [. . .] I felt that all the women here they are frightened to talk, and they are frightened to go out, so I think why shouldn't I start [. . .] with these boys and girls, these youth [. . .] who have strength. I think these people they will push their mothers outside, because if I am inside my house, I didn't want to go out, my child who is suffering from this problem told me "Mama, please go, go and work for me," of course I will go out. [. . .] There was a big demonstration in Jordan on the 14th of March [. . .] [and] people they were demonstrating for political issues, [. . .] and I put my banner like that in front of the Ministry of Interior [. . .]. Of course, at that time people started to talk and so many articles came out in the Jordanian online media, also in the media in general. I think I have made—I started the fire at that time, just started the fire.

From March 2011, the campaign began to hold regular protests and sit-ins on the street in front of the prime minister's office, the Royal Court, and on the Dakhaliyyeh Circle (which was also the site of the disbanded protest camp in 2011) (Sweis 2011; Husseini 2012b; Husseini 2012c; Husseini 2014d). In February 2013, a group of individuals (journalists, lawyers, women's rights activists, and other public figures) and organizations formed a coalition that included Nimeh's group and MOSAWA (a network of eighty-six women CBOs from across Jordan) called My Nationality Is the Right of My Family to lobby the government to change the law as well as to raise public awareness about the impacts of the existing law (Arab Women Organization et al. 2013: 2). In November 2013, the government formed a committee to look into "civil rights options" for the families of Jordanian mothers married to non-Jordanian men. In August 2014, Minister of Political and Parliamentary Affairs

Khaled Kalaldeh announced that the government would grant "services and privileges" to the children of Jordanian mothers married to foreign men, specifically, "free health and education services, as well as eas[ing] restrictions on driving licences, property ownership and investment opportunities" (Husseini 2014a). However, at the time of writing, the government continues to refuse to grant citizenship to the children of foreign husbands of Jordanian women.

The campaign to amend the nationality law to allow Jordanian women to pass on their nationality has met with considerable resistance from the government as well as nongovernmental actors—primarily, members of Jordan's tribes, who argue that to grant women the right to pass on their nationality would lead to more Palestinians obtaining Jordanian citizenship and Jordan becoming an "alternative Palestinian homeland," thereby helping Israel to prevent the right of Palestinian return, as well as "diluting" Jordanian identity, rooted in the tribes (Whitman 2013; Abuqudairi 2014). As previously mentioned, the regime is sensitive to this opposition because the tribes constitute the major pillar of support for the monarchy. Aroub Soubh, spokesperson for the My Nationality Is the Right of My Family coalition, who is also personally affected by the issue and has been writing about it for many years, was angry about the language used in the press to discuss the issue of Jordanian women married to foreign husbands:

> The bigger problem in my opinion and in the opinion of many friends in the coalition was that [...] between the lines, [the media] stated that giving the nationality to the children of Jordanian women would pose a threat to the basic component of the Jordanian society, which is the tribe. It's outrageous, actually, that they should mention that. First, they are limiting the Jordanian society to two components, tribes and male, in that crude way, and they are denying citizenship to a large part of society. And they are trying to pit people against each other; they are trying to create conflict in the society itself; they are endangering the national unity, which is something very dangerous, that the government doesn't care for the possible consequences of what they write, and what they wrote was very dangerous.

Interestingly, Aroub subverts the accusation that granting women's equal rights constitutes a "threat" to the nation by arguing that it is opponents of the change who threaten the nation by denying the diversity of Jordanian society. While campaigners welcomed the government's measures of "special privileges" in terms of easing economic burdens for Jordanian families with foreign fathers, protests and campaigning have continued. At the time of writing, families complain of continuing discrimination and bureaucratic hurdles, while activists insist that there must be equality between men and women in the nationality laws (Husseini 2017).

In Lebanon, women rights activists, led by CRTD-A, have also been campaigning for many years for a woman's right to pass on her nationality to her husband and children, and, as in Jordan, this right has been denied for "political reasons" (Abou-Habib 2003; Saidi 2015). As in Jordan, opponents of amending the nationality law to ensure gender equality, argue that naturalizing foreign husbands will undermine the "natural" demography of the country (Abou-Habib 2003). Moreover, Lebanese politicians raise the specter of *tawtin* (i.e., the permanent settlement of Palestinian refugees) as an argument against amending the nationality law or even granting privileges to the children of foreign fathers. Given that the confessional political system depends upon maintaining the myth of a particular demographic balance, amendments to the nationality law are viewed by all of the major political parties as a threat to the sectarian political order.

Another ongoing issue of importance for women activists in Lebanon, but that attracted wider public attention after 2011, was that of domestic violence. Here, campaigning efforts were led by KAFA: Enough Violence and Exploitation, an NGO that, in 2007, drafted a law to protect women from family violence. Forty-one civil society organizations, comprising the National Coalition for the Protection of Women from Family Violence, supported this draft law. In 2010, the cabinet approved the draft law and sent it to a parliamentary committee for consideration. However, its passage through parliament stalled due to opposition from religious authorities. When I interviewed KAFA's director Zoya Rouhana in November 2013, she told me: "We started to work on this draft law since 2007, and we passed through a very long period of resistance and confrontation [. . .] especially with the religious groups, the Sunnis in particular, who rejected the law and did not want the parliament to even study it. There was a huge campaign, and we succeeded and the law has passed the joint parliamentary committees and is now waiting for the general assembly to get approved." Sunni and Shi'a religious leaders argued that sharia already protects women's roles and status, and that the draft law copied Western laws, which were not appropriate for a Muslim society; it contravened sharia; and, most significantly, it conflicted with the Lebanese constitution that protects the personal status and religious affairs of all communities (IWSAW 2010–2011: 79–80). These arguments constructed an inner sphere of national sovereignty, governed by religion, and threatened by women's rights advocates. "Feminist secularist organizations" were criticized for "promot[ing] distorted interpretations of Western laws that only conform to the aggressive capitalist and individualistic values, and are in defiance of the religious principles, the moral values, as well as the oriental and Islamic customs and traditions" (IWSAW 2010–11: 80).

From 2011 onward, women's rights activists increasingly took their campaign to the street, holding several demonstrations to call on parliament to pass the legislation and to recognize marital rape as a crime (Mikdashi 2012; Qiblawi 2014). The largest demonstration was held on International Women's Day in 2014, when approximately five thousand people marched to call on parliament to pass anti–domestic violence legislation, undoubtedly provoked by two recent and much-publicized deaths of women at the hands of their husbands (Qiblawi 2014). Alongside this, KAFA launched a public campaign, which included billboards, public service announcements, and the use of social media, to reframe domestic violence as a public concern and to identify marital rape, a problem that was previously unrecognized in Lebanon, as a form of violence against women (Khoury 2015).

In April 2014, parliament finally passed a modified version of the law. Given the opposition among religious figures and the uncertain political situation, this was a major achievement that was undoubtedly due to the sustained civil society activism in support of the law. Thus, Lebanon's law is one of only a few in the Arab world criminalizing domestic violence. (Tunisia passed the most comprehensive law in the region in July 2017.) Reportedly, the law has encouraged women to seek support and enabled them to obtain protection orders from abusive husbands (Obeid 2017). However, before sending the draft law to parliament, a parliamentary subcommittee amended the bill to address concerns raised by religious authorities. It renamed the bill from the Law on the Protection of Women from Family Violence to the Law on the Protection of Women and other Family Members from Domestic Violence, thereby erasing the particular vulnerabilities of women caused by inequality within the family. It limited the crime of domestic violence to those acts already criminalized in Lebanese law, thereby excluding controlling behavior by abusive husbands and male relatives, such as forced marriage or restricting women's freedom of mobility, and, most significantly, removed the article criminalizing rape within marriage, replacing it with an article criminalizing a husband's use of threats or violence to claim "a marital right to intercourse." This was particularly alarming to women activists, since "a marital right to intercourse" did not previously exist in Lebanese law (Saghieh

2013). Moreover, the law reiterates the notion that the adjudication of family violence should not contradict the power of religious authorities, stating that all provisions considered contrary to the new law would be annulled except in cases of the personal status laws (and the Protection of Juvenile Offenders at Risk law) (HRW 2014a). In other words, the domestic violence law is careful not to unsettle the existing gender order underpinning the sectarian system and the power of religious leaders and politicians. Significantly, this is in a context of heightened political instability and insecurity resulting from the Syrian uprising, which exacerbated political divisions within Lebanon. Moreover, the continued existence of the personal status laws in their current form are a huge factor in rendering women vulnerable to violence, since women often stay with abusive husbands for the sake of retaining custody over children (Moussawi and Yassin 2017).

The case of Jordanian women married to foreigners and the domestic violence law in Lebanon demonstrate that, in the post–Arab Spring context, in which issues of rights and justice were at the top of the agenda of popular struggles and activists successfully brought their demands to the street, governments were obliged to respond in some way to campaigns for women's rights. The measures introduced by governments have contributed to mitigating some of the worst aspects of women's unequal citizenship status. However, they have stopped short of overturning the gender inequality that is crucial to the reproduction of the geopolitical order and that underpins regime authority. In the case of Lebanon, the domestic violence law even reiterated religious sovereignty over the inner sphere of the family. The limited nature of legal reforms functions to maintain regime alliances with key constituencies and guarantee their continued support for the geopolitical status quo in a context of regional instability, violence, and war.

CONCLUSION

At the time of writing, most commentators and many scholars have announced the death of the Arab Spring, understood as popular demands for democratic change (with the exception of Tunisia, which continues to be celebrated as the one Arab Spring success story). Certainly, the huge death toll and humanitarian catastrophes from the wars in Syria, Yemen, Iraq, and, to a lesser degree, Libya; the scale of repression and human rights abuses in Syria, Egypt, and Bahrain; and the lack of substantial political reforms in

Jordan, Lebanon, and Morocco tell a very pessimistic story about the out-comes of the Arab uprisings of 2011. Within this narrative, the fates of women and women's rights are often highlighted to illustrate just how bad things have become. Indeed, despite women's large presence in the protest movements and uprisings from the end of 2010 onward, they have faced con-siderable obstacles to secure their inclusion within political transition proc-esses, as well as concerted attacks on their rights and bodily integrity.

These gender-specific challenges were not only the result of the longer-term weakness of women's movements and/or the rise to power of political Islamists; more importantly, they were also constitutive of the political tran-sition process in which the control and regulation of women's bodies was a primary means by which political actors sought to (re)establish political order and maintain political authority in the face of political upheaval. This is why levels of violence and exclusion faced by women have differed in vari-ous geopolitical contexts. In Egypt, where protests led to regime change, political competition was fiercest and, therefore, battles over women's bodies were most violent. Meanwhile, in Jordan and Lebanon, where protests did not lead to regime change, the exclusion of women was less aggressive. Nevertheless, resistance to demands for women's rights and gender equality were part of regime calculations in maintaining power and authority.

However, it is dangerous to reduce the story of the Arab uprisings to one of backlash and exclusion. By unsettling the geopolitical status quo, the mass protests created opportunities for women to transgress dominant gender norms and to innovate new modalities of struggle, which, in the case of Egypt, constituted a significant rupture from state feminism and the NGO-ized model of women's rights activism. In particular, the uprisings helped to politicize and mobilize a new generation of women, who not only insisted on being part of political transformations but also succeeded, for the first time since the 1970s, in putting questions of women's rights and bodily integrity onto the agenda of political and social movements. In Egypt, incidents of mass rape against women protesters rendered women's rights to bodily integ-rity as an existential matter about the future of women's public participation. The levels of violence targeted against women were directly proportional to the extent to which women were challenging dominant gender norms and, with this, dominant geopolitical power, in the aftermath of the uprisings. Women's insistence on participation in political transformations, their fear-less subversion and resignification of norms of female respectability, and their embedding of women's rights demands within wider struggles for social justice and freedom not only unsettled the "patriarchy-as-normal" paradigm but contributed to if not dismantling, then certainly to renegotiating the boundaries of the inner/outer spheres that have been central to the postcolonial geopolitical imaginary. We see the legacies of these struggles in the establishment of anti–sexual harassment units at Cairo and Ayn Shams universities (Shalabi 2016) as well as women's continuing leadership in civil society, despite regime repression. In Jordan and Lebanon too, women have been increasingly speaking out about sexual harassment and violence. However, the retreat of the revolutionary movement and of popular struggles for political transformation after 2013 in the face of the renewal of authoritarianism in Egypt, the ongoing conflict in Syria, and the rise of the Islamic State across the region threatened the gains that women made as a result of their participation in revolutionary struggles. This is examined in the next chapter.

SEVEN

The Gendered Geopolitics of Fear
and Counterrevolution

THE ARAB UPRISINGS not only challenged the geopolitical order but, simultaneously, unleashed counterrevolutionary processes, giving rise to projects of authoritarian restoration, militarized repression, sectarian violence, religious extremism, regional power struggles, and imperialist interventions. Several writers have attempted to understand the failure of the Arab uprisings to achieve sustained political transformations by analyzing the global political economy, legacies of state building, interventions by regional and/or international powers, and/or tactical errors of local actors (Achcar 2016; Brownlee, Masoud, and Reynolds 2015; De Smet 2015; Hinnebusch 2015a, 2015b; Kamrava 2012; McMahon 2017).

This chapter explores the gendered dimensions of these counterrevolutionary processes, in terms of an embodied and emotional geopolitics of counterrevolution. Specifically, the chapter examines a "geopolitics of fear" (Pain and Smith 2008; Pain 2009) in relation to the Arab uprisings. The narratives of many women whom I interviewed reveal concerns about personal and communal security in the post-uprising period. While these fears were genuinely felt, they should not be viewed as a natural reaction to a priori threats. As Rachel Pain and Susan Smith argue, "Fear does not pop out of the heavens and hover in the ether before blanketing itself across huge segments of cities and societies: it has to be lived and made" (2008: 3). Fear is embedded in the everyday, including in the insecurities and marginalization produced through unequal social relations (Pain and Smith 2008; Pain 2009). These emotions are not only passively experienced but also constitutive of social and, hence, geopolitical relations. As Sara Ahmed notes, "It is through emotions, or how we respond to objects and others, that surfaces or boundaries are made: the 'I' and the 'we' are shaped by, and even take the shape of, contact with others" (Ahmed 2014: 10).

This chapter explores women's narratives of fearing for their rights, safety, and personal freedoms. It demonstrates how narratives of fear have served to reproduce gendered and racialized boundaries between "us" and "them"— with the latter cast as political Islamists and refugees. In this regard, I argue that fears about women's rights and personal safety have underwritten the use of exclusionary and coercive measures, and even violence, in the name of protecting "us" from "them." They have been appropriated by political elites and have contributed to strengthening counterrevolutionary projects of authoritarian restoration and militarization.

The chapter first focuses on Egypt, where, in the name of "saving Egypt" and "protecting the 25 January Revolution," the military successfully ousted the elected president, Mohammed Morsi, on 3 July 2013, paving the way for unprecedented state violence against the Muslim Brotherhood and almost total repression of any form of dissent. The chapter highlights the fears of women activists about the threats posed by the Muslim Brotherhood to women's rights and the future of Egypt and how, in turn, these fears were mobilized to legitimize the military's intervention and the post–July 2013 regime. The chapter also considers the implications of the military coup for women's rights activists, in terms of a weakening of independent activism and a shift toward either more depoliticized gender activism or a focus on "non-contentious" politics.

The second part of the chapter investigates women's fears about personal safety and women's rights in Jordan and Lebanon as a result of the Syrian conflict. These fears relate to the conflict and violence in Syria spilling over the border and the socioeconomic effects of the arrival of large numbers of Syrian refugees. As in Egypt, these fears have been mobilized in ways that may legitimize authoritarian and even violent measures as a means of protecting personal security. By contrast, other activists have been involved in solidarity activities, but these are generally based on humanitarian and/or depoliticized logics operating in tandem with, rather than in resistance to, the current geopolitical order.

EGYPT: GENDERING THE COUNTERREVOLUTION

In June 2012, Mohammed Morsi was elected as Egypt's first post-uprising president, winning 51 percent of the vote in a run-off with Ahmed Shafiq, a former member of the Mubarak regime. There soon emerged opposition to

Morsi and the rule of the Muslim Brotherhood, with many activists viewing him as little better than the dictatorship of Hosni Mubarak. After Morsi announced an executive decree in November 2012, the opposition organized protests outside the presidential palace (the Ittihadiyya) against what they viewed as the Brotherhood's power grab (Amar 2013a: 35–36). Mai Saleh, a member of the New Woman Foundation, participated in those protests:

> We were at Ittihadiyya at that time when the violence ensued and when the tents of the protestors were brought down. I won't lie to you, I cried at that moment. I was very worried about the country at that moment because we were two teams at Ittihadiyya, [. . .] the team of the revolutionary forces who saw [Morsi's presidential decree] as a dictatorial declaration and that Morsi was giving immunity to his decisions and that he was securing the path for a new dictator, and another team that was completely ignorant and had no idea what was going on. We were objecting to the constitutional declaration and they were shouting, "Egypt is Islamic," two very different subjects. [. . .] At that moment I felt like we were two different peoples, and I hated Morsi so much and hated the Muslim Brotherhood so much because they managed to divide the people.

Anti-Morsi protests continued throughout his period in office, in opposition to the proposed constitution, ongoing abuses by security forces, and what was perceived as the monopolization of power by the Brotherhood (Abdel-Baky 2013a). Opponents viewed the Muslim Brotherhood as betraying the goals of the 25 January Revolution, undermining the security of the state, and threatening Egyptian identity (see Pratt and Rezk 2019). Meanwhile, popular frustration with Morsi's rule grew because of the deteriorating economic situation (Abdel-Razek 2013). In May 2013, following months of antagonism and violent clashes between the opposition and supporters of the Muslim Brotherhood, youth activists launched the Tamarod ("rebel") campaign. By mid-June, they claimed to have collected fifteen million signatures supporting early presidential elections and calling for mass demonstrations on 30 June (Abdel-Baky 2013b). It has since been revealed that the Tamarod campaign was supported by the Egyptian security services (Ketchley 2017); yet, at the time, many of the women whom I interviewed were unaware of this association, signed the Tamarod petition, and participated in the protests of 30 June alongside millions of other Egyptians, demanding that Morsi step down.

In response to massive demonstrations, the military issued an ultimatum to Morsi to resolve the political crisis; when Morsi failed to act, it moved on 3 July to depose him. Flanked by leaders of the political opposition, Tamarod, the Coptic Pope, and others, the army announced a new transition roadmap, with the appointment of Judge Adly Mansour as interim president, the formation of a new cabinet, the cancellation of the 2012 (Muslim Brotherhood) constitution, and the establishment of a new constitution-drafting committee (Chulov and Kingsley 2013).

The ousting of Morsi ushered in a period of violence unprecedented in Egypt's postindependence history, with the army using lethal force against pro-Morsi demonstrations, while some of Morsi's supporters attacked Coptic Christians in revenge for what they regarded as the community's support for the military coup. Between 3 July and December 2013, fourteen hundred people were killed and thousands detained, the majority of whom were supporters of Morsi (Amnesty International 2014). The worst violence was perpetrated on 14 August, when security forces and the army launched an operation to forcibly clear the pro-Morsi sit-ins at Raba'a al-Adawiya Square, in Nasr City, and Nahda Square, in front of Cairo University, resulting in almost one thousand civilians killed (HRW 2014a). Since then, there have been unprecedented numbers of forced disappearances, reports of police torture, political prisoners, and mass death sentences (Amnesty International 2014, Guerin 2018). These shocking levels of police violence were brought to the attention of European audiences after an Italian, Giulio Regeni, a PhD student at Cambridge University, disappeared on 25 January 2016 and his mutilated body was later found, dumped by a highway, bearing the hallmarks of torture by Egyptian security services (*Mada Masr* 2016b).

Regime repression and harassment very quickly extended beyond Muslim Brotherhood supporters to also include activists, politicians, media, and human rights groups that criticized the Sisi regime. Magda Adli, a founding member of the Nadim Center for the Rehabilitation of Victims of Violence and Torture, was prescient in our interview in December 2013:

> So, since the dispersal of the sit-in at Raba'a, there has been a systemized attack on those organizations which denounced the killing of so many people [...] via newspapers and TV stations, even satellite channels. [...] There's a situation that anyone who doesn't acknowledge Sisi as a president is considered an enemy. We've always been against the military rule and against the Islamist rule, both of them. But when there are human rights violations regardless of who the perpetrators are, we take the side of the victims against the criminals, it's that simple really. Yet it's being distorted; from both sides. There has been severe political polarization after the authorization of Sisi on July third. So, there's an attack from all sides and these are the prelude to the coming "punch."

Following the passage in November 2013 of a law banning public protests, several non-Islamist protesters were arrested and tried, including high-profile revolutionary figures Alaa Abdel-Fattah, Ahmed Maher, Mohamed Adel, Ahmed Douma, and Mahinoor Masry, as well as other women activists, such as Yara Sallam and Sana Seif. The April 6 Movement, one of the youth groups that mobilized for the 25 January 2011 demonstration, was banned in 2014 (Afify 2016). In 2016, authorities reopened the so-called NGO foreign funding case, paving the way for a crackdown on NGOs for allegedly receiving funds illegally. As a result, sixty-one NGO workers were called for questioning, fifteen rights activists were charged, travel bans were implemented against twenty-seven activists, and the personal assets of ten activists and seven NGOs were frozen (HRW 2018). Among those targeted were Mozn Hassan, Azza Soliman, and Aida Seif El Dawla (*Mada Masr* 2016a, 2016c, 2016d; Michaelson 2016). Moreover, in 2017, Egyptian authorities closed El-Nadim Center, while Nazra for Feminist Studies was forced to close its office in 2018 because of the ongoing asset freeze. Despite the shocking levels of state violence and repression, Egyptians were overwhelmingly supportive of the army, which was widely seen as the "savior of Egypt" from the evil clutches of the Muslim Brotherhood (Chakravarti 2014; Pratt and Rezk 2019). A huge cult of personality developed around El-Sisi, with his face appearing on T-shirts, cupcakes, and even women's underwear (Chakravarti 2014), while women supporters declared their love for him (McTighe 2014; Rabie 2014).

Many (although definitely not all) of the women that I interviewed at the end of 2013 and beginning of 2014 were grateful for the army's removal of Morsi, out of fear for what the continued rule of the Muslim Brotherhood would have brought. For example, Nevine Ebeid of the New Woman Foundation, insisted, "If the army hadn't stepped in on July third, a civil war would've broken out that was even uglier than what we are seeing today. [. . .] If the army hadn't stepped in, it would've been much worse than this. We're in a phase of minimizing our losses and the bloodshed." Despite reservations about the increasing repression under the Sisi regime, Salma El-Naqqash, a member of Nazra for Feminist Studies and of the Socialist Popular Alliance Party also welcomed the removal of the Muslim Brotherhood:

> There is a legitimacy for the ending of the Islamist rule in Egypt, and there is a legitimacy for this transitional period. It's a very important political statement that I stick with all the time [. . .] because the Muslim Brotherhood is a genuine dictatorship. What they were trying to establish throughout the last year was a genuine dictatorship; [. . .] they are genuinely terrorists. We know

from our own research that in both sit-ins in Raba'a and Al-Nahda [Squares], there were a lot of weapons [. . .] and we know that terrorism is really a part of their ideology, and [. . .] violence is genuinely a part of their ideology, so I can't really defend them.

Several women activists highlighted the issue of women's rights to distinguish the post–July 2013 regime from Morsi's rule. Leftist political activist Elham Eidarous Al-Kassir, former member of the Socialist Popular Alliance Party and cofounder of the Aysh wa Horreya party, told me that despite the fact that the new constitution included an article preserving military trials of civilians, which activists had consistently opposed, she regarded the 2014 constitution as "much better" than the Muslim Brotherhood constitution, mainly because of the inclusion of women's rights: "It must be said that there were many developments regarding civil rights and women's rights, and it is incomparable to the previous situation. Previously, there was a huge battle regarding women's rights. So, you can't say that this constitution is the military's constitution, because [. . .] a battle ensued within the Committee of 50, in which many democratic elements were able to obtain some of their goals, but they couldn't change the situation regarding the privileges of the army." In particular, many women whom I interviewed mentioned Article 11, which explicitly commits the state to ensuring gender equality, women's parliamentary representation, women's participation in state institutions, and state protection from violence (Constitution of Egypt 2014), as an indicator of progress. Women's rights activist and university professor Hoda Elsadda, who was a member of the Committee of 50 tasked with drafting the 2014 constitution, told me:

> I really believe that if we had not had a revolution, there are some articles there [in the constitution] that would've never been [normally] written in the Egyptian constitution. [. . .] The article on women for example, I would argue that the majority, at least half if not more [. . .] of the fifty-member committee would not normally agree to this article, okay? [. . .] I really think it's because of this feeling that, you know, [. . .] we want rights for women; . . . there's a wave of rights that's going through society.

Karima El-Hefnawy, a founding member of the Egyptian Socialist Party, ascribed women's rights gains in the 2014 constitution to several years of efforts by women activists: "This is one of the benefits we got from the revolution."

Other women (as well as men) were more skeptical about the document. Some were disappointed that, while recognizing women's rights to hold public office, the constitution did not include any special measures, such as quotas, for ensuring women's increased presence in state institutions. Doaa Abdelaal, co-founder of the Ikhtiyar collective and member of Women Living Under Muslim Laws, saw this omission as highly problematic, arguing that it would not be possible to increase the number of women in the Egyptian parliament without a quota. She expressed frustration with the position of some other women's rights organizations:

> Some of the well-established women's rights activists, especially the ones affiliated with the National Council for Women, and even the Council itself, they will say we have reached the best we can for women's participation, [. . .] whilst [. . .] we think what we have reached is less than what we have advocated for and we need to go on. [. . .] We have to use the time we have now in keeping people engaged, [. . .] in supporting our agenda for change. [. . .] But actually seeing the National Council for Women coming and saying that [. . .] we should support the constitution is giving a kind of legitimacy to what is written there. And, it's like putting a full-stop, not helping us to continue bargaining or negotiating for the things we really want to do.

Meanwhile, others criticized the constitution for not going far enough to protect human rights (see also, EIPR 2013). One activist observed, "The chapter talking about the rights and freedoms, it improved immensely [. . .] but the problem is when you look at the other chapters talking about the judiciary and of course the chapter talking about the military institution, it is scary. It looks like you are giving me a lot more freedom and a lot more rights, but how am I supposed to implement them if you are going to let the military be such an immune institution?" In effect, the insertion of women's rights guarantees into a constitution that maintains special privileges for the military, against a backdrop of violent repression and authoritarian restoration, served to enshrine what Iris Marion Young calls a "logic of masculinist protection" (2003). By this she means the relationship between "security regimes" and their citizens, in which the former offers protection against enemies of the state on the condition of obedience, thereby compromising rather than promoting rights and autonomy (Young 2003). In the 2014 constitution, the granting of women's rights was implicitly dependent upon obedience to the military, with negative implications for the autonomy of women's activism.

The logics of masculinist protection served to reinscribe norms of female respectability. This was evident in the reframing of sexual violence after 2013. Whereas the post-2011 anti–sexual violence movement strove to present the issue as a question of women's rights to bodily integrity in political and protest spaces, by contrast, the Sisi regime's discourse on sexual violence resurrected the paradigm of "honor and shame" in relation to women's bodies. In a statement following sexual attacks that occurred at his presidential victory rally in June 2014 (which were filmed and went viral), El-Sisi declared, "Our honour is being assaulted in the streets. This is unacceptable and we can't allow one more incident like this to happen" (Kingsley 2014). Similarly, Mervat al-Tallawi, then NCW president, announced that the Council would sue Al-Jazeera network for using the issue of sexual harassment to "tarnish the image of Egypt" and discredit the "30 June Revolution" (*Mada Masr* 2014a). The much-publicized image of El-Sisi bringing a bouquet of red roses to the survivor of the attacks and declaring that "We'll get you your rights" (quoted in *Mada Masr* 2014b) also reduced the woman to "an object of love and guardianship," to borrow Young's terminology (2003: 19) and constructed El-Sisi as her male protector—thereby reproducing rather than challenging the relationship of power and subordination that underpins violence against women. By contrast, those women who have opposed the regime, particularly supporters of the deposed President Morsi, have been deprived of masculinist protection and, instead, are subject to numerous rights violations, including sexual violence, at the hands of security officers and police (Agosti 2018: 184–203; Biagini 2017a: 186–214; Amnesty International 2015).

As in the case of previous Egyptian regimes, El-Sisi's state feminism recognizes demands of the women's movement only to the extent that they do not threaten the gendered hierarchies of the nation state. However, in contrast to previous Egyptian regimes, El-Sisi's state feminism is embedded within the most repressive and militaristic project of authoritarian restoration seen in the history of modern Egypt. Meanwhile, the vast majority of Egyptians have experienced a significant deterioration in their living standards since El-Sisi came to power. The re-imbrication of women's rights with tyranny and corruption constitutes a setback for women's rights activists.

At the time of my visit to Egypt, the counterrevolution was winning and the revolutionary movement of the post-Mubarak period was in abeyance. Many individuals had withdrawn from public activism, some traumatized by all that they had experienced (see Matthies-Boon 2017). The only anti-regime street protests were ones organized by those opposing the military coup (Biagini 2017a: 186–214), usually in peripheral areas and working-class neighborhoods of Cairo (Wagdy 2016). Several activists had left the country to escape the depressing situation or to avoid arrest (see also Soliman and Nour 2016). The dissipation of activism was also a result of divisions among the coalition of activists who supported the 25 January Revolution over what position to take toward the military. For the first time since Mubarak's departure, women's rights activists did not organize a public march to celebrate International Women's Day in 2014. They were divided, with many refusing to comply with the protest law that required that the Ministry of the Interior be informed of any public gatherings, while others were rallying in support of Sisi's regime. I found tensions among members of the same organizations and parties toward events of the summer of 2013. Some, like Salma El-Naqqash, insisted on the legitimacy of the army's ouster of Morsi and its roadmap as legitimate and necessary to protect the revolution, but opposed or were deeply ambivalent about the scale of the regime's repression. Some considered the Muslim Brotherhood to be a terrorist organization and supported the military takeover and the violent repression of the organization. Others opposed the army's takeover as a threat to the goals of the revolution, while equally opposing the Muslim Brotherhood. However, attempts by some to forge an anti-military and anti-Brotherhood coalition under the banner of the Way of the Revolution were criticized by several women with whom I spoke because its members had backed Morsi against Ahmed Shafiq (a Mubarak-era politician) during the presidential election run-off in June 2012. Journalist and activist Salma Shukrallah summed up well the dilemmas of finding an independent position amid the deep polarization in the post-Morsi political moment:

It's very difficult. At the beginning [after 3 July], I was more hopeful. [. . .] Until now, I can say that I'm happy we got rid of the Brotherhood, because without that, this could have been a disaster. I think, no matter what the cost is, this had to happen. The fact that they lost so much popularity is actually positive. But now I'm more and more afraid of the old regime, the apparatuses of the old regime. They are coming back really strong. [. . .] I don't see myself either here nor there, which is making me a bit paralyzed, [. . .] but I think that there are a lot of people like me.

Nonetheless, I also met people who sought to reformulate or resist the fears generated by the aftermath of the 3 July coup through continued public activism. Elham Eidarous and Mona Ezzat were among 304 individuals who resigned from the Socialist Popular Alliance party in autumn 2013 because of its uncritical stance toward the military and security forces after 3 July (Salem 2013). They founded a new political party called Aysh wa Horreya (Bread and Freedom), recalling the original demands of the 25 January uprising. Mona, a journalist and member of the New Woman Foundation, told me how she saw the role of the party in the current environment:

> We feel that there is a group of people who took part in the revolution, who were calling for liberty and social justice and were therefore close to the ideas of the left, but without calling themselves leftists, and that they want to be active in public life. Our role is to try to be a voice for this group and be able to attract these people and these youth, and that can be a political platform for them that can work with other groups to continue the course of the revolution, to build a real foundation for democracy and for the security forces not to be involved in public life.

Amal Elmohandes, a member of Nazra for Feminist Studies, was continuing her work with the Front for the Defense of Egyptian Protesters, despite facing hostility from her friends and family:

> They are very aggressive. And of course, it's because it's the media. It's under this guise of nationalism and the war on terrorism and it's difficult. It's these polarizations. It's either you're this or that. Nothing in the middle. Like for example when my mom sees me going down to take supplies to the women who were arrested from Al-Azhar [university] clashes or whatever. She would get really angry and she was, like, "Why are you defending these terrorists?" And I'm like, "They're not terrorists." And 60 percent of the people that were arrested are actually people who have nothing to do with the Muslim Brotherhood. So, you know, she's like, "you're a traitor." [...] Even with friends, they're like, "So, what are you supporting the Muslim Brotherhood?" I'm like, "No, I'm not supporting the Muslim Brotherhood. I'm supporting rights in general." Period.

On the whole, since 2013, people have turned away from overt political activism and contentious politics, which have become high-risk activities under Sisi's repressive regime (as illustrated by the authorities' response to the demonstrations against the Red Sea Islands transfer in 2017 and the protests that briefly erupted in September 2019). Instead, I came across several individuals, particularly young women, who were involved in what could be called "non-contentious" activism—that is, activities that do not speak directly to political power or seek to address the government directly. These activities are concerned with "social" issues, particularly issues that concern gender and sexuality, and often use cultural and educational events and social media to raise awareness. For example, Ikhtiyar (meaning "choice") was created in 2013 as a feminist collective, aiming to create knowledge in Arabic about gender and a space for the exploration of gender and sexuality issues. Thawrat El Banat (Girls' Revolution) is a Facebook page that discusses gender-related issues, publishes testimonies from women of sexual violence and discrimination, and launches online campaigns to defend women's rights to bodily autonomy, including openly discussing the taboo topic of abortion. Popular culture is another arena in which young women (and men) seek to question dominant gender norms. For example, the Bussy project, modeled somewhat on *The Vagina Monologues*, began in 2010, as a platform for performing women's stories of their experiences of violence and discrimination and, when I visited Egypt in spring 2017, was continuing to perform in different cities around Egypt. The all-girl group Bint al-Masarwa, formed in 2016, write and perform songs based on women's testimonies of sexual violence and discrimination.[1]

Many people voiced their refusal to give up. As Amal Elmohandes told me, "A lot of people have sacrificed a lot, so for me to whine and complain and say 'there's no hope'—at least just keep trying!" Meanwhile, political activist Nagwan El Ashwal believed that there was an irreversible generational shift that made future change unavoidable:

> We learned a lot over these different periods [since 2011] and this is a positive thing. Things are not lost. We will no longer trust the older people: Baradei, Sabahi, and Abul Foutouh. [. . .] The youth are the only ones that can bring change to society. I believe in the Egyptian people. Even if they are now legitimizing the coup. I went to villages in Upper Egypt and listened to people talking. They have an awareness and refuse to be slaves of the state. I believe that there is a big revolution coming and we will do it. We can achieve the change. There are also changes happening inside Islamist movements, such as, the Muslim Brotherhood. The young generation is making a change in the MB. They are challenging the leadership, not just since Raba'a, but even during the Raba'a sit-in. They see that their leaders have made mistakes. And now you find a lot of women in the Muslim Brotherhood and they are organizing and leading people. Things cannot return to how they were in the past. Those who are feeling pessimistic now, hopefully they will feel the spirit of the revolution again. Even if we are defeated today, we are on the right track.[2]

Perhaps one of the most significant ways in which people were resisting the counterrevolution was by remembering the 25 January 2011 uprising in the face of regime efforts to rewrite history. In the words of Revolutionary Socialist Manar Abdel Sattar: "Even with what is happening now, which is 'almost tragic' and the counterrevolution is winning with a vengeance. But 'still' this moment [of the 25 January Revolution] will still be present in many people's memories, that we can do this and we can change things. We are not doomed to live in the current situation forever."

THE SYRIAN CONFLICT: GENDERING THE GEOPOLITICS OF FEAR IN JORDAN AND LEBANON

In March 2011, inspired by citizens of other Arab countries, Syrians began protest demonstrations against the regime of Bashar al-Assad. The regime labeled the protesters as terrorists and responded with a massive military crackdown. In response, the protests transformed from peaceful demonstrations into an armed insurgency, supported by Assad's regional enemies (Saudi Arabia, Qatar, and Turkey) as well as Western countries. In turn, Assad's allies, Iran, Hizbollah, and later, Russia, intervened militarily in support of the regime. The causes of the Syrian conflict, its disastrous humanitarian consequences, including the huge death toll and massive numbers of displaced, as well as the grave human rights violations and war crimes perpetrated overwhelmingly by the regime but also by non-state parties to the conflict, have been well-documented and analyzed (among others, Abboud 2015; Lister 2016; Lynch 2016; Phillips 2016; Yassin-Kassab and al-Shami 2016). This section considers the implications of the conflict for neighboring Jordan and Lebanon but, more specifically, the fears the Syrian conflict generated among Jordanian, Lebanese, and Palestinian women activists and the ways in which gender and women's rights came to enable exclusionary and authoritarian projects.

Due to Syria's strategic importance, the Syrian uprising has had massive implications for regional political actors. A victory for the Syrian opposition would not only unseat the Assad regime but would weaken Iranian influence across the Eastern Mediterranean, to the benefit of Saudi Arabia, Egypt, Jordan, Israel, and other international actors hostile to Iran (Hokayem 2014). In the Lebanese context, Assad's downfall would be a disaster for Hizbollah and a blessing for Hizbollah's domestic political rivals, the Future Movement, as well as Sunni Islamist groups (ICG 2012b, 2013; Salloukh 2017). Such political calculations shaped attitudes toward the Syrian uprising after 2011. Lina, a student and actor, criticized politicians for their self-interested attitudes toward the Arab uprisings:

When it was Egypt everyone was happy, or neutral, so it was a revolution. When it went to Syria it was a conspiracy theory for some and freedom for others. Like it depends if you have American or Iranian affiliations; if you're [with] Iran it's a Zionist scheme, if you're [Saad] Hariri [leader of the Future Movement] or American it's the call for freedom and suddenly Bashar Al-Assad became this monster whom they didn't see before, you know. Like now they just opened their eyes to all the crimes and all the facts and massacres that happened? So, it's ridiculous from both sides.

Palestinians in Lebanon were also divided over events in Syria. Haifa Jammal explained the calculations behind the positions of different Palestinians toward the conflict:

Hamas, for example, [...] now are against the [Syrian] regime, and they support the Islamic opposition. [...] But on the grassroots level [...] you find people who [...] feel they support the Syrian regime, not because they are happy with the Syrian regime, but because they [are against] Western interference; like America and France and Britain, most of the European countries, they interfere with the political crisis [in Syria] and they support the opposition. [...] Then they feel that, not the Syrian regime is the target but Syria as a country because Syria before the crisis was [...] very strong, economically and politically and on the military side.

Beyond political calculations, I found that the brutality of the Syrian regime and the magnitude of the humanitarian crisis undermined support for the Arab uprisings among people in Jordan and Lebanon. In Lebanon, a community activist in the Chouf told me that "security is more important than freedom" and that "it is better to achieve change through reform rather than revolution." In Jordan, writer Suhair al-Tal observed that: "Now, when the events unfolded in Syria the people got scared; they didn't want to form any movements. They saw King Abdullah, despite his corruption and the corruption of the regime, as a blessing compared to the killing and destruction taking place in Syria and Iraq." Similarly, Tereza Al-Rayan, from the Jordanian Women's Union, believed that, "today's cause isn't the cause of democracy but that of the people's personal safety. [...]. So many important issues were delayed because the people's safety and lives were endangered. So, this replaced even the issues of freedom and bread, not to mention the issues of women."

As in Egypt, an important source of fear generated by the uprisings was the perceived threat posed by Islamists. For example, women's rights activist

Joumana Merhy, in Lebanon, told me, "The Islamist groups are trying to push women back into their household roles and other traditional roles. Currently, there's more resistance from women, but the challenges they face are bigger than they used to be. To battle with the Islamists is no easy task. [...] The rise of political Islam is suffocating women's involvement in politics. They're also trying to give women traditional roles in politics, such as aid and social workers, instead of utilizing their political skills and their role in bringing about change." For some women, fears of political Islam shaped their assessment of the Arab uprisings. For example, when I asked Mirna Shidrawi about her thoughts on the Arab uprisings, she replied:

It was beautiful up until the Islamists took over the revolutions. [...] That's what's going to happen in Syria if the regime ever is toppled [...], which I doubt. Which we all hope for. [...] No matter how free or democratic or educated or good willed most of the Syrians are, it's going to be as ugly as Tunisia and Egypt. Then again what's happening in Egypt now with Sisi, I appreciate him, you know? But at the same time, he's still an army man and isn't that what you tried to change with Mubarak? I'm not optimistic at all today, so I don't think it's the right day to ask me about the revolutions.

Mirna was not the only person to express sympathy with the Egyptian army coup against Mohammed Morsi in July 2013 for the reasons of safeguarding women's rights and democracy. Similarly, fear of the Islamists created support for the Syrian regime against the growth of Islamic State, Jabhit al-Nusrah, and other Salafist-jihadist elements within the Syrian opposition. For example, Jordanian writer Rania Al Jabaari told me that she initially "had strong reservations against the Syrian regime because it's an oppressive regime," but as the conflict continued, she welcomed the interventions of Hizbollah and Russia in support of the regime in order to prevent the Salafists taking power. In her assessment, a victory for the Salafists against the Syrian regime would affect women's freedom: "In Jordan, women would've paid the price [...] because [...] we would be back to trying to get our basic rights which we had before, if the Salafists were victorious in Syria against the regime, that is. It would've become a dream to go out to the street, [...] to go out with my male friends [...]. So, I think the Arab Spring would be completed in the region when Syria survives what was plotted against it in the name of the Arab Spring."

Another issue mentioned by several women was that of the presence of significant numbers of Syrian refugees in their respective countries. At the time of writing, eight years since the uprising began, 5.6 million Syrians have fled their country, with most of them residing in neighboring countries. Lebanon hosts more than 991,000 Syrian refugees (down from a previous high of 1.1 million) and Jordan hosts almost 662,000 (UNHCR 2018). In addition, despite closing their borders to Palestinian refugees fleeing Syria, Jordan hosts 16,000 Palestinian refugees from Syria and Lebanon hosts 31,000 (UNRWA 2018). Many refugees are living in poverty or precarious conditions, vulnerable due to their insecure legal situation (see UNICEF 2018). Women and LGBTQ refugees face particularly challenging circumstances (Freedman Kivilcim, and Özgür 2017; International Rescue Committee 2014; Women's International League for Peace and Freedom et al. 2017).

Some of the women with whom I spoke, expressed fears about the effects of such large numbers of refugees. Initially, host communities in Lebanon and Jordan extended hospitality to the refugees. However, as their numbers rapidly increased due to the increasing violence in Syria, there emerged a growing resentment toward them. While fears about the implications of large numbers of refugees are understandable given that Lebanon hosts the most refugees per capita in the world (173 per 1,000), followed by Jordan (89 per 1,000) (McCarthy 2017), it is noteworthy that the specific fears expressed were gendered in ways that serve to reproduce existing geopolitical imaginaries and hierarchies of power. For example, some perceived Syrian refugees as a threat to social reproduction and to the gender order that underpins it (male breadwinner/female caregiver). In this respect, many women mentioned the impact of the refugees on the cost of living, housing, and social services. Ferial Abu Hamdan, an activist in the Chouf mountains told me:

> We feel very badly for the Syrian people, but the problem is [that] their numbers are over, much more than our number, so, and everything is getting very expensive, even the bakery, the bread, are, you know, getting too much, because, you know, now [. . .] they are double, triple [the number they were before] [. . .] there are supposed to be [places for] all those [Syrian] children in schools. But how? Who will be paying for them? Even if they put them in elementary public school, there are no places for them. Because their numbers are too much, so this is a big problem. And, you see, what will happen to us in the winter? When all these families are all cold, no jobs for them and no school for the children. So, I am praying that the problem in Syria will finish soon.

A Jordanian community development and social activist was especially worried about the impact of Syrian refugees on the labor market, as they were competing for scarce jobs with Jordanians: "The [Jordanian] Department of

Statistics says that the income of the average family is 500 to 800 Jordanian dinars, while the minimum monthly wage is currently JD 190, and with the arrival of the Syrian refugees, the minimum wage [for non-Jordanians] was reduced to JD 100. Thousands of Jordanian young men were replaced with Syrian refugees and immigrants who don't even have work permits." Arguably, such perceptions serve to mask the threats to social reproduction and human security posed by the political status quo, including lack of accountability and corruption; long-standing economic problems exacerbated by regional conflict and uncertainty; and, in the case of Lebanon, political divisions among the political elite that engender crisis. Additionally, particularly in Lebanon, several women expressed fears for their personal safety. For example, at the time of my visit to Lebanon in October–November 2013, a women's group in the Chouf Mountains had recently launched a campaign for personal security and safety, based on a questionnaire, in which I noted that one of the choices offered in response to a question about sources of insecurity was "Syrian refugees." When I asked one of the campaign organizers about this question, she told me that people feel insecure because Syrian refugees steal, while rival Syrian factions were involved in violent conflict within Lebanon. These fears of Syrian male violence and criminality function to erase (arguably greater) threats to women's personal safety and security emanating from male relatives, which are underpinned by state-sanctioned gender inequalities within the private sphere. The construction of such fears depends upon gendered and racialized notions of "other men" (as violent) and contribute toward legitimizing violence against and surveillance of Syrian refugee men.

None of the women I interviewed expressed support for forcibly returning refugees or withdrawing financial assistance from them. Nonetheless, these types of fears have echoed political and media discourses that have scapegoated refugees, particularly in Lebanon, for a range of social and economic problems, while also securitizing them as a threat to the "country's national fabric" (Chit and Nayel 2013; Fakhoury 2017: 689; Shebaya 2017), rendering Syrians targets of violence and exclusion. It is not only that a discourse presenting Syrian refugees as a threat serves to let governing elites "off the hook" for their mistakes, but also that such narratives reproduce particular notions of gender and gendered divisions of labor that, in turn, underpin gendered and racialized hierarchies, which are mobilized to construct boundaries between "us" and "them" and authorize a sectarian, authoritarian, and unjust political order.

However, fears about Syrian refugees also reflected the insecurities generated through the marginalization and exclusion of particular groups within society as a result of historical patterns of unequal development. In Lebanon, large numbers of refugees have settled in areas of the country that were already economically marginalized, such as the Beqaa Valley and north Lebanon. In Beirut, refugees have settled in Palestinian refugee camps, where the cost of living is lower than in the center of the city, and exacerbated already poor living conditions (Berti 2015; Mahmoud and Roberts 2018). For example, one Palestinian refugee woman helping to distribute food and financial aid in a Palestinian camp in Beirut, echoed the words of several other Palestinian refugees whom I met: "We are now very crowded. There are a lot of people. There are a lot of problems. Most houses have been rented out. [. . .] The aid that used to go to Palestinians now goes to the Syrians to help them. They took a lot of things from us."

I also found expressions of sympathy for the plight of Syrian refugees and various initiatives in support of them. For example, Nimat F., born in Lebanon and raised in Damascus, was continuing a longer tradition of women's voluntary work by raising money to support education for Syrian refugee children and other activities to improve the conditions of Syrian refugees in Lebanon, particularly those living in very basic conditions in informal camps. On a larger scale, several Lebanese, Jordanian, and Palestinian NGOs were aiding refugees fleeing Syria, including Palestinian refugees. Some activities specifically target Syrian women, principally in terms of "economic empowerment" (setting up small income-generation projects) or as victims of gender-based violence, including trafficking and early marriage. The JWU and AWO in Jordan and ABAAD and KAFA in Lebanon were the only women's rights organizations working with Syrian refugees (that I came across). However, all of these activities are donor-funded projects, embedded in depoliticized models of relief and assistance, in which Syrians are treated as beneficiaries. This can be contrasted with women's associational activities following the 1967 war, which were largely resignified as part of a movement in solidarity with Palestinian refugees, who themselves were considered political actors, in defiance of the geopolitical status quo.

CONCLUSION

We cannot understand the success of counterrevolutionary processes without understanding the ways in which the 2011 uprisings generated anxieties that were embedded in both everyday gendered experiences and longer-standing social and cultural constructions of gender. In general, the violence, instability, and uncertainty in the aftermath of the 2011 uprisings, particularly in Syria, undermined support for revolutionary movements and projects of radical sociopolitical change. Meanwhile, fears about women's rights and personal safety and security were mobilized and appropriated to support authoritarian renewal, military repression, and other violent and exclusionary projects. In Egypt, fears of Islamist rule and perceived threats to women's rights underpinned the support of many women for the military's ouster of Mohamed Morsi. Similarly, in Jordan and Lebanon, fears of the rise of jihadist-Salafists among the Syrian opposition and the perceived threats to women's rights led some women to express support for the Syrian regime. Meanwhile, threats to women's personal safety, security, and the well-being of their families, perceived to be the result of the presence of large numbers of Syrian refugees, have been articulated in ways that reproduce gendered and racialized hierarchies and legitimize the political status quo.

As previous chapters have demonstrated, women's rights may often be positioned in contradictory ways in relation to dominant power structures due to the complex ways in which gender, as a discourse and embodied enactment, is constantly reworked in relation to shifts in the geopolitical order. On the one hand, the 2011 uprisings opened up new opportunities for activists to voice women's rights demands and to insist that gender justice was integral to calls for freedom, dignity, and social justice. Yet, on the other hand, fears about women's rights were successfully mobilized and appropriated to legitimize highly repressive regimes and exclusionary and violent projects. In Egypt, in particular, a reformulated state feminism played an important role in legitimizing the Sisi regime. This seemingly paradoxical relationship between women's rights and authoritarianism can be understood as a legacy of the historical relationship of gender to modernity and sovereignty. As a marker of modernity, which, in turn, is performative of sovereignty, women's rights, including women's public visibility, may be articulated with both emancipatory and disciplinary projects dependent upon the geopolitical context. In a context of *anti*colonial or *anti*-geopolitical struggle, women's rights may become symbols of freedom and justice. However, in a context of *post*colonial state building or the rebuilding of geopolitical *order*, women's rights may become objects of securitization and masculinist protection. This means that, as feminist scholars and activists, we must always be attentive to the broader geopolitical context in which women's rights and personal safety are being advocated.

Despite high levels of repression in Egypt, women's activism continues. Nonetheless, it has largely (re)turned to depoliticized, NGO-ized activism in which women's rights are addressed in isolation of questions of authoritarianism and social justice. Alongside this, there exist examples of non-contentious activism, which, rather than addressing itself to formal political power, orients itself toward society, seeking to raise awareness of and discuss gender and sexuality issues through educational and cultural activities. Such trends highlight the resilience of women's activism and its ability to continue to question dominant gender relations and norms in adverse conditions. However, at the time of writing, women's activism is no longer part of a wider movement to transform politics and society, since such movements no longer exist. Meanwhile, women's activism continues unabated in Jordan, Lebanon, and many other countries in the MENA region, and women are highly visible in new movements that are challenging the geopolitical and sociopolitical status quo. More research is needed not only to document the various activities of a new generation of women but also to understand the ways in which their activism is challenging intersecting structures of power, from the personal to the global.

Conclusion

It's about creating that platform where you can actually be in community and in communion and you can, you find place, you find space. I think that's a very important aspect. When I was talking about the freedom to belong, I was talking about what are the risks individuals take in the process of creating change and the very difficult negotiations that make what you do very incremental [...] because [...] when you are living in this construct of the extended family and the security apparatus and the very conservative culture that's actually extremely patriarchal, you want to still be able to operate as a change agent, but you want to be able to [...] be part of the people and not isolate yourself fully and be in your bubble.

SAMAR DUDIN,
theater director and activist, Jordan

I BEGAN THIS BOOK BY OUTLINING my initial motivations for writing about women's activism in the MENA region. I set out to counter the Orientalist assumptions implicit in much commentary on the mass protests and uprisings of 2011, which tended to view women's involvement as novel or exceptional within the context of Middle East and North African "culture." By contrast, this book has captured some of the history of women's activism that long predates the 2011 uprisings. Indeed, rather than MENA "culture" being a barrier to women's activism, historically constructed gender norms of female respectability in relation to anticolonial and postcolonial projects of modernity and sovereignty enabled the emergence of women's public activism. Nevertheless, dominant gender norms have also regulated and constrained women's activism. At times, women activists have resisted these gender norms; at other times, they have contributed to reproducing them; and at yet other times, they have resignified them. However, as Samar's quote suggests, they cannot escape these gendered forms of power that are inextricably bound up with the wider sociopolitical and geopolitical context.

In particular, the book has highlighted the legacies of colonialism and anticolonial struggle in producing a certain geopolitical logic—consisting of the need to construct an "inner" domain of national/cultural difference, protected from ongoing violations of sovereignty by Western powers. This geopolitical logic continues to structure gender relations, identities, and norms and has informed the resistance of governing elites and some other social and political actors to legal reforms that would transform gender relations and norms. Laws that deeply affect gender relations, including personal status laws, nationality laws, and domestic violence laws are understood not as matters of citizenship rights but rather as issues that touch on the very fabric of the state and society, with repercussions for their future and stability. In other words, the personal is geopolitical and the geopolitical is personal. This has implications for how we practice transnational feminist solidarity, since support for women's struggles in the MENA may be perceived/constructed by their respective regimes as a violation of state sovereignty, met with measures that further strengthen rather than dismantle the boundaries of the "inner" domain that underpins gender hierarchies.

The geopolitical logic that gives rise to gender inequality has not prevented women activists from achieving some gains in women's rights, such as, the introduction of *khula'* divorce and laws criminalizing sexual harassment, as well as the repeal of the so-called "marry your rapist" laws. In advancing these rights, women activists have creatively leveraged notions of cultural difference as well as its flip side, desires for progress and modernization in the "outer" domain, in order to reform, rather than radically revise, gender relations. Hence, for the most part, the effects of women's activism are circumscribed and incremental, rather than fundamental or consistent. Hence, women's activism cannot be reduced to *either* resistance to *or* compliance with hegemonic power. This complexity challenges dichotomous representations of women in the Middle East and North Africa as either victims of patriarchy, authoritarianism, and war or as heroines courageously resisting oppression and violence. For the most part, agency and activism are not so clear cut, as power relations are multilayered and multiscalar. As scholars, we must avoid succumbing to the "romance of resistance" (Abu-Lughod 1990) as well as dismissing or ignoring those acts that do not meet expected notions of resistance; we must be aware of the different geographies of activism, its constraints, and its multiscalar effects. Women may simultaneously be victims and agents, depending upon the context. In this respect, the book has demonstrated the importance of considering women's activism in relation to specific historical moments and different regional and international orders, from decolonization to the US hegemony of the post–Cold War moment, as well as in relation to specific geopolitical projects, including anti-imperialist struggles and anti-regime uprisings. Women's activism may resist hegemonic power at, for example, the interpersonal level, while reinscribing it at the national or international levels.

It is only in exceptional moments that women activists have been able to resist multiple layers of power simultaneously. During periods of crisis, for example, in the aftermath of military defeat or regime breakdown, women have found themselves at the center of geopolitical contestations but also able to take advantage of the breakdown in the status quo to challenge not only hegemonic constructs of gender but the whole geopolitical edifice built upon these. This is especially the case when women's activism is part of wider movements for sociopolitical and geopolitical change, as occurred in the wake of the 1967 defeat and the 2011 uprisings. Since 2011, a significant feature of women's activism has been their insistence on ensuring that demands for gender justice are voiced alongside those for social justice, political accountability, and the end of corruption and sectarianism. This resolve was not only apparent in the mass mobilizations of 2011–13, but even more so in mass protests and uprisings after 2018 in Lebanon, Iraq, Algeria, and Sudan. The ability of women to achieve their demands depends on the success of the movements in which they are embedded. As the most powerful governments in the world ignore widely reported human rights abuses and enable militarized repression, violence, and conflict by continuing to arm state militaries and non-state military actors in the MENA region, activists have continued to face considerable challenges in realizing their demands. Moreover, it is also important to examine the role of the World Bank and the IMF, whose assistance to MENA governments is predicated on the continuation of economic policies that prevent social justice. In other words, the geopolitical and economic interests of the world's most powerful governments and organizations constitute significant obstacles to fundamental change that would support transformations in gender relations and norms in the MENA region.

The women whose narratives form the basis of this book do not represent all women in the MENA region, and it is not possible to generalize about the experiences, priorities, or desires of all based on the group of women interviewed here. Women's experiences differ across the MENA region, according to class, ethnicity, religious background, place of residence, citizenship status, nationality, and generation, while their perceptions of the world and events may depend upon their ideological and political outlooks. Therefore, the experiences of the particular women studied here should be understood as a partial view. However, this does not undermine the validity of their words. As Donna Haraway (1988) argues, all knowledge is situated and, therefore, partial. The impartial "view from nowhere" is a fiction. The narratives of women activists presented here contribute a view from "somewhere"—a positionality that is rarely considered in the study of the politics and international relations of the MENA region, which, instead, has long focused on the equally partial perspective and experience of (male) political leaders, armed actors, and economic elites.

Rather than trying to present a universal law about the relationship between women's activism and geopolitics, this book has demonstrated how the narratives of women activists can be an important means through which to understand how power operates at multiple scales from the personal to the global and how it may be reconfigured over time. In this respect, women's activism can be seen as a "diagnostic of power" (Abu-Lughod 1990: 95–96) that reveals power as a multilayered web over multiple sites, foregrounding "the links, the relationships, between the local and the global" and the ways in which "these links are conceptual, material, temporal, contextual, and so on" (Mohanty 2003: 242). Such an approach to studying the international relations in/of the MENA does not simply come down to "add women and stir." It invites us to ask more fundamental questions about the bases of power, how power is reproduced across time and space, and how it may be resisted or transformed. It obliges us to think about the normative implications of our research and whose interests it serves.

NOTES

INTRODUCTION

1. Laura Shepherd also discusses these examples to explore the relationship between performances of gender and global politics. She concludes that the Mothers of the Plaza de Mayo remained within the boundaries of acceptable gender behaviors while the Greenham Common women went beyond the boundaries of acceptable gender behavior and, therefore, were viewed as more threatening (2015: 29–31). While I find useful Shepherd's analysis of the ways in which the different sets of activists performed their gender identity in relation to their movement objectives, nevertheless, in terms of assessing the degree to which these activisms were transgressive, it is crucial to consider the particular geopolitical context in which each was performed. The activities of the Mothers of the Plaza de Mayo should be considered transgressive in the context of a military dictatorship in which opposition to the regime was very limited and high risk.

2. Not all nationalists supported the emancipation of women. For example, in Egypt, the Watani party, headed by Mustafa Kamil, viewed it as a Western imposition that threatened to undermine Egyptian society. Nonetheless, the issue of women's rights was part of a modernizing trend that was in the ascendancy (Badran 1991: 204–6).

3. For a discussion of the associated concept of "respectability" in the context of interwar Egypt, see Hammad (2017).

4. The boundaries of the states formed out of the former Ottoman Empire after World War I were largely decided by the British and French. The states of North Africa, including Egypt, had existed as autonomous provinces since before colonial encroachment, yet their state institutions were profoundly shaped by colonialism. Israel's pre-1967 borders were established on the basis of territories acquired in the 1948 Arab-Israeli war.

5. Only the personal status codes of Tunisia, Morocco, Algeria, and Libya do not use the term *obedience* (*nushuz*) with regard to a wife's obligations in marriage.

However, they still refer to the husband's obligation of financial maintenance (Welchman 2007: 94–96).

6. This law has been repealed in Egypt, Jordan, Lebanon, Morocco, and Tunisia.

7. For a discussion of how middle-class women in Bangladesh use clothing choices as "an embodied cultural capital and a site of negotiation of their identities and practices of both respectability and progressive new womanhood," see Hussein (2018: 106).

8. Other examples of narrative methods in the fields of feminist IR and feminist security studies include Wibben (2010), Shepherd (2012), and Duncanson (2013). Meanwhile, narratives have also been taken up in the field of critical IR as an alternative style of academic expression providing new insights into the relationships between the personal and the international (see Dauphinee 2013; Inayatullah 2011; Inayatullah and Dauphinee 2016).

9. In this respect, the Women and Memory Forum and the Emily Bisharat Studies and Documentation Center of the Jordanian Women's Union hold some private collections and memoirs but only of a few high-profile women activists. The AUC Library has digitized editions of the journal of the feminist organization Bint al-Nil Association (founded in 1948) but does not hold digitized collections of other organizations relevant to this study.

10. I conducted the interviews in English and Arabic. Those in English were transcribed, and those in Arabic were translated into English by Captivate Arabia (a company based in Jordan). An open-access digital archive of the audio and transcripts of most of these interviews (where consent has been given) will be made available through the School of Oriental and African Studies (University of London) Library to coincide with the publication of this book. See, https://digital.soas.ac.uk/mewa/all

11. Examples of events attended include: a seminar on women and security in Gharifeh, Lebanon, October 2013, organized by one of my interviewees, Ferial Abu Hamdan, a community activist in the Chouf mountains; a seminar launching a report on sexual violence against women in the wake of the 30 June 2013 demonstrations, held at the offices of Nazra for Feminist Studies, Cairo, Egypt, December 2013; and a reception for the Making Way for Young Women in the Middle East program, organized by a Swedish women's rights NGO, Kvinna til Kvinna, in Amman, Jordan, May 2014. Literature was collected from almost all of the organizations in which I interviewed women. See the appendix for a list of organizations relevant to the book.

12. For work on marginalized women's activisms, see, for example, Chatty and Rabo (1997), Hoodfar (1997), Richter-Devroe (2012), and Singerman (1997).

13. As Nadje Al-Ali's work on the Egyptian women's movement demonstrates, *secularism* is a term that takes on different meanings among women activists and should definitely not be interpreted to mean that women completely exclude religion from their activist concerns (2000: 128–48). Indeed, as discussed in

chapter 5, many "secular" women activists draw on religion to justify women's rights reforms.

14. For an in-depth exploration of the activism of the Egyptian Muslim Sisterhood during and after the 2011 uprising, see Biagini (2017a, 2017b).

15. See Deeb (2006) for further discussion of Hizbollah's gatekeeping practices.

16. A detailed list of interviewees and the dates and places of interviews can be found in the appendix. Interviewees were asked whether they would prefer to speak in Arabic or English. Approximately one-third of the interviews were conducted in Arabic or a mixture of Arabic and English. Interviews were mostly conducted in the offices of the organizations where individuals worked/volunteered or in coffee shops or restaurants. Some interviews were conducted in homes.

CHAPTER ONE. FEMALE RESPECTABILITY AND EMBODIED NATIONAL SOVEREIGNTY

1. While much of the focus of this press was on educating women to adopt "modern, hygienic, and rational principles for developing 'productive members of society'" (Shakry 1998: 126; see also Badran 1995: 62), this should not be interpreted as a conservative reaction against calls for the reform of women's roles. Rather, the modernization of women's domestic roles was deemed essential for the modernization of the family in order to overcome the nation's "backwardness" vis-à-vis Europe (Abu-Lughod 1998a, 1998b; Ahmed 1982; Baron 1994; Philipp 1978).

2. For a discussion of Lebanese working-class women's participation in strikes and protests against the French, see Abisaab 2010: 57–88.

3. The maternity leave and crèches only applied where companies hired more than one hundred female workers. In practice, many companies would hire less than one hundred women in order to avoid providing childcare facilities.

4. According to Emily Naffa in an interview with the author in Amman, 2007, this organization was closed by Glubb Pasha. Joseph Massad (2001: 96) also mentions this, based on an unpublished paper by Emily Naffa. However, she did not mention this in our interview in 2014. Nor is this mentioned in Suhair al-Tal's extensive account of the Jordanian women's movement (al-Tal 2014).

5. The only academic critique published in English of Lebanon before the outbreak of the civil war was Michael Hudson's *Precarious Republic* (1968). However, at the time, there were many political critiques of the system by the new ideological parties.

6. In 1943, an electoral law was passed allocating parliamentary seats at a ratio of 6:5, Christians to Muslims (Traboulsi 2007: 106). This balance was supposed to reflect the distribution of population among the religious sects according to the census of 1932 (the last census taken in the country), despite the fact that Lebanese demography had changed by 1943. Informally, it was agreed to award the presidency to a Maronite, the premiership to a Sunni, and the Speaker of Parliament to a Shi'ite.

This agreement of sharing out the main posts has continued until today, although the powers of the presidency were significantly reduced in the 1989 Ta'if agreement that ended Lebanon's civil war.

7. For the first time, in the May 2018 parliamentary elections, the Lebanese elected women who did not come from one of the big political families. See *New Arab* (2018).

8. Sana is critical of existing family laws. However, the LCW as a whole continues to avoid addressing this issue, which would threaten to divide the Council and provoke opposition from many political and religious leaders. On this issue see Aïssaoui 2002: 107–8; Khattab 2010: 102.

9. For a detailed discussion of women factory workers' strikes during this period, see Abisaab 2010.

CHAPTER TWO. THE 1967 DEFEAT AND ITS AFTERMATH: THE BREAKDOWN OF THE GENDER ORDER AND THE EXPANSION OF WOMEN'S ACTIVISM

1. Palestinians who fled during the 1967 war were predominantly from the West Bank, holding Jordanian citizenship, and, therefore, are considered "Internally Displaced Persons" by the Jordanian government, rather than refugees. However, those who were already displaced in 1948, in addition to those fleeing from the Gaza Strip, were registered with UNRWA as refugees. See Al Abed (2004) for more details on the different categories of Palestinians in Jordan.

2. "Jews" refers to Israelis.

3. Although sisters, Farida and Amina transliterate their family name, al-Naqqash, differently, with Farida's spelling following more closely Anglophone conventions and Amina's spelling, Francophone conventions.

4. Kamal Abu Eita, a long-standing union activist, was minister of labor between July 2013 and March 2014.

5. As an illustration of the stigma surrounding women's political activism, after being imprisoned in 1981, Farida El-Nakkash wrote a letter to her daughter expressing feelings of guilt over her separation from her children as a result of her political activities (see Booth 1987).

6. It is important to name these women and recognize their role in building the Palestinian movement in Lebanon. This role is completely ignored in histories of the PLO in Lebanon, such as Yezid Sayigh (1997) and Rex Brynen (1990). Meanwhile, Palestinian women's activism in Lebanon is never discussed in histories of the Lebanese women's movement (for example, Stephan 2012; Daou 2014).

7. The exact number of people killed is disputed and ranges from a few hundred to a few thousand. Bayan Nuwayhed al-Hout's painstaking research verified names of at least 1,390 victims (al-Hout 2004).

8. Fieldwork notes, Beirut, 29 October 2013.

CHAPTER THREE. THE GENDERED EFFECTS OF POLITICAL REPRESSION AND VIOLENCE IN THE 1970S AND 1980S

1. Farida's willingness to recognize Israel following its withdrawal from lands occupied after the 1967 war is reflective of the position of communist parties across the Arab world, which, in line with the Soviet Union, accepted the 1947 partition of the Mandate of Palestine (see Flores 1979).

2. Before his death, Nasser had already recognized the need to reform the state-led economy as part of the "March 30 Program," adopted in 1968. While this program paved the way for the reintroduction of private capital into the economy, it was on a rather more modest scale than Sadat's Open Door Policy.

3. CEDAW was ratified on 18 September 1981. The Egyptian government stated its compliance with all articles subject to them not contravening the sharia. This particularly pertains to the article on gender equality in marriage, divorce, and family life. United Nations Treaty Collection (n.d.).

4. Other organizations that emerged during this period were not founded by women activists from political movements and parties but rather by professional women influenced by ideas from the field of international development, such as women's empowerment, micro-credit, and legal awareness, such as, the Alliance for Arab Women (AAW) and the Association for the Development and Enhancement of Women (ADEW) (Al-Ali 2000: 160–64).

5. Israel remained in control of a twelve-mile wide swath of Lebanese territory along the border, which it designated as a "security zone," until 2000.

CHAPTER FOUR. THE POLITICAL ECONOMY AND GEOPOLITICS OF WOMEN'S ACTIVISM AFTER THE COLD WAR

1. In 2007, the Lebanese army destroyed Nahr El-Bared refugee camp, near Tripoli, in the course of battling against a militant Islamist group called Fateh al-Islam. Since then, Palestinians displaced from their homes have been living in temporary shelters and under highly repressive security surveillance by the Lebanese authorities. Among others, see Aboud 2009; Hanafi and Long 2010; Ramadan 2009.

2. Palestinian NGOs in Lebanon must register as Lebanese NGOs, since Palestinians do not have the right to form autonomous associations. This means that Lebanese citizens make up a large part of the NGO administration, but the NGO effectively works for the Palestinian community alone. Other NGOs serving the Palestinian community are foreign NGOs. See Suleiman 1997.

3. Other groups that, at the time of my interview, did not adhere to a formalized NGO structure were the Uprising of Women in the Arab World, a Facebook group

founded by Lebanese, Palestinian, and Egyptian women to raise awareness of women's issues in relation to the uprisings and promote solidarity among women activists across the Arab region, which really took off in 2012; Thawrat El Banat, a campaign group created mainly by young, Egyptian women in 2012, using social media to raise issues around women's bodily autonomy; and Ikhtiyar, a collective of young Egyptian women and men, created in 2013 to promote indigenous knowledge production about gender and sexuality.

4. Fieldwork notes, Beirut, 24 October 2013.

CHAPTER FIVE. WOMEN'S RIGHTS AS GEOPOLITICAL DISCOURSE: THE STRUGGLE OVER GEOGRAPHY IN THE POST–COLD WAR PERIOD

1. In interviews in 2007, several women in Jordan and Lebanon, including Palestinian women, mentioned their participation in conferences of the Women's International Democratic Federation (WIDF), which was founded in 1945 and was mainly active during the Cold War. The Federation's objectives included fighting fascism, and promoting equality between men and women and solidarity with women in anticolonial struggles. In particular, it played an important role in promoting anticolonial stances and highlighting the links between colonial oppression and women's oppression, including at the UN (Armstrong 2016; McGregor 2016). Egyptian women's participation in WIDF and other antiimperialist international women's conferences is documented in Botman (1988), Khater and Nelson (1988), and Bier (2011).

2. Egypt first established a national women's machinery in 1975, but it was largely ineffective (Tallawy 1997: 133).

3. At the time of writing, Article 340 and Article 98 remain on the books, enabling defendants to claim that they perpetrated murder either in defense of family honor or in a fit of rage, which affords a reduced sentence. However, the government introduced a special tribunal in 2009 to hear "honor" crimes, which has resulted in harsher sentences (Husseini 2010: 3).

4. Following the return of the parliament in 2003, many of these temporary laws were rejected by the lower house (Al-Atiyat 2012: 157–60). With regard to the minimum age of marriage, a judge may grant permission to marry to anyone over the age of fifteen, if it is believed to be in the individual's interests. In 2014, the children of Jordanian women and foreign fathers were granted special benefits, including ID cards allowing them to obtain free health care and education, driver's licenses, and work permits, but were refused Jordanian citizenship.

5. See Dana Olwan (forthcoming) for further details.

6. Corinne L. Mason uses the term *genderwash* to refer to the ways in which women's rights concerns are coopted for imperialist projects, mobilizing particular gender, sexual, and racial logics (Mason 2013: 63–65).

7. The Campaign against So-Called Honor Killings founded in 1999 and the No Honor in Crime (La sharaf fi-l-jarima) founded in 2009, both in Jordan, also refused external funding. See Husseini 2009; Nanes 2003; La sharaf fi-l-jarima website.

8. The pragmatic-instrumentalist approaches to religion discussed here should be differentiated from spiritual-holistic approaches to religion and women's rights. For example, self-identifying Islamic feminist Omaima Abou-Bakr, an Egyptian university professor and founding member of Women and Memory Forum, views Islamic feminism as an intellectual and philosophical project based on *ijtihad* (independent reasoning) to "produc[e] an Islamic knowledge that revives and emphasizes gender justice, equality, and partnership—a knowledge alternative to the processes of exclusion and sense of male superiority we find in most traditional discourses" (Abou-Bakr 2013: 4). Since 2011, Omaima Abou-Bakr has developed her project of Islamic feminism into a holistic ethical-political project (for example, see Abou-Bakr 2015). At the heart of this project is the Quran and "its mandate of moral agency for all humans" (Abou-Bakr 2013: 5). Heba Raouf Ezzat, a high-profile Egyptian Islamic thinker and political theorist, is also engaged in a broader project of Islamic revival, reinterpreting Islamic sources to create a holistic ethical project. Raouf Ezzat differs from Abou-Bakr in that she rejects the term *feminism*, which she regards as embedded within a particular, secular intellectual paradigm (El-Gowhary 1994; Raouf Ezzat 2009). Although Abou-Bakr and Raouf Ezzat are similarly engaged in an ethical and intellectual project to renew Islamic thinking that has political implications, it is not linked to a particular political or ideological group. Raouf Ezzat is adamant to maintain her political independence and views her public contributions, as she told me, in terms of "teaching people and making people more aware about their situation, more aware about how they can understand politics and society. But also understand themselves." Abou-Bakr briefly joined the Wasat Party after the ouster of Mubarak in 2011 but became gradually disillusioned and resigned from the party in early 2013. It is important to note that, in the Arab world, such an approach to women's rights within Islam has yet to become a wider social movement.

9. See also Valentine Moghadam (2002) for an attempt to reconcile the two sides of the debate in the context of Iran.

10. Not her real name.

CHAPTER SIX. THE STRUGGLE OVER GENDER AT THE HEART OF THE ARAB UPRISINGS

1. I use the term *Arab uprisings* to refer to the mass protests that spread across the Arab region, demanding social justice, freedom, and dignity, from the end of December 2010 onward. However, I recognize that not all participants in these protests identified as Arab and, moreover, many referred to them as "revolutions." For further discussions, see El Said et al. (2015b) and Hasso and Salime (2016), among others.

2. Fourth Circle is the location of the prime minister's office.

3. "Mawtini," meaning "My homeland," is a patriotic song based on a poem written c. 1934 by Palestinian poet Ibrahim Touqan and set to music by Lebanese composer Muhammed Flayfel. It served as Palestine's unofficial national anthem until 1996 and was adopted as Iraq's national anthem in 2004 (nationalanthems.info, n.d.).

4. In May 2008, following months of growing political tensions between the government (March 14 bloc) and the opposition (March 8 bloc), Hizbollah took over several parts of West Beirut, confronting the militia of the Future Movement and resulting in street battles that left eleven dead (BBC 2008).

5. Salma's mother is Anissa Hassouna, quoted in chapter 1.

6. Waleed Jumblatt is the long-standing leader of the Progressive Socialist Party (PSP)—the main Druze party. Marwan Hamadeh is a high-profile member of the PSP, who has served in many different cabinets since the 1980s. Here, Ferial underlines the futility of pitting herself against such seasoned politicians with vast networks of patronage among the Druze community.

7. This person requested anonymity in relation to this particular quote.

8. As discussed in the previous chapter, in 2005, women protesters spoke out against the use of sexual harassment by regime-hired thugs. In 2008, Noha al-Ostaz successfully prosecuted a man who groped her in public. In the same year, a coalition of sixteen NGOs launched a Taskforce for Combatting Sexual Violence and, in 2010, proposed a law to combat sexual violence. In 2009, the Egyptian Center for Women's Rights published the first survey on sexual harassment in Egypt. For an excellent summary of these efforts, see Abdelmonem (2015), Kirollos (2016).

CHAPTER SEVEN. THE GENDERED GEOPOLITICS
OF FEAR AND COUNTERREVOLUTION

1. See, Ikhtiyar: https://www.facebook.com/ikhtyarforgenderstudies/; Girls' Revolution: https://www.facebook.com/EgyGirlsRev/; Bint al-Masarwa: https://www.facebook.com/bntalmasarwa/?fref=mentions.

2. For an indepth discussion of the leadership role of women in the Muslim Brotherhood post-2013, see Biagini (2017a, 2017b).

INTERVIEWEES

This list states the affiliation/occupation of each individual at the time of the interview.

EGYPT

All interviews conducted between December 2013 and January 2014, except for those indicated with an asterisk, which were conducted in March 2013.

Abdel Waheb El Afify, Nadia, New Woman Foundation; Egyptian Social Democratic Party, b. Cairo, 1951

Abdelaal, Doaa, Ikhtiyar Collective; Women Living Under Muslim Laws, b. Cairo, 1976

Abdel Sattar, Manar Hussein, Revolutionary Socialist, b. Cairo, 1968

Abou-Bakr, Omaima, Women and Memory Forum, b. Alexandria, 1957

Abouelnaga, Shereen, professor of English literature, Cairo University, b. Cairo, 1966

Adli, Magda, El-Nadim Center for the Rehabilitation of Victims of Violence and Torture, b. Cairo, 1953

Ahmed, Shaima Abdel Rahman, Independent Teachers Union, b. Cairo, 1981

Al-Naccache, Amina, Tagammu' Party, b. Daqhaliyya, 1948

Assaad, Marie, FGM Taskforce, b. Cairo, 1932, died 2018.

Darwiche, Nawla, New Woman Foundation, b. Cairo, 1949

Ebeid, Nevine, New Woman Foundation, b. Cairo, 1972

Eidarous Al-Kassir, Elham, 'Aysh wa Horreya Party, b. Giza (Greater Cairo), 1980

El Ashwal, Nagwan, PhD researcher at the European University Institute (EUI), Italy, independent youth activist, b. Fayoum, 1980

El-Hefnawy, Karima, Egyptian Socialist Party, b. Cairo, 1953

El-Mahdi, Rabab, political activist; professor of political science, AUC, b. Saudi Arabia, 1974

Elmohandes, Amal, Nazra for Feminist Studies, b. Dubai, 1980

El-Nakkash, Farida*, Tagammu' (National Progressive Unionist) Party, b. Daqhaliyya, 1940

El-Naqqash, Salma, Nazra for Feminist Studies, b. Cairo, 1987

Elsadda, Hoda, professor of Arabic literature, Cairo University, and founder of Women and Memory Forum, b. Cairo, 1958

El Said, Maha F., professor of English language and literature, Cairo University, b. Cairo, 1960

El Shaker, Naglaa (pseudonym), Muslim Sisters, b. Cairo, 1978

Emam Sakory, Fatma, researcher, women's rights activist, b. Cairo, 1982

Ezzat, Mona, New Woman Foundation, 'Aysh wa Horreya Party, b. Cairo, 1974

Ezzeldin, Iman, assistant professor of drama and theater criticism, Ayn Shams University, b. Cairo, 1956

Fouad, Sanaa, Doctors' Syndicate, b. Cairo, 1951

Hassan, Mozn, Nazra for Feminist Studies, b. Saudi Arabia, 1979

Hassan, Maissan, Women and Memory Forum, b. Alexandria, 1985

Hassouna, Anissa Essam, Magdi Yacoub Foundation, b. Cairo, 1953

Helmi, Heba Ali, artist, Revolutionary Socialist, b. Cairo, 1969

Kamal, Hala, Women and Memory Forum, b. Kuwait, 1968

Kamel, Azza, Appropriate Communications Techniques for Development (ACT), b. Cairo, 1960

Loutfi, Arab, filmmaker and leftist activist, b. Sidon (Lebanon), 1953

Mitwalli, Noura (pseudonym), Muslim Sisters, b. Cairo, 1989

Nagy, Salma, Egypt Freedom Party, b. Cairo, 1980

Ramadan, Fatma, EIPR, Independent Union, b. Minufiyya, 1966

Raouf Ezzat, Heba, professor of political science, Cairo University, b. Cairo, 1965

Saad Zaghloul, Nihal, Imprint Movement/Haraket Bassma, b. Cairo, 1985

Saber, Kholoud, human rights activist; teaching assistant at Cairo University, b. Cairo, 1985

Saleh, Mai, New Woman Foundation, b. Cairo, 1982

Seif El Dawla, Aida, psychiatrist; Nadim Center for the Rehabilitation of Victims of Violence, b. Cairo, 1954

Shukrallah, Hala, Development Alternatives, b. Cairo, 1957

Shukrallah, Salma, journalist and activist, b. Cairo, 1985

Soueif, Laila, assistant professor of mathematics, Cairo University, b. London, 1956

Soliman, Azza, Center for Egyptian Women's Legal Assistance, b. Cairo, 1966

Wahba, Dina, women's rights activist; Egyptian Social Democratic Party, b. Cairo, 1986

Zohny, Sally, storyteller, feminist, b. Cairo, 1985

JORDAN

All interviews conducted in April–May 2014, except for *, interviewed in January 2014.

Abu Elba, Abla, secretary general of HASHD, b. Qalqilya, Palestine, early 1950s

Al-Bashir, Haifa, White Beds Society; Jordan Psychiatric and Rehabilitation Centre; Senior Citizens Forum, b. Nablus, Palestine, 1931

Al Jaabari, Rania, writer and journalist, b. Amman, 1980

Al-Rayan, Tereza, Jordanian Women's Union, b. Madaba, 1954

al-Saadi, Muyassar, Families Development Association, b. Haifa, Palestine, 1947

al-Tal, Suhair Salti, writer and researcher, b. Irbid, 1952

Al-Zuriekat, Adma, Teachers' Movement, b. Karak, 1967

Batshon, Dina, youth activist, b. Amman, 1989

Darwish, Maha, IBDAA Foundation, b. Ramallah, Palestine, approximately, 1960s

Dawany, Lubna, lawyer and human rights activist, b. Amman, early 1960s

Deeb, Hala, Jordanian Women's Union, b. Kuwait, 1971

Dudin, Samar, theater director and community organizer, b. Hebron, Palestine, 1962

Ejeilat, Lina, *7iber.com*, b. Amman, sometime in the 1980s

Habashna, Nimeh, blogger and writer; "My Mother is Jordanian and her nationality is my right" campaign, b. Lebanon, 1958, d. 2015

Jabiri, Afaf*, Jordanian Women's Union, academic, b. Baqa' Camp, 1972

Khader, Asma, women's rights activist, lawyer, b. West Bank, 1952

Masannat, Samah, social activist and voluntary worker, b. Karak, 1967

Musimi, Hayat, Islamic Action Front, b. Nablus, Palestine, 1962

Naffa, Emily, Arab Women Organization of Jordan, b. Salt, 1932

Naffa Hamarneh, Leila, Arab Women Organization of Jordan, b. Amman, 1944

Naffa, Randa, gender consultant and founder of SADAQA, b. Amman, approx. 1970s

Nasser, Lamis, independent consultant and researcher; Human Rights Forum for Women, b. Jerusalem, Palestine, 1943

Nims, Salma Elia, formerly Taqaddam Platform, incoming head of the Jordanian National Commission for Women, b. Amman, 1971

Shamroukh, Nadia, Jordanian Women's Union, b. Bethlehem, Palestine, 1957

Soubh, Aroub, media professional; spokesperson, Coalition for "My Nationality Is the Right of My Family," b. Amman, 1969

Tahboub, Dima, Shura Council, Islamic Action Front, b. Hebron, Palestine, mid-1960s

LEBANON

All interviews conducted October–November 2013.

Abu Hamdan, Ferial, Lebanese Committee for Peace and Freedom, b. Amman, 1955

Al-Yassir, Wafa Ali, Norwegian People's Aid, activist in field of Palestinian rights, b. Beirut, 1954

Ali, Leila, Association Najdeh, b. Shatila Refugee Camp, 1964

Anani, Ghida, director of ABAAD, b. Beirut, 1981

Anid, Nada, Women in Front, b. Beirut, 1962

Attieh, Romy Lynn, MA anthropology, AUB, b. USA, 1982

Bou Karroum, Joulia, NGO worker; human rights defender, activist, b. United Arab Emirates, 1980

Charafeddine, Fahima, women's rights activist, b. South Lebanon, 1940s

Dabbous, Dima, formerly Lebanese American University, b. Beirut, 1965

Daou, Bernadette, leftist activist, b. Beirut, 1979

Darwich, Lynn, queer and feminist activist, b. Beirut, 1986

Doughan, Iqbal Murad, lawyer, president of the Lebanese League for Working Women, former president of the Lebanese Council for Women, b. Beirut, 1940s

F., Nimat, humanitarian volunteer, b. Beirut, 1945

Fakhry, Rima, member of Political Bureau, Hezbollah, b. south Lebanon, 1966

Haidar, Diala, Uprising of Women in the Arab World Movement, b. Beirut, 1984

Jammal, Haifa, Norwegian People's Aid, Palestinian rights activist, b. Burj al-Shammali Refugee Camp, 1959

Jarar, Souad Amin, fashion designer, volunteer, b. Saudi Arabia, 1960

Khoury, Gisele, TV journalist, b. Beirut, 1961

Lina, student, singer, b. Beirut, 1982

Mahmoud, Olfat, Women's Humanitarian Organization, b. Burj al-Barajneh Refugee Camp, 1960

Makarem Hilal, May, teacher and social activist, b. Ras el Matn, 1948

Matar, Linda, Lebanese League for Women's Rights, b. Beirut, 1925

Merhy, Joumana, Arab Institute for Human Rights, b. Beirut, 1965

Rouhana, Zoya, KAFA: Enough Violence, b. Beirut, 1955

Saad, Mona, Marouf Saad Foundation, b. Beirut, 1949

Salah, Racha, Social Communication Center, b. Ain al-Hilweh Refugee Camp, 1973

Salah, Samira, member of the Palestinian National Council, b. Tiberias (Palestine), 1944

Salti, Nuha Nuwayri, Chronic Care Center, b. Beirut, 1942

Shidrawi, Mirna, ex-Lebanese Democratic Left, b. Beirut, 1979

Shuayb, Maha, sociology of education researcher, b. Beirut, 1979

Solh, Sana, Lebanese Council of Women, b. Brumanna, 1945, d. 2019

Suliemane, Amne, General Union of Palestinian Women, b. Shatila Refugee Camp, 1952

Zakharia, Leila, social development consultant, b. Beirut, 1945

ORGANIZATIONS

EGYPT

Women's Organizations, Groups and Networks

- Al-Ittihad al-Nissa'i al-Misri (Egyptian Feminist Union)(founded 1923)
- Bint al-Nil (Daughter of the Nile Union) (founded 1948)
- Jama'iyat Tadamun al-Mar'a al-'Arabiya (Arab Women's Solidarity Association) (founded 1982)
- Jama'at Bint al-Ard (Daughter of the Land Association) (founded 1982)
- Jama'at Dirasat al-Mar'a al-Jadida (New Woman Group) (which later became the New Woman Research Center, then New Woman Foundation, founded in the mid-1980s)
- Rabtat al-Mar'a al-'Arabiya (Alliance for Arab Women) (founded 1987)
- Jama'at Nuhud wa Tanmiyat al-Mar'a (Association for the Development and Enhancement of Women) (founded 1987)
- Ittihad al-Nissa'i al-Taqadummi (Progressive Women's Union) (founded approximately in the 1980s)
- Jama'at Dirasat al-Mar'a al-Jadida (New Woman Foundation, previously New Woman Research Center) (registered 2004)
- FGM Taskforce (founded 1994)
- Al-Mar'a wa-l-Zakira (Women and Memory Forum) (founded 1995)
- Markaz al-Musa'ada al-Qanuniya li-l-Mar'a al-Misriya (Center for Egyptian Women's Legal Assistance) (founded 1995)
- Al-Markaz al-Misri li-Huquq al-Mar'a (Egyptian Center for Women's Rights) (founded 1996)
- Muntada al-Mar'a fi-l-Tanmiya (Forum for Women in Development) (founded 1997)

- Nazra li-l-Darasat al-Naswiya (Nazra for Feminist Studies) (founded 2008)
- Operation Anti-Sexual Harassment (OpAntiSh) (founded 2012)
- Tahrir Bodyguards (founded 2012)
- Shuft Taharrush (I Saw Harassment) (founded 2012)
- Baheya Ya Masr (founded 2012)
- Thawrat El Banat (Girls' Revolution) (founded 2012)
- Basma Imprint Movement (founded 2012/13)
- Ikhtiyar: "Choice" for Gender Studies and Research (founded 2013)

Civil Society Organizations, Groups and Networks

- Jama'at al-Ikhwan al-Muslimin (Muslim Brotherhood) (founded 1928)
- Al-Munazama al-Misriya li-Huquq al-Insan (Egyptian Organization for Human Rights) (founded 1985)
- Markaz al-Nadim li-Munahida al-'Unf w-al-Ta'zib (Nadim Center for the Rehabilitation of Victims of Violence and Torture) (founded 1993)
- Markaz al-Wasa'il al-Ittissal al-Mula'ama min ajl al-Tanmiya (Appropriate Communication Techniques for Development) (founded 1990)
- Al-Mubadira al-Misriya li-l-Huquq al-Shakhsiya (Egyptian Initiative for Personal Rights) (founded 2002)
- Majmu'a al-Misriya al-Munahida al-'Awlima (Anti-Globalization Egyptian Group) (founded 2002)
- Al-Lajna al-Sha'biya al-Misriya li-l-Tadamun ma' al-Filastiniyin (Egyptian Popular Committee for Solidarity with the Palestinians) (founded 2002)
- Haraka 9 Maris li-l-Istiqlal al-Jami'at (9 March Movement for the Independence of the Universities) (founded, 2004)
- Kefaya—the Movement for Change (founded, 2004)
- Jibhat li-l-Difa'a 'an al-Muhtajiyin al-Misriyin (Front to Defend Egyptian Protesters) (founded 2010)

Political Parties

- Al-Hizb al-Shuyu'i al-Misri (Egyptian Communist Party) (founded 1921)
- Al-Hizb al-Watani al-Taqadummi al-Wahdawi (National Progressive Unionist Party) (Tagammu') (founded 1977)
- Al-Hizb al-Watani al-Dimuqrati (National Democratic Party) (founded 1978)
- Al-Hizb al-'Arabi al-Dimuqrati al-Nasiri (Arab Democratic Nasserist Party) (Hizb al-Nasiri) (founded 1992)
- Al-Ishtirakiyun al-Thawriyun (Revolutionary Socialists) (founded 1995)

- Hizb al-Wasat (Wasat Party) (founded 1996)
- Al-Hizb al-Misri al-Dimuqrati al-Ijtima'i (Egyptian Social Democratic Party) (founded 2011)
- Al-Hizb al-Ishtiraki al-Misri (Egyptian Socialist Party) (founded 2011)
- Hizb Misr al-Hurriya (Egypt Freedom Party) (founded 2011)
- Hizb al-Hurriya wa-l-'Adala (Freedom and Justice Party) (founded 2011)
- Hizb al-Dastour (Constitution Party) (founded 2012)
- 'Aysh wa Horreya (Bread and Freedom Party) (founded 2013)

Governmental Institutions

- Al-Majlis al-Qawmi li-l-Mar'a (National Council for Women) (founded 2000)

JORDAN

Women's Organizations, Groups and Networks

- Al-Ittihad al-Mar'a al-'Arabiya (Arab Women's Union) (founded 1954)
- Jama'iya al-Nisa' al-'Arabiyat fi-l-Urdunn (Arab Women Organization of Jordan) (founded 1970)
- Ittihad al-Mar'a fi-l-Urdunn (Women's Union in Jordan) (founded 1974)
- Al-Ittihad al-Nissa'i al-Urdunni al-'Am (General Federation of Jordanian Women) (founded 1981)
- Ittihad al-Mar'a al-Urdunniya (Jordanian Women's Union) (founded 1994)
- Jama'iya Mahid al-Dawli li-Tadamun al-Nisa' (Sisterhood Is Global Institute) (founded 1998)
- Campaign against So-Called Honor Killings (founded 1999)
- La Sharaf fi-l-Jarima (No Honor in Crime) (founded 2009)
- SADAQA: Nahu Bi'a 'Amal Sadiqa li-l-Mar'a (Toward a Woman-friendly Work Environment) (founded 2012)
- Umi Urdunniya wa Jinsiyat-ha Haqq Li ("My mother is Jordanian and her nationality is my right" campaign) (founded 2011)
- I'tilaf Jinsiyati Haqq l-'A'ilati (Coalition for My Nationality Is the Right of My Family) (founded 2013)

Civil Society Organizations

- Mizan Law Group for Human Rights (founded 1998)
- Jama'iya al-'Usra al-Tanmiya (Families Development Association) (founded 1999)

- Ruwwad Al-Tanmeya (founded 2005)
- Al-Nahda al-'Arabiya li-l-Dimuqratiya w-al-Tanmiya (Arab Renaissance for Democracy and Development) (founded 2008)

Political Parties

- Al-Hizb al-Shuyu'i al-Urdunni (Jordanian Communist Party) (founded 1948)
- Hizb al-Sha'b al-Dimuqrati al-Urdunni (Jordanian Democratic People's Party) (HASHD) (founded 1989)
- Jabhat al-'Amal al-Islami (Islamic Action Front) (founded 1992)

Governmental Organizations

- Al-Lajna al-Wataniya al-Urdunniya li-Shu'un al-Mar'a (Jordanian National Commission for Women) (founded 1992)

LEBANON

Women's Organizations, Groups and Networks

- Lajna Huquq al-Mar'a al-Lubnaniya (League for Lebanese Women's Rights) (founded 1947)
- Al-Majlis al-Nisa'i al-Lubnani (Lebanese Council for Women) (founded 1952)
- Bahithat: The Lebanese Association of Women Researchers (founded 1987)
- Rabta al-Mar'a al-'Amila (Working Women's League) (founded 1994)
- Al-Tajamu' al-Nisa'i al-Dimuqrati al-Lubnani (Lebanese Women Democratic Gathering) (founded 1976)
- Al-Lajna al-'Ahliya li-Mutab'a Qadaya al-Mar'a (Committee for the Follow-up on Women's Issues) (founded 1996)
- Al-Hay'a al-Lubnaniya li-Munahida al-'Unf did al-Mar'a (Lebanese Council to Resist Violence against Women) (founded 1997)
- Palestinian Women's Humanitarian Organization (founded 1993)
- KAFA 'Unf wa Istighlal: Enough Violence and Exploitation (founded 2005)
- Nasawiya (feminist collective) (founded around 2007)
- ABAAD: Resource Center for Gender Equality (founded 2012)
- Nisa' Ra'idat (Women in Front) (founded 2012)

Civil Society Organizations

- Association Najdeh (founded 1976)
- Mu'asasa Maarouf Saad al-Ijtima'iya w-al-Thaqafiya (Maarouf Saad Social and Cultural Foundation) (founded 1980)
- Al-Jama'iya al-Lubnaniya min ajl Dimuqratiya al-Intikhabat (Lebanese Association for Democratic Elections) (founded 1996)
- Majmu'a al-Abhath wa-l-Tadrib li-l-Amal al-Tanmawi (Collective for Research and Training on Development–Action) (CRTD-A) (founded 1999)

Political Parties, Coalitions, and Movements

- Al-Hizb al-Shuyu'i al-Lubnani (Lebanese Communist Party) (founded 1924)
- Al-Hizb al-Taqadummi al-Ishtiraki (Progressive Socialist Party) (founded 1949)
- Al-Haraka al-Wataniya al-Lubnaniya (Lebanese National Movement) (formed 1969)
- Munazama al-'Amal al-Shuyu'i fi Lubnan (Organization of Communist Action) (founded 1970)
- Jabhat al-Muqawama al-Wataniya al-Lubnaniya (Lebanese National Resistance Front) (formed around 1982)
- Hizbollah (formed 1985)
- Harakat al-Yassar al-Dimuqrati (Democratic Left Movement) (formed 2004)

Governmental Organizations

- Al-Hay'a al-Wataniya li-Shu'un al-Mar'a al-Lubnaniya (National Commission for Lebanese Women) (founded 1996)

PALESTINIAN ORGANIZATIONS

- Harakat al-Qawmiyin al-'Arab (Arab Nationalist Movement) (founded 1951)
- Munazama al-Tahrir al-Filastiniya (Palestine Liberation Organization) (founded 1964)
- Al-Jabha al-Sha'biya li-Tahrir Filastin (Popular Front for the Liberation of Palestine) (founded 1967)
- Al-Jabha al-Dimuqratiya li-Tahrir Filastin (Democratic Front for the Liberation of Palestine) (founded 1969)

- Al-Ittihad al-'Am li-Talaba Filastin (General Union of Palestinian Students) (founded 1959)
- Al-Ittihad al-'Am li-l-Mar'a al-Filastiniya (General Union of Palestinian Women) (founded 1965)

PAN-ARAB ORGANIZATIONS

- Lajnat al-Mar'a fi Ittihad al-Muhamin al-'Arab (Women's Committee of the Arab Lawyers' Union) (date founded unknown)
- Intifada al-Mar'a fi-l-'Alam al-'Arabi (Uprising of Women in the Arab World, Facebook group) (founded 2012)

REFERENCES

Ababneh, Sara. 2016. "Troubling the Political: Women in the Jordanian Day-Waged Workers Movement," *International Journal of Middle East Studies* 48(1): 87–112.

Abboud, Samer N. 2015. *Syria*. Oxford: Polity Press.

Abdalla, Ahmed. 1985. *The Student Movement and National Politics in Egypt 1923–1973*. London: Saqi Books.

Abdel-Baky, M. 2013a. "Protests Continue." *Al-Ahram Weekly Online*, 7–13 January. Accessed 15 April 2018. http://weekly.ahram.org.eg/News/1353.aspx.

———. 2013b. "Something Big Will Happen on 30 June." *Al-Ahram Weekly*, 13–19 June, Accessed 9 February 2018. https://www.masress.com/en/ahramweekly/102985.

Abdel-Latif, Omayma. 2008. *In the Shadow of the Brothers: The Women of the Egyptian Muslim Brotherhood*. Beirut: Carnegie Middle East Center.

Abdel-Razek, Sherine. 2013. "Unkept Promises." *Al-Ahram Weekly Online*, 27 June. Accessed 15 April 2018. https://www.masress.com/en/ahramweekly/103121.

Abdelaal, Doaa, and Eleonora Mura. 2014. "The League of Arab States and Gender: Political Participation and the Arab Woman." In *International IDEA, Inclusive Political Participation and Representation: The Role of Regional Organizations*, edited by Raul Cordenillo and Karin Gardes, 99–120. Stockholm: IDEA.

Abdelmonem, Angie. 2015. "Reconceptualizing Sexual Harassment in Egypt: A Longitudinal Assessment of el-Taharrush el-Ginsy in Arabic Online Forums and Anti-Sexual Harassment Activism." *Kohl: A Journal for Body and Gender Research* 1(1): 23–41.

Abdelrahman, Maha. 2009. "With the Islamists? Sometimes. With the State? Never! Cooperation between the Left and Islamists in Egypt." *British Journal of Middle Eastern Studies*. 36(1): 37–54.

———. 2013. "In Praise of Organization: Egypt between Activism and Revolution." *Development and Change* 44(1): 569–85.

———. 2015. *Egypt's Long Revolution: Protest Movements and Uprisings*. London: Routledge.

———. 2017. "Policing Neoliberalism in Egypt: The Continuing Rise of the 'Securocratic' State." *Third World Quarterly* 31(1): 185–202.

Abisaab, Malek Hassan. 2010. *Militant Women of a Fragile Nation*. Syracuse, NY: Syracuse University Press.

Abou-Bakr, Omaima. 2013. "Introduction: Why Do We Need an Islamic Feminism?" In *Feminist and Islamic Perspectives: New Horizons of Knowledge and Reform*, edited by Omaima Abou-Bakr, trans. Yasmin Motawy, 4–8. Cairo: Women and Memory Forum.

———. 2015. "Islamic Feminism and the Equivocation of Political Engagement: 'Fair Is Foul, and Foul Is Fair.'" In *Rethinking Gender in Revolutions and Resistance: Lessons from the Arab World*, edited by Maha El Said, Lena Meari, and Nicola Pratt, 181–204. London: Zed.

Abou-Habib, Lina. 2003. "Gender, Citizenship, and Nationality in the Arab Region." *Gender and Development* 11(3): 66–75.

Aboud, Samer. 2009. "The Siege of Nahr al-Bared and the Palestinian Refugee Camps in Lebanon." *Arab Studies Quarterly* 31(1–2): 31–48.

Abouelnaga, Shereen. 2015. "Reconstructing Gender in Post-Revolution Egypt." In *Rethinking Gender in Revolutions and Resistance: Lessons from the Arab World*, edited by Maha El Said, Lena Meari, and Nicola Pratt, 152–54. London: Zed.

———. 2016. *Women in Revolutionary Egypt: Gender and the New Geographics of Identity*. Cairo: American University in Cairo Press.

Aboulenein, Ahmed. 2012. "Gender Equality Only within Provisions of Shari'a, Says Constituent Assembly." *Daily News Egypt*, September 22. Accessed 22 September, 2014. http://www.dailynewsegypt.com/2012/09/22/gender-equality-only-within-provisions-of-sharia-says-constituent-assembly/.

Abu Ghazaleh, Veronique. 2014. "Lebanese Women Look to Play Bigger Role in Politics." *Al-Monitor*, November 20. Accessed 21 July 2015. http://www.al-monitor.com/pulse/politics/2014/11/lebanese-women-failing-to-get-into-politics.html.

Abu Hanieh, Hassan. 2008. *Women and Politics from the Perspective of Islamic Movements in Jordan*. Amman: Friedrich Ebert Stiftung.

Abu-Lughod, Lila. 1986. *Veiled Sentiments: Honor and Poetry in a Bedouin Society*. Berkeley: University of California Press.

———. 1990. "The Romance of Resistance: Tracing Transformations of Power through Bedouin Women." *American Ethnologist* 70(1): 41–55.

———. 1998a. *Remaking Women: Feminism and Modernity in the Middle East*. Princeton, NJ: Princeton University Press.

———. 1998b. "The Marriage of Feminism and Islamism in Egypt: Repudiation as a Dynamic of Postcolonial Cultural Politics." In *Remaking Women: Feminism and Modernity in the Middle East*, edited by Lila Abu-Lughod, 243–69. Princeton, NJ: Princeton University Press.

———. 2013. *Do Muslim Women Need Saving?* Cambridge, MA: Harvard University Press.

Abu-Odeh, Adnan. 1999. *Jordanians, Palestinians, and the Hashemite Kingdom in the Middle East Peace Process*. Washington, DC: United States Institute of Peace.

Abu-Odeh, Lama. 2015. "Holier Than Thou? The Anti-Imperialist versus the Local Activist." openDemocracy, 4 May. Accessed 12 November 2015. https://www

.opendemocracy.net/5050/lama-abu-odeh/holier-than-thou-antiimperialist
-versus-local-activist.

Abu-Rish, Ziad. 2012. "The Political Status Quo, Economic Development, and Protests in Jordan." In *The Dawn of the Arab Uprisings: End of an Old Order?*, edited by Bassam Haddad, Rosie Bsheer, and Ziad Abu-Rish, 237–47. London: Pluto Press.

Abu-Zayd, Gehan. 2002. "In Search of Political Power: Women in Parliament in Egypt, Jordan and Lebanon." In *Women in Parliament: Beyond Numbers*, edited by Azza Karam. Stockholm: International IDEA. Accessed 7 April 2016. http://www.idea.int/publications/wip/upload/CS_Egypt.pdf.

Abuqudairi, Areej. 2014. "Women Punished for Marrying Non-Jordanians." Al Jazeera, 20 December. Accessed 12 April 2016. http://www.aljazeera.com/news/middleeast/2014/12/women-punished-marrying-non-jordanians-20141215121425528481.html.

Achcar, Gilbert. 2013. *The People Want: A Radical Exploration of the Arab Uprising*. Berkeley: University of California Press.

———. 2016. *Morbid Symptoms: Relapse in the Arab Uprisings*. Stanford, CA: Stanford University Press.

Adams, Melinda. 2007. "'National Machineries' and Authoritarian Politics: The Case of Cameroon." *International Feminist Journal of Politics* 9(2): 176–97.

Adely, Fida. 2012. "The Emergence of a New Labor Movement in Jordan." *Middle East Report Online*, no. 264 (Fall). Accessed 5 August 2015. http://www.merip.org/mer/mer264/emergence-new-labor-movement-jordan.

Afary, Janet. 2004. "The Human Rights of Middle Eastern and Muslim Women: A Project for the 21st Century." *Human Rights Quarterly* 26(1): 106–25.

Afify, Heba. 2016. "April 6: From Saviours to Outlaws." *Mada Masr*, 6 April. Accessed 8 April 2016. http://www.madamasr.com/sections/politics/april-6-saviors-outlaws.

Afkhami, Mahnaz, and Erika Friedl. 1997. *Muslim Women and the Politics of Participation: Implementing the Beijing Platform*. Syracuse, NY: Syracuse University Press.

Agosti Pinilla, Marta. 2018. "The Female Protestor: Sexual Violence and the Making and Unmaking of the State in Egypt Post January 25, 2011." PhD thesis submitted to the Department of Anthropology and Sociology SOAS, University of London.

Ahmad Zaki, Hind, and Dalia Abdel Hamid. 2014. "Istabaha al-nisa' fi-l-majal al-'am 2." *Jadaliyya*, 10 January. http://www.jadaliyya.com/pages/index/15944 /استباحة-النساء-في-المجال-العام-2.

Ahmed, Leila. 1982. "Feminism and Feminist Movements in the Middle East, a Preliminary Exploration: Turkey, Egypt, Algeria, People's Democratic Republic of Yemen." *Women's Studies International Forum* 5(2): 153–68.

———. 1992. *Women and Gender in Islam*, New Haven, CT: Yale University Press.

Ahmed, Sara. 2014. *The Cultural Politics of Emotions*. Edinburgh: Edinburgh University Press.

Ahram Online. 2012a. "Political Forces Sign On ElBaradei Call for Constituent Assembly Boycott." *Ahram Online*, 29 September. http://english.ahram.org.eg/NewsContent/1/0/54250/Egypt/0/Political-forces-sign-on-ElBaradei-call-for-Consti.aspx.aspx.

———. 2012b. "Women Protest Against Constitution at Cairo University." *Ahram Online*, 19 December. http://english.ahram.org.eg/NewsContent/1/64/60860/Egypt/Politics-/Women-protest-against-constitution-at-Cairo-Univer.aspx.

———. 2014. "Egypt's Mansour Issues Law for Tougher Sexual Harassment Penalties." *Ahram Online*, 5 June. Accessed 29 January 2015. http://english.ahram.org.eg/NewsContent/1/64/103010/Egypt/Politics-/Egypts-Mansour-issues-law-for-tougher-sexual-haras.aspx.

Aïssaoui, Nadia Leïla. 2002. "Les femmes et la citoyenneté dans le Liban d'après-guerre: Image et représentation de la femme dans la sphère publique." Maîtrise de Sociologie, Département de Sciences Sociales, Faculté des Sciences Humaines et Sociales, Université René Descartes—Paris V, Sorbonne.

Al Abed, Oroub. 2004. "Palestinian Refugees in Jordan." *Forced Migration Online*. Accessed 27 April 2016. https://www.fmreview.org/palestine/elabed.

Al-Ali, Nadje, and Nicola Pratt, eds. 2009a. *Women and War in the Middle East*. London: Zed Books.

———. 2009b. *What Kind of Liberation? Women and the Occupation of Iraq*. Berkeley: University of California Press.

Al-Ali, Nadje. 2000. *Secularism, Gender and the State in the Middle East: The Egyptian Women's Movement*. Cambridge: Cambridge University Press.

———. 2007. *Iraqi Women: Untold Stories from 1948 to the Present*. London: Zed Books.

———. 2012. "Gendering the Arab Spring." *Middle East Journal of Culture and Communication* 5(1): 26–31.

———. 2014. "Reflections on (Counter) Revolutionary Processes in Egypt." *Feminist Review, Special issue: Revolutions* 106(1): 122–28.

Al-Arian, Abdullah. 2014. *Answering the Call: Popular Islamic Activism in Sadat's Egypt*. Oxford: Oxford University Press.

Al-Attiyat, Ibtissam. 2003. *The Women's Movement in Jordan: Activism, Discourses and Strategies*. Amman: Friedrich Ebert Stiftung.

———. 2005. "Participation in Public Life and Its Impact on Women in Jordan." In *Building Democracy in Jordan*, edited by Ziad Majed, 25–69. Stockholm: International IDEA.

———. 2012. "Harvests of the Golden Decades: Contemporary Women's Activism in Jordan." In *Mapping Arab Women's Movements: A Century of Transformations from Within*, edited by Pernille Arenfeldt and Nawar Al-Hassan Golley, 133–70. Cairo: American University in Cairo Press.

Al-Haytham, Yusif. 1976. "Lebanon Explodes: 'Battles of Survival'" *MERIP Reports* 44 (1): 3–14.

Al-Hout, Bayan Nuwayhed. 2004. *Sabra and Shatila: September 1982*. London: Pluto Press.

Al-Khatib, Hanifa. 1984. *Tarikh tatawwur al-haraka al-nisa'iyya fi lubnan 1800– 1975.* Beirut: Dar Al-Hadatha.

Al-Maaitah, Rowaida, Arwa Oweis, Muntaha Gharaibeh, Hmoud Olimat, and Hadeel al-Maaitah. 2013. "Arab Women and Political Development." In *Arab Spring and Arab Women: Challenges and Opportunities,* edited by Muhamad S. Olimat, 17–31. London: Routledge.

Al-Mutlaq, Eidah. 1996. "Women and Democracy, Political Performance of Jordanian Women." In *The Democratic Process in Jordan: Deliberations of the Conference on the "Democratic Process in Jordan—Realities and Prospects."* Conference held in Amman 31 May–2 June 1994, edited by Hani Hourani and Hussein Abu-Rumman, 249–61. Amman: Sindbad Publishing House.

Al-Rasheed, Madawi. 2013. *A Most Masculine State: Gender, Politics, and Religion in Saudi Arabia.* Cambridge: Cambridge University Press.

Al-Tahat, Jassar. 2017. "Lower House Approves Domestic Violence Protection Bill, Amendments to Banking Law." *Jordan Times,* 18 April. Accessed 10 November 2018. http://www.jordantimes.com/news/local/lower-house-approves-domestic-violence -protection-bill-amendments-banking-law.

al-Tal, Suhair Salti. 2014. *Tarikh al-Haraka al-Nisa'iya al-Urdunniya, 1944–2008.* Amman: Azmina li-l-nashr wa-l-tawzi'a.

Alaimo, Kara. 2015. "How the Facebook Arabic Page "We Are All Khaled Said" Helped Promote the Egyptian Revolution." *Social Media + Society* 1(1): 1–10.

Alatiyat, Ibtesam, and Hassan Barari. 2010. "Liberating Women with Islam? The Islamists and Women's Issues in Jordan." *Totalitarian Movements and Political Religions* 11(3–4): 359–78.

Alexander, Anne, and Farah Koubaissy. 2008. "Women Were Braver Than a Hundred Men." *Socialist Review,* 321 (January). Accessed 31 May 2020. https:// socialistreview.org.uk/321/women-were-braver-hundred-men.

Allam, Nermin. 2017. *Women and the Egyptian Revolution: Engagement and Activism during the 2011 Arab Uprisings.* Cambridge: Cambridge University Press.

Allinson, Jamie. 2015. *The Struggle for the State in Jordan: The Social Origins of Alliances in the Middle East.* London: I. B. Tauris.

Alvarez, Sonia E. 1990. *Engendering Democracy in Brazil: Women's Movements in Transition Politics.* Princeton, NJ: Princeton University Press.

———. 1999. "Advocating Feminism: The Latin American Feminist NGO 'Boom.'" *International Feminist Journal of Politics* 1(2): 181–209.

Amar, Paul. 2011. "Turning the Gendered Politics of the Security State Inside Out?" *International Feminist Journal of Politics* 13(3): 299–28.

———. 2013a. "Egypt." In *Dispatches from the Arab Spring: Understanding the New Middle East,* edited by Paul Amar and Vijay Prashad, 24–62. Minneapolis: University of Minnesota Press.

Amawi, Abla. 1992. "Democracy Dilemmas in Jordan." *Middle East Report,* no. 174 (January–February): 26–29.

———. 2000. "Gender and Citizenship in Jordan" In *Gender and Citizenship in the Middle East,* edited by Suad Joseph, 158–84. Syracuse, NY: Syracuse University Press.

Amin, Galal. 2000. *Whatever Happened to the Egyptians? Changes in Egyptian Society from 1950 to the Present.* Cairo: American University in Cairo Press.

Amin, S. 2011. "Egyptian General Admits 'Virginity Checks' Conducted on Protesters." CNN Online. Accessed 15 March 2013. http://edition.cnn.com/2011/WORLD/meast/05/30/egypt.virginity.tests/index.html.

Amnesty International. 2011a. "Egyptian Army Condemned over Tahrir Square Protest Breakup." Amnesty International, 9 March, http://www.amnesty.org/en/for-media/press-releases/egyptian-army-condemned-over-tahrir-square-protest-breakup-2011-03-09.

———. 2011b. "Egyptian Women Prisoners Forced to Take 'Virginity Tests.'" Amnesty International, 23 March. Accessed 17 January 2015. http://www.amnesty.org/en/news-and-updates/egyptian-women-protesters-forced-take-virginity-tests-2011-03-23.

———. 2011c. "Egypt: Military Pledges to Stop Forced 'Virginity Tests." Amnesty International, Accessed 7 September 2017. https://www.amnesty.org/en/press-releases/2011/06/egypt-military-pledges-stop-forced-virginity-tests/.

———. 2012. "Egypt: A Year after 'Virginity Tests', Women Victims of Army Violence Still Seek Justice." Amnesty International, 9 March. http://www.amnesty.org/en/news/egypt-year-after-virginity-tests-women-victims-army-violence-still-seek-justice-2012-03-09.

———. 2014. "Egypt: Roadmap to Repression: No End in Sight for Human Rights Violations." Amnesty International, 23 January. Accessed 30 January 2015. http://www.amnesty.org/en/library/asset/MDE12/005/2014/en/cddf8bfb-6dcb-45b2-b411-6d12190b7583/mde120052014en.pdf.

———. 2015. *"Circles of Hell": Domestic, Public and State Violence against Women in Egypt.* MDE 12/004/2015. London: Amnesty International.

———. 2017. "Egypt: NGO Law Threatens to Annihilate Human Rights NGOs." Amnesty International, 30 May. Accessed 16 August 2017. https://www.amnesty.org/en/latest/news/2017/05/egypt-ngo-law-threatens-to-annihilate-human-rights-groups/.

Anderson, Betty S. 2005. *Nationalist Voices in Jordan: The Street and the State.* Austin: University of Texas Press.

Andrews, Molly. 2007. *Shaping History: Narratives of Political Change.* Cambridge: Cambridge University Press.

Anonymous. 2005. "Nothing Less Than the Resignation of Habib El Adly" [statement issued in response to the events of 25 May 2005]. Indymedia, 1 June. Accessed 4 August 2015. http://www.beirut.indymedia.org/ar/2005/06/2710.shtml.

Arab Women Organization of Jordan. *Unveiling Gender-Based Violence against Syrian Women Refugees in Jordan and Lebanon.* https://www.peacewomen.org/sites/default/files/AWO%20Research%20on%20Syrian%20Refugees-English.pdf.

Arab Women Organization, MOSAWA, and members of the campaign "My Mother Is Jordanian and Her Nationality Is My Right." 2013. "Women's Rights in Jordan." Submitted to the Universal Periodic Review, the Human Rights Council, Amman-Jordan, February.

Arenfeldt, Pernille, and Nawar Al-Hassan Golley, eds. 2012. *Mapping Arab Women's Movements: A Century of Transformations from Within*. Cairo: AUC Press.

Armitage, Susan H. 2002. "The Next Step." In *Women's Oral History: The Frontiers Reader*, edited by Susan H. Armitage, Patricia Hart, and Karen Weathermon, 61–74. Lincoln: University of Nebraska, 2002.

Armstrong, Elisabeth. 2016. "Before Bandung: The Anti-Imperialist Women's Movement in Asia and the Women's International Democratic Federation." *Signs: Journal of Women in Culture and Society* 41(2): 305–31.

Arvin, Maile, Eve Tuck, and Angie Morrill. 2013. "Decolonizing Feminism: Challenging Connections between Settler Colonialism and Heteropatriarchy." *Feminism Formations* 25(1): 8–34.

Assaad, Marie Bassili. 1980. "Female Circumcision in Egypt: Social Implications, Current Research, and Prospects for Change." *Studies in Family Planning* 11(1): 3–16.

Associated Press. 2014. "Egypt Sentences 7 to Life for Sexual Assaults." *New York Times*, 16 July. Accessed 19 January 2015. http://www.nytimes.com/aponline /2014/07/16/world/middleeast/ap-ml-egypt.html?_r=0.

Associated Press in Cairo. 2011. "Egypt Clashes Continue into Third Day as Army Cracks Down." *The Guardian*, 18 December. Accessed 6 April 2016. http://www .theguardian.com/world/2011/dec/18/egypt-violence-day-three.

Association Najdeh. N.d. "Our Profile." Association Najdeh. http://www.association -najdeh.org/english/about.htm.

Aulas, Marie-Christine. 1978. "Egypt Confronts Peace." *MERIP Reports* no. 72(November): 3–11.

Ayubi, Nazih. 1991. *Political Islam: Religion and Politics in the Arab World*. London: Routledge.

———. 1995. *Over-Stating the Arab State: Politics and Society in the Middle East*. London: I. B. Tauris.

Azzi, Iman. 2011. "Lebanese Protesters Take Aim at Family Law System." *Women's News*, 24 March. Accessed 11 April 2016. http://womensenews.org/2011/03 /lebanon-protesters-take-aim-at-family-law-system/.

Baaklini, Abdo, Guilain Denoeux, and Robert Springborg. 1999. *Legislative Politics in the Arab World: The Resurgence of Democratic Institutions*. Boulder, CO: Lynne Rienner.

Badran, Margot. 1991. "Competing Agenda: Feminists, Islam and the State in 19th and 20th Century History." In *Women, Islam and the State*, edited by Deniz Kandiyoti, 201–36. Philadelphia: Temple University Press.

———. 1995. *Feminists, Islam, and Nation: Gender and the Making of Modern Egypt*. Princeton, NJ: Princeton University Press.

———. 2009. *Feminism in Islam: Secular and Religious Convergences*. Oxford: Oneworld.

———. 2011. "Egypt's Revolution and the New Feminism." SSRC, 3 March. Accessed 20 January 2015. http://blogs.ssrc.org/tif/2011/03/03/egypts-revolution -and-the-new-feminism/.

Baheya Ya Masr. N.d. Facebook page. https://www.facebook.com/BaheyaYaMasr/info?ref=page_internal.

Barnett, Michael N. 1998. *Dialogues in Arab Politics: Negotiations in Regional Order.* New York: Columbia University Press.

Baron, Beth. 1994. *The Women's Awakening in Egypt.* New Haven, CT: Yale University Press.

———. 2005. *Egypt as a Woman: Nationalism, Gender, and Politics.* Berkeley: University of California Press.

Baumann, Hannes. 2016. *Citizen Hariri: Lebanon's Neoliberal Reconstruction.* London: Hurst Publishers.

Bayat, Asef. 2013a. *Revolution without Revolutionaries: Making Sense of the Arab Spring.* Stanford, CA: Stanford University Press.

———, ed. 2013b. *Post-Islamism: The Changing Faces of Political Islam.* Oxford: Oxford University Press.

———. 2013c. "The Arab Spring and Its Surprises." *Development and Change* 44(3): 587–601.

BBC. 2005. "Egypt Anger over 'Grope Attacks.'" BBC News Online, 1 June. Accessed 26 September 2017. http://news.bbc.co.uk/1/hi/world/middle_east/4600133.stm.

———. 2008. "Hizbollah Takes Over West Beirut." BBC News, 9 May, Accessed 28 August 2017. http://news.bbc.co.uk/1/hi/world/middle_east/7391600.stm.

Beckman, Bjorn. 1993. "The Liberation of Civil Society: Neo-Liberal Ideology and Political Theory." *Review of African Political Economy* 58(1): 20–33.

Beder, Sharon. 2002. "Environmentalists Help Manage Corporate Reputation: Changing Perceptions Not Behaviour." *Ecopolitics: Thought and Action* 1(4): 60–72.

Beinin, Joel. 2001. *Workers and Peasants in the Modern Middle East.* Cambridge: Cambridge University Press.

———. 2012. *The Rise of Egypt's Workers.* Washington, DC: Carnegie Endowment for International Peace.

Beinin, Joel, and Marie Duboc. 2013. "A Workers' Social Movement on the Margin of the Global Neoliberal Order, Egypt 2004–2011." In *Social Movements, Mobilization and Contestation in the Middle East and North Africa*, edited by Joel Beinin and Frederic Vairel, 2nd edition, 181–201. Stanford, CA: Stanford University Press.

Beinin, Joel, and Hossam El-Hamalawy. 2007. "Strikes in Egypt Spread from Center of Gravity." *Middle East Report Online* (May 9). https://merip.org/2007/05/strikes-in-egypt-spread-from-center-of-gravity/.

Benford, Robert, and David Snow. 2000. "Framing Processes and Social Movements: An Overview and Assessment." *Annual Review of Sociology* 26(1): 611–39.

Bernal, Victoria, and Inderpal Grewal, eds. 2014. *Theorizing NGOs: States, Feminisms, and Neoliberalism.* Durham, NC: Duke University Press.

Berti, Benedetta. 2015. "The Syrian Refugee Crisis: Regional and Human Security Implications." *Strategic Assessment.* 17(4): 41–53.

Biagini, Erika. 2017a. A Revolution of Their Own: The Activism of the Egyptian Muslim Sisterhood and Its Evolution since the Arab Spring (1928–2014). PhD thesis submitted to the School of Law and Government Dublin City University, Ireland.

———. 2017b. The Egyptian Muslim Sisterhood between Violence, Activism and Leadership, *Mediterranean Politics* 22(1): 35–53.

Bier, Laura. 2011. *Revolutionary Womanhood: Feminisms, Modernity, and the State in Nasser's Egypt*. Stanford, CA: Stanford University Press.

Blaydes, Lisa, and Safinaz El Tarouty. 2009. "Women's Electoral Participation in Egypt: The Implications of Gender for Voter Recruitment and Mobilization." *The Middle East Journal* 63(3): 364–380.

Boctor, Lillian. 2011. "Organizing for No Military Trials for Civilians: Interview with Egyptian Activist Shahira Abouellail." 6 November, *Jadaliyya*. http://www.jadaliyya.com/pages/index/3069/organizing-for-no-military-trials-for-civilians_in.

Boddy, Janice. 2007. *Civilizing Women: British Crusades in Colonial Sudan*. Princeton, NJ: Princeton University Press.

Booth, Marilyn. 1987. Prison, Gender, Praxis: Women's Prison Memoirs in Egypt and Elsewhere. *Middle East Report*, no. 149 (December): 35–41.

———. 2001. *May Her Likes Be Multiplied: Biography and Gender Politics in Egypt*. Berkeley: University of California Press.

Botman, Selma. 1988. "The Experience of Women in the Egyptian Communist Movement, 1939–1954." *Women's Studies International Forum* 11(2): 117–26.

Brand, Laurie. 1988. *Palestinians in the Arab World: Institution Building and the Search for State*. New York: Columbia University Press.

———. 1995a. "In the Beginning was the State . . . The Quest for Civil Society in Jordan." In *Civil Society in the Middle East*, edited by Augustus Richard Norton, 148–85. Leiden: E.J. Brill.

———. 1995b. "Palestinians and Jordanians: A Crisis of Identity." *Journal of Palestine Studies* 24(4): 46–61.

———. 1998. *Women, the State, and Political Liberalization: Middle Eastern and North African Experiences*. New York: Columbia University Press.

———. 1999. "Al-Muhajirin w-al-Ansar: Hashemite Strategies for Managing Communal Identity in Jordan." In *Ethnic Conflict and International Politics in the Middle East*, edited by Leonard Binder. Gainseville: University Press of Florida.

Browers, Michaelle L. 2009. *Political Ideology in the Arab World: Accommodation and Transformation*. Cambridge: Cambridge University Press.

Brown, Nathan, and Stilt, Kristen. 2011. "A Haphazard Constitutional Compromise." Carnegie Endowment, 11 April. Accessed 12 January 2015. http://carnegieendowment.org/2011/04/11/haphazard-constitutional-compromise.

Brownlee, Jason. 2011–12. "Peace before Freedom: Diplomacy and Repression in Sadat's Egypt." *Political Science Quarterly* 126(4): 641–68.

———. 2012. *Democracy Prevention: The Politics of the US-Egyptian Alliance*. Cambridge: Cambridge University Press.

Brownlee, Jason, Tarek E. Masoud, and Andrew Reynolds. 2015. *The Arab Spring: Pathways of Repression and Reform.* New York: Oxford University Press.

Brownmiller, S. 1975. *Against Our Will: Men, Women and Rape.* New York: Fawcett Columbine.

Brynen, Rex. 1990. *Sanctuary and Survival: The PLO in Lebanon.* Boulder, CO: Westview Press.

Bunch, Charlotte. 1990. "Women's Rights as Human Rights: Toward a Re-Vision of Human Rights." *Human Rights Quarterly* 12(4): 486–98.

Bush, George. 1998. "Toward a New World Order." In *The Geopolitics Reader* edited by Gearóid Ó Tuathail, Simon Dalby and Paul Routledge, 131–35. London: Routledge.

Butler, Judith. 1999. *Gender Trouble: Feminism and the Subversion of Identity.* New York: Routledge.

———. 2004. *Undoing Gender.* New York: Routledge.

Carapico, Sheila. 2000. "NGOs, INGOs, GO-NGOs and DO-NGOs: Making Sense of Non-Governmental Organizations." *Middle East Report,* no. 214 (Spring). Accessed 23 August 2015.http://www.merip.org/mer/mer214/ngos-ingos-go-ngos-do-ngos.

———. 2014. *Political Aid and Arab Activism: Democracy Promotion, Justice, and Representation,* Cambridge: Cambridge University Press.

Chakrabarty, Dipesh. 1997. "The Difference-Deferral of a Colonial Modernity: Public Debates on Domesticity in British Bengal." In *Tensions of Empire: Colonial Cultures in a Bourgeois World,* edited by Frederick Cooper and Ann Laura Stoler, 373–405. Berkeley: University of California Press.

Chakravarti, Leila Zaki. 2014. "From Strongman to Superman: Sisi the Saviour of Egypt." openDemocracy, 28 April. Accessed 27 January 2015. https://www.opendemocracy.net/5050/leila-zaki-chakravarti/from-strongman-to-superman-sisi-saviour-of-egypt.

Chappel, Louise. 2006. "Contesting Women's Rights: Charting the Emergence of a Transnational Conservative Counter-network." *Global Society* 20(4): 491–520

Charafeddine, Fahmieh. 2006. *Al-haraka al-nisa'iyya fi lubnan.* Beirut: ESCWA.

Charara, Beydoun Azza. 2002. *Nisa' wa jama'iyyat lubnaniyyat bayna insaf al-that wa khidmat al-ghayr.* Beirut: Dar Annahar.

Charrad, Munira. 2001. *States and Women's Rights: The Making of Postcolonial Tunisia, Algeria, and Morocco.* Berkeley: University of California Press.

Chatterjee, Partha. 1989. "The Nationalist Resolution of the Women's Question." In *Recasting Women: Essays in Colonial History,* edited by Kumkum Sangari and Sudesh Vaid, 233–52. Delhi: Kali for Women.

———. 1993. *The Nation and Its Fragments: Colonial and Postcolonial Histories.* Princeton, NJ: Princeton University Press.

Chatty, Dawn, and Annika Rabo, eds. *Organizing Women: Formal and Informal Women's Groups in the Middle East.* London: Bloomsbury.

Chen, Martha Alter. 1995. "Engendering World Conferences: The International Women's Movement and the United Nations." *Third World Quarterly* 16:(3): 477–93.

Chit, Bassem, and Mohamad Ali Nayel. 2013. "Understanding Racism against Syrian Refugees in Lebanon." Civil Society Knowledge Center, Lebanon Support, 28 October. http://cskc.daleel-madani.org/paper/understanding-racism-against -syrian-refugees-lebanon.

Choudry, Aziz, and Dip Kapoor. 2013. "Introduction: NGOization: Complicity, Contradictions and Prospects." In *NGOization: Complicity, Contradictions and Prospects*, edited by Aziz Choudry and Dip Kapoor, 1–23. London: Zed Books.

Chowdhry, Geeta. and Sheila Nair, eds. 2004. *Power, Postcolonialism and International Relations: Reading Race, Gender and Class*. New York: Routledge.

Christophersen, Mona. 2013. "Protest and Reform in Jordan: Popular Demand and Government Response 2011 to 2012." Fafo Report. https://www.fafo.no /zoo-publikasjoner/fafo-rapporter/item/protest-and-reform-in-jordan.

Chulov M., and P. Kingsley. 2013. "Egypt's Military Arrest Muslim Brotherhood Supreme Leader." *The Guardian*, 4 July, Accessed 9 February. 2018. https://www .theguardian.com/world/2013/jul/04/egypt-military-arrest-warrants-muslim -brotherhood.

Clark, Janine A. 2004. *Islam, Charity, and Activism: Middle-Class Networks and Social Welfare in Egypt, Jordan, and Yemen*. Bloomington: Indiana University Press.

Clark, Janine Astrid, and Jillian Schwedler. 2003. "Who Opened the Window? Women's Activism in Islamist Parties." *Comparative Politics* 35(3): 293–312.

Coalition of Egyptian Feminist Organizations. 2011a. "National Council for Women Doesn't Represent Egyptian Women. Call for Rapid Dissolution." February. https://nazra.org/en/2011/02/call-rapid-dissolution-national-council -women.

———. 2011b. "Coalition of Egyptian Feminist Organizations Open Letter to Prime Minister." 5 March. http://www.wluml.org/node/7020.

———. 2011c. "Statement on the Proposed Constitutional Amendments." 13 March. Accessed 13 January 2015. http://nwrcegypt.org/en/?p=3615.

———. 2011d. "Statement by the Coalition of Egyptian Feminist Organisations Regarding the Attacks at the Cabinet Sit-in." December. https://www.wmf.org .eg/en/statement-by-the-coalition-of-egyptian-feminist-organisations-regarding -the-attacks-at-the-cabinet-sit-in/.

———. 2012. "Statement by the Coalition of Egyptian Feminist Organizations on the General Strike." February. Last accessed 2014. http://www.wmf.org.eg/en /node/981.

Coleman, Isabel. 2011. "Is the Arab Spring Bad for Women?" *Foreign Policy*, 20 December. Accessed 16 July 2016. http://foreignpolicy.com/2011/12/20/is-the -arab-spring-bad-for-women/.

———. 2012. "Women and the Elections in Egypt." Council on Foreign Relations, 12 January, Accessed 10 April 2016. http://blogs.cfr.org/coleman/2012/01/12 /women-and-the-elections-in-egypt/.

Constitution of Egypt. 2013. "Constitution of The Arab Republic of Egypt." http:// www.sis.gov.eg/Newvr/Dustor-en001.pdf, Accessed 27 January 2015.

Cook, Steven A. 2011. *The Struggle for Egypt: From Nasser to Tahrir Square*. Oxford: Oxford University Press.

Cooke, Miriam. 1996. *Women and the War Story*. Berkeley: University of California Press.

———, 1999. "'Mapping Peace,' in Women and War. In *Lebanon*, edited by Lamia Rustom Shehadeh, 73–88. Gainesville: University of Florida Press.

Corm, Georges. 1988. "Myths and Realities of the Lebanese Conflict." In *Lebanon: A History of Conflict and Consensus*, edited by Nadim Shehadi and Dana Haffar Mills, 258–74. London: I. B. Tauris.

Dabashi, Hamid. 2012. *The Arab Spring and the End of Postcolonialism*. London: Zed Books.

Dann, Uriel. 1989. *King Hussein and the Challenge of Arab Radicalism: Jordan. 1955–1967*. Oxford: Oxford University Press.

Daou, Bernadette. 2014. "Les féminismes au Liban: Un dynamisme de positionnement par rapport au patriarcat et un renouvellement au sein du 'Printemps Arab.'" Master's thesis, Université Saint Joseph, Beirut, Lebanon.

Daou, Mark. 2015. "The Lebanese Left: Three Phases since the Civil War." 30 April Accessed 17 August 2015. https://now.mmedia.me/lb/en/commentary/565197 -the-lebanese-left-three-phases-since-the-civil-war.

Dauphinee, Elizabeth. 2013. *The Politics of Exile*. London: Routledge.

De Smet, Brecht. 2015. *Gramsci on Tahrir: Revolution and Counter-Revolution in Egypt*. London: Pluto Press.

Deeb, Lara. 2006. *An Enchanted Modern: Gender and Public Piety in Shi'i Lebanon*. Princeton, NJ: Princeton University Press.

Dekmejian, Richard Hrair. 1978. "Consociational Democracy in Crisis: The Case of Lebanon." *Comparative Politics* 10(2): 251–66.

Diamond, Larry. 1999. *Developing Democracy: Toward Consolidation*. Baltimore: Johns Hopkins University Press.

Dixon, Deborah P., and Sallie A. Marston. 2011. "Introduction: Feminist Engagements with Geopolitics." *Gender, Place & Culture* 18(4): 445–53.

Doty, Roxanne L. 1996a. "Sovereignty and the Nation: Constructing the Boundaries of National Identity." In *State Sovereignty as a Social Construct*, edited by T. Biersteker and C. Weber, 121–47. Cambridge: Cambridge University Press.

———. 1996b *Imperial Encounters: The Politics of Representation in North-South Relations*. Minneapolis: University of Minnesota Press.

Dowler, Lorraine, and Joanne Sharp. 2001. "A Feminist Geopolitics?" *Space and Polity* 5(3): 165–76.

Duboc, Marie. 2013. "'Where Are the Men? Here Are the Women!' Surveillance, Gender, and Strikes in Egyptian Textile Factories." *Journal of Middle East Women's Studies* 9(3): 28–53.

Duffield, Mark, and Vernon Hewitt, eds. 2013. *Empire, Development and Colonialism: The Past in the Present*. Woodbridge, UK: James Currey.

Duncanson, Claire. 2013. *Forces for Good? Military Masculinities and Peacebuilding in Afghanistan and Iraq*. London: Palgrave Macmillan.

The Economist. 2005. "Democracy Stirs in the Middle East." 3 March. https://www
.economist.com/leaders/2005/03/03/democracy-stirs-in-the-middle-east.

ECWR (Egyptian Centre for Women's Rights). 2011a. "Egypt: Women Excluded
from Constitutional Committee." ECWR, 17 February. http://www.pambazuka
.net/en/category/wgender/71060.

———. 2011b. "The Victory of the Revolution Shall Be Achieved by Preserving
Human Rights and Not by Repealing Them." ECWR, 7 April. http://ecwronline
.org/?p=1133.

———. 2011c. "The Revolution Will Not Be Complete without Women's Participation." ECWR, 8 April http://ecwronline.org/?p=1131.

———. 2011d. "The Training for the Female Candidates of the Revolution Council
(People's Assembly 2011) Ends." ECWR, November. Accessed 14 January 2015.
http://ecwronline.org/?p=1082.

———. 2012a. "Egyptian Women's Status Report 2011." ECWR, 24 March.
Accessed 13 January 2015. http://ecwronline.org/?p=4573.

———. 2012b. "ECWR Completely Refuses Draft of Constitution." ECWR,
8 December. Accessed 15 December 2015. http://ecwronline.org/?p=719.

———. 2013. "Egypt's New Constitution a Victory for Women's Rights to Full Citizenship." ECWR, 2 December. Accessed 16 April 2018. http://ecwronline.org
/?p=1886.

———. "Women's Lines Challenge the Terrorism of the Muslim Brotherhood. And
They Welcomed the First Day of the Referendum with Singing." ECWR,
14 January. http://ecwronline.org/?p=1908.

Edwards, Michael, and David Hulme eds. 1996. 'Introduction: NGO Performance
and Accountability'. In *Beyond the Magic Bullet: NGO Performance and Accountability in the Post-Cold War World*. West Hartford, CT: Kumarian Press.

Eggert, Jennifer Philippa. 2018a. "'The Mood Was an Explosion of Freedom': The
1968 Movement and the Participation of Women Fighters during the Lebanese
Civil War." In *Women, Global Protest Movements and Political Agency: Rethinking the Legacy of 1968*, edited by Sarah Colvin and Katharina Karcher, 152–67.
Abdingdon, UK: Routledge.

———. 2018b. "Female Fighters and Militants during the Lebanese Civil War:
Individual Profiles, Pathways, and Motivations." *Studies in Conflict and Terrorism.* doi: 10.1080/1057610X.2018.1529353.

Egypt Penal Code. N.d. Accessed 10 September 2017. http://hrlibrary.umn.edu
/research/Egypt/criminal-code.pdf.

EIPR (Egyptian Initiative for Personal Rights). 2011a. "On the Third Day of the
Cabinet Confrontations between Security Forces and Demonstrators: The Latest
Toll of Wounded and Arrested." EIPR, 19 December. Accessed 29 January 2015.
http://eipr.org/en/pressrelease/2011/12/19/1342.

———. 2011b. "In an Investigation by the EIPR: Bullets of the Ministry of
Interior Were Aimed to Leave Demonstrators Permanently Disabled." EIPR,
26 November, Accessed 29 January 2015. http://eipr.org/en/pressrelease/2011
/11/26/1294.

————. 2013. "Comment on the Final Draft of the Constitution: Despite Some Improvements, EIPR Finds That the 2013 Constitution Falls Short of Expectations." EIPR, 18 December. Accessed 3 May 2018. https://www.eipr.org/en/press/2013/12/comment-final-draft-constitution-despite-some-improvements-eipr-finds-2013.

————. 2014. "Weeks of Killing: State Violence, Communal Fighting, and Sectarian Attacks in the Summer of 2013." June, Cairo: EIPR. http://eipr.org/sites/default/files/reports/pdf/weeks_of_killing_en.pdf

EISA (Electoral Institute for Sustainable Democracy in Africa). 2012. "Egypt: Women Elected to the People's Assembly in 2012." Accessed 9 January 2014. http://eisa.org.za/WEP/egy2012women.htm.

El Saadawi, Nawal. (1980) 2015. *The Hidden Face of Eve: Women in the Arab World.* London: Zed Books.

El Said, Maha, Lena Meari, and Nicola Pratt, eds. 2015. *Rethinking Gender in Revolutions and Resistance: Lessons from the Arab World.* London: Zed Books.

El-Awady, Mehrinaz. 2014. "Women's Political Participation in Egypt: Beyond the Numbers." *Association of Middle East Women's Studies E-Bulletin* 12(1): 1–5.

El-Din, Gamal Essam. 2013. "Shura MPs Fault Protesters for Tahrir Square Rapes, Sexual Harassment." *Ahram Online.* Accessed 15 March 2013. http://english.ahram.org.eg/NewsContent/1/64/64552/Egypt/Politics-/Shura-MPs-fault-protesters-for-Tahrir-Square-rapes.aspx

El-Gowhary, Karim. 1994. "It's Time to Launch a New Women's Liberation Movement—An Islamic One: An Interview with Heba Raouf Ezzat." *Middle East Report*, no. 191(November–December): 26–27.

El-Guindi, Fadwa. 1981. "Veiling Infitah with Muslim Ethic: Egypt's Contemporary Islamic Movement" *Social Problems* 28(4): 465–85.

El-Hage, Sandy. 2013. "Transnational Activism in Lebanon's Women's Movement: Between Fitna, Fawda, and Feminism." Master's thesis submitted to the School of Arts and Sciences, Lebanese American University.

El-Hamalawy, Hossam. 2009. "1977 Bread Uprising." Master's thesis, American University in Cairo.

El-Husseini, Rola. 2012. *Pax Syriana.* Syracuse, NY: Syracuse University Press.

El-Khoury, Bachir. 2017. "Lebanon's Civil Society Groups Gear Up for 2018 Elections." *Al-Monitor,* June 19. Accessed 27 August 2017. http://www.al-monitor.com/pulse/originals/2017/06/lebanon-civil-society-non-partisans-prepare-for-elections.html.

El-Khoury, Joseph. 2008. "No Frontiers: The Birth of Independent Activism at AUB. "Accessed 17 August 2015. http://www.arabdemocracy.com/2008/11/no-frontiers-birth-of-independent.html.

El-Mahdi, Rabab. 2009. "Enough! Egypt's Quest for Democracy." *Comparative Political Studies* 42(8): 1011–39.

————. 2010. "Does Political Islam Hinder Gender-Based Mobilization? The Case of Egypt." *Totalitarian Movements and Political Religions* 11(3–4): 379–96.

————. 2011. "Labour Protests in Egypt: Causes and Meanings." *Review of African Political Economy* 38(129): 387–402.

El-Mahdi, Rabab, and Phil Marfleet, eds. 2009. *Egypt: The Moment of Change*. London: Zed Press.

El-Nadeem Center for the Rehabilitation of Victims of Torture and Violence, Nazra for Feminist Studies, and New Woman Foundation. 2013. *Sexual Assault and Rape in Tahrir Square and Its Vicinity: A Compendium of Sources 2011–2013.* Cairo. Accessed 1 July 2014. http://nazra.org/sites/nazra/files/attachments /compilation-_of_sexual-violence_-testimonies_between_20111_2013_en.pdf.

El-Nahhas, Mona. 2012. "A Trail of Broken Promises." *Al-Ahram Weekly* Online, 2–8 August. http://weekly.ahram.org.eg/2012/1109/eg10.htm.

El-Tibi, Manal. 2012. "Manal El-Tibi's Resignation Letter to the Constituent Assembly." Translated by Bassem Sabry. *Ahram Online*, 26 September. http:// english.ahram.org.eg/NewsContent/1/64/53896/Egypt/Politics-/Manal-ElTibis -resignation-letter-to-Egypts-Constit.aspx.

Elsadda, Hoda. 2011. "Women's Rights Activism in Post-January 25 Egypt: Combating the Shadow of the First Lady Syndrome in the Arab World." *Middle East Law and Governance* 3: 84–93.

————. 2013. "A War against Women: The CSW Declaration and the Muslim Brotherhood Riposte." openDemocracy. Accessed 8 April 2013. http://www .opendemocracy.net/5050/hoda-elsadda/war-against-women-csw-declaration -and-muslim-brotherhood-riposte.

————. 2015. "Article 11: Feminists Negotiating Power in Egypt." openDemocracy, 5 January. Accessed 26 January 2015. https://opendemocracy.net/5050/hoda -elsadda/article-11-feminists-negotiating-power-in-egypt.

Elshtain, Jean Bethke. 1982. "On Beautiful Souls, Just Warriors and Feminist Consciousness." *Women's Studies International Forum* 5 (3–4): 341–48.

Enloe, C. 1988. *Does Khaki Become You? The Militarization of Women's Lives*. London: Pandora.

————. 1990. "Women and Children: Making Feminist Sense of the Persian Gulf Crisis." *The Village Voice*, 25 September.

————. 1993. *The Morning After: Sexual Politics at the End of the Cold War*. Berkeley: University of California Press.

————. 2000. *Manoeuvers: The International Politics of Militarizing Women's Lives*. Berkeley: University of California Press.

————. 2004. *The Curious Feminist: Searching for Women in a New Era of Empire*. Berkeley: University of California Press.

————. 2005. 'What If Patriarchy Is "the Big Picture"? An Afterword'". In *Gender, Conflict and Peacekeeping*, edited by D. Mazurana, A. Raven-Roberts, and J. Parpart, 280–84. Lanham, MD: Rowman & Littlefield.

————. 2007. *Militarism and Globalisation: Feminists Make the Link*. Lanham, MD: Rowman & Littlefield.

————. 2010. *Nimo's War, Emma's War: Making Feminist Sense of the Iraq War*. Berkeley: University of California Press.

————. 2014. *Bananas, Beaches and Bases: Making Feminist Sense of International Politics.* 2nd ed. Berkeley: University of California Press.

ERTU (Egyptian Radio and TV Union) 1965. "Gamal Abdel-Nasser on the Muslim Brotherhood." YouTube video. Accessed 16 December 2016. www.youtube.com/watch?v=TX4RK8bj2Wo.

Eschle, Catherine, and Bice Maiguashca. 2010. *Making Feminist Sense of the Global Justice Movement.* Lanham, MD: Rowman & Littlefield.

Esposito, John L. 1984. *Islam and Politics.* Syracuse, NY: Syracuse University Press.

Esposito, John L., and Natana J. DeLong-Bas, eds. 2001. *Women in Muslim Family Law.* New York: Syracuse University Press.

Essaid, Salim. 2013. "In Jordan, Women Fight for Full Citizenship Rights." *Time*, 13 May. http://world.time.com/2013/05/13/in-jordan-women-fight-to-pass-on-their-citizenship/.

Essam El-Din, Gamal. 2012. "A Weight of Contradiction." *Al-Ahram Weekly*, 4–10 October. https://www.masress.com/en/ahramweekly/30811.

Ezzat, Dina. 2012. "'Like Mohamed, Like Fatemah': Egyptian Women's Fight for Equality." *Ahram Online*, 5 October. http://english.ahram.org.eg/NewsContent/1/64/54791/Egypt/Politics-/Like-Mohamed,-like-Fatemah-Egyptian-womens-fight-f.aspx.

Fakhoury, Tamirace. 2017. "Governance Strategies and Refugee Response: Lebanon in the Face of Syrian Displacement." *International Journal of Middle East Studies* 49(4): 681–700.

Falk, Richard. 1999. *Predatory Globalization: A Critique.* Cambridge: Polity Press.

Farag, Fatemah. 2000. "Palestinian Flag over the Nile." *Al-Ahram Weekly Online*, 19–25 October. Accessed 17 March 2018. http://weekly.ahram.org.eg/Archive/2000/504/pal62.htm.

————. 2002. "The Many Faces of Solidarity." *Al-Ahram Weekly Online.* 2–8 May. Accessed 6 August 2015. https://www.masress.com/en/ahramweekly/23086.

Farsoun, Samih. 1973. "Student Protests and the Coming Crisis in Lebanon." *MERIP Reports*, no. 19 (August): 3–14.

Fecteau, Andre. 2012. "A Graffiti Campaign Brings Strong Female Voices to the Streets." *Egypt Independent*, 10 March. http://www.egyptindependent.com//news/graffiti-campaign-brings-strong-female-voices-streets.

Fisher, Julie. 1988. *Nongovernments: NGOs and the Political Development of the Third World.* West Hartford, CT: Kumarian Press.

Fisk, Robert. 2002. *Pity the Nation.* 4th ed. Oxford: Oxford Paperbacks.

Fleischmann, Ellen L. 1999. "The Other 'Awakening': The Emergence of Women's Movements in the Modern Middle East, 1900–1940." In *A Social History of Women and Gender in the Modern Middle East*, edited by Margaret L. Meriwether and Judith E. Tucker, 89–139. Boulder, CO: Westview Press.

Flores, Alexander. 1979. "The Arab CPs and the Palestine Problem," *Khamsin* no. 7, 21–40. Accessed 17 June 2019 https://libcom.org/book/export/html/48209.

Foucault, Michel. 1977. *Discipline and Punish*. Translated by A. Sheridan. New York: Vintage.

———. 1980. *Power/Knowledge: Selected Interviews and Other Writings 1972–1977*. Edited by Colin Gordon. New York: Pantheon Books.

———. 1998. *The Will to Knowledge: The History of Sexuality, Volume One*. Translated by Robert Hurley. London: Penguin Books.

Freedman, Jane, Zeynep Kivilcim, and Nurcan Özgür Baclacioglu, eds. 2017. *A Gendered Approach to the Syrian Refugee Crisis*. London: Routledge.

Frisch, Michael. 1990. *A Shared Authority: Essays on the Craft and Meaning of Oral and Public History*. Albany: State University of New York Press.

Gallagher, Nancy. 2000. "Women's Human Rights on Trial in Jordan: The Triumph of Toujan al-Faisal." In *Faith and Freedom: Women's Human Rights in the Muslim World*, edited by Mahnaz Afkhami 209–31. London: I. B. Tauris.

Gandolfo, Luisa. 2012. *Palestinians in Jordan: The Politics of Identity*. London: I. B. Tauris.

Garcia-Navarro, Lourdes. 2012. "In Egypt's New Parliament, Women Will be Scarce." NPR, January 19. Accessed 10 April 2016. http://www.npr.org/2012/01/19/145468365/in-egypts-new-parliament-women-will-be-scarce.

Garner, Karen. 2013. *Gender and Foreign Policy in the Clinton Administration*. Boulder, CO: Lynne Rienner.

Gelvin, James. 2012. *The Arab Uprisings: What Everyone Needs to Know*. Oxford University Press, Oxford.

George, Alan. 2005. *Jordan: Living in the Crossfire*. London: Zed Books.

Gerges, Fawaz. 2012. "The Transformation of Arab Politics: Disentangling Myth from Reality." In *The 1967 Arab-Israeli War: Origins and Consequences*, edited by William Roger Louis and Avi Shlaim, 285–314. Cambridge: Cambridge University Press.

Gharaybah, Ibrahim. 1997. *Jama'at al-Ikhwan al-Muslimin fi-l-Urdunn 1946–1996*. Amman: Al-Urdunn al-Jadid.

Ghodsee, Kristen 2010. "Revisiting the United Nations Decade for Women: Brief Reflections on Feminism, Capitalism and Cold War Politics in the Early Years of the International Women's Movement." *Women's Studies International Forum* 33(1): 3–12.

Giles, Wenona, and Jennifer Hyndman. 2004. "New Directions for Feminist Research and Politics." In *Sites of Violence: Gender and Conflict Zones*, edited by Wenona Giles and Jennifer Hyndman, 301–16. Berkeley: University of California Press.

Global Fund for Women. 2013. "Egyptian Women Want Democracy, Not 'Ballotocracy.'" Global Fund for Women, 8 July, Accessed 27 January 2015. http://www.globalfundforwomen.org/impact/news/183-2013/2067-egyptian-women-want-a-democracy-not-a-qballotocracyq.

Gluck, Sherna Berger, and Daphne Patai, eds. 1991. *Women's Words: The Feminist Practice of Oral History*. London: Routledge.

Göle, Nilüfer. 1997. "The Gendered Nature of the Public Sphere." *Public Culture* 10(1): 61–81.

Grewal, Inderpal. 2005. *Transnational America: Feminisms, Diasporas, Neoliberalisms.* Durham, NC: Duke University Press.

Grewal, Inderpal, and Caren Kaplan. 1994. "Introduction: Transnational Feminist Practices and Questions of Postmodernity." In *Scattered Hegemonies: Postmodernity and Transnational Feminist Practices*, edited by Inderpal Grewal and Caren Kaplan, 1–33. Minneapolis: University of Minnesota Press.

Guerin O. 2018. "The Shadow over Egypt." BBC, 23 February. Accessed 7 March 2018. http://www.bbc.co.uk/news/resources/idt-sh/shadow_over_egypt.

Gulhane, Joel, and Mohamed Omar. 2013. "In Pictures: Egyptian Women March on International Women's Day." *Daily News Egypt*, 8 March. Accessed 7 April 2016. http://www.dailynewsegypt.com/2013/03/08/in-pictures-egyptian-women -march-on-international-womens-day/.

Hafez, Sherine. 2011a. "Women Developing Women: Islamic Approaches for Poverty Alleviation in Rural Egypt." *Feminist Review* 97(1): 56–73.

———. 2011b. *An Islam of Her Own: Reconsidering Religion and Secularism in Women's Islamic Movements.* New York: New York University Press.

———. 2014. "The Revolution Shall Not Pass through Women's Bodies: Egypt, Uprising and Gender Politics." *Journal of North African Studies* 19(2): 172–85.

———. 2019. *Women of the Midan: The Untold Stories of Egypt's Revolutionaries.* Bloomington: Indiana University Press.

Halliday, Fred. 2005. *The Middle East in International Relations.* Cambridge: Cambridge University Press.

Hammad, Hanan. 2016. "Arwa Salih's 'The Premature': Gendering the History of the Egyptian Left." *Arab Studies Journal* 24(1): 118–42.

———. 2017. "Disreputable by Definition: Respectability and Theft by Poor Women in Urban Interwar Egypt." *Journal of Middle East Women's Studies* 13(3): 376–94.

Hammami, Rema. 1995. "NGOs: The Professionalisation of Politics." *Race and Class* 37(2): 51–63.

Hanafi, Sari, and Linda Tabar. 2006. *The Emergence of a Palestinian Globalized Elite: Donors International Organizations and Local NGOs.* Ramallah: Institute of Jerusalem Studies and Muwatin, The Palestinian Institute for the Study of Democracy.

Hanf, Theodor. 1993. *Coexistence in Wartime Lebanon: Decline of a State and Rise of a Nation.* London: I.B. Tauris.

Hanieh, Adam. 2013. *Lineages of Revolt: Issues of Contemporary Capitalism in the Middle East.* London: Haymarket.

Haraway, Donna. 1988. "Situated Knowledges: The Science Question in Feminism and the Privilege of Partial Perspective." *Feminist Studies* 14(3): 575–99.

Harstock, Nancy C.M. 1983. "The Feminist Standpoint: Developing the Ground for a Specifically Feminist Historical Materialism." In *Discovering Reality: Femi-*

nist Perspectives on Epistemology, Metaphysics, Methodology, and Philosophy of Science, edited by S. Harding and M. Hintikka, 283–310. Dordrecht: D. Reidel.

Hasso, Frances S. 2000. "Modernity and Gender in Arab Accounts of the 1948 and 1967 Defeats." *International Journal of Middle East Studies* 32(4): 491–510.

———. 2005a. *Resistance, Repression, and Gender Politics in Occupied Palestine and Jordan*. Syracuse, NY: Syracuse University Press.

———. 2005b. "Problems and Promise in Middle East and North Africa Gender Research." *Feminist Studies* 31(3): 653–78

———. 2009. "Empowering Governmentalities Rather Than Women: The Arab Human Development Report 2005 and Western Development Logics." *International Journal of Middle East Studies* 41(1): 63–82.

———. 2011. *Consuming Desires: Family Crisis and the State in the Middle East*. Stanford, CA: Stanford University Press.

Hasso, Frances, and Zakia Salime, eds. 2016a. *Freedom without Permission: Bodies and Space in the Arab Revolutions*. Durham, NC: Duke University Press.

———. 2016b. "Introduction." In *Freedom without Permission: Bodies and Space in the Arab Revolutions*, edited by Frances Hasso and Zakia Salime, 1–24. Durham, NC: Duke University Press.

Hatem, Mervat. 1988. "The Enduring Alliance of Nationalism and Patriarchy in Muslim Personal Status Laws: The Case of Egypt." *Feminist Issues* 6 (1): 19–43.

———. 1992. "Economic and Political Liberation in Egypt and the Demise of State Feminism." *International Journal of Middle East Studies* 24 (2): 231–51.

———. 1998. "Secularist and Islamist Discourses on Modernity in Egypt and the Evolution of the Postcolonial Nation-State." In *Islam, Gender, and Social Change*, edited by Yvonne Yazbeck Haddad and John L. Esposito, 85–99. Oxford: Oxford University Press.

———. 1999. "Modernization, the State, and the Family in Middle East Women's Studies." In *A Social History of Women and Gender in the Modern Middle East*, edited by Margaret L. Meriwether and Judith E. Tucker, 63–88. Boulder, CO: Westview Press.

———. 2000. "The Pitfalls of the Nationalist Discourses on Citizenship in Egypt." In *Gender and Citizenship in the Middle East*, edited by Suad Joseph, 33–57. Syracuse, NY: Syracuse University Press.

———. 2006. "In the Eye of the Storm: Islamic Societies and Muslim Women in Globalization Discourses." *Comparative Studies of South Asia, Africa and the Middle East* 26(1): 22–35.

———. 2013. "Gender and Counterrevolution in Egypt." *Middle East Report* no. 268 (Spring): 10–17.

Hatem, Yasmina. 2013. "10 Questions for Nasawiya: Interview with Rola Yasmine." 5 August 2013. Accessed 29 June 2015. https://now.mmedia.me/lb/en /Interview/10-questions-for-nasawiya.

Haugbolle, Sune. 2010. *War and Memory in Lebanon*. Cambridge: Cambridge University Press.

————. 2017. "The New Arab Left and 1967." *British Journal of Middle Eastern Studies* 44(4): 497–512.

Hearst, David, and Abdel-Rahman Hussein. 2012. "Egypt's Supreme Court Dissolves Parliament and Outrages Islamists." *Guardian Online*, 14 June, Accessed 9 January 2014. http://www.theguardian.com/world/2012/jun/14/egypt-parliament-dissolved-supreme-court.

Helfont, Samuel, and Tally Helfont. 2011. "Jordan's Protests: Arab Spring Lite?" Foreign Policy Research Centre, July. http://www.fpri.org/articles/2011/07 /jordans-protests-arab-spring-lite.

Helie-Lucas, Marie-Aimee. 1994. "The Preferential Symbol for Islamic Identity: Women in Muslim Personal Status Laws." In *Identity Politics and Women: Cultural Reassertions and Feminisms in International Perspective*, edited by Valentine Moghadam, 391–407. Boulder, CO: Westview Press.

Hewitt de Alcantara, Cynthia. 1998. "The Uses and Abuses of the Concept of Governance." *International Social Science Journal* 50 (155): 105–33.

Hijab, Nadia. 1988. *Womanpower: The Arab Debate on Women at Work*. Cambridge: Cambridge University Press.

Hinnebusch, Raymond. 2003. *The International Politics of the Middle East*. Manchester: Manchester University Press.

————, ed. 2015a. "From Arab Spring to Arab Winter: Explaining the Limits of Post-Uprising Democratization." Special issue of *Democratization* 22(1): 2.

————. 2015b. "Globalization, Democratization and the Arab Uprising: The International Factor in MENA's Failed Democratization." *Democratization* 22(2): 335–57.

Hirst, David. 1977. "Egyptians Riot over Price Rises." *The Guardian*, January 19.

Hokayem, Emile. 2014. "Iran, the Gulf States and the Syrian Civil War." *Adelphi Series* 54(447–48): 39–70.

Hoodfar, Homa. 1997. *Between Marriage and the Market: Intimate Politics and Survival in Cairo*. Berkeley: University of California Press.

Hourani, Albert. 1983. *Arabic Thought in the Liberal Age: 1798–1939*. Cambridge: Cambridge University Press.

Hourani, Hani, and Hussein Abu-Rumman. 1996. *The Democratic Process in Jordan: Deliberations of the Conference on the "Democratic Process in Jordan—Realities and Prospects."* Conference held in Amman 31 May–2 June 1994. Amman: Sindbad Publishing House.

Howard-Merriam, Kathleen. 1981. "Egypt's Other Political Elite." *The Western Political Quarterly* 34(1): 174–87.

Howeidy, Amira. 2002a. "Solidarity in Search of a Vision." *Al-Ahram Weekly Online*, 11–17 April 2002. Accessed 6 August 2015. https://www.masress.com/en /ahramweekly/23162.

————. 2002b. "Continuing Solidarity." *Al-Ahram Weekly Online*, 16–22 May. Accessed 6 August 2015. https://www.masress.com/en/ahramweekly/23028.

————. 2014. "Sexual Violence, Will the Noise Die Down?" *Al-Ahram Weekly*, 12 June. Accessed 19 January 2015. https://www.masress.com/en/ahramweekly /106483.

HRW (Human Rights Watch). 2005. "Egypt: Calls for Reform Met with Brutality." 26 May. Accessed 12 January 2015. http://www.hrw.org/news/2005/05/25 /egypt-calls-reform-met-brutality.

———. 2011. "Work on Him Until He Confesses." Impunity for Torture in Egypt. January. Accessed 17 January 2015. http://www.hrw.org/sites/default/files /reports/egypt0111webwcover.pdf.

———. 2012. *World Report: Events of 2011.* Washington, DC: Human Rights Watch.

———. 2013a. "Egypt: Epidemic of Sexual Violence." 3 July. Accessed 6 April 2016. https://www.hrw.org/news/2013/07/03/egypt-epidemic-sexual-violence.

———. 2013b. *World Report: Events of 2012.* Washington, DC: Human Rights Watch.

———. 2014a. "All According to Plan: The Rab'a Massacre and Mass Killings of Protesters in Egypt." Accessed 14 January 2018. https://www.hrw.org/report /2014/08/12/all-according-plan/raba-massacre-and-mass-killings-protesters -egypt.

———. 2014b. "Lebanon: Domestic Violence Law Good, but Incomplete." 3 April. Accessed 28 August 2017. https://www.hrw.org/news/2014/04/03/lebanon -domestic-violence-law-good-incomplete.

———. 2014c. "Lebanon: Rising Violence Targets Syrian Refugees." 30 September. http://www.hrw.org/news/2014/09/30/lebanon-rising-violence-targets-syrian -refugees.

———. 2016. "Human Rights Watch Statement on Proposed Amendments to Jordan's 2008 Law on Associations." 7 August. Accessed 16 August 2017. https:// www.hrw.org/news/2016/08/07/human-rights-watch-statement-proposed -amendments-jordans-2008-law-associations.

———. 2018. "Egypt: Events of 2017." Accessed 9 March 2018. https://www.hrw .org/world-report/2018/country-chapters/egypt.

Hudson, Michael C. 1968. *The Precarious Republic: Political Modernization in Lebanon.* Boulder, CO: Westview Press.

———. 1977. *Arab Politics: The Search for Legitimacy.* New Haven, CT: Yale University Press.

———. 1988. "The Problem of Authoritative Power in Lebanese Politics: Why Consociationalism Failed." In *Lebanon: A History of Conflict and Consensus,* edited by Nadim Shehadi and Dana Haffar Mills, 224–39. London: I. B. Tauris.

Hulme, David, and Edwards, Michael. 1997. "NGOs, States and Donors: An Overview." In *NGOs, States and Donors: Too Close for Comfort?,* edited by D. Hulme and M. Edwards, 275–84. New York: St. Martin's Press.

Hunt, Krista, and Kim Rygiel. 2006. *Engendering the War on Terror: War Stories and Camouflaged Politics.* Aldershot, UK: Ashgate.

Hussein, Mahmoud. 1972. "The Revolt of the Egyptian Students." *MERIP* 11(1): 10–14.

Hussein, Nazia. 2018. "Bangladeshi New Women's Smart Dressing: Negotiating Class, Culture and Religion." In *Rethinking New Womanhood: Practices of*

Gender, Class, Culture and Religion in South Asia, edited by N. Hussein, 97–122. London: Palgrave.

Husseini, Rana. 2009. *Murder in the Name of Honour*. Oxford: Oneworld Publications.

———. 2010 "Jordan." In *Women's Rights in the Middle East and North Africa: Progress Amid Resistance*, edited by Sanja Kelly and Julia Breslin, 193–222. New York: Freedom House.

———. 2012a. "Activists to Press for 30 Per Cent Female Parliament." *Jordan Times*, 8 May. http://jordantimes.com/activists-to-press-for-30-per-cent-female -parliament.

———. 2012b. "Activists Urge PM to Commit to Statement on Reviewing CEDAW Reservations." *Jordan Times*, 16 November. http://jordantimes.com/activists -urge-pm-to-commit-to-statement-on-reviewing-cedaw-reservations.

———. 2012c. "Activists Vow to Keep Fighting for Equal Rights." *Jordan Times*, 7 March. http://jordantimes.com/Activists+vow+to+keep+fighting+for+equal +rights++-45869.

———. 2013. "2012 a Grim Year for Women in Jordan—Activists." Jordanian National Commission for Women, 5 January. http://women.jo/en/news_details .php?news_id=2673.

———. 2014a. "Activists Reject Gov't Move to Scrap 10% Women Quota in Politi- cal Parties." *Jordan Times*, 23 August. http://jordantimes.com/activists-reject -govt-move-to-scrap-10-women-quota-in-political-parties.

———. 2014b. "Gov't Announces Privileges for Children of Jordanian Women Married to Foreigners." *Jordan Vista*, 9 November. Accessed 12 April 2016. http:// vista.sahafi.jo/art.php?id=dcd832e583bcddbd74a3b00cf3f96d765394697b.

———. 2014c. "Granting Service-Related Privileges to Children with Non-Jordanian Fathers 'a Matter of Time'—Kalaldeh." *Jordan Times*, 11 August. http://jordantimes .com/granting-service-related-privileges-to-children-with-non-jordanian-fathers -a-matter-of-time----kalaldeh.

———. 2014d. "Protesters Demand Full Citizenship Rights for Children with Foreign Fathers." *Jordan Times*, 16 June. http://jordantimes.com/protesters -demand-full-citizenship-rights-for-children-with-foreign-fathers.

Husseini, Rana. 2017. "Activists to 'Continue Struggle' for Rights of Jordanian Women Married to Foreigners." *Jordan Times*, 20 August. Accessed 27 August 2017. http://jordantimes.com/news/local/activists-continue-struggle'-rights -jordanian-women-married-foreigners.

Hutchings, Kimberly. 2013. "Choosers or Losers? Feminist Ethical and Political Agency in a Plural and Unequal World." In *Gender, Agency and Coercion*, edited by Sumi Madhok, Anne Philipps, and Kalpana Wilson, 14–28. London: Palgrave Macmillan.

Hyndman, Jennifer. 2001. "Towards a Feminist Geopolitics." *The Canadian Geog- rapher / Le Geographe canadien*, 45(2): 210–22.

———. 2004. "Mind the Gap: Bridging Feminist and Political Geography through Geopolitics." *Political Geography* 23(1): 302–22.

Ibrahim, Arwa. 2016. "Egypt Witnessed Hundreds of Labour Protests in 2015." *Middle East Eye*, 12 January. Accessed 13 April 2016. http://www.middleeasteye .net/news/egypt-witnessed-hundreds-labour-protests-2015-report-113115708.

Ibrahim, Saad Eddin. 1995. "Civil Society and Prospects of Democratization in the Arab World." In *Civil Society in the Middle East*, edited by Augustus Richard Norton, 27–54. Leiden: E.J. Brill.

ICG (International Crisis Group). 2012a. *Popular Protest in North Africa and the Middle East (IX): Dallying with Reform in a Divided Jordan*. Middle East/North Africa Report No.118, 12 March. https://www.crisisgroup.org/middle-east-north -africa/eastern-mediterranean/jordan/popular-protest-north-africa-and-middle -east-ix-dallying-reform-divided-jordan.

———. 2012b. *A Precarious Balancing Act: Lebanon and The Syrian Conflict*. ICG Report No.132, 22 November. https://www.crisisgroup.org/middle-east-north -africa/eastern-mediterranean/lebanon/precarious-balancing-act-lebanon-and -syrian-conflict-0.

———. 2013. *Too Close for Comfort: Syrians in Lebanon*. ICG Report No. 141, 13 May. Accessed 12 April 2016. https://www.crisisgroup.org/middle-east-north -africa/eastern-mediterranean/lebanon/too-close-comfort-syrians-lebanon.

———. 2015. "Lebanon's Self-Defeating Survival Strategies." 20 July. Accessed 12 April 2016.http://www.crisisgroup.org/en/regions/middle-east-north-africa /syria-lebanon/lebanon/160-lebanon-s-self-defeating-survival-strategies.aspx.

Identity Centre. 2014. "Map of Political Parties and Movements in Jordan, 2013/14." Netherlands Institute for Multiparty Democracy. http://www.nimd.org/wp -content/uploads/2014/01/Map-of-the-Political-Parties-and-Movements-in -Jordan-2013-2014.pdf.

IFES (International Foundation for Electoral Systems). 2011. "Elections in Egypt: Analysis of the 2011 Parliamentary Electoral System." Washington DC: IFES, 1 November. https://www.ifes.org/publications/analysis-egypts-2011-parliamentary -electoral-system.

Immenkamp, Beatrix 2017a. "Briefing: Syrian Crisis: Impact on Jordan, European Parliament." Europarl, February. Accessed 20 April 2018. http://www.europarl .europa.eu/RegData/etudes/BRIE/2017/599258/EPRS_BRI%282017%29599258 _EN.pdf.

———. 2017b. "Briefing: Syrian Crisis: Impact on Lebanon, European Parliament." Europarl, March. Accessed 20 April 2018. http://www.europarl.europa.eu /RegData/etudes/BRIE/2017/599379/EPRS_BRI%282017%29599379_EN.pdf.

Inayatullah, Naeem, ed. 2011. *Autobiographical International Relations: I, IR*. London: Routledge.

Inayatullah, Naeem, and Elizabeth Dauphinee, eds. 2016. *Narrative Global Politics: Theory, History and the Personal in International Relations*. London: Routledge.

International Rescue Committee. 2014. *Are We Listening? Acting on Our Commitments to Women and Girls Affected by the Syrian Conflict*. New York: International Rescue Committee.

Ismael, Tareq Y., and Jacqueline S. Ismael, eds. 1994. *The Gulf War and the New World Order: International Relations of the Middle East*, Gainseville: University of Florida Press.

IWSAW (Institute for Women's Studies in the Arab World). 2010–2011. "Responses to the Draft Law to Protect Women from Family Violence." *Al-Raida* 131–132(1): 77–88.

Jabiri, Afaf. 2016. *Gendered Politics and the Law in Jordan*. London: Palgrave.

Jabri, Vivienne. 2012. *The Postcolonial Subject: Claiming Politics / Governing Others in Late Modernity*. London: Routledge.

Jacobs, Susie, Ruth Jacobson, and Jennifer Marchbank, eds. 2000. *States of Conflict: Gender, Violence and Resistance*. London: Zed Books.

Jad, Islah. 2005. "Between Religion and Secularism: Islamist Women of Hamas." In *On Shifting Ground: Muslim Women in the Global Era*, edited by Fereshteh Nouraie-Simone. New York: Feminist Press at the City University of New York.

———. 2007. "The NGO-ization of Arab Women's Movements." In *Feminisms in Development: Contradictions, Contestations and Challenges*, edited by Andrea Cornwall, Elizabeth Harrison, and Ann Whitehead, 177–90. London: Zed Books.

———. 2018. *Palestinian Women's Activism: Nationalism, Secularism, Islamism*. Syracuse, NY: Syracuse University Press.

Jadaliyya Reports. 2011. "Jordan's March 24 Youth Sit-In Violently Dispersed." *Jadaliyya*, 26 March. Accessed 11 April 2016. http://www.jadaliyya.com/pages/index/1012/jordans-march-24-youth-sit-in-violently-dispersed-.

Jayawardena, Kumari. 1986. *Feminism and Nationalism in the Third World*. London: Zed Books.

———. 1995. *The White Woman's Other Burden*. London: Routledge.

Jeffrey, Alex. 2013. "Non-Governmental Organisations." In *The Ashgate Research Companion to Critical Geopolitics*, edited by Klaus Dodds, Merje Kuus, and Joanne P. Sharp, 387–403. Farnham, UK: Ashgate.

Joachim, Jutta. 2003. "Framing Issues and Seizing Opportunities: The UN, NGOs, and Women's Rights." *International Studies Quarterly* 47(2): 247–74.

Johnson, Michael. 1986. *Class and Client in Beirut: The Sunni Muslim Community and the Lebanese State, 1840–1985*. London: Ithaca Press.

———. 2001. *All Honourable Men: The Social Origins of War in Lebanon*. London: I. B. Tauris.

Johnson, Peter. 1973. "Egyptian Student Revolt Moves from Streets to Chambers." *Middle East Report and Information Project*, no. 15 (March): 28.

Joseph, Suad. 1991. "Elite Strategies for State Building: Women, Family, Religion and the State in Iraq and Lebanon." In *Women, Islam and the State*, edited by Deniz Kandiyoti, 176–200. Philadelphia: Temple University Press.

———. 1997. "Shopkeepers and Feminists: The Reproduction of Political Process among Women Activists in Lebanon." In *Organizing Women: Formal and Informal Groups in the Middle East*, edited by Dawn Chatty and Annika Rabo, 57–80. New York: Berg.

————. 2000a. "Civic Myths, Citizenship, and Gender in Lebanon." In *Gender and Citizenship in the Middle East*, edited by Suad Joseph, 107–36. Syracuse, NY: Syracuse University Press.

————. 2000b. "Introduction." In *Gender and Citizenship in the Middle East*, edited by Suad Joseph, 3–30, Syracuse, NY: Syracuse University Press.

Joshi, Sanjay. 2001. *Fractured Modernity: Making of a Middle Class in Colonial North India*. Oxford: Oxford University Press.

Joyce, Miriam. 2008. *Anglo-American Support for Jordan: The Career of King Hussein*. London: Palgrave MacMillan.

Kamrava, Mehran. 2012. The Arab Spring and the Saudi-Led Counterrevolution. *Orbis* 56(1): 96–104.

Kandil, Hazem. 2012. *Soldiers, Spies, and Statesmen: Egypt's Road to Revolt*. London: Verso Books.

Kandiyoti, Deniz. 1988. "Bargaining with Patriarchy." *Gender and Society* 2 (3): 274–90.

————. 1991a. "Identity and Its Discontents: Women and the Nation." *Millennium*, 20(3): 429–43.

————. 1991b. "Introduction." In *Women, Islam and the State*, edited by Deniz Kandiyoti, 1–21. Philadelphia: Temple University Press.

————. 1997. "Gendering the Modern: On Missing Dimensions in the Study of Turkish Modernity." In *Rethinking Modernity and National Identity in Turkey*, edited by Sibel Bozdoğan and Reşat Kasaba. Seattle: University of Washington Press.

————. 2013. "Fear and Fury: Women and Post-revolutionary Violence." openDemocracy, 14 January. Accessed 31 August 2017. http://www.opendemocracy.net/5050 /deniz-kandiyoti/fear-and-fury-women-and-post-revolutionary-violence.

————. 2015. "The Triple Whammy: Towards the Eclipse of Women's Rights." openDemocracy, 19 January. https://www.opendemocracy.net/en/5050 /triple-whammy-towards-eclipse-of-womens-rights/.

Kaplan, Caren. 1994. "The Politics of Location as Transnational Feminist Practice." In *Scattered Hegemonies: Postmodernity and Transnational Feminist Practices*, edited by I. Grewal, and C. Kaplan, 137–52. Minneapolis: University of Minnesota Press.

Kaplan, Caren, Norma Alarcon, and Minoo Moallem, eds. 1999. *Between Woman and Nation: Nationalisms, Transnational Feminisms, and the State*, Durham, NC: Duke University Press.

Kapur, Ratna. 2002. "The Tragedy of Victimization Rhetoric: Resurrecting the Native Subject in International/Postcolonial Feminist Legal Politics." *Harvard Human Rights Law Journal* 15(1): 1–37.

Karam, Azza M. 1997. "Women, Islamisms, and the State." *In Muslim Women and the Politics of Participation: Implementing the Beijing Platform*, edited by Mahnaz Afkhami and Erika Friedl, 18–28. Syracuse, NY: Syracuse University Press.

Karam, Karam. 2005. "Civil Associations, Social Movements, and Political Participation in Lebanon in the 1990s." In *NGOs and Governance in the Arab World*, edited by Sarah Ben Néfissa, Nabil Abd al-Fattah, Sari Hanafi, and Carlos Milani. Cairo: American University in Cairo Press.

Kardam, Nuket. 2004. "The Emerging Global Gender Equality Regime from Neoliberal and Constructivist Perspectives in International Relations." *International Feminist Journal of Politics* 6(1): 85–109.

Kassem, Fatma. 2011. *Palestinian Women: Narrative Histories and Gendered Memory*, London: Zed Books.

Keck, Margaret, and Kathryn Sikkink. 1998. *Activists beyond Borders: Advocacy Networks in International Politics*, Ithaca. NY: Cornell University Press.

Kelly, L., and J. Radford. 1996. "'Nothing Really Happened': The Invalidation of Women's Experiences of Sexual Violence." In *Women, Violence and Male Power*, edited by L. Kelly and J. Radford, 19–33. Philadelphia: Open University Press.

Kerr, Malcolm. 1971. *The Arab Cold War: Gamal Abd al-Nasir and His Rivals, 1958–1970*. Oxford: Oxford University Press.

Ketchley N. 2017. "How Egypt's Generals Used Street Protests to Stage a Coup." *Washington Post*, 3 July. Accessed 9 February 2018. https://www.washingtonpost .com/news/monkey-cage/wp/2017/07/03/how-egypts-generals-used-street -protests-to-stage-a-coup/?utm_term=.cf19b77836be.

Khader, Asma. 1996. "Women and Democracy, The Democratic Experiment in Jordan (1989–1993)." In *Democratic Process in Jordan—Realities and Prospects* (Conference in Amman, Jordan, 31 May–2 June 1994), edited by Hani Hourani and Hussein Abu-Rumman, 263–68. Amman: Sindbad Publishing House.

Khafagi, Fatma. 2001. "Breaking Cultural and Social Taboos: The Fight against FGM in Egypt." *Development* 44(3): 74–78.

Khafagy, Fatma. 2012. *National Women Machineries*. Cairo: UN Women Egypt Country Office.

Khalidi, Rashid. 2009. *Sowing Crisis: The Cold War and American Dominance in the Middle East*. Boston: Beacon Press.

Khalidi, Walid. 1979. *Conflict and Violence in Lebanon: Confrontation in the Middle East*. Cambridge, MA: Harvard Center for International Affairs.

Khalil, Andrea, ed. 2015. *Gender, Women and the Arab Spring*. London: Routledge.

Khalili, Laleh. 2007. *Heroes and Martyrs of Palestine: The Politics of National Commemoration*. Cambridge: Cambridge University Press.

Khater, Akram, and Cynthia Nelson. 1988. "Al-Harakah Al-Nissa'iyyah: The Women's Movement and Political Participation in Modern Egypt." *Women's Studies International Forum* 11(5): 465–83.

Khattab, Lara. 2010. "Civil Society in a Sectarian Context: The Women's Movement in Post-war Lebanon." MA thesis, submitted to the School of Arts and Sciences, Lebanese American University.

Khayat, Karma. 2012. "The Left: Can It Be Right for Lebanon?" MA thesis, Lebanese American University.

Khoury, Doreen. 2013. "Women's Political Participation in Lebanon." Heinrich Boll Stiftung, 23 September. Accessed 21 July 2015. http://lb.boell.org/en/2013/09/23 /womens-political-participation-lebanon.

Khoury, Nicole. 2015. "Enough Violence: The Importance of Local Action to Transnational Feminist Scholarship and Activism." *Peitho Journal*, 18(1): 113–39.

Kilani, Sa'eda. 2003. "Boycott Fever in Jordan." *Middle East Report*, no. 226 (Spring): 24–27.

Kingsley, Patrick. 2014 "Egypt's President in Hospital Photo-Call in Effort to Tackle Sexual Violence." *The Guardian Online*, 11 June. http://www.theguardian.com/world/2014/jun/11/egypt-president-sisi-tackle-sexual-violence.

———. 2015. "Female Protester's Death Prompts Rare Condemnation in Egypt's State Media." *Guardian Online*, 26 January. Accessed 30 January 2015. http://www.theguardian.com/world/2015/jan/26/egypt-female-protester-death-condemnation-egyptian-state-media.

Kirollos, Mariam. 2013a. "Sexual Harassment in Tahrir: A Message from Mariam Kirollos." *Tahrir Squared*, 1 July. http://www.tahrirsquared.com/node/5131.

———. 2013b. "Sexual Violence in Egypt: Myths and Realities." *Jadaliyya*, 16 July. http://www.jadaliyya.com/pages/index/13007/sexual-violence-in-egypt_myths-and-realities.

———. 2016. "The Daughters of Egypt Are a Red Line." *24 SUR: International Journal on Human Rights* 13(24): 137–54.

Knudsen, Are. 2003. "Islamism in the Diaspora: Palestinian Refugees in Lebanon." *Journal of Refugee Studies* 18(2): 216–34.

Koopman, Sara. 2011. "Alter-geopolitics: Other Securities Are Happening." *Geoforum* 42(3): 274–84.

Korany, B., and R. El-Mahdi, eds. 2013. *Arab Spring in Egypt: Revolution and Beyond*. Cairo: American University in Cairo Press.

Kortam, Hind. 2013. "Essam El-Haddad: Tahrir Crowds Are Out of Control." *Daily News Egypt*, 30 June. Accessed 19 January 2015. http://www.dailynewsegypt.com/2013/06/30/essam-el-haddad-tahrir-crowds-are-out-of-control/.

Krayem, Hassan. 1997. "The Lebanese Civil War and the Taif Agreement." In *Conflict Resolution in the Arab World: Selected Essays*. Edited by Paul Salem. Beirut: American University of Beirut. Accessed 14 June 2019. http://ddc.aub.edu.lb/projects/pspa/conflict-resolution.html.

Kubursi, Atif. 1999. "Reconstructing the Economy of Lebanon." *Arab Studies Quarterly* 21(1): 69–96.

Kurtulus, Ersun N. 2009. "'The Cedar Revolution': Lebanese Independence and the Question of Collective Self-Determination." *British Journal of Middle Eastern Studies* 36(2): 195–214.

La sharaf fi-l-jarima. Accessed 9 November 2015. http://www.lasharaffiljareemah.net/?page_id=724.

Lachapelle, Jean. 2012. "Lessons from Egypt's Tax Collectors." *Middle East Report Online*, no. 264 (Fall). Accessed 5 August 2015. http://www.merip.org/mer/mer264/lessons-egypts-tax-collectors-0.

Lang, Sabine. 1997. "The NGOization of Feminism." In *Transitions, Environments, Translations: Feminisms in International Politics*, edited by Joan W. Scott, Cora Kaplan, and Deborah Keates, 101–20. London: Routledge.

Langohr, Vickie. 2004. "Too Much Civil Society, Too Little Politics: The Case of Egypt and the Arab Liberalizers." *Comparative Politics* 36(2): 181–204.

———. 2011. "How Egypt's Revolution Has Dialed Back Women's Rights." *Foreign Affairs*, 22 December. Accessed 14 January 2015. http://www.foreignaffairs.com /articles/136986/vickie-langohr/how-egypts-revolution-has-dialed-back-womens -rights.

———. 2013. "'This Is Our Square' Fighting Sexual Assault at Cairo Protests." *Middle East Report*, no. 268 (Fall). Accessed 20 January 2015. http://www.merip.org /mer/mer268/our-square.

———. 2014. "New President, Old Pattern of Sexual Violence in Egypt." *Middle East Research and Information Project* (7 July). Accessed 19 January 2015. http:// www.merip.org/mero/mero070714?ip_login_no_cache=f031ea0367397fd02c8 0838a7e111283c.

Larzilliere, Penelope. 2016. *Activism in Jordan*. Translated by Cynthia Schoch, London: Zed Books.

Layne, Linda L. 1989. "The Dialogics of Tribal Self-Representation in Jordan." *American Ethnologist* 16(1): 24–39.

Lebanon Opposition. 2004. "Bristol Declaration: Full Text." Lebanon Wire, 18 December. Accessed 18 August 2015. http://www.lebanonwire.com/0412 /0412180Ibristol_declaration.asp.

Leenders, Reinoud. 2012. *Spoils of Truce: Corruption and State-Building in Postwar Lebanon*. Ithaca, NY: Cornell University Press.

Leila, Reem. 2012a. "Moving Backwards." *Al-Ahram Weekly Online*, 25–31 October. http://weekly.ahram.org.eg/2012/1120/eg5.htm.

———. 2012b. "'Two Steps Back.'" *Al-Ahram Weekly Online*, 20 December. http:// weekly.ahram.org.eg/News/625/24/Two-steps-back.aspx

Levine, Mark. 2013. "The Human Rights Situation in Egypt: An Interview with Aida Seif al-Dawla." *Jadaliyya*, 23 January. http://www.jadaliyya.com/pages /index/9740/the-human-rights-situation-in-egypt_an-interview-w.

Levitt, Peggy, and Merry, Sally. 2009. "Vernacularization on the Ground: Local Uses of Global Women's Rights in Peru, China, India and the United States." *Global Networks* 9(4): 441–61.

Liddle, Joanna, and Shirin Rai. 1998. "Feminism, Imperialism, and Orientalism: The Challenge of the Indian Woman." *Women's History Review* 7(4): 495–520.

Lijphart, Arendt. 1968. "Typologies of Democratic Systems." *Comparative Political Studies* 1(1): 3–44.

Lister, Charles. 2016. *The Syrian Jihad: Al-Qaeda, the Islamic State and the Evolution of an Insurgency*. Oxford: Oxford University Press.

LLWR (Lebanese League for Women's Rights). 1987. *Mahatat 'ala tariq al-nidal min 'ajl al-masawa w-al-hurriya w-al-dimuqratiya w-al-salam, 1948–1987*. Beirut: Lebanese League for Women's Rights.

Louis, Wm. Roger, and Avi Shlaim, eds. 2012. *The 1967 Arab-Israeli War: Origins and Consequences*. Cambridge: Cambridge University Press.

Lubitow, Amy, and Mia Davis. 2011. "Pastel Injustice: The Corporate Use of Pink-washing for Profit." *Environmental Justice* 4(2): 139–44.

Lugones, Maria. 2007. "Heterosexualism and the Colonial/Modern Gender System." *Hypatia* 22 (1): 186–209.

———. 2010. "Towards a Decolonial Feminism." *Hypatia* 25 (4): 742–59.

Lynch, Marc. 2007. "Blogging the New Arab Public." In *Arab Media & Society*, 1 (Spring): 3. Accessed August 2015 http://www.arabmediasociety.com/?article =10..

———. 2013. *The Arab Uprising: The Unfinished Revolutions of the New Middle East*. New York: Public Affairs.

———. 2016. *The New Arab Wars: Uprisings and Anarchy in the Middle East*. New York: Public Affairs.

Macleod, Arlene Elowe. 1991. *Accommodating Protest: Working Women, the New Veiling, and Change in Cairo*. New York: Columbia University Press.

Mada Masr. 2014a. "National Women's Council Says Assault Is Used to Discredit Women." 10 June. https://madamasr.com/en/2014/06/10/news/u/national -womens-council-says-assault-is-used-to-discredit-women/.

———. 2014b. "Sisi Visits Tahrir Square Mob Sexual Assault Victim in Hospital." 11 June. Accessed 9 September 2017. https://www.madamasr.com/en/2014/06/11 /news/u/sisi-visits-tahrir-square-mob-sexual-assault-victim-in-hospital/.

———. 2016a. "Authorities Ban Rights Defender Aida Seif al-Dawla from Traveling." 23 November. Accessed 15 April 2018. https://www.madamasr.com/en/2016/11/23 /news/u/authorities-ban-rights-defender-aida-seif-al-dawla-from-traveling/.

———. 2016b. "Italian Newspaper Sheds Light on Hundreds of Forced Disappearances in Egypt." 4 April. Accessed 8 April 2016. https://madamasr.com /en/2016/04/04/news/u/italian-newspaper-sheds-light-on-hundreds-of-forced -disappearances-in-egypt/.

———. 2016c. "Nazra for Feminist Studies Summoned for Investigation in Re-opened NGO Case." 20 March. Accessed 8 April 2016. http://www.madamasr .com/news/nazra-feminist-studies-summoned-investigation-re-opened-ngo -case.

———. 2016d. "2011 NGO Case Reopened against Hossam Bahgat, Gamal Eid and Others." 17 March, Accessed 8 April 2016. http://www.madamasr.com /news/2011-ngo-case-reopened-against-hossam-bahgat-gamal-eid-and-others.

Mahadeen, Ebtihal. 2014. "Beyond Modesty: Fighting Sexual Harassment in Jordan." *The New Arab.* Accessed 10 April 2016. https://www.alaraby.co.uk /english/comment/2014/12/21/beyond-modesty-fighting-sexual-harassment-in -jordan.

Mahfouz, Asmaa. 2011. "Vlog." YouTube, 2 February. Accessed 29 March 2016. https://www.youtube.com/watch?v=eBg7O48vhLY.

Mahmood, Saba. 2005. *Politics of Piety: The Islamic Revival and the Feminist Subject*. Princeton, NJ: Princeton University Press.

Mahmoud, Olfat, and Rebecca Roberts. 2018. "One Camp, Three Refugee Groups: Challenges for Local NGOs." *Forced Migration Review* 57(1): 7–9.

Makdisi, Jean Said. 1996. "The Mythology of Modernity: Women and Democracy in Lebanon." In *Feminism and Islam: Legal and Literary Perspectives* edited by Mai Yamani. 231–50. New York: New York University Press.

Manea, Elham. 2011. *The Arab State and Women's Rights: The Trap of Authoritarian Governance.* London: Routledge.

Marfleet, Philip. 2016. *Egypt: Contested Revolution.* London: Pluto Press.

Martin, Roger L., and Sally Osberg. 2007. "Social Entrepreneurship: The Case for Definition." *Stanford Social Innovation Review* (Spring).

Mason, Corinne L. 2013. Global Violence against Women as a National Security "Emergency," *Feminist Formations* 25(2): 55–80.

Massad, Joseph A. 2001. *Colonial Effects: The Making of National Identity in Jordan.* New York: Columbia University Press.

Matthies-Boon, Vivienne. 2017. "Shattered Worlds: Political Trauma amongst Young Activists in Post-revolutionary Egypt." *Journal of North African Studies* 22(4): 620–44.

Mayer, Ann Elizabeth. 1995. "Rhetorical Strategies and Official Policies on Women's Rights: The Merits and Drawbacks of the New World Hypocrisy." In *Faith and Freedom: Women's Human Rights in the Muslim World*, edited by Mahnaz Afkhami, 104–32. London: I. B. Tauris.

———. 1997. Aberrant "Islams" and Errant Daughters: The Turbulent Legacy of Beijing in Muslim Societies. In *Muslim Women and the Politics of Participation: Implementing the Beijing Platform*, edited by Mahnaz Afkhami and Erika Friedl, 29–42. Syracuse, NY: Syracuse University Press.

McCarthy, Niall. 2017. "Lebanon Still Hosts the Most Refugees per Capita by Far." *Forbes*, 3 April. Accessed 3 May 2018. https://www.forbes.com/sites /niallmccarthy/2017/04/03/lebanon-still-has-hosts-the-most-refugees-per-capita -by-far-infographic/#1761114f3970.

McClintock, Anne. 1993. "Family Feuds: Gender, Nationalism and the Family." *Feminist Review* 44: 61–80.

———. 1995. *Imperial Leather: Race, Gender and Sexuality in the Colonial Contest.* London: Routledge.

McGregor, Katharine. 2016. "Opposing Colonialism: The Women's International Democratic Federation and Decolonisation Struggles in Vietnam and Algeria 1945–1965." *Women's History Review.* 25(6): 925–44.

McLarney, Ellen Anne. 2015. *Soft Force: Women in Egypt's Islamic Awakening.* Princeton, NJ: Princeton University Press.

McMahon, Sean. 2017. *Crisis and Class War in Egypt: Social Reproduction, Factional Realignments, and the Global Political Economy.* London: Zed Books.

McRobbie, Angela. 2004. "Post-feminism and Popular Culture." *Feminist Media Studies* 4(3): 255–64.

McTighe, Kristen. 2014. "'I Love Him Like My Own Dad': El-Sisi Wins the Hearts of Egyptian Women." *The National*, 25 May. Accessed 7 September 2017. https://www .thenational.ae/world/i-love-him-like-my-own-dad-el-sisi-wins-the-hearts-of -egyptian-women-1.243298.

Meijer, Roel. 2002. *The Quest for Modernity: Secular, Liberal and Left-Wing Thought in Egypt, 1945–1958*. London: Routledge Curzon.

Meintjes, Sheila, Anu Pillay, and Meredith Turshen, eds. 2001. *The Aftermath: Women in Post-Conflict Transformation*. London: Zed Books.

MERIP Reports. 1971. "Amman '71: Long Hot Summer." *MERIP* 1(2): 1–2.

Meriwether, Margaret, and Judith E. Tucker. 1999. "Introduction." In *A Social History of Women and Gender in the Modern Middle East*, edited by Margaret L. Meriwether and Judith E. Tucker, 1–24. Boulder, CO: Westview Press.

Merry, Sally Engle. 2003. "Constructing a Global Law: Violence against Women and the Human Rights System." *Law and Social Inquiry* 28(4): 941–77.

———. 2006. *Human Rights and Gender Violence: Translating International Law into Local Justice*. Chicago: University of Chicago Press.

Michaelson, R. 2016. "Arrest of Leading Egyptian Feminist Azza Soliman Sparks Anger." *The Guardian*, 7 December. Accessed 9 March 2018. https://www.the guardian.com/world/2016/dec/07/womens-rights-activist-azza-soliman -arrested-in-egypt.

Mikdashi, Maya. 2012. "Sexual Violence Is a Crime Sometimes." *Jadaliyya*, 11 January. Accessed 10 April 2016. http://www.jadaliyya.com/pages/index/4001 /sexual-violence-is-a-crime-sometimes.

———. 2013. "Lebanon." In *Dispatches from the Arab Spring: Understanding the New Middle East*, edited by Paul Amar and Vijay Prashad, 266–81. Minneapolis: University of Minnesota Press.

———. 2014. "Quick Thoughts: Maya Mikdashi on the Current Situation in Lebanon." *Jadaliyya*, 24 June. http://photography.jadaliyya.com/pages/index/18272 /quick-thoughts_maya-mikdashi-on-the-current-situat.

———. 2015. "Lebanon August 2015: Notes on Paralysis, Protests and Hope." *Jadaliyya*, 26 August, Accessed 13 April 2016. http://www.jadaliyya.com/pages /index/22491/lebanon-august-2015_notes-on-paralysis-protests-an.

Mikhail, Amira. 2014. "The Obliteration of Civil Society in Egypt." openDemocracy, 6 October. Accessed 30 January 2015.https://www.opendemocracy.net /arab-awakening/amira-mikhail/obliteration-of-civil-society-in-egypt.

Mitchell, Richard P. 1969. *The Society of the Muslim Brothers*. Oxford: Oxford University Press.

Moghadam, Valentine, ed. 1994. *Gender and National Identity: Women and Politics in Muslim Societies*. London: Zed Books.

———. 2002. "Islamic Feminism and Its Discontents: Towards a Resolution of the Debate." *Signs* 27(4): 1135–71.

———. 2005. *Globalizing Women: Transnational Feminist Networks*. Washington, DC: The Johns Hopkins University Press.

———. 2012. *Globalization and Social Movements: Islamism, Feminism, and the Global Justice Movement*. 2nd ed. Lanham, MD: Rowman & Littlefield.

———. 2013. *Modernizing Women: Gender and Social Change in the Middle East*. Boulder, CO: Lynne Rienner.

Moghissi, Haideh. 1999. *Feminism and Islamic Fundamentalism: The Limits of Postmodern Analysis*. London: Zed Books.

Mohanty, Chandra Talpade. 1991. "Under Western Eyes: Feminist Scholarship and Colonial Discourses." In *Third World Women and the Politics of Feminism*, edited by Chandra Talpade Mohanty, Ann Russo, and Lourdes Torres, 51–80. Bloomington: Indiana University Press.

———. 2003. *Feminism without Borders: Decolonizing Theory, Practicing Solidarity*. Durham, NC: Duke University Press.

Mojab, Shahrzad. 2001. "Theorizing the Politics of 'Islamic Feminism.'" *Feminist Review* 69(1): 124–46.

Moser, Caroline, and Fiona Clark, eds. 2001. *Victims, Perpetrators or Actors? Gender, Armed Conflict and Political Violence*. London: Zed Books.

Moussawi, Fatima, and Nasser Yassin. 2017. "Dissecting Lebanese Law 293 on Domestic Violence: Are Women Protected?" Policy Brief no. 5, August, AUB Policy Institute.

Muasher, Marwan. 2011. "Jordan's Proposed Constitutional Amendments: A First Step in the Right Direction." *Carnegie Endowment for International Peace*, 17 August. http://carnegieendowment.org/2011/08/17/jordan-s-proposed -constitutional-amendments-first-step-in-right-direction.

Muhammad Taha, Rana. 2012. "Women Cut Their Hair in Protest of New Constitution." *Daily News Egypt*, 25 December. Accessed 15 January 2015. http:// www.dailynewsegypt.com/2012/12/25/women-cut-their-hair-in-protest-of-new -constitution/.

Muhanna, Aitemad. 2015b. "Secular and Islamic Women's Activism and Discourses in Post-Uprising Tunisia." In *Rethinking Gender in Revolutions and Resistance: Lessons from the Arab World*, edited by Maha El Said, Lena Meari, and Nicola Pratt, 205–31. London: Zed Press.

Muhanna-Matar, Aitemad. 2014. "New Trends of Women's Activism after the Arab Uprisings: Redefining Women's Leadership." LSE Middle East Centre Working Paper. http://eprints.lse.ac.uk/68134/.

Mustafa, Hala. 2005. "Women, Politics and Modernization in Egypt." In *Building Democracy in Egypt*, edited by Ziad Majed, 19–29. Stockholm: International IDEA.

Mutawi, Samir A. 1987. *Jordan in the 1967 War*. Cambridge: Cambridge University Press.

Mutua, Makau. 2001. "Savages, Victims, and Saviors: The Metaphor of Human Rights." *Harvard International Law Journal* 42(1): 201–45.

Nader, Aya. 2014. "Government Body to Implement New Strategy to Protect Women against Violence." *Daily News Egypt*, 7 July. Accessed 19 January 2015. http://www.dailynewsegypt.com/2014/07/07/government-body-implement-new -strategy-protect-women-violence/.

Najmabadi, Afsaneh. 1991. "Hazards of Modernity and Morality: Women, State and Ideology in Contemporary Iran." In *Women, Islam and the State*, edited by Deniz Kandiyoti, 48–76. Philadelphia: Temple University Press.

Nanes, Stefanie Eileen. 2003. "Fighting Honor Crimes: Evidence of Civil Society in Jordan." *Middle East Journal* 57(1): 112–29

Naples, Nancy, and Manisha Desai, eds. 2002. *Women's Activism and Globalization: Linking Local Struggles and Transnational Politics.* New York: Routledge.

Nasr, Salim. 1978. "Backdrop to Civil War: The Crisis of Lebanese Capitalism." *MERIP Reports*, no. 73 (December): 3–13.

Nasser, Lamis. 2010. *Economic, Social, Political and Psychological Implications on Jordanian Women Married to Non-Jordanians and Their Families.* Amman: Arab Women Organization of Jordan. http://www.el-karama.org/wp-content /uploads/2013/10/Citizenship_Report-EN1.pdf.

National Council for Women. 2015. "National Report on Beijing +20." Cairo, Accessed 1 September 2015. http://www.unwomen.org/~/media/headquarters /attachments/sections/csw/59/national_reviews/egypt_review_en_beijing20 .ashx.

National Front for Reform. 2011. "Khatut al-'aridha li-birnamij al-jabha al-wataniya." Outlines of the National Front Programme. http://jordanreform.org/.

nationalanthems.info. n.d. "Palestine." Accessed 28 August 2017. http://www .nationalanthems.info/ps.htm.

Nauphal, Naila. 1997. *Post-war Lebanon: Women and Other War-Affected Groups.* Geneva: International Labour Organization. http://www.nzdl.org /gsdlmod?e=d-00000-00---off-0aedl--00-0----0-10-0---0---0direct-10---4------ 0-1l--11-en-50---20-about---00-0-1-00-0--4----0-0-11-10-outfZz-8-00&a=d&c=a edl&cl=CL2.6.1&d=HASH012ff8edo2d4edb40e4d69b6.2.

Naylor, Hugh. 2012. "Jordan's Rural Poor the Loudest Critics of 'Corrupt' Politics." *The National*, 2 July. http://www.thenational.ae/news/world/middle-east /jordans-rural-poor-the-loudest-critics-of-corrupt-politics#page1#ixzz3EDavfvTy.

Nazra for Feminist Studies. 2011. "Egyptian Human Rights Organizations Stop Their Participation in an International Campaign against Gender Based Violence." 25 November. http://nazra.org/en/2011/11/we-stopped-our-participation -intl-campaign-against-gender-based-violence.

———. 2012a. "The President, His Group, and the Government Must Cease Their Policy of Targeting Female Activists and Excluding Women from the Public Sphere." 12 December. http://nazra.org/en/2012/12/president-his-group-must -cease-their-policy-targeting-female-activists-excluding-women.

———. 2012b. "She and Elections: Mentoring on the Ground with the Candidates 2011/2012." April. Accessed 14 January 2015. http://nazra.org/sites/nazra/files /attachments/nazra_she_and_elections_report_april2012_en.pdf.

———. 2012c. "Sixteen Female Candidates for the People's Assembly Elections 2011/2012." 3 September. Accessed 14 January 2015.http://nazra.org/sites/nazra/files /attachments/candidates_profiles_people_assembly_elections_2011_2012 _en.pdf.

———. 2013a. *Al-'unf al-ijtima'i did al-nisa' ba'd 30 yunio.* Cairo: Nazra for Feminist Studies.

———. 2013b. "The Dispersion of the Rab'aa Sit-in and Its Aftermath." 10 September. Accessed 27 January 2015. http://nazra.org/sites/nazra/files/attachments /report_on_police_treatment-with_women_protesters_en.pdf.

———. 2013c. "Position Paper on Sexual Violence against Women and the Increasing Frequency of Gang Rape in Tahrir Square and Its Environs." 4 February, Accessed 19 January 2015. http://nazra.org/en/2013/02/position-paper-sexual -violence-against-women-and-increasing-frequency-gang-rape-tahrir.

———. 2014. "Feminist Groups and Organizations Collaborate Together in Order to Present Their Vision for a National Strategy to Combat Violence against Women and Adopt a Holistic and Broad Perspective to Eradicate These Crimes from Their Roots." 10 December. Accessed 28 January 2015. http://nazra.org /en/2014/12/feminist-groups-and-organizations-collaborate-together-order -present-their-vision-national.

New Arab. 2018. "The Six Lebanese Women Voted into Parliament." 8 May. Accessed 11 February 2019. Available at: https://www.alaraby.co.uk/english/news/2018/5/8 /the-six-lebanese-women-voted-into-parliament.

New York Times. 1986. "Communist Party Raided in Jordan." 20 May. http://www .nytimes.com/1986/05/21/world/communist-party-raided-in-jordan.html.

Newsweek. 2005. "Across the Arab World: People Power." 6 March.

Norton, Augustus Richard, ed. 1995. *Civil Society in the Middle East*. Volume 1. Leiden: E.J. Brill.

———, ed. 1996. *Civil Society in the Middle East*. Volume 2. Leiden: E.J. Brill.

Noueihed, L., and A. Warren. 2013. *The Battle for the Arab Spring: Revolution, Counter-Revolution and the Making of a New Era*. New Haven, CT: Yale University Press.

Ó Tuathail, Gearóid. 1996. *Critical Geopolitics: The Politics of Writing Global Space*. Minneapolis: University of Minnesota Press.

O'Brian, Robert, Anne Marie Goetz, Jan Aart Scholte, and Marc Williams. 2000. *Contesting Global Governance: Multilateral Economic Institutions and Global Social Movements*. Cambridge: Cambridge University Press.

Obeid, Ghinwa. 2017. "Parties Seek to Amend Domestic Violence Law." *The Daily Star*, 8 April.

OCHA. (United Nations Office for Coordination of Humanitarian Affairs). 2018. "UNICEF Syria Crisis Situation Report—2017 Humanitarian Results." OCHA Reliefweb, January. Accessed 27 April 2018. https://reliefweb.int/report/syrian -arab-republic/unicef-syria-crisis-situation-report-2017-humanitarian-results.

O'Donnell, Guillermo, Philippe Schmitter, and Laurence Whitehead, eds. 1986. *Transitions from Authoritarian Rule (4 vols)*. Baltimore: Johns Hopkins University Press.

Olimat, Muhamad S. ed. 2013. *Arab Spring and Arab Women: Challenges and Opportunities*. London: Routledge.

Olwan, Dana M. Forthcoming. "At the Limits of Legal Justice: Reforming the Law, Modernizing the Jordanian State." In *Gendered Violence and the Transnational Politics of the "Honor" Crime*.

O'Rourke, Catherine. 2013. *Gender Politics in Transitional Justice*. London: Routledge.

Ottaway, Marina. 2004a. "Avoiding the Women's Rights Trap in the Middle East." Carnegie Endowment for International Peace. 20 July. Accessed 31 August 2015. http://carnegieendowment.org/sada/?fa=21227.

———. 2004b. *Women's Rights and Democracy in the Arab World*. Carnegie Paper no. 42, February. Washington, DC: Carnegie Endowment for International Peace.

———. 2012. "Egypt: Death of the Constituent Assembly?" *Carnegie Endowment for International Peace*, 13 June. Accessed 15 January 2015. http://carnegieendowment.org/2012/06/13/egypt-death-of-constituent-assembly/brzn.

Otterman, Sharon. 2007. "Publicizing the Private: Egyptian Women Bloggers Speak Out." Arab Media Society. Accessed 10 August 2015. http://www.arabmediasociety.com/topics/index.php?t_article=28&p=0.

Otto, Dianne. 1996. "Holding up Half the Sky, but for Whose Benefit: A Critical Analysis of the Fourth World Conference on Women." *Australian Feminist Law Journal* 6(1): 7–30.

Owen, Roger. 2000. *State, Power and Politics in the Making of the Modern Middle East*, 2nd ed. London: Routledge.

Pain, Rachel. 2009. "Globalized Fear? Towards an Emotional Geopolitics." *Progress in Human Geography* 33(4): 466–86.

Pain, Rachel, and Susan J. Smith, eds. 2008. *Fear: Critical Geopolitics and Everyday Life*. Aldershot, UK: Ashgate.

Pankhurst, Donna. 2004. "The "Sex War" and Other Wars: Towards a Feminist Approach to Peace Building." In *Development, Women, and War: Feminist Perspectives*, edited by Haleh Afshar and Deborah Eade, 8–42. Oxford: Oxfam.

Parla, Ayse. 2001. "The 'Honor' of the State: Virginity Examinations in Turkey," *Feminist Studies* 27(1): 65–89.

Parpart, Jane L., and Marysia Zalewski, eds. 2008. *Rethinking the Man Question: Sex, Gender and Violence in International Relations*. New York: Zed Books.

Passerini, Luisa. 1979. "Work, Ideology and Consensus under Italian Fascism." *History Workshop Journal* 8(1): 82–108.

———. 1987. *Fascism in Popular Memory: The Cultural Experience of the Turin Working Class*. Cambridge: Cambridge University Press.

Pateman, Carole. 1988. *The Sexual Contract*. Stanford, CA: Stanford University Press.

Paul, Katie. 2012. "In Jordan's Tafilah, Demands Escalate for King's Downfall." *Almonitor*, 16 November. http://www.al-monitor.com/pulse/originals/2012/al-monitor/jordan-king-talifah.html#.

Perthes, Volker. 1997. "Myths and Money: Four Years of Hariri and Lebanon's Preparation for a New Middle East." *Middle East Report*, no. 203 (Spring): 16–21.

Peteet, Julie. 1991. *Gender in Crisis: Women and the Palestinian Resistance Movement*. New York: Columbia University Press.

—————. 1996. "From Refugees to Minority: Palestinians in Post-War Lebanon." *Middle East Report* no. 200 (July): 27–30.

—————. 2005. *Landscape of Hope and Despair: Palestinian Refugee Camps*. Philadelphia: University of Pennsylvania Press.

Peterson, V. Spike. ed. 1992a. *Gendered States: Feminist (Re)visions of IR Theory*. Boulder, CO: Lynne Rienner Publishers.

—————. 1992b. "Security and Sovereign States: What Is at Stake in Taking Feminism Seriously?" In *Gendered States: Feminist (Re)Visions of International Relations Theory*, edited by V. Spike Peterson, 31–64. Boulder, CO: Lynne Rienner

—————. 1999. "Sexing Political Identities: Nationalism as Heterosexism." *International Feminist Journal of Politics* 1(1): 34–65.

Peterson, V. Spike., and Anne Sisson Runyan. 2010. *Global Gender Issues in the New Millennium*. Boulder, CO: Westview Press.

Petras, James. 1997. "NGOs and Imperialism." *Monthly Review* 49(7): 10–27.

Pettman, Jan Jindy. 1996. *Worlding Women: A Feminist International Politics*. London: Routledge.

—————. 1997. "Body Politics: International Sex Tourism." *Third World Quarterly* 18(1): 93–108.

Philipp, Thomas. 1978. "Feminism and Nationalist Politics in Egypt." In *Women in the Muslim World*, edited by Lois Beck and Nikkie Keddie. Cambridge, MA: Harvard University Press.

Phillips, Christopher. 2016. *The Battle for Syria: International Rivalry in the New Middle East*. New Haven, CT: Yale University Press.

Pietrobelli, Marta. 2013. "In Whose Interests? The Politics of Gender Equality in Jordan." PhD thesis, SOAS, University of London.

Pollard, Lisa. 2005. *Nurturing the Nation: The Family Politics of Modernizing, Colonizing, and Liberating Egypt, 1805–1923*. Berkeley: University of California Press.

Portelli, Alessandro. 1991. *The Death of Luigi Trastulli and Other Stories: Form and Meaning in Oral History*. Albany: State University of New York Press.

Povey, Tara. 2015. *Social Movements in Egypt and Iran*. London: Palgrave Macmillan.

Prashad, Vijay. 2007. *The Darker Nations: A People's History of the Third World*. New York: The New Press.

Pratt, Nicola. 2002. "Globalization and the Postcolonial State: Human Rights NGOs and the Prospects for Democratic Governance in Egypt." Unpublished PhD thesis, University of Exeter (UK).

—————. 2004. "Bringing Politics Back In: Examining the Link between Globalization and Democratization." *Review of International Political Economy* 11(2): 311–36.

—————. 2005. "Identity, Culture and Democratisation: The Case of Egypt." *New Political Science* 27(1): 69–86.

—————. 2006. "Human Rights NGOs and the Foreign Funding Debate in Egypt." In *Human Rights in the Arab World*, edited by Anthony Tirado-Chase and Amr Hamzawy, 114–26. Philadelphia: University of Pennsylvania Press.

————. 2007. "The Queen Boat Case in Egypt: Sexuality, National Security and State Sovereignty." *Review of International Studies* 33(1): 129–44.

————. 2011. "Debating the Future of the Arab Revolutions in Cairo: Democracy, Imperialism and Neoliberalism." *Jadaliyya*, 29 June. Accessed 29 March 2016. http://www.jadaliyya.com/pages/index/2011/debating-the-future-of-the-arab-revolutions-in-cai.

————. 2012a. "Bringing the Revolution to Campus: An Interview with March 9 Activist Laila Soueif." 10 May, *Jadaliyya*. Accessed 5 August 2015. http://www.jadaliyya.com/pages/index/5457/bringing-the-revolution-to-campus_an-interview-wit.

————. 2012b. "The Gender Logics of Resistance to the 'War on Terror': Constructing Sex-Gender Difference through the Erasure of Patriarchy in the Middle East." *Third World Quarterly* 33(10): 1821–36.

————. 2013a. "Egyptian Women: Between Revolution, Counter-Revolution, Orientalism and Authenticity." *Jadaliyya*. 6 May. Accessed 26 January 2015.http://www.jadaliyya.com/pages/index/11559/egyptian-women_between-revolution-counter-revoluti.

————. 2013b. "Ranking Violence against Arab Women Feeds Tired Stereotypes." *The Conversation*, 14 November. http://theconversation.com/ranking-violence-against-arab-women-feeds-tired-stereotypes-20173.

————. 2013c. "Reconceptualizing Gender, Reinscribing Racial-Sexual Boundaries in International Security: The Case of UN Security Council Resolution 1325 on "Women, Peace and Security." *International Studies Quarterly* 57(4): 772–83.

————. 2014. *From Revolution to Repression: Egyptian Universities on the Frontline of Protest* [Egypt Solidarity Pamphlet]. https://egyptsolidarityinitiative.files.wordpress.com/2014/05/es-pamphlet-for-web.pdf.

————. 2015. "A History of Jordanian Women's Activism." *7iber.com*, 23 May. http://www.7iber.com/society/a-history-of-womens-activism-in-jordan-1946-1989/.

————. 2016. "How the West Undermined Women's Rights in the Arab World." *Jadaliyya*. 25 January. http://www.jadaliyya.com/pages/index/23693/how-the-west-undermined-women's-rights-in-the-arab.

Pratt, Nicola, and Dina Rezk. 2019. "Securitizing the Muslim Brotherhood: State Violence and Authoritarianism in Egypt after the Arab Spring," *Security Dialogue*, 50(3): 239–56.

Pruzan-Jørgensen, Julie Elisabeth. 2012. *Islamic Women's Activism in The Arab World: Potentials and Challenges for External Actors*. Copenhagen: Danish Institute for International Studies.

Puar, Jasbir. 2007. *Terrorist Assemblages: Homonationalism in Queer Times*. Durham, NC: Duke University Press.

————. 2011. "Citation and Censorship: The Politics of Talking about the Sexual Politics of Israel." *Feminist Legal Studies* 19(1): 133–42.

————. 2013. "Rethinking Homonationalism." *International Journal of Middle East Studies* 45(1): 336–52.

Qiblawi, Tamara. 2014. "Women Decry Lebanon's Domestic Violence Law." Al Jazeera, 15 April. Accessed 10 April 2016. http://www.aljazeera.com/indepth /features/2014/03/women-decry-lebanon-domestic-violence-law-2014327115352486894 .html.

Quandt, William. 1978. *Decade of Decisions: American Policy Toward the Arab-Israeli Conflict, 1967–1977*. Berkeley: University of California Press.

———. 1984. "Reagan's Lebanon Policy: Trial and Error." *Middle East Journal* 38(2): 237–54.

Quilty, Jim. 2005. "The Changing Face of the Lebanese Left: Democratic Left Movement Vice President Ziad Majed on Lebanon's Smallest High-Profile Party." *Middle East Transparent*, 19 July. Accessed 18 August 2015. http://www.metransparent .net/old/texts/ziad_majed_interview.htm,

Rabie, Dalia. 2014. "Sisi and His Women." *Mada Masr*. 25 May. Accessed 7 September 2017. https://www.madamasr.com/en/2014/05/25/feature/politics/sisi-and -his-women/.

Radsch, Courtney. 2008. "Core to Commonplace: The Evolution of Egypt's Blogosphere." *Arab Media and Society*, 6(Fall). Accessed 3 August 2015. http://www .arabmediasociety.com/?article=692.

Rai, Shirin M. 2002. *Gender and the Political Economy of Development*. Cambridge: Polity Press.

———. 2003a. "Introduction."' In *Mainstreaming Gender, Democratizing the State: Institutional Mechanisms for the Advancement of Women*, edited by Shirin Rai, 1–11. Manchester, UK: Manchester University Press.

———. 2003b. "Institutional Mechanisms for the Advancement of Women: Mainstreaming Gender, Democratizing the State?" In *Mainstreaming Gender, Democratizing the State: Institutional Mechanisms for the Advancement of Women*, edited by Shirin Rai, 15–39. Manchester, UK: Manchester University Press.

Raouf Ezzat, Heba. 2009. "Rethinking Secularism, Rethinking Feminism." IkhwanWeb, 28 September. Accessed 28 March 2016. http://www.ikhwanweb .com/article.php?id=21136.

Rashwan, Nada Hussein. 2011. "Teachers' Strike Reaches Unprecedented Heights in March on the Cabinet." *Ahram Online*, 24 September. http://english.ahram .org.eg/NewsContent/1/64/22374/Egypt/Politics-/Teachers-strike-reaches -unprecedented-heights-in-m.aspx.

Rice, John. 1986. "Protesters, Press Bear Brunt of Jordan's New Restrictions." *The Palm Beach Post*, 27 June. http://news.google.com/newspapers?nid=1964&dat =19860627&id=zUojAAAAIBAJ&sjid=Mc8FAAAAIBAJ&pg=953,6306178.

Richards, Alan, and John Waterbury. 1998. *A Political Economy of the Middle East*. 2nd ed. Boulder, CO: Westview Press.

Richter-Devroe, Sophie. 2012. "Defending Their Land, Protecting Their Men." *International Feminist Journal of Politics*" 14(2): 181–201.

Risse, Thomas, Stephen C. Ropp, and Kathryn Sikkink, eds. 1999. *The Power of Human Rights: International Norms and Domestic Change*. Cambridge: Cambridge University Press.

Roberts, Rebecca. 2010. *Palestinians in Lebanon: Refugees Living with Long-Term Displacement*. London: I. B. Tauris.

Robins, Philip. 2004. *A History of Jordan*. Cambridge: Cambridge University Press.

Rofel, Lisa. 1999. *Other Modernities: Gendering Yearnings in China after Socialism*. Berkeley: University of California Press.

Rose, Aaron. 2014. "Demonstrators Rally against Sexual Harassment." *Daily News Egypt*, 15 June. http://www.dailynewsegypt.com/2014/06/15/demonstrators-rally-sexual-harassment-2/.

Sabbagh, Amal. 2005. "The Arab States: Enhancing Women's Political Participation." In *Women in Parliament: Beyond Numbers* (revised edition), edited by Julie Ballington and Azza Karam, 52–71. Stockholm: International IDEA.

———. 2006. *A Critical Assessment of NWMs: The Case of Jordan*. Study for the European Commission for the Project on the Role of Women in Economic Life in the Mediterranean.

Safa, Oussama. 2006. "Lebanon Springs Forward." *Journal of Democracy*, 17(1): 22–37.

Saghieh, Nizar. 2013. "Lebanon's Law to Protect Women: Redefining Domestic Violence." *The Legal Agenda*, 23 December. Accessed 28 August 2017. http://legal-agenda.com/en/article.php?lang=en&id=571.

Said, Atef. 2015. "We Ought to Be Here: Historicizing Space and Mobilization in Tahrir Square." *International Sociology* 30(4): 348–66.

Said, Edward. 1978. *Orientalism*. London: Routledge and Kegan Paul.

———. 1993. *Culture and Imperialism*. London: Chatto & Windus.

Saidi, Mira. 2015. "Lebanon's Sexist Citizenship Law Hurts Mothers and Babies." Al Jazeera America, May 10. Accessed 12 April 2016. http://america.aljazeera.com/opinions/2015/5/lebanons-sexist-citizenship-law-hurts-mothers-and-babies.html.

Salem, Elise. 2003. *Constructing Lebanon: A Century of Literary Narratives*. Gainesville: University Press of Florida.

Salem, Mostafa. 2013. "Social Popular Alliance Party Shaken by 304 Resignations." *Daily News Egypt*, 9 November. Accessed 17 April 2018. https://www.dailynewsegypt.com/2013/11/09/social-popular-alliance-party-shaken-by-304-resignations/.

Salem, Mostafa, Fady Ashraf, and Joel Gulhane. 2013. "NoMilTrials Protest Dispersed; Prominent Activists Detained." *Daily News Egypt*, 26 November. http://www.dailynewsegypt.com/2013/11/26/nomiltrials-protest-dispersed-prominent-activists-detained/.

Salibi, Kamal. 2006. *The Modern History of Jordan*. London: I. B. Tauris.

Salime, Zakia. 2010. "Securing the Market, Pacifying Civil Society, Empowering Women: The Middle East Partnership Initiative." *Sociological Forum* 25(4): 725–45.

———. 2011. *Between Feminism and Islam: Human Rights and Sharia Law in Morocco*. Minneapolis: University of Minnesota Press.

———. 2012. "A New Feminism? Gender Dynamics in Morocco's February 20th Movement." *Journal of International Women's Studies* 5(5): 101–14.

Salkind, Michele, and Nadeem Abdel-Samad. 1977. "Lebanese Communist Party: Interview with Nadeem Abdel-Samad." *Middle East Report*, no. 61 (October): 15–16.

Salloukh, Bassel F. 2017. "The Syrian War: Spillover Effects on Lebanon." *Middle East Policy* 24(1). Accessed 20 April 2018. http://www.mepc.org/journal/syrian-war-spillover-effects-lebanon.

Sami, Hala. 2015. "A Strategic Use of Culture: Egyptian Women's Subversion and Re-signification of Gender Norms." In *Rethinking Gender in Revolutions and Resistance: Lessons from the Arab World*, edited by Maha El Said, Lena Meari, and Nicola Pratt, 86–105. London: Zed.

Sawalha, Jacky. 2011. *Voices: The Pioneering Spirit of Women in Jordan*. Amman: Jordan Ministry of Culture.

Sayigh, Rosemary. 2007. *The Palestinians from Peasants to Revolutionaries*. London, Zed.

Sayigh, Yezid. 1997. *Armed Struggle and the Search for a State: The Palestinian National Movement, 1949–1993*. Oxford: Oxford University Press.

Sayigh, Yezid, and Avi Shlaim, eds. 1997. *The Cold War and the Middle East*. Oxford: Clarendon Press.

Sbaiti, Ahmed. 1994. "Reflections on Lebanon's Reconstruction." In *Peace for Lebanon? From War to Reconstruction*, edited by Deidre Collings, 163–78. Boulder, CO: Lynne Rienner.

Schemm, Paul. 2003. "Egypt Struggles to Control Anti-War Protests." *Middle East Report Online*, 31 March. Accessed 15 August 2015. http://www.merip.org/mero/mero033103.

Schulman, Sarah. 2011. "Israel and Pinkwashing." *New York Times*, 22 November.

Schwedler, Jillian. 2003. "More Than a Mob: The Dynamics of Political Demonstrations in Jordan." *Middle East Report*, no. 226 (Spring):18–23.

———. 2012. "The Political Geography of Protest in Neoliberal Jordan." *Middle East Critique* 21(3): 259–70.

———. 2013. "Jordan." In *Dispatches from the Arab Spring: Understanding the New Middle East*, edited by Paul Amar and Vijay Prashad, 243–81. Minneapolis: University of Minnesota Press.

Schwedler, Jillian, and Sam Fayyaz. 2010. "Locating Dissent: Space, Law, and Protest in Jordan." In *Policing and Prisons in the Middle East: Forms of Coercion*, edited by Laleh Khalili and Jillian Schwedler. London: Hurst & Co.

Seif El Dawla, Aida. 1999. "The Political and Legal Struggle over Female Genital Mutilation in Egypt: Five Years since the ICPD." *Reproductive Health Matters* 7(13): 128–36.

Seikaly, Sherine. 2013. "The Meaning of Revolution: On Samira Ibrahim." *Jadaliyya*, 28 January. www.jadaliyya.com/pages/index/9814/the-meaning-of-revolution_on-samira-ibrahim#.

Shakry, Omnia. 1998. "Schooled Mothers and Structured Play: Child Rearing in Turn-of-the-Century Egypt." In *Remaking Women: Feminism and Modernity in the Middle East*, edited by Lila Abu-Lughod, 126–70. Princeton, NJ: Princeton University Press.

Shalabi, Samir. 2016. "Egypt's Ain Shams University Launches Unit to Combat Sexual Harassment." *Egyptian Streets*, 12 April. Accessed 13 April 2016. http://egyptianstreets.com/2016/04/12/ain-shams-university-launches-unit-to-combat-sexual-harassment/.

Shalhoub-Kevorkian, Nadera. 2007. *Militarization and Violence against Women in Conflict Zones in the Middle East: A Palestinian Case Study*, Cambridge: Cambridge University Press.

Shami, Seteney, and Lucine Taminian. 1990. "Women's Participation in the Jordanian Labour Force: A Comparison of Rural and Urban Patterns." In *Women in Arab Society: Work Patterns and Gender Relations in Egypt, Jordan and Sudan*, edited by Seteney Shami, Lucine Taminian, Soheir A. Morsy, Zeinab B. El Bakri and El-Wathig M. Kameir, 1–86. Munich: Berg Publishers/UNESCO.

Sharafeldin, Marwa. 2013. "Challenges of Islamic Feminism in Personal Status Law Reform: Women's NGOs in Egypt between Islamic Law and International Human Rights." In *Feminist and Islamic Perspectives: New Horizons of Knowledge and Reform*, edited by Omaima Abou-Bakr, 58–82. Cairo: Women and Memory Forum.

Sharara, Yolla Polity. 1978. "Women and Politics in Lebanon." *Khamsin: Journal of Revolutionary Socialists in the Middle East*, no. 6: 6–15. https://libcom.org/library/women-politics-lebanon.

Sharp, Jeremy M. 2016. *Jordan: Background and US Relations*. Washington, DC: Congressional Research Service.

Sharp, Joanne P. 2000. "Remasculinising Geo-politics? Comments on Gearoid O Tuathail's Critical Geopolitics." *Political Geography* 19(1): 361–64.

———. 2007. Geography and Gender: Finding Feminist Political Geographies, *Progress in Human Geography* 31(3): 381–87.

Shebaya, Halim. 2017. "Xenophobia Will Not Solve Lebanon's Refugee Crisis." Al-Jazeera English, 31 May. Accessed 30 April 2018. https://www.aljazeera.com/indepth/opinion/2017/05/xenophobia-solve-lebanons-refugee-crisis-170523092620345.html.

Shehadeh, Lamia Rustum. 1999a. "Women before the War." In *Women and War in Lebanon*, edited by Lamia Rustom Shehadeh, 7–44. Gainesville: University of Florida Press.

———. 1999b. "Women in the Lebanese Militias." In *Women and War in Lebanon*, edited by Lamia Rustom Shehadeh, 145–166. Gainesville: University of Florida Press.

———. 1999c. "Women in the Public Sphere." In *Women and War in Lebanon*, edited by Lamia Rustom Shehadeh, 45–72. Gainesville: University of Florida Press.

Shehadi, Nadim. 2007. "Riviera vs Citadel: The Battle for Lebanon." OpenDemocracy, 13 July. Accessed 29 March 2018. https://www.opendemocracy.net/conflict-middle_east_politics/riviera_citadel_3841.jsp.

Shepherd, Laura. J. 2012. *Gender, Violence and Popular Culture: Telling Stories*. London: Routledge.

———. 2015. "Sex or Gender? Bodies in Global Politics and Why Gender Matters." In *Gender Matters in Global Politics: A Feminist Introduction to International Relations*, edited by Laura J. Shepherd, 24–35. London: Routledge.

Sholkamy, Hania. 2011. "Creating Conservatism or Emancipating Subjects? On the Narrative of Islamic Observance in Egypt." *IDS Bulletin* 42(1): 47–55.

———. 2012. "Women Are Also Part of This Revolution." In *Arab Spring in Egypt: Revolution and Beyond*, edited by Bahgat Korany and Rabab El-Mahdi. Cairo: AUC Press.

Shukrallah, Salma. 2011. "10,000 Egyptian Women March against Military Violence and Rule." *Ahram Online*, 20 December. Accessed 20 January 2015. http://english.ahram.org.eg/NewsContent/1/0/29824/Egypt/0/,-Egyptian-women-march-against-military-violence-a.aspx.

———. 2014. "More Egyptians Killed Post-Morsi Than During 2011 Revolution: Rights Groups." *Ahram Online*, 4 January. Accessed 30 January 2015. http://english.ahram.org.eg/NewsContent/1/64/90800/Egypt/Politics-/More-Egyptians-killed-postMorsi-than-during--revol.aspx.

Sika, Nadine. 2014. "An Egyptian Spring for Women?" In *Arab Spring and Arab Women: Challenges and Opportunities*, edited by Muhamad S. Olimat, 61–69. London: Routledge.

Singerman, Diane. 1997. *Avenues of Participation: Family, Politics, and Networks in Urban Quarters of Cairo*, Princeton, NJ: Princeton University Press.

———. 2004. "Women and Strategies for Change: An Egyptian Model." Carnegie Endowment for International Peace, 20 July. Accessed 31 August 2015. http://carnegieendowment.org/sada/?fa=21228.

———. 2005. "Rewriting Divorce in Egypt: Reclaiming Islam, Legal Activism, and Coalition Politics." In *Remaking Muslim Politics: Pluralism, Contestation, and Democratization*, edited by Robert Hefner, 161–88. Princeton, NJ: Princeton University Press.

Skalli, Loubna Hanna. 2014. "Young Women and Social Media against Sexual Harassment in North Africa." *Journal of North African Studies* 19(2): 244–58.

Smith, Fiona M. 2001. "Refiguring the Geopolitical Landscape: Nation, 'Transition' and Gendered Subjects in Post–Cold War Germany." *Space and Polity* 5(3): 213–35.

Smith, Sara, Nathan W Swanson, and Banu Gökarıksel. 2016. "Territory, Bodies and Borders." *Area* 48(3): 258–61.

SMIWPM (Suzanne Mubarak International Women's Peace Movement). N.d. "Vision." Accessed 9 November 2015. http://www.sm-womenforpeace.org/Vision.asp.

Solidarity Center. 2010. *Justice for All: The Struggle for Worker Rights in Egypt.* Washington DC: The Solidarity Center.

Soliman, D., and A. Nour. 2016. "Egypt's Revolutionaries: Where Are They Now?" BBC News, 25 January. Accessed 9 March 2018. http://www.bbc.co.uk/news/world-middle-east-35401868.

Sonbol, Amira El-Azhary. 2003. *Women of Jordan: Islam, Labor, and the Law.* Syracuse, NY: Syracuse University Press.

Sonneveld, Nadia. 2012. *Khula' Divorce in Egypt: Public Debates, Judicial Practices, and Everyday Life*, Cairo: American University in Cairo Press.

Sowers, Jeannie Lynn, and Chris Toensing, eds. 2012. *The Journey to Tahrir: Revolution, Protest, and Social Change in Egypt*, London: Verso Books.

Spivak, Gayatri. 1988. "Can the Subaltern Speak?" In *Marxism and the Interpretation of Culture*, edited by Cary Nelson and Lawrence Grossberg, 271–313. Basingstoke, UK: Macmillan Education.

Spivak, Gayatri Chakravorty. 1996. "'Women' as Theatre: United Nations Conference on Women," Beijing 1995, *Radical Philosophy* 75 (January–February): 2–4.

Staton, Bethan. 2016a. "Jordan's Women Fight for Political Representation." Al Jazeera, 8 March, accessed 11 April 2016. http://www.aljazeera.com/news/2016/03/jordan-women-fight-political-representation-160306101829565.html.

———. 2016b. "Jordan University Students Vow to Continue Protests." Al Jazeera, 2 April. Accessed 13 April 2016. http://www.aljazeera.com/news/2016/04/jordan-university-students-vow-continue-protests-160401080135573.html.

Stephan, Rita. 2012. "Women's Rights Movement in Lebanon." In *Mapping Arab Women Movements: A Century of Transformation from Within*, edited by Nawar Al-Hassan Golley and Pernille Arenfeldt. Cairo: American University of Cairo Press.

———. 2014. "Four Waves of Lebanese Feminism." E-International Relations. 7 November. http://www.e-ir.info/2014/11/07/four-waves-of-lebanese-feminism/.

Stevens, Janet. 1978. "Political Repression in Egypt," Middle East Research and Information Project Report." 66(1): 18–21.

Stork, Joe. 1983. "Report from Lebanon." *Middle East Report*, no. 118 (October): 3–13, 22.

Suleiman, Jaber. 1997. "Palestinians in Lebanon and the Role of Non-Governmental Organizations." *Journal of Refugee Studies* 10(3): 397–410.

Swash, Rosie. 2012. "How Egyptians are Fighting Harassment on the Streets." *The Guardian*, 5 November. Accessed 20 January 2015. http://www.theguardian.com/lifeandstyle/2012/nov/05/egyptians-fighting-harassment-streets.

Sweis, Rana. 2011. "In Jordan, a Struggle for Gender Equality." *New York Times*, 30 November. http://www.nytimes.com/2011/12/01/world/middleeast/in-jordan-a-struggle-for-gender-equality.html?pagewanted=all&_r=0.

Tadros, Mariz. 2010. "Between the Elusive and the Illusionary: Donors' Empowerment Agendas in the Middle East in Perspective." *Comparative Studies of South Asia, Africa, and the Middle East* 30(2): 224–37.

———. 2011. "Introduction: Gender, Rights and Religion at the Crossroads." *IDS Bulletin* 42(1): 1–9.

———. 2012. "*The Muslim Brotherhood in Contemporary Egypt: Democracy Defined or Confined?*" London: Routledge.

———. 2013a. "The Politics of Sexual Violence in Protest Spaces." openDemocracy, 4 July. Accessed 19 January 2015. https://www.opendemocracy.net/5050/mariz-tadros/egypt-politics-of-sexual-violence-in-protest-spaces.

————. 2013b. "Growing Anger with Western Opinion." openDemocracy, 22 July. Accessed 30 January 2015. https://www.opendemocracy.net/5050/mariz-tadros /egypt-growing-anger-with-western-opinion.

————. 2014. *Reclaiming the Streets for Women's Dignity: Effective Initiatives in the Struggle against Gender-Based Violence in between Egypt's Two Revolutions.* IDS Evidence Report 48, Brighton, UK: IDS.

Taha, Rana Mohammed. 2013. "No Military Trials Calls upon Constituent Assembly to Ban Military Trials for Civilians." *Daily News Egypt*, 23 September. http:// www.dailynewsegypt.com/2013/09/23/no-military-trials-calls-upon-constituent -assembly-to-ban-military-trials-for-civilians/.

Tallawy, Mervat. 1997. "International Organizations, National Machinery, Islam, and Foreign Policy." In *Muslim Women and the Politics of Participation: Implementing the Beijing Platform*, edited by Mahnaz Afkhami and Erika Friedl, 128–40. Syracuse, NY: Syracuse University Press.

Taraki, Lisa. 1996. "Jordanian Islamists and the Agenda for Women: Between Discourse and Practice." *Middle Eastern Studies* 32(1): 140–58.

Tax, Meredith. 2014. "The Antis: Anti-imperialist or Anti-feminist?" open Democracy, 19 November. https://www.opendemocracy.net/en/5050/antis -antiimperialist-or-antifeminist-0/.

Tell, Tariq. 2013. *The Social and Economic Origins of Monarchy in Jordan.* London: Palgrave.

Thomas, Lynn. 2000. "Ngaitana (I Will Circumcise Myself): Lessons from the Colonial Campaign to Ban Excision in Meru, Kenya." In *Female Circumcision in Africa: Culture, Controversy and Change*, edited by B. Shell-Duncan and Y. Herlund, 129–50. Boulder, CO: Lynne Rienner Publishers.

Thompson, Elizabeth. 2000. *Colonial Citizens: Republican Rights, Paternal Privilege, and Gender in French Syria and Lebanon.* New York: Columbia University Press.

————. 2003. "Public and Private in Middle Eastern Women's History." *Journal of Women's History* 15(1): 52–69.

Thompson, Paul. 1988. *The Voice of the Past: Oral History.* Oxford: Oxford University Press.

Thomson Reuters. 2013. "Women's Rights in the Arab World." 13 November. http:// blog.thomsonreuters.com/index.php/thomson-reuters-foundation-poll-graphic -of-the-day/.

Tickner, J. Anne. 1992. *Gender in International Relations: Feminist Perspectives on Achieving Global Security.* New York: Columbia University Press.

Tohamy, Ahmed. 2016. *Youth Activism in Egypt: Islamism, Political Protest and Revolution.* London: I. B. Tauris.

Tomlin, Julie. 2011. "Egypt Election: No Revolution for Women," Guardian Online, 1 December. Accessed 9 January 2015. http://www.theguardian.com/world/2011 /dec/01/egypt-revolution-women-elections.

Traboulsi, Fawwaz. 2003. "An Intelligent Man's Guide to Modern Arab Feminism." *Al-Raida*, 20(100): 15–19.

——. 2007. *A History of Modern Lebanon*, London: Pluto.

Trew, Bel. 2012. "Breaking the Silence: Mob Sexual Assault on Egypt's Tahrir." *Ahram Online*, 3 July. Accessed 20 January 2015. http://english.ahram.org.eg/News ContentPrint/1/0/46800/Egypt/0/Breaking-the-silence-Mob-sexual-assault-on -Egypts-.aspx.

Tripp, Charles. 2013. *The Power and the People: Paths of Resistance in the Middle East*. Cambridge: Cambridge University Press.

True, Jacqui. 2018. "Bringing Back Gendered States: Feminist Second Image Theorizing of International Relations." In *Revisiting Gendered States: Feminist Imaginings of the State in International Relations*, edited by Swati Parashar, J. Ann Tickner, and Jacqui True, 34–47. Oxford: Oxford University Press.

True, Jacqui, and Michael Mintrom. 2001. "Transnational Networks and Policy Diffusion: The Case of Gender Mainstreaming." *International Studies Quarterly* 45(1): 27–57.

Tucker, Judith. 1978. "While Sadat Shuffles: Economic Decay, Political Ferment in Egypt." *MERIP Reports*, no. 65(March): 3–9, 26.

——. 2008. *Women, Family and Gender in Islamic Law*. Cambridge: Cambridge University Press.

UN Fourth World Conference on Women. 1995. "Platform for Action." Beijing, September. Accessed 22 August 2017. http://www.un.org/womenwatch/daw/beijing /platform/institu.htm.

UN Women. 2015. "Assessment of National Women Machineries," Amman. UN Women, July. Accessed 1 September 2015. http://jordan.unwomen.org/~/media /field%20office%20jordan/attachments/what-we-do/financing/a-assessment% 20of%20national%20women%20machineries-1%20(1).pdf.

UNDP. 2006. *Arab Human Development Report 2005: Towards the Rise of Women in the Arab World*. New York: Regional Bureau of Arab States, cosponsored with the Arab Fund for Economic and Social Development and the Arab Gulf Programme for United Nations Organizations.

UNHCR (United Nations High Commissioner for Refugees). 2016. "Syria Regional Refugee Response." July. Accessed 12 April 2016. http://data.unhcr.org /syrianrefugees/regional.php#.

——. 2018. "Syrian Regional Refugee Response." July. Accessed 19 April 2018. https://data2.unhcr.org/en/situations/syria.

United Nations Treaty Collection. N.d. Accessed 25 July 2017. https://treaties.un.org /Pages/ViewDetails.aspx?src=TREATY&mtdsg_no=IV-8&chapter=4 &lang=en#EndDec.

UNRWA (United Nations Relief and Works Agency). 2018. "Syria Crisis." Accessed 20 April 2018. https://www.unrwa.org/syria-crisis.

Vairel, Frederic. 2013. "Protesting in Authoritarian Situations: Egypt and Morocco in Comparative Perspective." In *Social Movements, Mobilization and Contestation in the Middle East and North Africa*, 2nd edition, edited by Joel Beinin and Frederic Vairel, 33–48. Stanford, CA: Stanford University Press.

Van Raemdonck, An. 2013. "Egyptian Activism against Female Genital Cutting as Catachrestic Claiming." *Religion and Gender* 3(2): 222–39.

Vatikiotis, P. J. 1991. *The History of Modern Egypt.* 4th ed. London: Weidenfeld and Nicolson.

Wagdy, Belal. 2016. "Inside Egypt's Continuing Protests. Panorama." *Mada Masr,* 21 January. Accessed 8 April 2016. https://madamasr.com/en/2016/01/21/panorama/u/inside-egypts-continuing-protests/.

Walker, R. B. J. 1993. *Inside/Outside: International Relations as Political Theory.* Cambridge: Cambridge University Press.

Wallace, Tina. 2004. "NGO Dilemmas: Trojan Horses for Global Neoliberalism?" *Socialist Register* 40(1): 202–19.

Warrick, Catherine. 2009. *Law in the Service of Legitimacy: Gender and Politics in Jordan.* Farnham, UK: Ashgate.

Watenpaugh, Keith David. 2006. *Being Modern in the Middle East: Revolution, Nationalism, Colonialism and the Arab Middle Class.* Princeton, NJ: Princeton University Press.

Waterbury, John. 1983. *The Egypt of Nasser and Sadat: The Political Economy of Two Regimes.* Princeton, NJ: Princeton University Press.

Waylen, Georgina. 1994. "Women and Democratization: Conceptualizing Gender Relations in Transition Politics." *World Politics* 46(3): 327–54.

———. 2007. *Engendering Transitions: Women's Mobilization, Institutions, and Gender Outcomes.* Oxford: Oxford University Press.

Weber, Cynthia. 1995. *Simulating Sovereignty: Intervention, the State and Symbolic Exchange.* Cambridge: Cambridge University Press.

———. 1998. "Performative States." *Millennium: Journal of International Studies* 27(1): 77–95.

The Weekly Standard. 2005. "Party in Beirut—Pass It On." 14 March.

Weinbaum, Marvin G. 1985. "Egypt's 'Infitah' and the Politics of US Economic Assistance." *Middle Eastern Studies* 21(2): 206–22.

Welchman, Lynne. 2007. *Women and Muslim Family Laws in Arab States: A Comparative Overview of Textual Development and Advocacy.* Amsterdam: Amsterdam University Press.

Welchman, Lynn, and Sara Hossain, eds. 2005. *"Honour": Crimes, Paradigms, and Violence against Women.* London: Zed Books.

Whitman, Elizabeth. 2013. "Jordan's Second-Class Citizens." *Boston Review,* 14 October. http://www.bostonreview.net/world/whitman-jordan-citizenship.

———. 2014. "As Jordanian Women Leave the Home, Sexual Harassment Reaches Unprecedented Levels." *The Nation,* 18 March. Accessed 10 April 2016. http://www.thenation.com/article/jordanian-women-leave-home-sexual-harassment-reaches-unprecedented-levels/.

Wibben, Annick T. R. 2010. *Feminist Security Studies: A Narrative Approach.* London: Routledge.

Wikipedia. N.d.a. "Faten Hamama." Wikipedia (last edited 27 June 2016). Accessed 17 July 2016. http://en.wikipedia.org/wiki/Faten_Hamama.

————. N.d.b. "Munira Solh." Wikipedia (last edited 26 May 2016). Accessed 17 July 2016. http://en.wikipedia.org/wiki/Mounira_Solh.

Wiktorowicz, Quintan. 2000. "Civil Society as Social Control: State Power in Jordan." *Comparative Politics* 33(1): 43–61.

Women and Memory Posters. Facebook https://www.facebook.com/media/set /?set=a.1386642768252510.1073741831.1385907074992746&type=3.

Women's International League for Peace and Freedom, Amnesty International UK, Women Now for Development, and Gender Action for Peace and Security 2017. "Syria Response Consultations on the UK National Action Plan on Women, Peace and Security." May. Accessed 10 September 2017. Available at: http://gaps -uk.org/wp-content/uploads/2017/06/Syria-NAP-Consultations-report-EN.pdf.

Working Group on Women and the Constitution. 2011. "Muktaharat bi muwad dasturiya fi-l-dastur al-masri al-jadid." Cairo. Accessed 12 January 2015. http://www.wmf.org.eg /sites/default/files/files/مقترحات20%بمواد20%في20%الدستور20%المصري20%الجديد .pdf.

World Bank. 2004. *Gender and Development in the Middle East and North Africa.* Washington, DC: World Bank.

————. 2006. "Gender Equality as Smart Economics: A World Bank Group Gender Action Plan." Accessed 6 November 2017. https://siteresources.worldbank .org/INTGENDER/Resources/GAPNov2.pdf.

————. 2017. *Progress Towards Gender Equality in the Middle East and North Africa.* Washington, DC: World Bank.

Yapp, Malcolm E. 1987. *The Making of the Modern Near East 1792–1923.* London: Longman.

————. 1996. *The Near East Since the First World War: A History to 1995.* London: Longman.

Yassin-Kassab, Robin, and Leila al-Shami. 2016. *Burning Country: Syrians in Revolution and War.* London: Pluto Press.

Yegenoglu, Meyda. 1998. *Colonial Fantasies: Towards a Feminist Reading of Orientalism.* Cambridge: Cambridge University Press.

Young, Iris Marion. 2003. "The Logic of Masculinist Protection: Reflections on the Current Security State." *Signs: Journal of Women in Culture and Society* 29 (1): 1–25.

Young, Michael. 1998. "Two Faces of Janus: Postwar Lebanon and Its Reconstruction." *Middle East Report* 209 (Winter): 4–7, 44.

Youngs, Gillian. 1996. "Beyond the Inside/Outside Divide." In *Identities in International Relations,* edited by Jill Krause and Neil Renwick, 22–37. London: Palgrave Macmillan.

————. 2004. "Feminist International Relations: A Contradiction in Terms? Or Why Women and Gender are Essential to Understanding the World We Live In." *International Affairs* 80(1): 75–87.

Youssry, Moustafa. 2011. "The Islamisation of Human Rights: Implications for Gender and Politics in the Middle East." *IDS Bulletin* 42(1): 21–25.

Yuval Davis, Nira. 1997. *Gender and Nation,* London: Sage.

Yuval-Davis, Nira, and Floya Anthias, eds. 1989. *Woman-Nation-State*. London: Macmillan.

Zaalouk, Malak. 1989. *Power, Class and Foreign Capital in Egypt: The Rise of the New Bourgeoisie*. London: Zed Books.

Zahran, Zainab. 2011. "Nurse Education in Jordan: History and Development." *International Nursing Review* 59(1): 380–86.

Zalzal, Marie Rose. 1997. "Secularism and Personal Status Codes in Lebanon: Interview with Marie Rose Zalzal." *Middle East Report*, 203 (Spring): 37–39.

Zuhur, Sherifa. 1992. *Revealing Reveiling: Islamist Gender Ideology in Contemporary Egypt*. Albany: State University of New York Press.

———. 2002. "Empowering Women or Dislodging Sectarianism: Civil Marriage in Lebanon," *Yale Journal of Law and Feminism* 14(1):177–208. http://digital commons.law.yale.edu/yjlf/vol14/iss1/5.

Zwingel, Susanne. 2012. "How Do Norms Travel? Theorizing Women's Rights in Transnational Perspective." *International Studies Quarterly* 56(1): 115–29.

———. 2016. *Translating International Women's Rights: The CEDAW Convention in Context*. London: Palgrave Macmillan.

INDEX

Notes are indicated by page numbers followed by n.

Al-Yassir, Wafa Ali, 76, 108
al-Zayyat, Latifa, 37
Al-Zuriekat, Adma, 99, 144–45
Amal, 79, 107, 140
American University of Beirut (AUB), 47, 49, 54, 76, 138, 139
Amin, Qasim, 35
Anani, Ghida, 127
Anglo-Jordanian Treaty, 45
Anid, Nada, 184
anticolonial nationalism: class hierarchies in, 36; female respectability and, 33, 36, 39, 56; inner/outer sphere and, 42, 222; modernization and, 38; nationalist boundaries and, 10; "woman question" and, 56; women's activism and, 33, 35–36
Appropriate Communications Techniques for Development Center (ACT), 159
April 6 Movement, 205
Arab Cold War, 33
Arab Lawyers' Union, 103
Arab-Muslim culture, 3
Arab nationalism, 45, 59, 100, 102. See also pan-Arabism
Arab Nationalist Movement, 54–55, 74
Arab Renaissance for Democracy and Development (ARDD), 128–29
Arab Socialist Union, 42
Arab Spring, 2, 20, 178, 194, 198, 214. See also 25 January 2011 uprising; Arab uprisings
Arab states: criticisms of NGOs in, 116–18; Egypt-Israel peace treaty consequences and, 86, 89–90, 105; international gender equality regime, 152–58; liberation of Palestine and, 59, 62; modernization programs in, 39, 54; pan-Arabism and, 33, 39, 93, 105, 111; popularity of Nasser in, 55; state feminism in, 15; United States influence in, 113–14; Western interventions and, 112; women's education in, 35, 49, 227n1. See also Middle East and North Africa (MENA); post-1967 crisis; specific country names
Arab University Women Graduates' Club, 103

Arab uprisings: authoritarian renewal and, 15, 31, 202; counterrevolutionary processes and, 201; defining, 231n1; failure to sustain political transformation, 199–201; fear of political Islam and, 214; freedom of expression and, 175–76; geopolitical dynamics of, 18, 20, 170–71, 201; Jordanian protests, 175–78; Lebanese protests, 178; narratives of fear and, 201; resistance to gender equality and, 199; significance of gender to, 170–71; state feminism and, 15; Tahrir Square demonstrations, 171–74; in Tunisia, 175, 178; women's participation in, 2–4, 20, 172–79, 199–200; women's rights and, 171, 198–200, 222. See also 25 January 2011 uprising
Arab Women Organization, 70–71, 130, 148, 166, 183, 194
Arab Women's Union, 43–45, 57, 101–2
Arafat, Yasser, 63
ARDD. See Arab Renaissance for Democracy and Development (ARDD)
Assaad, Marie, 36, 161
Assad, Bashar al-, 212
Association Najdeh, 124
Aysh wa Horriya Party, 206, 209
Ayubi, Nazih, 87

Baghdad Pact, 44–45, 54
Baheya Ya Masr, 187–88
Barakat, Huda, 80
Basma Imprint Movement, 192
Batshon, Dina, 176
bayt al-ta'a, 41
Beijing Platform for Action, 153
Beinin, Joel, 138
Bier, Laura, 40–41
Bila Hudud (No Frontiers), 138
Bint al-Masarwa, 211
Bint al-Nil organization, 37
Bint Talal, Basma, Princess, 153
Bisharat, Emily, 43
Black September conflict, 97–99
Brand, Laurie, 101
bread uprising, 93–94, 134
Britain: Baghdad Pact and, 44; Egyptian uprising against, 36–38; Jordanian

decolonization: ban on women's activism and, 38; female respectability and, 56; geopolitical upheaval and, 38–39; state formation and, 11, 13; women's activism and, 4, 33, 38, 56, 83

Democratic Front for the Liberation of Palestine (DFLP), 72, 123

Democratic Gathering Bloc, 139–140

Democratic Left Movement (DLM), 139–141

domestic violence: criminalization of, 193, 197–98; Jordanian legislation and, 154; Lebanese legislation and, 197; Lebanese women's activism and, 159, 184, 193, 196–98; NWMs and, 158. *See also* violence against women

Doty, Roxanne, 11, 14

Doughan, Iqbal Murad, 54–55, 163, 184

Douma, Ahmed, 205

Duboc, Marie, 144

Dudin, Samar, 98–99, 221–22

Ebeid, Nevine, 205

effendiya, 22

Egypt: Arab Cold War and, 33; attack on lands occupied by Israel, 88–89; backlash against women's rights, 181–82; bread uprising and, 93–94; British occupation of, 26; Camp David Accords and, 89; CEDAW and, 153, 229n3; civil society organizations in, 240; companionate marriage and, 40–41; counterrevolutionary processes in, 201–11; criticisms of NGOs in, 117–18; cultural difference markers and, 11; divorce rights and, 92, 154, 162; female genital mutilation (FGM) in, 14–15; female respectability and, 91–92; female veiling and, 87–88; FGM/FGC in, 14–15, 161; gendered hierarchies and, 42–43; gender norms and, 40; Gulf War of 1990–91, 113; Infitah policies and, 90–91, 93; Islamist movement in, 87–88, 92–93, 111; map of, xiv; modernization programs in, 39–40; modern-yet-modest women and, 42; Non-Aligned Movement and, 26, 39; NWMs and, 153–54, 157–58; personal status laws and, 37, 41–42, 92, 153–54; political Islam in, 22–23; political parties in, 188–190, 240–41; political repression and, 93–95, 204–5; popular movements in, 59; post-1967 antiregime movements in, 60–61, 66–69; post-1967 women's activism, 66–69; post-2000 protest movements, 132–38, 144, 146; post-Morsi violence in, 204–5; public sector corruption in, 91; sexual violence against women activists in, 31, 143, 145, 180, 190–92, 199; social mobility and, 90–91; state feminism in, 15, 26, 39–43, 92–93, 155, 208; state formation in, 26, 39; student movements in, 67–69; suppression of women's activism in, 38, 42, 57; Tahrir Square demonstrations, 171–74; United States support for, 94–95; uprising against the British, 36–38; violence against women in, 159; "woman question" in, 40; women's education in, 40; women's organizations in, 239–240; women's political exclusion, 36; women's rights and, 153–54, 162; workers' strikes in, 137–38, 144; working women in, 40–42, 92. *See also* 25 January 2011 uprising; 30 June 2013 protests; Egyptian women's activism; violence against women

Egyptian Communist Party, 124

Egyptian constitution (1923), 36

Egyptian constitution (1956), 39

Egyptian constitution (1971), 87

Egyptian constitution (2012), 181

Egyptian constitution (2013), 203–4

Egyptian constitution (2014), 206–7

Egyptian constitutional amendments (2005), 143

Egyptian constitutional revisions (2011), 179–180

Egyptian Feminist Union (EFU), 37

Egyptian National Council for Women (NCW), 153

Egyptian Organization for Human Rights, 95–96

Egyptian Popular Committee for Solidarity with the Palestinians (EPCSP), 133–34

Egyptian Social Democratic Party (ESDP), 189

Egyptian Socialist Party, 206

Egyptian women's activism: anti-Morsi protests, 203, 218; anti-SCAF protests, 185–88; civil society organizations and, 95–96, 172; counterrevolutionary resistance, 211–12; divorce rights and, 92–93; female respectability and, 36–38, 42–43, 57, 88, 92, 143–45, 178, 188, 199; gender-specific agendas and, 96–97; international development ideas and, 229n4; Islamist movement and, 93, 95; masculinist protection and, 207–8; noncontentious, 210–11, 219; personal status laws and, 92–93; political activism and, 57–58, 97, 188–190; political inclusion and, 179–180; political polarization and, 174, 204, 209–10; political repression and, 95–96, 204–5; post-1967 crisis, 66–69; post-2011 anti–sexual violence movement, 190–93, 207; post-Morsi, 205–11; in post-Mubarak period, 179–182, 185–190; sexual violence against, 31, 137, 143, 145, 180, 199; state suppression of, 42, 57, 204–11; student movements and, 67–69, 84; Tahrir Square demonstrations, 172–74; testimony of violence survivors, 192, 211; violence against protesters, 31, 180–81, 186–88; voluntary and charitable activities, 42; "woman question" and, 96; women's rights and, 153–54, 162, 173, 177, 179–190

Egypt-Israel peace treaty, 89–90, 105, 112

Eidarous Al-Kassir, Elham, 206, 209

Ejeilat, Lina, 137, 175–76

El Ashwal, Nagwan, 186, 211

El Baramawy, Yassmine, 192

El Dawla, Aida Seif, 68, 87–88, 97, 205

elections: anti-Morsi protests and, 203, 209; Egyptian women's participation in, 96, 167, 179, 183; Jordanian women's participation in, 167, 183; Lebanese women's participation in, 51, 184–85, 228n7; NGOs and, 122; women's parliamentary quotas in, 184, 207

El-Hefnawy, Karima, 67, 136, 206

El Hilo, Jihan, 74

El Hilo, Shadia, 74

El-Mahdi, Rabab, 136, 143, 145

Elmohandes, Amal, 172, 210–11

El-Nakkash, Farida, 40, 42, 66–67, 89, 96, 125, 152

El-Naqqash, Salma, 205, 209

El-Saadawi, Nawal, 93

Elsadda, Hoda, 162, 181, 189, 206

El Said, Maha, 189

El Shaker, Naglaa, 167

embodied geopolitics, 3–8, 17

Engineers for Democracy, 136

Enloe, Cynthia, 4, 31, 171

European powers: colonial rule and, 8–9, 11, 34, 38; cultural difference and, 10, 34, 36, 38; encroachment on Middle East, 35, 56; geopolitical order and, 38; indigenous resistance to, 38, 57; "new woman" discourse and, 9–10, 57; "Oriental woman" discourse and, 9, 34–35; state formation and, 11; state formation by, 27

Ezzat, Mona, 209–10

Ezzeldin, Iman, 91, 135

Facebook, 172, 175–76, 178, 194, 211, 229n3

Families Development Association, 120

Fateh, 62, 73–74

Fawwaz, Zaynab, 35

fear narratives: gendered/racialized dimensions of, 202; Syrian conflict and, 212–14, 218; Syrian refugees and, 216, 218; threat of political Islam and, 213–14, 218; women's rights and, 218

fedayeen: Black September conflict, 97–99; challenges to Jordanian regime, 97; expulsion of, 86, 90, 99; Jordanian attacks on, 86, 97–99; Lebanese Civil War and, 78; Lebanese opposition and, 64–65; PLO and, 64–65; popularity in Jordan, 71; support in Lebanon, 64

female genital mutilation/cutting (FGM/FGC), 14–15, 154, 160–61

female respectability: anticolonialism and, 39; Egyptian Infitah and, 88, 91–92; Egyptian protests and, 178, 188, 199; Egyptian state feminism and, 42–43; Egyptian worker strikes and, 144–45;

female respectability (*continued*)
gender norms and, 7, 18, 22, 121; hijab
and, 92; inner/outer sphere and, 40, 42,
48; Islamist movement and, 88, 92;
Jordanian activism and, 46–48; Lebanese activism and, 52–54; legitimization
of regime authority and, 47–48, 53, 57;
masculinist protection and, 207; modesty-modernity boundary and, 38, 41,
121; political exclusion and, 36, 38;
political repression and, 86; postcolonial state and, 33–34, 56–57; protest
movements and, 115, 143; public violence
and, 191; reproduction of, 57; resignification of, 37, 145; resistance to, 34; transgression of, 36–37; voluntary activities
and, 121; weaponization in protests,
143–46; women in public service and,
18, 34, 57; women's activism and, 36, 57,
60, 77, 221
feminist geopolitics, 3–4
FGM/FGC. *See* female genital mutilation/
cutting (FGM/FGC)
FGM Taskforce, 161
Forum for Women in Development, 125
Freedom and Justice Party (FJP), 182
Front to Defend Egyptian Protesters, 173,
210
Future Movement, 212

Geagea, Sethrida, 51
gender: colonialism and, 8–10; embodied
geopolitics and, 3–6; hegemonic, 6–7;
modernity and, 31, 167, 218; organization of geopolitical power and, 5–6;
performativity of, 6–7
gender identity, 7, 142, 225n1
gender inequalities: cultural difference and,
12, 15; inner/outer sphere and, 165; in
the Middle East, 12; NWMs and, 153;
personal status laws and, 13; reproduction of geopolitical order and, 7, 198; use
of international instruments against,
115; Western interventions and, 12, 17
gender norms: cultural difference and, 11;
embodied enactment of, 17–18; female
respectability and, 7, 18, 121, 221;
geopolitical upheaval and, 18–19, 31;

geopolitics of, 5–8, 12, 17, 26, 185;
modesty-modernity boundary and, 10,
121, 185; "natural state" and, 12–13, 34,
58, 84; popular culture and, 40, 211;
postwar challenge to, 37; radical political movements and, 44; regime authority and, 185; reproduction of, 47–48, 82,
222; resignification of, 7, 29, 82, 222;
state policies and laws, 6, 12–16; transgression of, 29–30, 34, 36, 174, 222;
women's activism and, 7, 16, 56, 221
genderwashing, 156–58, 164, 230n6
General Federation of Jordanian Women
(GFJW), 102–4
General Union of Palestinian Students, 71,
74
General Union of Palestinian Women
(GUPW), 70–72, 74–76, 107, 123–24
geopolitics: feminist, 3–4; gendered dimensions of, 5–6; gender norms and, 5–8, 12,
17, 26, 185; genderwashing and, 156;
women's activism and, 5, 8, 26, 34–38,
111–12, 224; women's rights and, 152. *See
also* embodied geopolitics
geo-power: idealized Self/demonized
Other and, 149–150, 168; international
women's rights norms and, 149–150, 155,
158, 168
Global North, 4, 11, 116–17. *See also* West,
The
Global South, 11, 116, 151, 160
Glubb, John Bagot (Pasha), 45
Greek Orthodox Christians, 27
Gulf War of 1990–91, 113
GUPW. *See* General Union of Palestinian
Women (GUPW)

Habashna, Nimeh, 193–94
Habashna, Shadyah, 74
Haidar, Diala, 178
Hamarneh, Leila Naffa. *See* Naffa, Leila
Hamas, 166, 213
Haraway, Donna, 224
Hariri, Bahia, 51
Hashemite Kingdom. *See* Jordan
Hassan, Mozn, 129, 173, 190, 192, 205
Hasso, Frances, 155
Hassouna, Anissa Essam, 41

National Front for Reform, 177
nationality laws: in Egypt, 154; gender inequalities in, 26, 29, 193, 196; in Jordan, 129–130, 154, 183; in Lebanon, 51; "natural state" and, 14; personal status laws and, 153; women married to foreigners and, 14, 193–96
National Socialist Party (Jordan), 45
National Women's Machineries (NWMs), 153–55, 157–58
nation state: cultural difference and, 10, 12, 26, 155; gendered boundaries and, 5–6; genderwashing and, 156; reproduction of gender norms and, 27, 182; women's activism and, 5. See also state sovereignty
"natural state": gender norms and, 12, 34, 58, 84, 185; nationality laws and, 14; reproduction of, 185; state formation and, 11–14, 17
Nazra for Feminist Studies, 129, 173, 190, 205, 210
neoliberalism: authoritarianism and, 15–16, 152–53, 157–58; NGOs and, 115–16, 120, 127; protest movements against, 114; women's empowerment and, 24, 151
New Woman Foundation, 122, 159, 188–89, 205, 210
NGO-ization: resistance to, 130–31; women's activism and, 114–120; women's political activism and, 121–27; young women's social entrepreneurialism and, 127–132
NGOs. See nongovernmental organizations (NGOs)
Non-Aligned Movement, 26, 39
nongovernmental organizations (NGOs): anti-geopolitics and, 124, 126; civil society and, 114–15, 118, 129; colonial legacies and, 117; criticisms of, 115–18; demobilization of popular movements by, 116; depoliticization of social change and, 116, 121, 124–28; gender-specific agendas and, 30; geopolitical structures and, 131; Global North funding for, 116–17, 126; human rights and, 117–18, 122; leftist/radical politics and, 121–25;

neoliberal mitigation and, 115–16, 119–120, 127, 146; Palestinian refugees and, 123–24, 229n2; professional activists and, 127–131; selective donor funding and, 126–27; Western influence and, 121; women's activism and, 114–132, 146; women's rights and, 118, 125, 129, 142; women's voluntary activities and, 119–121
Norwegian People's Aid, 124
NWMs. See National Women's Machineries (NWMs)

Olwan, Dana, 155
OpAntiSH (Operation Anti-Sexual Harassment), 191–92
Organization of Communist Action, 56
Otto, Diane, 151
Ottoman societies, 34–35
Ó Tuathail, Gearoid, 149
Oxfam, 128

Pain, Rachel, 201
Palestine, 38, 43, 54, 62
Palestine Liberation Organization (PLO): gender inequalities and, 72; GUPW and, 70; in Lebanon, 64, 73; Palestinian Revolution and, 63; post-1967 political movements and, 59, 65; recruitment of women, 73, 76; war with Jordanian military, 28; withdrawal from Lebanon, 78–79, 106, 108; women's activism and, 72. See also fedayeen
Palestinian movement, 71–73, 76–77
Palestinian organizations, 243–44
Palestinian refugees: displacement from West Bank, 62, 70; Islamist groups and, 108; in Jordan, 70; in Lebanese refugee camps, 63–65, 74, 106–8, 123–24; NGOs and, 123–24; radical political movements and, 62–63; resistance movement, 71–73; social and economic rights in Lebanon, 124; terror campaign against, 106–7; War of the Camps, 107–8
Palestinian Resistance Movement, 71–73, 99
Palestinian Revolution, 63, 75, 78

Palestinian women activists: challenges to
gender norms, 77–78; defense of refugee communities, 107–8; humanitarian
work and, 75; narratives of fear, 212;
national movement and, 60, 73–76, 84,
228n6. *See also* General Union of Palestinian Women (GUPW)
Palestinian Women's Union, 74
pan-Arabism: Egypt-Israel peace treaty
consequences and, 105; Nasser and, 33,
93; postindependence and, 38–39;
weakening of, 111; women's activism
and, 34
pan-Arab organizations, 244
Pankhurst, Donna, 110
personal status laws: cultural difference
and, 13, 165, 182; gender inequalities
and, 13, 56, 153; Lebanese sectarian,
50–52, 56–57, 110, 163; regime consolidation and, 14; sharia and, 93, 161–62,
165, 182; women's activism and, 13;
women's divorce rights and, 92, 154, 162
Peteet, Julie, 72, 76, 106
PFLP. *See* Popular Front for the Liberation
of Palestine (PFLP)
pinkwashing, 156
PLO. *See* Palestine Liberation Organization (PLO)
political activism: Egyptian women and,
57–58, 97; Jordanian women and,
57–58, 71–73, 105; Lebanese women
and, 51, 57–58, 75–76, 83; NGOs and,
125–27; rise of political Islam and, 214;
women's disillusionment with, 124–26;
women's rights and, 125–26
Popular Committee of Women, 103
Popular Front for the Liberation of Palestine (PFLP), 74–75, 77, 82, 97
Popular Nasserite Organization, 65
post-1967 crisis: antiregime movements
and, 60–62, 64–73; Egyptian modernization and, 60–61; Egyptian student
movements and, 67–69; Egyptian
women's activism and, 66–69; gendered
dimensions of, 59–60, 66, 83; Jordanian
women's activism and, 70–73; Lebanese
women's activism and, 74–83; Palestinian refugees and, 62–65, 70, 84; popular

movements and, 59; protest movements
and, 61, 65, 68–69, 80, 88–89; women's
activism and, 66, 83–84. *See also* Lebanese Civil War
post-2000 protest movements: 9 March
Movement and, 135–36; anti-Iraq War,
134–35, 139; anti-Syrian, 138–140, 143,
146; blogging communities and, 137;
Cedar Revolution, 140, 143; challenges
to neoliberalism, 146–47; challenges to
US hegemony, 146; in Egypt, 132–38,
146; gendered dimensions of, 141–47; in
Jordan, 133, 137, 144–46; Kefaya, 136–37,
143, 145; in Lebanon, 138–140, 146;
pro-Palestine, 132–34, 139; role of
women in, 133–147; sexual violence
against women activists in, 137,
143; student movements and, 139;
weaponization of female bodies in,
143–46; women's rights NGOs
and, 142; workers' strikes, 137–38,
144
post-Cold War period: geopolitics and
gender in, 169; international women
activist cooperation and, 150–51; international women's rights norms and,
149–164, 168; Islamist resistance to,
164–68; neoliberal authoritarianism
and, 152–53, 156; religious arguments
for women's rights, 162; reproductive
freedom and, 164; sexual rights and,
164; state feminism in, 152–53, 156
postcolonial state: cultural difference and,
11–12; female respectability and, 33–34,
56–57; gendered hierarchies and, 149–
150; inner/outer sphere and, 11–12, 42;
personal status laws and, 56; state
feminism in, 56; struggle for sovereignty, 11
postfeminism, 158
Prashad, Vijay, 85, 111, 147
Progressive Socialist Party (PSP), 55, 64
Progressive Women's Union (PWU), 93,
96–97, 125
protest movements: post-1967 crisis and, 61,
65, 68–69, 80, 88–89; post-Cold War
period, 114–15; Sadat's policies and,
93–95; women's participation in,

132–34. *See also* Arab uprisings;
post-2000 protest movements
Puar, Jasbir, 156
public sphere: colonialism and, 9; elite
women and, 35–36, 38; international
women's rights and, 16; Islamist women
and, 23; middle-class women and,
21–22; modernity-modesty boundaries
and, 10, 16, 18, 29, 42, 49, 92; state
feminism and, 15; women's activism
and, 2–3, 21

Qarnayel association, 119, 121
Qornet Shahwan Gathering, 139–140

Ramadan, Fatma, 2
Rania, Queen, 120, 154, 157
Raouf Ezzat, Heba, 231n8
Regeni, Giulio, 204
regime authority: gender inequalities and,
155; international women's rights norms
and, 149; "natural state" and, 185; reproduction of female respectability and,
47–48, 53, 57, 121; reproduction of
inner/outer sphere and, 155, 164, 182;
sectarian personal status laws and, 50,
56, 110; threat of women's activism to,
57–58, 171; vernacularization strategies
and, 164; women's NGO activism and,
131
Rouhana, Zoya, 128, 159, 161, 196
Ruwwad, 176

Saad, Ma'ruf, 65
Saad, Mona, 65, 110
Sabra and Shatila Massacre, 79, 106
SADAQA, 129
Sadat, Anwar al-: 1973 Arab-Israeli War
and, 88–89; assassination of, 95; Camp
David Accords and, 89; criminalization
of dissent, 89–90, 93; protests against,
93–94; recovery of Sinai Peninsula and,
88–90; reversal of Nasserist policies,
86–87, 90–93; security expenditures
and, 94–95; sharia and, 87; turn
towards the West, 26, 90; unpopular
policies of, 93, 95; women's rights
and, 92

Said, Edward, 3, 149, 168
Said, Khaled, 137, 172
Salafist-jihadists, 214, 218
Salah, Racha, 105
Salah, Samira, 74–75, 77, 82, 105
Saleh, Mai, 203
Salime, Zakia, 167
Sallam, Yara, 205
Salti, Nuha Nuwayri, 1, 49
Sami, Hala, 188
Saudia Arabia, 113
Sawt al-Ma'ra al-Urdunniya, 44
SCAF. *See* Supreme Council of the Armed
Forces (SCAF), Egypt
Second Palestinian Intifada, 133–34
secularism, 168, 226n13
Seif, Sana, 205
Seif El Dawla, Aida, 68, 87–88, 97
sexual harassment, 187, 190–92, 200, 208,
232n8
sexual violence: in Egypt, 190, 232n8;
against Egyptian women protesters, 31,
137, 143, 145, 180, 190–92; honor and
shame discourse, 208; marital rape and,
193, 197; post-2011 movement against,
190–93, 207–8; testimonies of, 192, 211;
virginity testing and, 180, 192; in war,
66; women's bodily integrity and,
192–93; youth-led interventions, 191–92.
See also violence against women
Shafik, Doria, 37, 42
Shafiq, Ahmed, 202, 209
Shahbender, Ghada, 137
Shamroukh, Nadia, 73, 100, 125–26, 159
Shamun, Kamil, 49, 65
Sharara, Yolla, 55
Sha'rawi, Huda, 36
Shayfeen.com, 137
Shehadeh, Lamia Rustum, 81
Shepherd, Laura, 225n1
Shidrawi, Mirna, 138–141, 144, 214
Shidyaq, Ahmad Faris al-, 35
Shihab, Fuad, 20, 49
Shoft Taharrosh, 192
Shukrallah, Hala, 1, 68–69, 74, 188
Shukrallah, Salma, 171, 209
Siege of Beirut (1982), 78–80, 105–6
Sikkink, Kathryn, 115, 117

Sinai Peninsula, 88–90
Sir Magdy Yacoub Foundation, 41
Sisi, Abdel-Fattah El, 26, 180, 205, 208–10, 218
Smith, Susan, 201
Sneid, Muhammad, 145
Socialist Popular Alliance Party, 205–6, 209
social welfare, 20, 57
Society of the Jordanian Women's Union, 37
Society of the Supporters of the Palestinian Revolution, 67
Solh, Munira, 52
Solh, Riyad al-, 27, 52
Solh, Sana al-, 52
Solh, Wahid al-, 52
Soliman, Azza, 205, 207
Soubh, Aroub, 195
Soueif, Laila, 2, 60, 133, 135
sovereignty effect, 11–12, 17, 58
Soviet Union, 98, 111, 113, 149, 151
Spivak, Gayatri, 9, 151
state feminism: authoritarian renewal and, 208; development projects and, 155–56; Egypt and, 15, 26, 39–43, 92–93, 155; female respectability and, 42–43; gendered hierarchies and, 42–43; inner/outer sphere and, 56–57, 155; Jordan and, 15, 26, 29, 155; Lebanon and, 15, 26, 155; legitimization of Sisi and, 218; modernity and, 56; neoliberal authoritarianism and, 15, 152–53; neoliberal restructuring and, 156; post-Cold War period, 152–53, 156; women in the workforce and, 15, 40–42
state formation: colonialism and, 8–9, 225n4; Egypt and, 26, 39; gender and, 8–9; Jordan and, 27–29; Lebanon and, 27; nation state and, 12; "natural state" and, 11–14, 17; personal status laws and, 14; racial hierarchy and, 9
state sovereignty: inner/outer sphere and, 10–12, 165; modernity-modesty boundaries and, 21, 29, 31, 33, 40, 218, 221; outer/inner sphere and, 165; postcolonial struggles for, 11; self-rule and, 10; Westphalian model of, 8; women's

bodies and, 10–11. *See also* nation state; sovereignty effect
Suez Crisis/Tripartite Aggression (1956), 39, 45, 54–55
Suliemane, Amne, 74, 107, 123
Supreme Council of the Armed Forces (SCAF), Egypt, 179–180, 185
Syria: 1967 Arab-Israeli War and, 60; abandonment of pan-Arabism, 105; attack on lands occupied by Israel, 88–89; attacks on Palestinians, 107; Bush on "axis of evil", 140, 146; civil war in, 212–18; Gulf War of 1990–91, 113; humanitarian crisis and, 212–13; Lebanese Civil War and, 79; Lebanese protests against, 138–141, 143, 146; refugees from, 214–17; regional impact of conflict in, 212–14; state formation and, 27; Ta'if Agreement oversight, 109; toppling of pro-Western regime in, 39; withdrawal from Lebanon, 141
Syrian refugees, 214–18

Tagammu' Party, 89, 93–96, 125
Tahboub, Dima, 166, 167, 168
Tahrir al-ma'ra (Qasim Amin), 35
Tahrir Bodyguards, 191
Tahrir Square demonstrations, 171–74, 180–81
Ta'if Agreement, 109–10, 138
Tamarod campaign, 203
Thawrat El Banat (Girls' Revolution), 211
Third World Project, 85, 111, 147
Thompson, Elizabeth, 50
Tunisia, 13, 175, 178
Turkey, 13

UN Conference on Environment and Development, 150
UN Convention on the Elimination of all forms of Discrimination against Women (CEDAW): activist use for gender equality, 115; Egyptian ratification of, 92, 153, 229n3; Islamist opposition to, 165–66, 168, 183; Jordanian ratification of, 103, 153–54; Lebanese ratification of, 153, 155; MENA government reservations on, 13, 16, 150, 153, 155,

229n3; ratification as modernity marker, 26

UN Declaration to Eliminate Violence against Women, 191

UN International Conference on Population and Development (ICPD), 159

UN International Women's Conference, 101–2, 150–51, 153, 159, 168

United States: influence on Arab states, 113–14; international women's rights agenda and, 151; Middle East intervention and, 85–86, 142, 151; military interventions and, 30, 151–52; political repression and, 30; support for Egypt, 94–95; support for Jordan, 45, 98; support for political repression, 111–12; support for war on Hizbollah, 141. *See also* Gulf War of 1990–91; Iraq War

UN Relief and Works Agency (UNRWA), 62–63

Uprising of Women in the Arab World, 178–79

USAID, 126

US Middle East Partnership Initiative (MEPI), 157

vernacularization, 150, 159–163

violence against women: breakdown of gender norms and, 191; conservative defense of, 160; honor killings, 120, 154, 160, 230n3, 231n7; international women's rights norms and, 159–162; as justification for Western intervention, 160; nationalist ideology and, 66; neocolonial discourse and, 160; organizations combatting, 128, 232n8; postcolonial feminism and, 159–160; refusal to acknowledge, 159–160; religious argument against, 161, 169; sexual violence, 31, 66, 137, 143, 145, 180, 190–93; vernacularization of, 160–62; women protesters and, 31, 137, 143, 180–81, 186–88, 190. *See also* sexual violence

Wahba, Dina, 172, 189

War of the Camps, 107–8

War on Terror, 132, 151, 157, 160

Watenpaugh, Keith, 22

Weber, Cynthia, 11

West, The: on Arab women activists, 2–3; Egyptian turn towards, 26, 90; instrumentalization of women's empowerment, 24, 112, 120, 151, 157; international dominance of, 11; interventions for women's rights, 12, 17, 142, 160; role in defeat of radical/revolutionary movements, 30, 111–12; state formation and, 8; undermining of gender equality, 111–12. *See also* Global North; United States

White Ribbon Apology Campaign, 137

"woman question", 35, 40, 44, 56

Woman's Committee in the Bar Association (Jordan), 103

women: colonial discourse and, 34–35; empowerment and, 24, 112, 120, 151, 157; modern-yet-modest, 29, 42, 57; narratives of fear, 202; personal narratives and, 19–25; public work by elite, 35–36; transgression of gender norms, 29–30; unpaid labor and, 20; workers, 40, 53–54, 82–83, 92, 102, 120, 122, 137, 144, 227n3, 228n9. *See also* female respectability

women activists: Arab-Muslim culture and, 3; elite women as, 35–36; Islamic attacks on, 166; Islamist, 165–68; leftist parties and, 18, 53–55, 67, 72–73, 82–83, 95, 97, 112, 116, 121, 124–25, 136, 139, 144, 188, 210; middle-class women as, 21–22; modernity/modesty boundary and, 18; in public service, 18, 46–48, 52; resistance to power, 4–5, 7; secular, 158–165, 168; violent targeting of, 31; younger professional, 127–131

Women and Constitution Study Group, 182

Women and Memory Forum, 162, 182, 189

Women for Democracy, 145

Women in Front, 131, 184

women's activism: charitable/welfare, 36–38; contestation over, 23–24; criticisms of national machineries, 157–58; cultural difference and, 222; decolonization and, 33; as embodied geopolitics, 3–8, 17; female respectability and, 36, 57,

women's activism (*continued*)
60, 221; gendered hierarchies and,
144–45; gender norms and, 16, 34, 37,
56, 221; geopolitical context for, 26,
34–38, 111–12, 224; hegemonic power
and, 7, 222–23; inner/outer sphere and,
17–18; international conferences and,
150–51; international instruments for
equality and, 115; modern-yet-modest,
36, 185; narratives of, 19–25; nationality
laws and, 14; nation state and, 5–6;
NGOs and, 114–132, 146; performance
of gender identity, 7, 225n1; personal
status laws and, 13; political activism
and, 124–25; political protests and, 37,
185; political repression and, 111–12;
post-2000 protest movements, 133–145;
as power diagnostic, 224; protest movements and, 114, 132; secularism and, 168,
226n13; sociopolitical/geopolitical
movements and, 222. *See also* Egyptian
women's activism; humanitarian work;
Jordanian women's activism; Lebanese
women's activism; Palestinian women
activists; women's voluntary activism
Women's Affairs Committee (Arab Lawyers' Union), 103
Women's Awakening League, 44
women's bodies: collective honor and, 192;
collective morality and, 143; colonialism
and, 9; control in MENA states, 12;
cultural difference and, 10, 12; geopolitics and, 3–8, 12, 17; Islamist discourse
and, 192; modesty and, 10, 13, 16;
protests and weaponization of, 143;
regulation of, 171; state sovereignty
and, 10–11, 16
Women's Humanitarian Organization, 124
Women's International Democratic Federation (WIDF), 230n1
women's organizations, 239–244
women's rights: changes over time in, 16;
contestation over, 16; cultural difference
and, 16; culturally relevant discourse

and, 145; dominant power structures
and, 218; Egyptian constitution (1923),
36; Egyptian constitution (1956), 39;
Egyptian constitution (1971), 87;
Egyptian constitution (2012), 181–82;
Egyptian constitution (2014), 206–7;
Egyptian constitutional revisions (2011),
179–180; Egyptian rollback of, 181–82;
geopolitical upheaval and, 149; governmentality and state power over, 155;
Islamist rejection of, 16; Islamist women
activists and, 165–68; marginalization
by leftist groups, 125–26; masculinist
protection and, 207–8; modernization
and, 167–68; narratives of fear and, 218;
NGOs and, 118, 125, 129, 142; as part of
imperialist/neoliberal agendas, 142;
policing of sexuality, 14–15; religious
arguments for, 162–64, 169, 231n8; rise
of political Islam and, 199; universalist
discourse and, 145; US military interventions and, 151–52; Western interventions and, 12, 17, 142, 160; women's
activism and, 22. *See also* international
women's rights norms; nationality laws;
personal status laws; state feminism
women's sexuality, 14–15
Women's Union in Jordan (WUJ), 101–2
women's voluntary activism: Egyptian
state feminism and, 42; female respectability and, 121; gendered hierarchies
and, 48; in Jordan, 46–47; NGOs and,
119–121; Palestinian refugees and, 76,
108
workers' strikes, 93, 137–38, 144
Working Women's League, 184
Writers for Change, 136

Yapp, Malcolm, 78
Young, Iris Marion, 192, 207–8
Youth for Change, 136

Zakharia, Leila, 2, 76, 106
Zohney, Sally, 174, 187

Founded in 1893,
UNIVERSITY OF CALIFORNIA PRESS
publishes bold, progressive books and journals
on topics in the arts, humanities, social sciences,
and natural sciences—with a focus on social
justice issues—that inspire thought and action
among readers worldwide.

The UC PRESS FOUNDATION
raises funds to uphold the press's vital role
as an independent, nonprofit publisher, and
receives philanthropic support from a wide
range of individuals and institutions—and from
committed readers like you. To learn more, visit
ucpress.edu/supportus.